Neighborhood and Life Chances

The City in the Twenty-First Century

Eugenie L. Birch and Susan M. Wachter, Series Editors

A complete list of books in the series is available from the publisher.

Neighborhood and Life Chances

How Place Matters in Modern America

Edited by

Harriet B. Newburger,
Eugenie L. Birch, and Susan M. Wachter

UNIVERSITY OF PENNSYLVANIA PRESS

PHILADELPHIA

Published by
University of Pennsylvania Press
Philadelphia, Pennsylvania 19104-4112

Printed in the United States of America on acid-free paper
10   9   8   7   6   5   4   3   2   1

Library of Congress Cataloging-in-Publication Data

Neighborhood and life chances : how place matters in modern America / edited by Harriet B. Newburger, Eugenie L. Birch, and Susan M. Wachter.
    p.   cm.— (The city in the 21st century)
  Includes bibliographical references and index.
  ISBN 978-0-8122-4258-4 (hardcover : alk. paper)
  1. Cities and towns—United States. 2. Neighborhoods—United States. 3. Place (Philosophy). I. Newburger, Harriet. II. Birch, Eugenie Ladner. III. Wachter, Susan M.
HT123.N355 2010
304.2'30973—dc22

                                                 2010004564

Contents

Abbreviations

CHA   Chicago Housing Authority
CPS   Chicago Public Schools
ECLS   U. S. Department of Education's Early Childhood
          Longitudinal Study
EITC   Earned Income Tax Credit
HOPE VI   Housing Opportunities for People Everywhere VI
HUD   U.S. Department of Housing and Urban Development
ITT   Intent-to-Treat Effects
LEP   Limited English Proficiency
LIHTC   Low-Income Housing Tax Credit
MINCS   Mixed-Income New Communities Strategy
MSA   Metropolitan Statistical Area
MTO   Moving to Opportunity Demonstration
MWTP   Marginal Willingness to Pay
NAEP   National Assessment of Educational Progress
NCDB   Neighborhood Change Database
NELS   National Education Longitudinal Study
NFHA   National Fair Housing Alliance
NHANES   National Health and Nutrition Examination Surveys
NPO   Nonprofit Organization
PHA   Public Housing Authority
PMSA   Primary Metropolitan Statistical Area
PRWORA   Personal Responsibility and Work Opportunity
          Reconciliation Act
PSID   Panel Study of Income Dynamics
SFA   Success for All Program
SOR   Spanish Origin Record
TAAS   Texas Assessment of Academic Skills
TANF   Temporary Assistance for Needy Families
TOT   Treatment-on-Treated Effects
TSMP   Texas Schools Microdata Panel
TSP   Texas Schools Project
UCR   FBI Uniform Crime Reports
WSR   Whole School Reform

Preface

Eugenie L. Birch, Harriet B. Newburger, and Susan M. Wachter

Place matters. Embedded in this apparently simple statement are a host of complex questions about *how* and *why* place matters. Does one's childhood address determine one's health as an adult? Does the place a student goes home to *after* school matter as much as the school she actually attends? To what degree is the success of my neighbor implicated in the fortunes of my own family? One overarching question summarizes many of our concerns about place: Does a child from a poor family, where low income may severely restrict residential options, face a double burden in getting ahead—his opportunities constrained not only by the family's limited resources but also by the conditions in the neighborhood where he lives?

Over the past two decades, the possibility of this double burden has stimulated a great deal of research aimed at understanding the relation between residential location and life chances. Yet despite the common wisdom that place matters, it has proven extremely difficult to pin down just how and how much it matters. Indeed, even definitively documenting that it *does* matter is beset by difficulties in sorting out the effects of residential location from the effects of other factors on individual and household outcomes, by difficulties in defining and measuring the neighborhood characteristics most relevant to these outcomes, and by difficulties in tracking effects of residential location that may unfold over long time periods.

The problem of "selection bias," in particular, has plagued researchers engaged in charting the effects of place. We might observe, for example, that children from poor families who grow up in low-poverty neighborhoods are ultimately more successful in the labor market than poor children from high-poverty neighborhoods. But it will be difficult to sort out how much of that greater success is due to living in a low-poverty neighborhood and how much is due to some household characteristic such as high parental motivation which cannot be easily observed, but which may be particularly prevalent among poor families who successfully search for housing in low-poverty neighborhoods.

In recent years, however, researchers have benefited from new tools, in the form of higher quality data and improved methodologies, to address such problems. *Neighborhood and Life Chances* reviews the recent literature and showcases new research on how residential environments, particularly in urban areas, affect the lives of the people who live in them. It also highlights new work on the efficacy of policies designed to improve the quality of opportunities available to households living in high-poverty neighborhoods. Finally, it provides a useful glimpse into the debates currently going on among researchers of "neighborhood effects," as the impacts of residential location are often termed.

Residential location affects outcomes in many of the spheres of human experience that are critical in determining individual and household well-being, including health, education, and crime. As these essays make clear, there are multiple pathways by which these effects may operate. Those living in high-poverty neighborhoods may tend to have poorer health because they are more likely to experience conditions that negatively affect health, such as pollution or crime-related stress, or because they are less likely to have access to products and activities that promote health, such as fresh produce or safe recreational opportunities. Young adults living in poor neighborhoods may be more likely to engage in criminal behavior because of the poor schooling and limited job opportunities that their neighborhoods provide, but also because of the greater likelihood that their social interactions expose them to others involved in criminal activity. But whatever the complexities of sorting through the sources of neighborhood effects, the evidence presented in this volume provides convincing support for the argument that the environment of one's early years is a factor in one's lifelong prospects.

What can be done? A wide range of programs have attempted to improve the standard of living of poor children and their families, and we continue to learn more about both the potential and the limitations of such programs. For example, a number of educational interventions in schools that serve poor children, some involving an increase in school resources and some involving a restructuring of the learning process, appear to provide improved life outcomes over the long term that justify their costs. But even successful interventions only narrow the gap between disadvantaged students and their peers, rather than eliminating it.

Other evidence indicates that in the 1990s, low-income central city neighborhoods were considerably more likely to show large economic gains than to experience large economic losses, reversing the pattern of previous decades; exploratory analysis suggests that this result is consistent with activity in a number of federal programs targeted to low-income families, such as the Earned Income and Low Income Housing Tax Credits. As in the case of educational interventions, however, the finding that low-income neighborhoods showed improvement in the 1990s comes with a caveat: economic gain in a neighborhood over the course of a decade does not indicate whether low-income households who lived there at the start of the decade are better or worse off.

Particularly interesting in the context of this volume are programs and policies that, by design, attempt to provide poor households with neighborhood environments that are richer in opportunities. Place-based investment in neighborhoods where opportunities are limited is one such strategy. Mixed-income housing, a particular form this strategy might take, has received considerable attention in recent years and is represented on a large scale by Chicago's Plan for Transformation, in which public housing projects are typically redeveloped as mixed-income developments with a reduced amount of public housing. While Plan for Transformation activities have by no means been completed, public housing tenants who have moved back to redeveloped projects report improved quality of life, though a substantial number do not expect the income mix to provide opportunities beyond improved housing. Because the reduction in public housing units means that not all former residents will return, a full analysis of the costs and benefits from this type of neighborhood revitalization for poor families must ultimately take account of the experiences of those who do not return as well as those who do.

An alternative to place-based investment as a strategy to improve options for households whose neighborhoods provide poor opportunities is to help them move to places where opportunities are better. Perhaps the best known example of this strategy is HUD's Moving to Opportunity Demonstration (MTO). MTO aimed at testing whether the strategy would improve the well-being of poor families and in furtherance of this goal, was structured according to an experimental design: Whether or not a participating family was offered assistance in moving from an initial high poverty neighborhood and whether actual receipt of such assistance was conditioned on the family's moving to a low poverty neighborhood were both determined randomly. While a final evaluation of MTO is not yet complete, findings from a 2003 interim evaluation are mixed. They provide evidence that neighborhood affects the physical and mental health of adults and that better neighborhood environments can lower psychological distress among teenage girls, but do not provide evidence of neighborhood effects in other areas, including employment, earnings, and children's school achievement.

The MTO demonstration and its interim evaluation results loom large in current discussions among researchers on the effect of neighborhood conditions on family and individual outcomes. MTO's central role in the debate on neighborhood effects is based on its experimental design; in particular, its random assignment of households to "treatment groups" was intended to overcome the problem of selection bias, which, as we have noted earlier, has made it so difficult to untangle the effects of household characteristics from those of neighborhood characteristics. Random assignment is considered by some to be the gold standard for the study of program effects and, in turn, the fact that the interim MTO evaluation found no evidence of neighborhood effects in key areas such as employment and school achievement has taken on considerable importance. For others, this importance is overstated. They note, for example, that MTO was designed as an experimental study of a particular housing program rather than an experimental study of neighborhood effects in general and argue that certain features of its design mean that it is not necessarily well-suited for the latter purpose, and also believe that the focus on MTO obscures real contributions that non-experimental research makes to our understanding of neighborhood impacts. The debate is a healthy one, particularly to the extent that it stimulates further research that deepens our understanding of neighborhood effects and the circumstances under which they are most likely to be observed. As many of the essays in this volume demonstrate, that effort is well underway.

Just as the study of neighborhood effects considers the impact of context on individual outcomes, it must also consider the role of context on neighborhood conditions themselves, for these conditions do not arise in a vacuum. They are determined, at least in part, by the characteristics of the larger geographies—cities or metropolitan areas, for example—in which the neighborhoods are located. In American cities, the level of residential segregation is a metropolitan characteristic that has been particularly salient in shaping the distribution of opportunities across neighborhoods, with negative effects for African Americans that have been well-documented. In addition, segregation appears to be associated with some negative outcomes that span the entire metropolitan area. For example, higher segregation in cities is associated with lower longevity for both blacks and whites. The essays in this volume sound some notes of optimism on the possibilities for decreased levels of segregation going forward. African American segregation has declined somewhat over recent decades, while white attitudes toward integration have become more positive. Tipping points—thresholds for neighborhood minority share beyond which white flight is precipitated—have risen over recent decades, allowing greater room for neighborhoods where some degree of integration can persist over time. At the same time, however, segregation of Hispanics and Asians, while lower than that of African Americans, has increased over the past two decades, though this may in part be associated with the large increases in these populations during the time period. And despite recent improvements, African American segregation remains very high. To the extent that minority segregation continues to affect access to opportunities as it has done in the past, it will remain an issue that must be considered by those concerned with overcoming the negative effects of place.

An earlier social science literature distinguished between people prosperity and place prosperity in its analysis of policies designed to alleviate poverty and poverty's effects. This volume makes clear that in today's urban environments such a dichotomy makes little sense. People and place prosperity go hand in hand. The policy-maker who wants to improve the life chances of poor families and their children cannot ignore the effects that place has on those chances. The scholars whose work is assembled here make this point through careful documentation of the many ways in which place matters and through thoughtful analysis of policies that aim to change the distribution of opportunities across both populations and places. These scholars also raise questions that will guide future research. They identify our need to know more about the precise mechanisms through which neighborhood effects are transmitted; about the distribution of benefits and costs of neighborhood revitalization; about which strategies are most effective under which situations; and about which programs most effectively complement each other. These are the types of questions that we must answer if we are to translate our recognition that place matters into policies that are able to counter the disadvantages that a place that is poor in opportunities may impose.

PART I

People and Places

Health, Education, and Safety

Chapter 1
Health and Residential Location

Janet Currie

Residents of poor neighborhoods are in worse health, on average, than residents of richer neighborhoods. In order to know whether improving the physical environment in a neighborhood will make people better off, it is first necessary to know whether the relationship between place and outcomes is causal. Residents of poor neighborhoods have many characteristics that are associated with worse health on average, such as lower incomes. And if neighborhoods do literally make people sick, then we need to know which aspects of the neighborhood are at fault.

This essay provides a selective overview of the literature on residential location and health, highlighting work that seeks to identify causal relationships. The first section provides a brief framework for thinking about the "production" of health. The remaining sections discuss the possible mechanisms that underlie the relationship between residential location and health. These mechanisms include the disease environment, the relationship between location and socioeconomic status, the effects of pollution, the effects of neighborhoods on obesity, the effects of crime, and the effects of stressful environments.

Health Production

The most common model of health production was created by Grossman (2000). In this model, it is assumed that individuals and families try to make themselves as well off as possible (maximize utility). The decision makers in a household value their own health and that of their family members, but they also value health because it enhances their earnings capacity and the ability to do other things that make them happy. Households face budgets and prices (including the wages they can command in the market). They make choices about which items they will buy (where "items" can include leisure, which has a price in terms of foregone wages). Some items are bought to be enjoyed in their own right, while others (such as vaccinations) can be regarded as investments in future health. Things that are inputs or investments in future health can be combined in certain ways that are determined by the technology available to the household. Every person starts out with an "endowment" of health. This endowment can be expected to depreciate over time in the absence of investments. This simple framework highlights the many ways in which residential location can influence health, as well as the distinction between the causal effects of location and the effects of other characteristics of the families that live in those locations.

First, as discussed above, people in poor neighborhoods are likely to be poor, which limits the amounts and types of health inputs that they can purchase. But this is not an effect of the neighborhood per se.

Second, if people in poor neighborhoods have more difficulty finding jobs, or if they face higher prices (e.g., because they have higher transportation costs), then this is a neighborhood effect that will tend to reduce the extent to which they can invest in their health. For example, it is often alleged that fresh fruits and vegetables are more expensive in poor neighborhoods. This is a characteristic of a neighborhood that would affect the household's budget constraint.

Third, as people in poor neighborhoods are less educated on average, then they may not combine health inputs as effectively as those in richer neighborhoods in order to produce health. Alternatively, people in poor neighborhoods may have different tastes for investments in health (Fuchs 1993). Differences in the ability to produce health or in tastes should not be attributed to neighborhoods.

Fourth, if certain health technologies are not available in poor neighborhoods, then limited access to these technologies would be a characteristic of the neighborhood. For example, poor neighborhoods may lack playgrounds with recreation equipment that challenges children safely.

Finally, it is possible that living in a poor neighborhood affects one's health endowment as well as one's ability to make health investments, the family's budget, and the prices the household faces. Poorer children seem to be more subject than richer children to health shocks, which can change the productivity of future investments in child health. Again, a shock such as a serious accident could be due to the physical environment, or it might be due to other factors, such as lack of proper supervision in the family, which would remain the same were the family to relocate to a different neighborhood.

Heckman (2007) recently extended the Grossman (2000) model by focusing on the dynamics of the process. He argued that a model in which there are "dynamic complementarities" and "self-productivity" fits the available evidence well. Dynamic complementarities imply that investments in the current period are more productive when there is a high level of capability in preceding periods. Self-productivity implies that higher levels of capacity in one period create higher levels of capacity in future periods. If this model is correct, then it implies that any effects of residential location on children's health are likely to be more serious when children are young, and that they are likely to have cumulative and increasing impacts over time. For example, if a child has a traumatic brain injury because of unsafe conditions in the neighborhood, this may have long-term consequences for schooling attainment. In this case, while it may be possible to take the child out of a bad neighborhood, it may not be possible to take the neighborhood out of the child in the sense that material deprivation associated with the neighborhood will have permanent effects on the health of the individual.

Many studies by David Barker and others show that fetal conditions are related to adult risk of disease. Gluckman and Hanson (2005) offered a more recent summary of work on this idea, which has come to be known as the "fetal origins hypothesis." This work can be seen in the broader context of research investigating the interplay between genes and environment (see, for example, Rutter 2006). The idea is that genes may predispose a person to a condition, but that it generally takes an environmental trigger to activate the expression of the gene. Moreover, genes that are associated with pathology in one set of circumstances may have protective functions in other contexts, which may explain why they persist in the genome. Thus, poor children may have poor health at birth because of the circumstances surrounding their births, rather than because their parents have "inferior" genetic endowments, and residential location may be an important early life circumstance.

The Disease Environment

Most contemporary threats to health are considerably more subtle than the major infectious diseases that used to account for a large share of deaths, especially in urban areas. Cutler and Miller (2005) discussed the huge improvement in health that occurred during the late nineteenth and early twentieth centuries. In 1900, 39.3 percent of deaths were due to infectious diseases such as typhoid, while by 1936, this percentage had fallen to 17.9. This improvement eliminated a "health penalty" that had been associated with living in large cities. Using variations in the timing of the adoption of clean water technologies across major U.S.

cities, they showed that clean water can explain half of the total mortality reduction in large cities and two-thirds of the reduction in child mortality.

Similarly, recent work has shown that malaria eradication campaigns in the United States, which took place in the 1920s, had long-term effects on the labor market productivity of affected cohorts of children (Bleakley 2007).

These examples should remind us that the health of people in cities is contingent on a certain level of public health expenditures and investments. Just as city leaders were able to reduce disease by focusing on innovations such as clean water, a better understanding of contemporary threats to health may suggest actions that municipal leaders can take to improve the health of urban dwellers.

Poverty, Income, and Health: The Role of Neighborhoods

Poor families are likely to live in less desirable neighborhoods because they are cheaper. But does the causality run in the reverse direction? Are families more likely to be poor or stay poor because of where they live? This question is important because of the strong and extremely well-documented relationship between poverty and poor health. This section discusses the effects of poverty on health, whether poverty affects health indirectly through impacts on other outcomes (such as income), and the direct effects of neighborhoods on health, in both the short and longer run.

Many authors have documented the fact that poor children suffer more insults to their health than richer ones. For example, Newacheck (1994), Brooks-Gunn and Duncan (1997), Newacheck and Halfon (1998), and Case, Lubotsky, and Paxson (2002) all showed that poor children are more likely to have many chronic conditions. Currie and Lin (2007) updated these analyses and showed that there are large gaps in measures of mental health and in acute conditions as well. Currie (2009) provides a survey of the relationship between socioeconomic status and child health.

Disparities between rich and poor children in the extent to which they are limited by their conditions are much greater than disparities in the reported prevalence of conditions between poor and nonpoor children: 11.4 percent of poor children say that they are limited by chronic conditions compared to 7.0 percent of higher income children. The fraction of children with a limitation due to a chronic condition rises with age, and rises more sharply for poor children than for others. By the teenage years, poor children have almost double the probability of being limited by a chronic condition: 14.1 percent compared to 7.8 percent of other children (Currie and Lin 2007). Using data from the third National Health and Nutrition Examination Survey, Bhattacharya and Currie (2001) showed that family income below 1.3 times the U.S. poverty line is a significant predictor of high blood cholesterol and high body mass index, even conditional on other demographic variables.

Health disparities between rich and poor grow as people age. Overall, premature death is three times more likely for people at the bottom of the economic ladder in the United States (those with incomes less than $10,000 in 1999) compared to those at the top (Adler and Stewart 2007), so any neighborhood factors that affect socioeconomic status are likely to also affect health.

Can neighborhoods actually cause poverty? The importance of neighborhoods may seem self-evident, but there is actually intense debate among social scientists about whether neighborhoods have an effect on children over and above the influence of their own families. People who move into a given neighborhood differ from those in other neighborhoods before they arrive, and those who leave differ from those who stay. So even if it appears that children from bad neighborhoods do worse than other children, one cannot assume that it is the neighborhood rather than the family that matters.

Wilson (1987) argued that the increasing concentration of poor black children in neighborhoods with few positive role models has had devastating consequences. A second potential mechanism for neighborhoods to cause poverty has been dubbed the "spatial mismatch" hypothesis. The idea is that jobs have moved away from poor neighborhoods so that a mismatch between the location of residences and the location of jobs makes it difficult for the poor to find work. However, Ellwood (1986) pointed out that black and white teens living in the same neighborhood can have dramatically different unemployment rates. More recent work by Raphael and Stoll (2002) found blacks to be more segregated from their jobs than others, though this does not prove that blacks are less likely to be employed because of this. Briggs and colleagues in this volume provide a further discussion of spatial mismatch.

Large public housing projects have received special attention as particularly bad neighborhoods that might be likely to breed poverty. However, the most careful studies have found surprisingly little negative effect of living in projects (or, alternatively, surprisingly small positive effects of moving out of them). Currie and Yelowitz (2000) found that families with a boy and a girl were more likely to live in public housing than those with two same-sex children, because they were entitled to larger apartments. This finding can be used to separate the effect of living in public housing from the effect of being in a poor family because the sex of the first two children born is random. They found that children in projects were 11 percent less likely to have repeated grades than other similar children, and that they lived in housing that was less crowded. However, they were unable to determine health outcomes in their data.

Jacob (2004) studied students displaced by demolitions of the most notorious Chicago high-rise projects. Congress passed a law in 1996 that required local housing authorities to destroy units if the cost of renovating and maintaining them was greater than the cost of providing a voucher for twenty years. Jacob argued that the order in which doomed buildings were destroyed was approximately random. For example, in January 1999, the pipes froze in some buildings in the Robert Taylor Homes, which meant that those buildings were demolished before others in the same complex. By comparing children who stayed in buildings scheduled to be demolished to others who had already been displaced by demolitions, he obtained a measure of the effect of living in high-rise public housing. Despite the fact that the high rises in Jacob's study were among the most notorious public housing projects in the country, he found very little effect of relocation on children's educational outcomes. Again, he was unable to examine health.

The most exhaustive examination of the effects of giving vouchers to project residents is an ongoing experiment called "Moving to Opportunity" (MTO). MTO is a large-scale social experiment that is being conducted in Chicago, New York, Los Angeles, Boston, and Baltimore (see Orr et al. 2003). Between 1994 and 1998, volunteers from public housing projects were assigned by lottery to one of three groups. The first group received a voucher that could only be used to rent housing in a low-poverty area (a census tract with a poverty rate less than 10 percent). This group also received help locating a suitable apartment. The second group received a normal Section 8 voucher, which they could use to rent an apartment in any neighborhood. The third group was the control and received no vouchers or assistance, although they were eligible to remain in their project apartment.

Families in the first group did move to lower-poverty neighborhoods, and the new neighborhoods of the first group were also considerably safer. Contrary to expectations, however, the move to new neighborhoods had little effect on family earnings. Girls in the MTO and Section 8 groups were much less likely to have ever been arrested than controls. In contrast, boys in the experimental group were 13 percent more likely than controls to have ever been arrested. This finding is particularly striking, since one might expect the lower-poverty neighborhoods to which the boys moved to have less crime. This increase was due largely to increases in property crimes. These results indicate that moving boys from housing projects to wealthier neighborhoods is not a panacea.

In addition, research on MTO also found evidence that boys in the experimental group also reported more risky behaviors such as drug and alcohol use. And boys in the MTO and voucher groups were more likely to suffer injuries. However, girls in the first group were more likely than controls to graduate from high school and were much less likely to suffer from anxiety. Girls in the regular Section 8 group also experienced improvements in mental health relative to the controls. These differences between boys and girls are apparent even within families (Orr et al. 2003). Among adult women, moving to better neighborhoods was associated with a 10.8 percent decline in the probability of being obese, and a 7.3 percent reduction in reports of psychological distress after four or five years (Orr et al. 2003).

It remains to be seen how the long-term outcomes of the MTO children will differ from controls. Oreopoulos (2003) used data from Canadian income tax records to examine the earnings of adults who lived in public housing projects in Toronto as children. There are large differences between projects in Toronto, in terms of both the density of the projects and the poverty of the neighborhoods. The type of project a family lives in is approximately randomly assigned, because the family is offered whatever happens to be available when they get to the top of the waiting list. Oreopoulos found that once the characteristics of the family were controlled, the neighborhood had no effect on future earnings or on the likelihood that someone worked.

Several recent studies show that the neighborhoods that mothers were exposed to when they were growing up can have long-run effects on the health of their infants. For example, areas with greater educational opportunities encourage mothers to receive more education, which in turn has effects on infant health.

Currie and Moretti (2003) showed that the opening of a new college in a woman's county of birth when she was 17 had a significant effect on her education. Using national data from birth certificates, they show that this increase in education increased the birth weight and gestational age of the children who were later born to these women. It also increased the probability that a new mother was married, reduced the number of children each woman bore, increased the use of prenatal care, and substantially reduced smoking, suggesting that these are all important pathways for the ultimate effect on health.

Carneiro, Meghir, and Parey (2007) examined the effect of maternal education using data from the National Longitudinal Survey of Youth. They used the presence of a four-year college and college tuition at age 17 in the county where the mother lived when she was 14 years old to explain educational attainment. They found strong effects of maternal education on measures of children's behavior problems, which might be regarded as a proxy for or correlate of mental health conditions. They concluded that the effects of increases in maternal education are large relative to the effects of other interventions designed to affect child outcomes.

Currie and Moretti (2007) examined the intergenerational transmission of low birth weight using a large data set of birth records from California. The data allowed them to identify both the mothers and the grandmothers of children born after 1989. It was also possible to identify mothers who are sisters in the data. They defined the mother's socioeconomic status by examining income in the zip code of the hospital where she was born. They found that compared to their own sisters, mothers who were born in poor areas were both more likely to have been low birth weight and about 6 percent more likely to eventually deliver a low birth weight baby themselves. These examples suggest that location can not only reflect socioeconomic status but also influence it, and that location can have direct and long-lasting effects on health.

Residential Location, Pollution, and Health

A number of scientists have been investigating "environmental justice," the question of whether minorities and those with low income are disproportionately exposed to pollutants. Many of their studies have reported, as expected, that poor and minority households are more likely to reside near emitters or in highly polluted areas. For example, Perlin, Sexton, and Wong (1999, 2001) examined data for three metro areas at the census tract level. They found that blacks and the poor (including poor whites) are more likely to live next to facilities that emit toxic releases and are more likely to live less than two miles from multiple emitting facilities. Similarly, Ash and Fetter (2004) used data from census block groups combined with information about urban air quality and found that African Americans and Hispanics live in more polluted areas within cities, as do poor people.

But it is not clear how to interpret these findings. Once again, the problem is that if people dislike living near pollution sources, then housing prices will fall to reflect this so that the people living near such sources will be lower income on average than those who live farther away. Using data from Massachusetts, Bui and Mayer (2003) examined the prediction that housing prices would fall and found no effect of toxic releases on house prices at the zip code level. But Oberholzer-Gee and Mitsunari (2006) found that average house prices in five Philadelphia-area counties fell after the U.S. government began publishing information on plant emissions from the Toxic Release Inventory in June 1989, and that they fell most in houses a quarter to a half mile from an emitting plant. The contrasting findings of these two studies suggest that even aggregation at the zip code level may mask the effects of toxic releases on housing prices.

But does exposure to toxic releases at the level that now generally occurs in the population have negative health effects? Data on possible human health effects generally come either from animal studies or from disastrous accidental releases. Woodruff (1998) ran 1990 data from the U.S. Environmental Protection Agency's Toxic Release Inventory through a dispersion model and calculated that 90 percent of census tracts have concentrations of several chemicals greater than cancer benchmarks. This suggests that American children (and others) may be at risk from toxic releases but does not establish any direct relationship between releases and health effects.

Vrijheid (2000) looked at the question of whether residence near a hazardous waste site has health effects and highlighted some of the methodological weaknesses of existing studies. Some studies control for some observable confounding factors, but there is still a possibility that there are unobservable characteristics of people who live close to hazardous waste sites that would tend to cause bad outcomes. An additional problem is that the number of hazardous waste sites analyzed in many of the previous studies is small, so that some "results" may actually be due to sampling variability. These problems plague much of the literature on toxic effects so that it is quite difficult to measure effects of pollution on health, let alone show that there are long-term consequences of exposures.

Some scourges of childhood, such as lead poisoning, have seen huge improvement with the adoption of public health measures such as banning lead in paint and gasoline. Before the regulation of lead, children were exposed to lead from paints, water pipes, gasoline, and canned food. Evidence from the National Health and Nutrition Examination Surveys (NHANES) showed that 88.2 percent of children aged one to five had lead levels above 10 microg/dl in 1976 to 1980, 8.6 percent had lead levels above the threshold in 1988–1991, and only 2.2 percent had levels this high in 1999–2000. These figures imply that the number of children with unsafe lead levels declined from 13.5 million to less than one half million over this period (U.S. Centers for Disease Control 2003), a public health triumph.

Lead has been shown to decrease IQ by two to five points for each 10 to 20 microg/dl above the current standard (Pocock, Smith, and Baghurst 1994), and the majority of affected children are low income.

Indeed, the government tracks lead poisoning by looking for areas with a combination of older housing stock and low-income households. Lead may also have negative effects on children's mental health, making them more prone to antisocial behavior (Needleman and Gastsonis 1991). Reyes (2005) used variation in prenatal lead exposure caused by the Clean Air Acts on infant health outcomes and found that even small amounts of lead are associated with adverse outcomes.

In two important and innovative works, Chay and Greenstone (2003a, b) used changes in regulation to identify pollution's effects on infant mortality. They argued that the 1970 and 1977 Clean Air Acts caused exogenous changes in pollution levels, and that the changes were different in different areas. These changes can be used to examine pollution's effects on housing markets and infant mortality. They found that a $1mg/m^3$ reduction in total suspended particulates (a common measure of overall pollution at that time) resulted in 5–8 fewer deaths per 100,000 live births.

Currie and Neidell (2005) examined the effects of air pollution on infant deaths in the 1990s. They used individual-level data and within-zip code variation in pollution over time to identify the effects of pollution. They included zip code-fixed effects to account for omitted characteristics like ground water pollution and socioeconomic status, and found that reductions in two pollutants—carbon monoxide and particulate matter consisting of particles of 10 micrometers or less (PM_{10})—in the 1990s saved over one thousand infant lives in California.

Pollution may also have many negative health effects without causing deaths. Many observers believe that high rates of asthma among inner-city children are related to levels of air pollution. However, much of the existing evidence is indirect. For example, McConnochie et al. (1999) examined hospital admissions for asthma in suburban, urban, and inner-city neighborhoods. They found that admission rates varied from 1.05 per 1000 child years in the suburbs to 5.21 per 1000 child years in the inner city. Moreover, the fraction of cases that were judged to be "severe" was approximately the same across the three types of areas, suggesting that the differences were not driven by differences in hospital admitting patterns. Blaisdell et al. (2007) examined emergency room visits for asthma and upper and lower respiratory tract infections in Baltimore and found that patterns of admissions do not correlate perfectly, suggesting that there are factors that are specific to asthma.

Neidell's (2004) study is one of the first to attempt to measure the causal link between air pollution and hospitalizations for asthma. As in his later (2005) study with Currie, Neidell used within-zip code variation in pollution levels in California to provide evidence that air pollution does increase hospitalizations for asthma.

These studies show that pollution can have causal effects on child health, but there has been little investigation of whether these negative health effects have long-term consequences for children's outcomes. The National Children's Study, which was authorized by the Children's Health Act of 2000, will attempt to remedy this situation by examining the effects of environmental exposures on 100,000 children who will be followed from birth to age 21 (http://www.nationalchildrensstudy.gov).

Residential Location and Characteristics of the "Built Environment"

Much of the research on the built environment argues that features such as low population density, lack of sidewalks, and unconnected streets (e.g., cul-de-sacs) are associated with increases in obesity and decreases in physical activity. These are all characteristics of suburban communities. However, compared to suburbanites, inner-city residents have higher obesity rates and are less physically active (Lopez and Hynes 2006).

Lopez and Hynes argued that this apparent paradox may be explained in part by the quality of urban amenities. For example, if sidewalks are cracked and broken, parks are not maintained, or vacant buildings provide havens for criminals, then outdoor activity will be less attractive to residents. Taylor et al. (1998) found that children in highly vegetated playgrounds play longer and more creatively than those playing in nonvegetated areas.

Many poor neighborhoods lack full-service grocery stores, which may mean that fresh food, and especially fresh fruit and vegetables, is expensive and/or hard to come by. Instead of grocery stores, poor neighborhoods often have large numbers of corner stores and fast-food establishments. It has been argued that these features of poor neighborhoods have a causal effect on the diets of the poor, leading to a higher incidence of obesity and obesity-related disorders such as diabetes and heart disease (see, for example, Morland 2002; Zenk et al. 2005; and Moore and Roux 2006). Horowitz et al. (2004) reported that while 58 percent of food stores in New York's wealthy Upper East Side stocked low-fat, high fiber foods, only 18 percent of stores in East Harlem stocked these foods. Similarly, fast-food restaurants are more likely to be located in poor neighborhoods, though this could be in part because these neighborhoods are also more urban, on average.

However, these correlations do not prove that there is a causal relationship running from what food stores stock to what local residents eat. The direction of causality might well be reversed—it might be the case that the stores stock what their customers wish to buy. One reason for low-income people to prefer energy-dense foods (i.e., "junk" foods that have a lot of calories per unit) is that they are cheaper per calorie. In a study conducted in Seattle supermarkets in 2004 and 2006, Monsivais and Drewnowski (2007) found that foods in the highest quintile of energy density cost $1.76 per 1,000 kilocalories compared to $18.16 for foods in the lowest quintile of energy density. Moreover, the price gap between foods in the two categories widened over the period of the study, with prices for the most energy-dense foods actually falling slightly.

In the case of fast food, Cutler, Glaeser and Shapiro (2003) used data from food diaries in the United States to show that the biggest increase in calories consumed over time has involved snacks consumed at home, so that fast food is not likely to be the major explanation for higher rates of obesity among low-income people.

The MTO results discussed above suggested that moving people from poor to nonpoor neighborhoods does lower obesity. This is perhaps the strongest evidence that characteristics of the neighborhood matter, but it is unclear whether it is increased opportunities for recreation, access to healthy food, or even changes in social norms that matter.

Injuries rather than illnesses are the leading cause of death among children in the U.S. as in other developed countries, and they continue to be a leading cause of death for prime age adults (Bonnie, Fulco, and Liverman 1999). Unintentional injuries, or accidents, may be caused by many features of the built environment in poor neighborhoods, such as older housing stock, lack of sidewalks, unsafe roadways, hazards such as abandoned houses or businesses, and a lack of safe or supervised places to play for children.

Still, in the United States accidental deaths among children 0 to 19 have declined very rapidly, falling by 47 percent between 1980 and 1998 (Currie and Hotz 2004). This decline represents a remarkable public health triumph that is not well understood. It is not clear how much of the overall improvement can be attributed to local regulations mandating such safety measures as fall bars on windows, fencing around swimming pools, and lower temperatures on hot water heaters, though all of these regulations have been shown to save lives. More general innovations in the safety of products as well as consumer product regulations (such as childproof caps on medicines) are also likely to have been important.

Glied (2001) discussed many important regulations affecting product safety, including the Poison Prevention Packaging Act of 1970 and laws mandating the use of infant and child safety seats in cars, which were first introduced in 1977 and had been adopted by all states by 1984. She argued, however, that these regulations cannot explain all of the declining trend in accident rates. A remarkable feature of the decline is that it has occurred across all categories of accidental death, from drownings in outdoor bodies of water to drownings in bathtubs to house fires. It is certainly clear that the measures she discussed are unlikely to account for declining death rates in recent years, since they were passed many years ago now.

It is extremely difficult to directly test the hypothesis that regulation is responsible for declines in accident rates, given the myriad regulations at federal, state, and even local levels. Glied argued that younger children should benefit most from new product regulation, or, conversely, that children with older siblings may be more at risk from dangerous older products. However, the Vital Statistics mortality data do not identify whether or not children have siblings, so this test cannot be directly implemented.

In addition to regulation, efforts by epidemiologists, public health agencies, and safety advocacy groups have increased the supply of information about possible hazards in everyday life and about strategies for preventing illness and accidents. These developments are disseminated to the public through public service announcements, product labeling (which is generally regulated, so that there is an overlap between regulation and information dissemination), school safety education programs, and other media. These efforts may also account for some of the decline in accidental deaths of children.

Other Effects of Neighborhoods on Health

A number of recent studies have suggested that people's behavior is influenced by the behavior of neighbors in their social group. It is important to know if this is the case with respect to health interventions, because if network effects are important, then public health interventions targeted to particular networks will have larger effects than those that are spread evenly over geographic areas.

In some cases, the social group may be defined by geographical proximity as well as by membership in a particular ethnic or demographic group (see, for example, Bertrand, Luttmer, and Mullainathan 2000); Aizer and Currie (2004) asked whether women from different racial or ethnic groups are influenced by the behavior of similar women from their zip codes when they decide whether or not to make use of publicly funded maternity care programs. They found that while there are strong correlations in the behaviors such as use of Medicaid-funded prenatal care among women from the same ethnic backgrounds and neighborhoods, these correlations are driven by the fact that women of different backgrounds attend different hospitals for delivery, even if they live in the same neighborhoods. Different hospitals make it more or less easy to enroll in public programs and are also more or less welcome to people of different ethnicities (for example, they may or may not offer translation services). Hence, it is possible that constraints on the services available, rather than network effects, explain the observed correlations in behavior. There have been few other attempts to identify network effects as they relate to health behaviors.

Neighborhood crime can have both direct and indirect effects on health. Intentional injuries are a leading cause of death, especially among some groups such as young black men (Currie and Hotz 2004). Studies have also shown that fear of crime can limit people's activities. For instance, a study of one of Boston's most crime-ridden public housing projects found that 63 percent of residents reported that they were afraid of violence in their neighborhood, and 60 percent forbade children to play outside because of the fear of violence (Levy et al. 2004).

Residents of public housing projects who volunteered to participate in the MTO study were largely motivated by fear of crime in their neighborhoods. Therefore, the mental toll exacted by fear of violence may at least partially explain the significant improvement in mental health outcomes in the MTO "treatment" group.

As discussed above, fear of crime can cause psychological stress, but it may not be the only source of stress in urban environments. Noise, grime, and crowding are all possible causes of stress. Os (2004) summarized recent literature linking urban environments to the onset of psychosis, schizophrenia, and major depression.

Studies of the effects of noise are particularly interesting because, other than the direct effect on hearing, noise has health effects mainly by causing stress. Schell and Denham (2003) summarize many studies showing effects of noise. For example, in a study of elementary school children, Bronzaft and McCarthy (1975) found that children in classrooms near a busy railroad track had reading scores a quarter of a year behind children in classrooms on the other side of the school. Evans, Bullinger, and Hygge (1998) compared children living near a new airport in Munich to controls in quieter neighborhoods, before and after the airport opened. They found that prior to the airport opening, the children had similar levels of stress hormones in their blood (epinephrine and norepinephrine). After the opening, the children near the airport had levels significantly higher than the control children. Similarly, Ando (1988) showed that the frequency of low birth weight increased along with the amount of jet activity at an airport in Japan. These studies suggest that measures to reduce the stress of urban life through, for example, noise abatement, might have significant health effects.

Conclusions

There are many reasons to suppose that residential location matters to health. But the fact that people choose their locations makes it difficult to identify causal relationships between features of locations and health outcomes. The poor are more likely to live in areas with undesirable features, such as pollution, and are also more likely to engage in negative health behaviors. We must be cautious about assuming that correlations imply causality. Jumping to conclusions can cause policymakers to pursue initiatives that, while they may be desirable for other reasons, will have little effect on health.

Still, the experimental MTO evaluation suggests that moving poor people to better neighborhoods can have important effects on health independent of any effects on income or employment. At this point, we do not really know why, though this finding could reflect lowered exposure to pollution, crime, and other disamenities of urban life, or improved access to health inputs such as healthy food. Determining the mechanisms underlying these health improvements is an important topic for future research.

Chapter 2

The Place of Race in Health Disparities
How Family Background and Neighborhood Conditions in Childhood Impact Later-Life Health

Rucker C. Johnson

Health is distributed unevenly, following a gradient that is a function of socioeconomic advantage and mirrors the pattern of neighborhood disadvantage. Among the steepest of such gradients is that of the United States, where there are large differences across people on measures of neighborhood environments, early childhood experiences, education, income, and housing quality.

Persistent residential segregation of poor and minority populations has spurred a growing number of studies that investigate the effects of community background on a variety of socioeconomic outcomes. However, the role of the physical and socioeconomic neighborhood in contributing to health disparities has been relatively unexplored. Analyses of health disparities have instead focused largely on individual- and family-level determinants of health outcomes. Over the past decade, however, we have witnessed a renewed research and policy interest and recognition of the salience of nonmedical determinants of health, especially the socioeconomic determinants of health that derive from differential neighborhood quality (Schoeni et al. 2008). Previous research has shown that such individual health behaviors as cigarette smoking, alcohol use, diet, and exercise explain a relatively small amount of race and socioeconomic differences in health status (Lantz et al. 2001), but it leaves open the question of the importance of parental socioeconomic status via its effect on access to neighborhood amenities.

This chapter reports on recent research by the author on the influence of neighborhood conditions on health over the life course, with a particular focus on how childhood neighborhoods affect health later in life. In this research I take the perspective that disadvantaged neighborhood exposures may both accumulate and beget future exposures due to links between neighborhood characteristics and the socioeconomic mobility process. In particular, in the United States, there are substantial racial differences in the incidence and persistence of exposure to high-poverty neighborhoods (Johnson 2008b). Moreover, in terms of health, blacks can expect to live six fewer years than whites, and can expect to live more years with chronic health problems (Hayward and Heron 1999), with most of the black-white difference in life expectancy stemming from racial differences in mortality rates prior to age 65. Racial disparities in neighborhood exposures, in childhood and adulthood, and the relationship between these disparities and those in health provide an important backdrop and motivation for this inquiry.

Stressful neighborhood conditions due to high poverty rates, crime, violence, and weaker sources of social support may lead to increased risk of high blood pressure and accelerated rates of health deterioration more generally. There are well-known differences across neighborhoods in the amount of perceived safety; availability and quality of public spaces and recreational facilities; tobacco advertising; liquor stores; and availability and cost of nutritious foods. The empirical question is whether differences across neighborhoods in the prevalence of particular health conditions do in fact reflect causal processes operating over the life course. Given the known lengthy latency periods before most health effects manifest (e.g., hypertension), it is important to examine whether later-life racial health disparities are rooted in early-life childhood circumstances. It is also important to examine whether racial differences in adult health status are the result of a long-term cumulative process of socioeconomic environmental exposures over the life cycle. The selected studies highlighted in this chapter seek to identify causal influences on the life cycle trajectory of health inequality using innovative research designs to separate causal impacts of neighborhoods from correlations arising from familial selection into neighborhoods.

The typical analytical approach used in neighborhood studies is to regress individual level outcomes such as health on neighborhood-level factors such as census tract mean income, poverty rates, or rates of single motherhood. But attempts to estimate causal effects of neighborhood context have faced well-documented challenges. The problem of endogeneity of residential location (in the form of "selection bias") has received perhaps the most attention in the literature (Manski 1993) and is a paramount concern because families choose where to live in part based on the characteristics they value. Thus, families who care more about investing in health-promoting activities may be less likely to choose to reside in a community with a poor health care system or high pollution. Many of the multidimensional aspects that influence residential location decisions are cannot be easily measured, which makes it particularly difficult to disentangle the causal influences of a child's family, school, and neighborhood. Few studies have used convincing identification strategies to overcome this challenge, exceptions being experimental evaluations such as Katz, Kling, and Liebman (2001) and Leventhal and Brooks-Gunn (2000). (See Gennetian et al. in this volume.)

Other challenges also complicate attempts to examine causal effects of neighborhood context. One such challenge is the difficulty of obtaining accurate measures of neighborhood characteristics. Another problematic characteristic of many neighborhood studies is that they examine the relationship between contemporaneous health and neighborhood conditions without regard to changing circumstances during the life cycle or the persistence of exposure to neighborhood conditions. If exposure to neighborhood conditions at an earlier stage of the life cycle influences current health but is not accounted for, then the estimated relationship between contemporaneous neighborhoods and health may be misleading. Finally, causality between economic and health status runs in both directions in adulthood and has proven notoriously difficult to sort out empirically (Adda, Chandoln, and Marmot 2003). By focusing on childhood socioeconomic conditions, we can more easily identify causal impacts on subsequent health because reverse causality is a relatively minor concern (i.e, poor child health is not a significant factor in most cases that leads to low parental income or neighborhood disadvantage).

The studies highlighted in this chapter employ a different approach than those typically used to address these challenges by exploiting a unique feature of the Panel Study of Income Dynamics (PSID). Specifically, the initial PSID sample in 1968 was highly clustered, with most original sample families having several other sample families living on the same block and who were subsequently followed over significant shares of the life course. This allows one to compare the similarity in adulthood health outcomes between siblings who grew up together versus unrelated individuals who grew up in the same narrowly defined neighborhood.

Estimating the overall scope of any such causal links of neighborhood environments is of substantial policy importance because the residential locations of both the poor and the affluent are influenced by public policies related to crime, subsidized housing, zoning, tax subsidies for home ownership, and school districting, among other things. Moreover, understanding how the effects of neighborhood conditions differ over the life cycle is critical to helping policymakers develop interventions (e.g., early childhood interventions or targeted policies for the geographic deconcentration of the poor) that build a bridge between childhood and early adulthood for impoverished families, so that fewer individuals arrive at the doorstep of retirement with accumulated exposures that are irreversible.

In the next section, I provide an overview of the ways that neighborhoods, as well as families, may directly and indirectly affect an individual's health trajectory in adulthood and then summarize previous research on a number of topics relevant to my research. The third section lays out the methodological hurdles in estimating causal effects of neighborhood conditions, while the fourth summarizes recent research findings using innovative approaches that address these methodological challenges across a range of health outcomes over the life course. The final section discusses the policy implications and interventions that show the most promise to promote population health in order to build a more comprehensive and efficient health system.

Why Might Neighborhood and Family Background Matter?

Family background can have direct effects on health status over the life course through several mechanisms. Transmission of genetic traits from parents to children clearly plays an important role. Parental socioeconomic and demographic characteristics most likely influence children's health status (Case, Lubotsky, and Paxson 2002), which in turn carries through to health status in adulthood. The transmission of health lifestyle orientation—eating habits, or exercise and smoking behaviors, for example—across generations may also translate into disparities in adult health.

Similarly, it has been hypothesized that neighborhood background can have direct effects on health. Childhood neighborhood factors such as water and air quality, sanitation, pollution and environmental toxins, crime, health care and social services, and public schools most likely have some influence on childhood health. Health lifestyle orientation may have a neighborhood component as well, with peer groups and role models within communities or neighborhoods influencing children's opportunities and preferences (Johnson 2007).

Perhaps equally or more important for health dynamics, both neighborhood and family background may indirectly affect health over the life course through their effects on the socioeconomic mobility process. The degree of socioeconomic mobility has direct connections to the resemblance of an individual's childhood and adult family characteristics, such as income and education, which may in turn affect health. Since economic status is a major determinant of residential choice, persistence in economic status is likely to lead to persistence in neighborhood quality as well; that is, the lower the economic mobility, the greater the correlation between childhood and adult neighborhood characteristics.

Previous Research

My recent research on the ways in which family and neighborhood background may affect health over the life course integrates a number of strands in the existing literature, including the life course perspective on health, the impact of stress on long-term health, the health effects of residential segregation, and the relationship between neighborhood conditions and intergenerational mobility. Each of these strands is briefly discussed below.

Life Course Perspective on Health

Research has shown that socioeconomic status and health status are highly correlated. This strong association holds for a variety of health status measures, is true in countries with varying levels of economic development and government-sponsored medical care, and has existed as far back in time as data are available. The association also holds across the entire life course, although the gap appears to widen with age through about age 60, and then declines (Smith 2004).

It is most likely the case that health causally affects economic status and economic status causally affects health, although the magnitude of each effect is uncertain (Smith 1999). If causality runs in both directions, then a life course model would imply that health problems early in life could affect health later in life because the problem is chronic, because the health shock damaged health stock making it more susceptible to deterioration later in life, and also because the health problem affects socioeconomic outcomes such as education which in turn influences health later in life (Kuh and Wadsworth 1993).

Impact of Stress on Health

Emerging research has sought to identify whether and how early-life differences in exposures to stressful life conditions get under the skin. There are compelling theoretical reasons to expect chronic stress linked to neighborhood environments to influence health trajectories. Recent findings in neuroscience demonstrate that prolonged exposure to stress hormones (e.g., cortisol) can suppress the body's immune response and cause greater vulnerability to chronic health conditions. Early life experiences of toxic stress, even in the womb, may have profound implications for later life health (Aizer, Stroud, and Buka 2008; Johnson and Schoeni 2007). Other research indicates that early-life risk factors compound over the life cycle—often-cited examples of the adaptive cost of stress-induced wear and tear ("weathering") include pushing the endocrine system toward diabetes or the cardiovascular system toward coronary artery disease and hypertension (Halfon and Hochstein 2002). Blacks appear to face more stress than comparable whites (Geronimus et al. 2006; Cohen et al. 2006), as evidenced in studies that document higher cortisol levels among blacks even after accounting for family income (DeSantis et al. 2007).

Recent findings in neuroscience also indicate that developmental health trajectories can be altered more readily during sensitive periods of rapid developmental change than during other periods. Heckman (2007) emphasized that "common developmental processes are at work where some cognitive and non-cognitive skills and health capabilities at one stage in childhood cross-fertilize the productivity of investment at later stages." Research evidence from this field increasingly supports the notion that the greatest opportunities to invest in health occur during the first twenty years of life. This suggests a need to shift some of the emphasis on treatment in later stages of disease toward the promotion of earlier, more effective prevention and an investment-oriented approach to health spending targeted to its most productive uses.

Metropolitan Form: Segregation and Fragmentation

No consensus among researchers has been reached on the assessment of the role of neighborhood quality versus overall residential segregation patterns in contributing to racial health disparities. Prior work has uncovered puzzling issues about the role of race in explaining spatial differences in morbidity and mortality that have yet to be resolved. In particular, people die younger in cities and states that are more segregated and have a higher fraction of African Americans in their populations; not only do blacks die younger than whites, but *both* blacks and whites die younger in places where the population is more heavily black and segregated (Deaton and Lubotsky 2002).

Hart et al. (1998) showed that metropolitan areas characterized by metropolitan governance had lower black mortality rates than areas characterized by municipal fragmentation and that housing segregation mediated the effect of metropolitan governance on black male mortality. Previous research has shown that fragmented local governance structures lead to greater black-white residential segregation within U.S. metropolitan areas.

Intergenerational Mobility

Research indicates that socioeconomic mobility tends to be lower among blacks than whites. Poor black children are less likely to escape poverty than poor white children (Bhattacharya and Mazumder 2007). In particular, Hertz (2005) found that 17 percent of whites in the bottom decile of family income remain there as adults compared to 42 percent of black children.

With a few exceptions, the role of neighborhood factors in contributing to this difference has received little attention in the literature. Intergenerational mobility literature has focused almost exclusively on cognitive skills and investments in education in understanding the process behind intergeneration persistence in economic status. Even in this work, however, the mechanisms by which effects are transmitted has not been identified.

One paper that *does* consider the role of neighborhoods on intergenerational mobility is that of Card and Rothstein (2006); they argued that differences in childhood neighborhood conditions and school quality may contribute to the lower rates of socioeconomic mobility observed among blacks. More recently, Johnson (2008b) has examined the relationship between residential and socioeconomic mobility. Johnson documented significantly higher rates of persistent exposures to poor neighborhoods from childhood through midlife among blacks. In particular, this work, using nationally representative data, shows that among cohorts born between 1951 and 1970, the average black child spent about one-fourth of his or her childhood years in high-poverty neighborhoods (i.e., neighborhood poverty rates in excess of 30 percent), and about one-third of the early to mid-adulthood years (ages 30–50) in high-poverty neighborhoods, while only roughly 15 percent of these adult years were lived in low-poverty neighborhoods (i.e., less than 10 percent of households in poverty). In addition, Johnson (2008b) demonstrated that childhood neighborhood poverty and related dimensions of childhood neighborhood disadvantage significantly influence mobility prospects and explain part of black-white differences in rates of upward mobility from poor families.

Methodological Challenges in Estimating Neighborhood Effects

The primary methodological challenge in estimating the causal effects of neighborhoods on health status is that unobserved factors that affect health may also be correlated with neighborhood factors, leading to biased estimates of neighborhood effects. This can arise from the self-selection associated with residential location. Namely, individuals and families choose where they live based on the characteristics they value (Tiebout 1956), although constraints such as racial discrimination and exclusionary zoning may be placed on that decision. In this context, families and individuals who care more about their health will be less likely to choose to live in an area with high crime, pollution, or a poor health care system; that is, they will tend to self-select into neighborhoods with "health-promoting" characteristics. In turn, if we observe that children who live in areas that score highly on health-promoting characteristics have better health than children who do not, it is difficult to determine the extent to which this is due to neighborhood characteristics and the extent to which it reflects their parents putting a high value on good health and taking a range of actions to foster it. This task is made particularly difficult because we do not actually observe the value that different households put on good health. Oakes (2004) argued that the lack of attention to the issue of self-selection in neighborhood choice implies that the resulting estimates of neighborhood effects "will always be wrong" (p. 1941).

The most powerful way to address self-selection is through a randomized trial of the type used in the MTO demonstration, where an experimental design is used to estimate the effects of offering housing assistance that allows individuals to move out of low-income neighborhoods (see Gennetian et al. in this volume). Evidence from two sites—Boston and New York—demonstrates that MTO had beneficial effects on the health of children and adults (Katz, Kling, and Liebman 2001; Leventhal and Brooks-Gunn 2000).

But research that can draw on an experimental design is rare. In turn, most studies have attempted to address self-selection using nonexperimental methods. The most common approach is the use of instrumental variable techniques (e.g., Evans, Oates, and Schwab 1992; Case and Katz 1991), where the exclusion restrictions are tenuous. An alternative nonexperimental approach is comparing siblings who have been raised in different neighborhoods at different ages because their parents have moved (Aaronson 1998; Plotnick and Hoffman 1999). But this approach is not satisfying either, because the key assumption is that the family effect is fixed, not time-varying. If, for example, families' preferences change as their children get older, and they become more interested in living in neighborhoods that are less risky for their children's health, then they might move to neighborhoods with less crime or pollution, which may in turn lead to better health outcomes for their kids. But if the underlying change in their preferences toward health outcomes not only caused them to change neighborhoods but also to spend more time encouraging their children to practice good health behaviors, then the neighborhood "effect" might actually be representing all of these other factors and not the true causal effects of neighborhoods per se.

The typical methods by which economists solve endogeneity problems are particularly ill suited for examining the question of whether and how neighborhood socioeconomic features influence long-run health trajectories. Difficulties in measuring neighborhood characteristics also become especially problematic when addressing this question. If health outcomes are a product of cumulative exposures to advantaged/disadvantaged environments spanning decades or exhibit long latent periods before problems manifest, as is hypothesized here, the connection between current neighborhood and current health may say little about the overall influence of neighborhood factors over the life cycle. As well, it may be important to conceptualize neighborhood effects as cumulative and variable over the life course as opposed to isolated and unchanging. Because most methods for overcoming endogenous neighborhood choice are based on small, short-run changes in the neighborhood environment, these approaches might be limited to uncovering effects only for rapidly responding intermediate outcomes such as health behaviors (e.g., smoking/drinking, exercise/diet). An additional issue is that neighborhood variables of the underlying neighborhood feature of interest are notoriously measured with a great deal of error. The neighborhood attributes of interest change slowly over time, so most year-to-year variations in the characteristic are comprised of measurement error.

Summary of New Evidence

I have recently conducted a series of studies that employ an empirical strategy that largely sidesteps the pitfalls of neighborhood studies in confronting the endogeneity of residential location by exploiting unique features of the Panel Study of Income Dynamics (PSID). The PSID is the longest-running nationally representative longitudinal study of the United States, spanning 1968–2005. These studies are among the first to use nationally representative data from the United States to analyze the persistence in neighborhood quality over the life course and investigate its health consequences later in life. The analysis utilizes the PSID, spanning nearly four decades, and follows two study samples: a cohort born between 1951 and 1970 from childhood through midlife, and older cohorts born between 1920 and 1949 followed from young to mid-adulthood through late life. I examine several different health outcomes, including self-assessed health status, risky health behaviors and risk preference formation in childhood, the onset of health-limiting conditions, the onset of hypertension, and mortality.

The research findings that emerge from this array of health outcomes at different stages of the life cycle provide corroborating evidence on the role of neighborhood environments over the life course on health. The consistency of findings across the study samples and health outcomes at different stages of the life course paints a cohesive portrait of the influence of neighborhood disadvantage earlier in the life cycle on health later in life.

Key Features of the Empirical Approach

The first goal of the analysis is focused on an overall assessment of the relative contributions of individual, childhood family, and neighborhood effects on health in childhood and early to mid-adulthood. A key to the empirical strategy and research design employed is that the initial PSID sample in 1968 was highly clustered, with most PSID families having several other sample families living on the same block. This survey design allows a comparison of the similarity in health from childhood through midlife between siblings versus unrelated individuals who grew up in the same neighborhood (using the younger cohort sample), and also allows us to compare the similarity in late-life health between spouses, versus unrelated individuals who were living in the same narrowly defined neighborhood during their young adult years (using the older cohort sample). This approach avoids the difficulty of defining neighborhood quality and instead compares sibling correlations with neighbor correlations, placing an upper bound on the neighborhood influence and allowing a comparison of the relative magnitudes of child neighborhood versus family effects.

The intuition behind this strategy is that if family background and residential community are important determinants of health outcomes, there will be a strong correlation between siblings in their health outcomes, as compared to two arbitrarily chosen individuals. Sibling correlations in health outcomes reflect the influence of all family and neighborhood background factors shared by siblings—measured and unmeasured—that may have an impact on health outcomes, such as the socioeconomic status of parents, genetic traits, and family structure, as well as neighborhood quality. And, if the neighborhood where the child grew up is important, it will show up as a strong correlation between *neighboring* children's subsequent health outcomes.

The overarching logic of the analytic approach is that if the neighbor correlations prove to be substantial, then that provides greater rationale for the further investigation of which neighborhood features matter and explain the lasting importance of childhood neighborhood conditions. Upon discovering substantial child neighbor correlations in adult health outcomes, I analyze the relative contribution of a rich array of measured individual, family, and neighborhood covariates to the total variation from each of these three components and test hypotheses about the effects of specific characteristics of families and neighborhoods.

The comparison of sibling and child neighbor correlations in adult health, and the comparisons between spousal and adult neighbor correlations in late-life health, allow an assessment of the relative magnitudes of the effects of the childhood neighborhood and family environments on adult health, as well as an assessment of the effects of neighborhood environment in adulthood versus family characteristics in adulthood. The findings are based on the estimation of four-level hierarchical random effects models of various dimensions of health.

There are four primary reasons why the approach taken in this work may be able to detect neighborhood effects in ways previous studies have been unable to do. First, in contrast to the experimental evidence and previous observational studies, the analysis examines effects over a much longer time horizon, using data over the life course spanning nearly four decades. This is particularly important for most health outcomes, as there is likely a long lag between poor neighborhood quality and the manifestation of health effects. Second, instead of focusing on contemporaneous neighborhood effects, I analyze the lasting effects of neighborhood environments earlier in the life cycle, which include cumulative exposure to neighborhood conditions that may vary over the life cycle. Third, I use the census block as the definition of neighborhood, which comprises a much smaller geographic area than previous studies utilize. Finally, I use estimates of neighbor correlations as an omnibus measure of the potential effects of neighborhood quality (including unmeasured characteristics), rather than initially focusing the analysis on particular observable neighborhood attributes.

Two unique aspects of the project findings include the relationship between cumulative neighborhood exposures over the life course and later-life health and the role of neighborhood environments in contributing to socioeconomic and racial health disparities. The innovative research design and unique measures collected on aspects of neighborhood physical, service, and social environments—including neighborhood poverty and crime, income and education, county per-pupil school expenditures, birth weight and health insurance, race and residential segregation, health behaviors, housing quality, and connectedness to informal sources of support—help illuminate what lies along the chain of causation from poverty to health outcomes over the life course.

Below, I summarize key findings that emerge from these studies by life cycle stage.

Key Findings

First, the overall scope of childhood family and neighborhood influences on health implied by the estimated sibling and child neighbor correlations in health outcomes over the life course is substantial. The results show that sibling correlations in general health status are roughly 0.6 through at least the first fifty years of life—suggesting that three-fifths of adult health disparities may be attributable to family and neighborhood background. I also find childhood neighbor correlations in adult health that are substantial (net of the similarity arising from similar observable family characteristics). The results suggest that disparities in neighborhood background account for between one-third and 40 percent of the variation in health status in midlife. The estimates indicate that a child who grows up in a neighborhood at the tenth percentile of the neighborhood quality distribution has roughly a 0.3 chance of falling in the bottom decile of the adult health distribution and has only a 0.15 chance of rising above the median.

The overall scale of both childhood family and neighborhood factors on health through midlife (implied by the sibling and child neighbor correlations in health) provided the impetus for further investigation of what aspects of childhood family and neighborhood features influence subsequent health trajectories and explain their lasting impacts. The full set of findings from this inquiry is reported in Johnson (2007), and summarized below.

What Aspects of Childhood Neighborhood and Family Socioeconomic Status Matter?

The results indicate that the composite neighborhood effects reflected in the significant child neighbor correlations in adult health appear to emanate both from the direct effects of neighborhood quality during childhood on child health, which may carry over into adulthood, and from indirect effects via the economic mobility process. Differences in developmental health trajectories explain much of the variance in the nature and rate of later declines in health.

The socioeconomic gradient in health is not fully accounted for by differentials in education, access to health care, or health behaviors; and childhood neighborhood conditions play a role in explaining the steepening of the gradient through midlife, indicating the lasting importance of childhood conditions. Significant child health and adult health status differences are associated with child and family characteristics, including parental income and education, parental expectations for child achievement, child health insurance coverage, birth weight, and parental health status, and with child neighborhood characteristics, including child neighborhood poverty and crime, racial composition and childhood residential segregation, school district per-pupil spending, and neighborhood housing quality. Child neighborhood poverty was found to be the single most salient neighborhood characteristic that influenced the subsequent health trajectory. The results reveal several patterns: (1) children growing up in poverty experience significantly higher rates of problematic health throughout life; (2) exposure to concentrated neighborhood poverty during childhood and cumulative exposure through midlife is highly predictive of adult health status problems at midlife; and (3) the socioeconomic gradient in health appears to widen over the life course, as the health deterioration rate is more rapid in adulthood among those who grew up in more disadvantaged child neighborhood and family environments. The results also reveal substantial persistence in health status across generations that is linked in part to low intergenerational economic mobility.

The results indicate that exposure to concentrated neighborhood poverty over the life course has significant deleterious impacts on later-life health, with the size of the effects varying with age. The largest neighborhood effects were identified during childhood and to some degree in young adulthood, with a far lesser role for contemporaneous neighborhood exposures in contemporaneous health outcomes. The widely discussed correlation between contemporaneous neighborhood conditions in adulthood and adult health status arises mostly because it is *lifetime neighborhood exposures* that have cumulative effects on health and mortality risk, and lifetime neighborhood quality and family resources are strongly positively related to contemporaneous neighborhood environments in adulthood. Most health outcomes are a product of cumulative exposures to advantaged/disadvantaged environments spanning decades or exhibit long latent periods before problems manifest. Therefore, the connection between current neighborhood and current health says relatively little about the overall influence of neighborhood factors over the life cycle. These research findings also point more generally to the importance of conceptualizing neighborhood effects as cumulative and variable over the life course as opposed to isolated and unchanging.

Causality Versus Selection Bias

Conditions of persistent exposures to disadvantaged neighborhoods, particularly high-poverty neighborhoods, appear to be responsible to a significant degree for the patterns of accelerated health deterioration and the socioeconomic gradient. Is this causal inference justified, or does it reflect selection bias? While there is no single perfect solution to address the endogeneity of residential location, there are ways to determine if selection bias is driving the results. The fact that the effect of concentrated neighborhood poverty is weaker when the duration of exposure is brief and parents know few of their neighbors suggests that selection bias is not driving these results. If effects simply represented unmeasured family factors, then the number of years in the neighborhood and the number of neighbors known by name should not be associated with the strength of these effects. But that is not the case here.

To probe the robustness of a causal inference, I also employed a novel empirical approach, recently proposed by Altonji, Elder, and Taber (2005), to gauge how sensitive estimates of the effects of neighborhood poverty are to selection on unobserved variables. The results reveal that even a large amount of selection on unobservable factors does not eliminate the significant effect of neighborhood poverty on health status later in life.

Toward Understanding Sources of Adult Racial Health Disparities

Another important contribution of my work is its systematic analysis of the evolution of racial health disparities over the life course and its attempt to explain the level of sibling and neighbor correlations and the way that these correlations evolve with age. In the results reported in Johnson (2007), general health status in childhood and adulthood through midlife is the key outcome analyzed, while the likelihood of onset of hypertension in adulthood is the health condition analyzed in Johnson (2008a). Both studies found that racial differences in adult health can be accounted for by childhood family and neighborhood factors, while contemporaneous adult economic factors account for relatively little of this gap.

Findings on hypertension are of particular interest because it is a major risk factor for heart disease and stroke, the leading causes of death in the United States. Blacks' higher prevalence of cardiovascular disease-related risk factors account for more than half of the racial disparity in longevity (Barghaus et al. 2007), with hypertension the leading culprit. I found that childhood neighborhood poverty and its attendant stressors play an influential role in shaping risks of onset of hypertension in middle age. Other notable neighborhood factors that were shown to influence risks of onset of hypertension in adulthood include childhood neighborhood crime exposure and county per-pupil school expenditures; notable child and family background factors include birth weight, parental health status, and parental socioeconomic status. These effects appear linked, in part, to low intergenerational economic mobility, particularly among blacks. The results indicate that racial differences in these early-life neighborhood conditions and family background characteristics play a significant role in explaining racial disparities in hypertension through at least age 50, while contemporaneous economic factors account for relatively little of the racial disparities in this health condition in adulthood. Findings such as these facilitate the identification of the antecedents of health at midlife and provide us with a better understanding of the early risk factors for health decline among older adults.

Mid- to Late-Life Health

The focus to this point has been on childhood to midlife. Johnson, Schoeni, and Rogowski (2008) and Johnson (2008c) sought to identify origins of health disparities at older ages, again with emphasis on the influence of the neighborhood environment and residential segregation. The results show that black men have a 79 percent higher mortality hazard in mid- to late life, relative to white men. The black-white gap in mortality risk is cut by about half after inclusion of controls for childhood and young adult family socioeconomic factors, including income, educational attainment, health insurance coverage, and to a lesser extent health behaviors. Furthermore, the study found that racial differences in longevity can be fully accounted for by childhood and young adult family *and* neighborhood socioeconomic factors, particularly neighborhood poverty and crime. The results highlight the significant role of neighborhood poverty in shaping adult mortality risks. I found that living in a high-poverty neighborhood during young adulthood increases subsequent mortality risks by 56 percent, relative to living in a low-poverty neighborhood.

The results demonstrate that the average health status of a 55-year-old who lived in a high-poverty neighborhood during young adulthood is roughly at the same level of health as a 70-year-old who lived in a low-poverty neighborhood during young adulthood. The implied difference in the rates of health deterioration by neighborhood poverty status is on par with the effect size of the well-known college-high school education gradient in health status. The study thus highlights substantial race differences in the incidence and duration of exposure to concentrated poverty over the life course with grave health consequences. The work also reveals high rates of immobility from poor neighborhoods over the life course, especially among African Americans.

Policy Implications and Directions for Future Research

The US leads the world as the most technologically advanced in clinical research and medical practice. We spend more on medical care than any other nation (now more than 16 percent of GDP), but our health system produces inferior health outcomes relative to many other developed countries. The performance gaps in our current system include: (1) the more than 45 million uninsured; (2) escalating medical costs; (3) the highly variable quality of health care; and (4) the failure to invest in measures to promote long-term health.

As emphasized by Chernichovsky and Liebowitz (2008), the singular focus on expanding health insurance ignores the necessity to design a health system that integrates preventive care and population-wide health initiatives over the life course. There remains a significant imbalance between resources devoted to public and population health with those spent on personal medical care. For example, 95 percent of the trillion dollars we spend on health goes to direct medical care services, while just 5 percent is allocated to population-wide health improvement (McGinnis, Williams-Russo, and Knickman 2002). It has been estimated that 10–15 percent of preventable mortality could be averted by better availability and higher quality of medical care. This suggests that a more substantial share of deaths may be caused by exposures (and behaviors formed) earlier in life that could be modified by preventive interventions.

If we want to expand our investments in promoting health, thereby reducing the demand for spending to restore health, what types of public policy interventions show the most promise, and at what stage of the life cycle? There may be critical periods early in life that represent windows of opportunity to affect neighborhood conditions that can have a profound impact on economic mobility patterns and health later in life. The research discussed here tests for differential effects of socioeconomic neighborhood conditions by life cycle stage, and the results highlight childhood as a critical period, in part because it sets the stage for a socioeconomic mobility process that has far-reaching impacts on later-life health.

Current health policies, however, do not reflect the implications of these research findings. From a public policy perspective, we have allowed a mismatch to develop between the opportunity for positively influencing an individual's healthy development during childhood, when this development is most malleable, and the other public investments we make in health services in later-stage adulthood. Overall, U.S. health policy has traditionally taken a rehabilitative approach that includes an emphasis on programs aimed at increasing access to health insurance and medical care services, rather than a preventive approach that might be more likely to incorporate consideration of childhood neighborhood conditions. In short, we have traditionally appealed to medical care access to remedy what disadvantaged neighborhood and family environments produce.

In contrast, the research findings underscore the potential for targeting neighborhood conditions as a means of improving population health and confronting health inequality. A shift in resources from expanding health care delivery expenditures for individuals at later ages to targeting disadvantaged neighborhoods at earlier stages of the life course may be a promising (and cost-effective) avenue for increasing population health and reducing racial/ethnic disparities.

Future research findings must help advance our understanding of the optimal ways to allocate resources between family-focused access to medical care and alternative policy programs that improve population health and reduce health disparities, including some that are not traditionally thought of as health programs. It is critical to examine whether society allocates resources in an optimal way across different health-improving policy levers. Unless the government spends in such a way that the marginal benefit (health improvement achieved from the last dollar spent) is the same for each activity, society will not be promoting population health in the most cost-effective manner. Neighborhoods research has promise to yield new insights that may point to reallocating resources toward approaches with higher payoffs, which may increase health for a given level of expenditure.

Housing and Income Policies Are Health Policies

Promoting good health cannot be the purview of the health care system alone. Many prevention initiatives depend upon policy changes that are outside the traditional health policy domain. There is a need, for purposes of targeting efficiency, to understand the geography of health, and there is also a need to assess health impacts of policies outside of the health care sector (e.g., road building, the built environment, environmental toxins).

It is particularly important to understand how housing policy affects health. Federal, state, and local governments intervene in the housing market by providing, subsidizing, or constraining the purchase, location, or rental of housing in a variety of ways, including tax policy, zoning law, and the provision of housing for low-income families. Evaluation of housing policy on health has focused on factors related to the built physical environment (such as exposure to lead and air pollution). However, less attention has been paid to how housing policy affects health through its effects on socioeconomic neighborhood conditions.

Housing mobility programs and demonstrations (e.g., the Yonkers scattered site public housing program), implemented for their potential impacts on racial and economic desegregation, have received far less attention for their potential longer-run (unintended) beneficial health effects. In the case of mixed-income housing policies, mixed-income developments have been shown to help alleviate the geographic concentration of urban poverty, but the verdict is still out on the potential for mixed-income housing development as a means of helping lift families in U.S. inner cities out of poverty and improving their future health trajectories. We are particularly interested in trying to better articulate the possible health impacts of mixed-income developments on low-income families. Why do we expect mixed-income neighborhood development to promote health, a higher quality of life, and upward mobility for low-income families? How might specifying our expectations for the benefits of this strategy more clearly inform current policy debates on how best to invest in health for disadvantaged families?

Future research should work toward providing an empirical assessment of whether our current policy of increased reliance on medical interventions at later ages and declining spending on housing and social welfare programs that come into play at earlier stages of the life cycle is the best way to spend our health-promoting dollars. Targeted housing and income-support policy for the poor to reduce highly concentrated poverty may be more cost-effective, at prevailing levels of expenditure, for improving population health than spending the same amount of funds on a (weak) health care delivery system.

How big are the health effects of income-support and housing policy targeted toward childhood conditions compared with effects of explicit health interventions? Future work should evaluate the cost and health-improving potential of housing and income-support programs. Further, it should attempt to set forth conditions under which a shift in resources from expanding health care delivery expenditures at later ages to targeting disadvantaged families and neighborhoods at earlier stages of the life course would lead to an increase in population health and reduction in racial/ethnic health disparities.

A policy that is based on evidence from research on the social determinants of health and that integrates housing and income-support policies at various stages of the life cycle would not just strengthen overall health status and the stock of human capital but may also improve educational attainments, reduce income inequality, and promote economic growth. If we really want to reduce the economic and social costs of health disparities, then we must confront its early roots. This chapter has summarized the accumulating research evidence underscoring the role of childhood family and neighborhood conditions.

In order to provide more specific policy prescriptions, we need a better understanding of the pathways through which neighborhoods and families affect health. We must recognize that policies that operate through access to medical care such as health insurance coverage, policies that operate primarily through family income such as Earned Income Tax Credits and minimum wages, and policies that work at the neighborhood level through improving the quality of neighborhoods, housing, local hospitals, and schools in inner cities operate through different pathways and may influence health outcomes in different ways. And as we must also recognize that even when we narrow our focus to neighborhood influences on health, peer group effects, role model effects, and the multilayered interaction of family and community factors represent distinct influences under the umbrella of neighborhood effects, and each has different policy implications. Disentangling the causal sources of neighborhood effects is extremely difficult (Manski 1993; Moffitt 1998), but the attempt to understand the mechanisms of why neighborhoods matter is an important area for future research.

Chapter 3

Educational Interventions
Their Effects on the Achievement of Poor Children

Brian A. Jacob and Jens Ludwig

Low-income children in the United States face an elevated risk for a variety of adverse educational outcomes. According to the 2007 National Assessment of Educational Progress (NAEP), only 16 percent of fourth-grade students eligible for free lunch score at proficient levels in reading compared with 44 percent of fourth graders whose family incomes are above the eligibility cutoff for free lunch. The disparity in math scores is even larger, 21 percent versus 53 percent (NCES 2007). One potential explanation for these disparities is that low-income children, particularly low-income minority children, are disproportionately likely to live in our nation's most disadvantaged urban neighborhoods (Jargowsky 1996, 2003). Many observers contend that the concentration of poverty exacerbates poor children's schooling difficulties through a variety of mechanisms, including low-quality schools and damaging peer influences. This possibility of "neighborhood effects" on children's schooling outcomes has generated interest in mobility interventions of the sort discussed elsewhere in this volume (for example, see Gennetian et al.). An alternative strategy, and the focus of the present chapter, is to identify ways of directly improving the quality of schooling in disadvantaged urban neighborhoods.

The question of how to improve the quality of schooling received by disadvantaged children has been the source of considerable debate within the social sciences from at least the 1966 publication of the so-called Coleman Report. The 1964 Civil Rights Act required a study of inequality in educational opportunities "by reason of race, color, religion, or national origin," which in turn led to the most massive nationwide education data collection effort that had ever been attempted, headed by the distinguished sociologist James Coleman. This landmark study revealed that most of the variation in student test scores is within, rather than across, schools. The Coleman Report also found that family background is the strongest predictor of academic achievement, and that most measurable school inputs—with the exception perhaps of a school's socioeconomic composition—are weakly correlated with student outcomes. A subsequent series of disappointing evaluation studies of educational interventions contributed to the sense of pessimism (see, for example, Levin 1977; Glazer 1986; Jencks 1986). Since then, however, our ability to uncover moderately sized program impacts within the messy context of school outcomes has been enhanced by a dramatic improvement in the technology of education policy evaluation.

The literature on educational interventions is often dominated by contentious, highly ideological debates about what should guide school reform efforts—one of the most prominent being whether improving student learning requires additional resources. The surprising findings of the Coleman Report contributed to a gradual shift from a focus on reforms that involve the inputs to schooling to those that emphasize improving the efficiency of schooling, and to evaluating those reforms on the basis of schooling "outputs," the most important being student learning.

Among strategies that seek to improve the efficiency of schooling, some strive to change school organization, curriculum, and instructional practices in very specific ways. These reforms operate at the school or classroom level. Other efficiency-oriented strategies target what one might describe as "macro" or "structural" aspects of schooling. These reforms do not prescribe specific practices but rather seek to change the market structure and/or incentives within which educators work, under the assumption that given the proper incentives and/or institutional arrangements, school administrators and teachers will be able to implement the reforms best suited to their particular needs.

In this chapter, we offer a message of tempered optimism. Rigorous research has identified several intervention strategies that seem capable of improving the schooling outcomes of disadvantaged children. The available evidence provides some support for both input- and output-oriented approaches. There do seem to be some inefficiencies within the existing public school system. There are several strategies for improving student outcomes that do not require large amounts of additional spending. For example, changing the incentives facing school administrators, teachers, and students can change behavior. Given the evidence of unintended consequences, the design and implementation of accountability programs are crucial to their success. At the same time, research also provides support for the idea that additional educational investments can improve student outcomes even without substantial changes in the structure or incentives of the existing K-12 schooling system. Reducing class sizes in the early grades seems like a promising intervention, assuming this can be done in a way that does not compromise teacher quality. Additional investments in disadvantaged children during the preschool years also seem quite promising. While these interventions will require additional resources, there is good reason to believe that the benefits that result, to the children themselves and to society as a whole, will be large enough to justify the costs.

Our optimism is tempered by the recognition that even the most successful education policy interventions will reduce, but not eliminate, disparities in educational outcomes across lines of race and social class. The average achievement scores for minority students in the United States lag behind white students by around one standard deviation, with even greater disparities between the most disadvantaged minority children and the average white student.[1] Even the most successful education policy interventions described below would improve test scores by no more than about a quarter of a standard deviation, enough to pass a cost-benefit test but not enough to equalize educational opportunity for all American children. This is not a reason for despair, but it does suggest that schooling interventions and social programs should be viewed as complements rather than substitutes.

Early Childhood Interventions

A growing body of research in neuroscience, developmental psychology, economics, and other fields suggests that the earliest years of life may be a particularly promising time to intervene in the lives of low-income children (Shonkoff and Phillips 2000; Carniero and Heckman 2003; Knudsen et al. 2006). One set of research has focused on small-scale, intensive intervention programs such as the Perry Preschool and Abecedarian programs. The Perry Preschool intervention provided one or two years of part-day educational services and home visits to a sample of low-income, low-IQ African American children aged 3 and 4 in Ypsilanti, Michigan, during the 1960s. Perry Preschool hired highly educated teachers (with at least a B.A.) and was implemented as a randomized experiment. Some mothers and their children were randomly assigned to the Perry program, while others were assigned to a control group that did not receive the same interventions.

When the children entered school, those who had participated in the Perry program scored .9 standard deviations higher on IQ tests than those who had not (Schweinhart et al. 2005). These IQ effects, however, disappeared by third grade. Nevertheless, the program produced lasting effects on reading and math achievement test scores as well as subsequent employment, earnings, and criminal participation. As for the last follow-up, when the participants were 40 years of age, those children who had participated in the Perry Preschool program had higher employment rates (76 percent compared with 62 percent) and earnings (median annual earnings of $20,800 compared with $15,300 in 2000 dollars) and substantially lower likelihood of ever having been arrested (29 percent of the participating children reached age 40 without an arrest as compared with 17 percent of the control group).

Another highly touted "model" intervention was the Abecedarian program. The Abecedarian program, which began in 1972 and served a sample of low-income, mostly African American women from Chapel Hill, North Carolina, was even more intensive than Perry. Mothers and children assigned to the Abecedarian "treatment" received year-round, full-time care for five years, starting with the child's first year of life. The Abecedarian preschool program included transportation, individualized educational activities that changed as the children aged, and low child-teacher ratios (3:1 for the youngest children and up to 6:1 for older children). Abecedarian teachers followed a curriculum that focused on language development and explained to teachers the importance of each task as well as how to teach it. High-quality health care, additional social services, and nutritional supplements were also provided to participating families (Ramey and Campbell 1979; Campbell et al. 2002; Barnett and Masse 2007).

Abecedarian was a high-cost, high-quality program run by researchers rather than by a government agency. It cost about $18,000 a year for each of a child's first five years and produced dramatic effects on the future life outcomes of its participants (Currie 2001). As with the Perry Preschool program, Abecedarian was evaluated as a random assignment study. Treatment and control-group children had IQ scores that averaged about 1 standard deviation below the mean at baseline, as would be expected for children from economically disadvantaged backgrounds. By the time the Abecedarian children reached age 5, however, their IQ scores were close to the national average, and roughly two-thirds of a standard deviation higher than scores of children who did not participate. Similarly large effects were observed for achievement on verbal and quantitative tests (Ramey and Campbell 1984).

Although IQ effects faded somewhat over time with Abecedarian, other long-term effects were dramatic and arguably just as important for reducing poverty. For example, children who received the Abecedarian program entered college at 2.5 times the rate of the control group. The Abecedarian intervention also reduced rates of teen parenthood and marijuana use by nearly half (Campbell et al. 2002). Although employment rates were not statistically different between the Abecedarian and control groups (64 percent compared with 50 percent), children who had participated in the program were about two-thirds more likely to be working in a skilled job (67 percent compared with 41 percent), a difference that is statistically significant. Despite its substantial cost and the need to discount benefits accrued in the distant future, the total economic value of Abecedarian's benefits seems to far exceed the costs of the program (Barnett and Masse 2007).

Evidence from the existing publicly funded early education programs is also encouraging. A recent random-assignment evaluation of Head Start found positive short-term effects of program participation on elementary prereading and prewriting skills equal to about 0.3 and 0.2 of a standard deviation, respectively. Head Start participation also increased parent-reported literacy skills of children by around 0.45 of a standard deviation. The Head Start experimental study evaluated all of the impacts separately for 3- versus 4-year-olds, given the possibility that program impacts might be larger for younger children. Statistically significant effects on other outcome domains were typically concentrated among 3-year-olds, with effect sizes of 0.15 for vocabulary and 0.20 for problem behaviors.

While the short-run achievement gains are impressive, the crucial question from a policy perspective is whether the effects of the large-scale early childhood education programs persist over time. In order to explore the longer-run impacts of such programs, one must rely on nonexperimental studies of children who participated in Head Start several decades ago. While this work is necessarily subject to certain limitations, there are several studies of the long-run impacts of Head Start that are able to control for many potentially confounding factors (Currie and Thomas 1995; Garces, Thomas, and Currie 2002; Ludwig and Miller 2007; Deming 2007). These studies suggest lasting improvements in schooling attainment and perhaps less likelihood of criminal activity, although test score effects appear to fade out over time. Like Abecedarian and Perry, these effects are large enough to generate benefits that likely outweigh the program costs. While there remains some uncertainty about what is the "best" early childhood program model and the extent to which the effects will persist, it seems clear that preschool interventions in general represent a promising way to improve the life chances of poor children.

Class Size Reduction

An alternative way to improve student learning during the early grades is to reduce average class sizes, which may enable teachers to spend more time working with individual students, tailor instruction to match children's needs, and make it easier for teachers to monitor classroom behavior. Class size reductions are not cheap, however. Reducing class sizes requires hiring additional teachers and in some cases expanding a school's physical space. But the best available evidence suggests that class size reduction can improve student outcomes by enough to justify these additional expenditures, with benefits that are particularly pronounced for low-income and minority children.

The best available evidence on the effects of reducing class size comes from Tennessee's Project STAR, which randomly assigned a total of 11,600 students in grades K-3 and 1,330 teachers to small classes (13–17 students), regular size classrooms (22–25 students), or regular-size classrooms that also included a teacher's aide.[2] Importantly, teachers were randomly assigned to different classroom environments as well as students. This ensures that the average quality of teachers in small versus regular size classrooms is the same.

Analysis of the Project STAR data suggests that class size reductions of around one-third during these early grades increased Stanford-9 reading and math scores by around .12 standard deviations for whites and .24 standard deviations for blacks. These impacts seem to be driven by larger impacts on students attending mostly black schools, although even within such schools, black students seem to benefit somewhat more than do whites (Krueger and Whitmore 2002). Similarly, impacts are somewhat larger for students eligible for the free lunch program. The STAR demonstration increased test scores by about the same amount for boys and girls, which is important, given evidence from some other interventions like Perry Preschool or residential mobility interventions that gains may be concentrated largely among girls (Schweinhart et al. 2005; Anderson 2008; Kling, Ludwig, and Katz 2005; Kling, Liebman, and Katz 2007a).

Follow-up evaluation of STAR found that test score impacts persisted through eighth grade, although the impacts declined by one-half to two-thirds (Achilles et al. 1993; Nye et al. 1995; Krueger and Whitmore 2001). Follow-up scores, like the short-term impacts, again revealed larger gains among low-income and minority students. STAR also provides evidence of even longer-term impacts of attending a smaller class in the early grades. Black students in the treatment group were roughly 5 percentage points (or 15 percent) more likely to take a college entrance exam (i.e., the SAT or ACT) during high school (Krueger and Whitmore 2001, 2002). Examination of other outcomes such as criminal involvement or teen births yielded point estimates that are in the direction of beneficial impacts, but these were imprecisely estimated (Schanzenbach 2006/7).

Figuring out whether STAR passes a benefit-cost test is complicated by the difficulty of calculating the value of test score gains that occur during the school years on longer-term life outcomes such as earnings, health, crime, citizenship and civic involvement, parenting quality, and so on. With this caveat in mind, the available evidence suggests that the test score gains induced in STAR were probably large enough to justify the costs, even when we focus just on the benefits that arise from test scores on future earnings alone (Krueger 2003; Krueger and Whitmore 2001; Schanzenbach 2006/7).

The results from Project STAR are encouraging, but it is important to keep in mind that they come from a controlled experiment that managed to hold the quality of teachers constant. A sobering example of the challenges of taking class size to scale comes from Jepsen and Rivkin (2002), who examined California's experience with trying to reduce classes statewide. The effort in California required schools to hire a large number of new teachers. The policy was implemented over a very short time period and was not accompanied by an increase in teacher salaries. As a result, many low-income school districts found it difficult to hire highly qualifed teachers to staff the new classrooms. Jepsen and Rivkin found that a large share of the benefits of class size reduction in California was lost because of reductions in average teacher quality, particularly in lower-income urban school districts.

California's example suggests that efforts focused on improving outcomes for low-income minority students may wish to implement class size reduction in areas serving those students, although this strategy may generate less political support compared to a more widespread class size reduction policy. And regardless of how widely or narrowly a new policy is targeted, the experiences in California suggest that additional resources may be required to ensure an adequate pool of high-quality teacher candidates. This means that the costs of class size reduction found in STAR will understate the costs we should expect with a larger-scale policy, although as noted above, estimates of the dollar value of benefits from STAR are almost surely also understated because they ignore all of the benefits that higher test scores generate for individuals and society as a whole beyond increased earnings.

Curricular and Instructional Interventions

The benefits of preschool intervention may be squandered if disadvantaged children spend time in low-quality elementary or high schools. There is a vast literature within education that studies the efficacy of classroom-based interventions, including curricula, pedagogical strategies, professional development approaches and features of school organization that are directly related to teaching and learning. Unfortunately, very few of these programs have been rigorously evaluated, and as a result, there have been many heated debates about the relative effectiveness of these interventions (What Works Clearinghouse 2007a and 2007b; Dynarski et al. 2007).

A particularly interesting and conceptually appealing subset of interventions is commonly referred to as comprehensive or Whole School Reform (WSR) models. As their name suggests, these programs simultaneously attempt to improve a variety of different aspects of the school at the same time. For example, a WSR model may combine curriculum materials, professional development, teacher mentoring, reorganization of the school day (e.g., block scheduling), and changing the school structure (e.g., schools-within-a-school).

At the elementary level, there is evidence to suggest that a few models may improve student outcomes. Perhaps the most promising intervention is Success for All (SFA). SFA is a comprehensive whole-school reform model that operates in more than 1,200 mostly high-poverty Title I schools. SFA focuses on reading, with a particular emphasis on prevention and early intervention. A number of studies have found SFA to have large, positive effects on student achievement. A recent random assignment evaluation of SFA provides more compelling evidence of the program's effectiveness (see Borman et al. 2007). At the end of three years, students in the treatment schools scored roughly .2 standard deviations higher than students in the control schools. These effects were statistically significant and substantial in magnitude (i.e., .2 standard deviations is equivalent to about one-fifth the gap between low and high socioeconomic-status children).

At the high school level, a number of popular WSR models incorporate similar features. Perhaps the most common feature of high school WSR models involves a reorganization of the larger high school into smaller learning communities, which are referred to under a number of different names, including "small schools," "schools within a school," and "learning academies." The goal of small learning communities is to provide a more personalized learning environment that will serve to engage and motivate students and prevent at-risk students from falling through the cracks.

While these models are promising in many respects, there is little rigorous evidence that, as currently implemented, these approaches improve student outcomes. The most rigorous evaluation of a high school WSR is the random assignment study of career academies, which was initiated in 1993 and is continuing to this day. Career academies are generally organized as small learning communities of between 150 and 200 high school students (often housed within larger, comprehensive high schools) that focus on a specific occupation or industry. The research firm MDRC conducted a random assignment study of career academies in nine high schools across the country (Kemple and Scott-Clayton 2004). Early results indicated a substantial impact on earnings among high-risk students.

Education Accountability

Class size reduction is an example of an "input-based" educational intervention, which is based on the assumption that schools will perform better with additional resources. The SFA program seeks to improve schooling outcomes with a prescriptive approach that lays out a new and hopefully more effective set of teaching strategies. A different approach is to instead incentivize teachers to identify more effective pedagogical strategies on their own or motivate them to implement whatever strategies they are using more effectively. This bottom-up approach is at the heart of education accountability reform, which allows for some heterogeneity in what constitutes best practice across schools, classrooms, and individual children.

The Chicago accountability reform of the late 1990s has been particularly well studied. Jacob (2005) examined the impact of an accountability policy implemented in the Chicago Public Schools (CPS) in 1996–97. In 1996 the CPS introduced a comprehensive accountability policy designed to raise academic achievement. The first component of the policy focused on holding students accountable for learning, by ending a practice commonly known as "social promotion" whereby students are advanced to the next grade regardless of ability or achievement level. Students who do not meet minimum standards are required to attend a six-week summer school program, after which they retake the exams. Note that eighth graders who failed to meet the promotion requirements were not able to graduate elementary school and move with their cohort to high school. Conversations with students and teachers indicate that this provided eighth grade students with a particularly strong incentive to improve their performance.

In conjunction with the social promotion policy, the CPS also instituted a policy designed to hold teachers and schools accountable for student achievement. Under this policy, schools in which fewer than 15 percent of students scored at or above national norms on reading exams were placed on probation. If they did not exhibit sufficient improvement, these schools could be reconstituted, which involved the dismissal or reassignment of teachers and school administrators.

Using a panel of student-level, administrative data, Jacob (2005) found that math and reading achievement increased sharply following the introduction of the accountability policy. However, for younger students, the policy did not increase performance on a state-administered, low-stakes exam. An item-level analysis suggests that the observed achievement gains were driven by increases in test-specific skills and student effort. Various studies suggest that test preparation associated with high-stakes testing may artificially inflate achievement, producing gains that are not generalizable to other exams (Linn et al. 1990; Shepard 1990; Koretz et al. 1991; Koretz and Barron 1998; Stecher and Barron 1999; Klein et. al. 2000).

Teacher Labor Markets

An alternative approach to enhancing students' classroom experience is to change the mix of teachers working in schools serving disadvantaged students or to change the compensation offered to existing teachers. If we could give disadvantaged children access to the most effective teachers, that may make a substantial difference in narrowing disparities in schooling outcomes. In this section, we review the research relating to teacher labor markets and discuss several policies relating to teacher hiring, promotion, and compensation that might be able to improve the distribution of teachers across schools (Jacob 2007; Hill 2007).

There is a large body of evidence documenting the fact that teacher qualifications vary dramatically across schools and districts, and that less qualified teachers are disproportionately likely to teach in higher-poverty schools. However, a growing body of research focuses not on teacher qualifications but rather on teacher effectiveness at raising student achievement. These studies estimate teacher effectiveness by comparing changes in student achievement scores across classrooms, controlling for student, classroom, and school characteristics that would be expected to influence student achievement regardless of the teacher. In this way, these studies attempt to isolate the value that an individual teacher "adds" to student achievement, and are thus commonly referred to as "teacher value-added" studies. These value-added studies find that there is substantial variation in teacher effectiveness, both within and across schools. According to a recent analysis of New York City elementary school math teachers, for example, students whose teacher falls in the top quarter of effectiveness learn roughly .33 test score standard deviations more in a single year than students whose teachers are in the bottom quarter (Kane, Rockoff, and Staiger 2006; see also Harris and Sass 2007; Hanushek et al. 2005; Aaronson, Barrow, and Sander 2007).

The policy challenge in the domain of teacher labor markets is to induce more highly effective teachers to teach in schools serving the most disadvantaged children, knowing that effectiveness cannot easily be measured by common markers such as the certification status or educational background of the teacher. Here we discuss several policy options: alternative certification, targeted salary bonuses, and hiring and promotion policies. Dozens of studies have explored the relative effectiveness of teachers with traditional versus alternative (or no) certification. The emerging consensus is that differences between the groups are relatively small, so that creating routes toward alternative certification can help improve teacher supply without reducing quality (Boyd et al. 2005a; Kane et al. 2006).

Another strategy is to entice teachers to work in hard-to-staff schools and/or subjects through financial incentives—namely, targeted salary increases or bonuses. While there have been a number of calls for such proposals and many states have adopted some sort of financial assistance (e.g., loan forgiveness programs, mortgage assistance, salary supplements), there has been very little systematic evaluation of these programs (Imazeki 2007; Guarino, Santibanez, and Daley 2006; Glazerman et al. 2006). Recent evaluations of targeted bonuses in North Carolina and California provide some evidence that such measures can induce teachers to work in high-need schools (Steele, Murnane, and Willet 2008; Clotfelter, Ladd, and Vigdor 2006), but more rigorous evaluation is certainly needed. Key questions include whether such programs will be able to induce teachers who would not otherwise have taught, and how long such teachers will remain. Moreover, financial incentives that are not tied to teacher performance run the risk of inducing ineffective teachers to locate in hard-to-staff schools.

Policies focusing on teacher hiring, promotion, and dismissal may also be important levers for improving the quality of public schools. Given the wide variation in effectiveness, policies that help school officials identify and hire the best applicants could have an important impact on student outcomes. Unfortunately, there is little guidance that researchers can provide in this area. On the other hand, there is ample evidence that certain political and bureaucratic aspects of the teacher hiring process drive many qualified applicants out of high-poverty urban districts.

Whatever system is used to hire teachers, it is inevitable that some teachers will not perform well in the classroom. Recognizing that the hiring process is imperfect, virtually all school systems today place new teachers on probation for several years and subject them to an up-or-out tenure review. However, in practice, public schools do not seem to take advantage of the opportunity provided by the probationary period to obtain additional information about teacher effectiveness and weed out lower-quality teachers.

One possible fix to this problem is to raise the tenure bar for new teachers and to deny tenure to those teachers who are not effective at raising student achievement. Some have suggested that this type of evaluation should be based at least in part on teacher value-added scores (e.g., Gordon, Kane, and Staiger 2006). Moreover, while commonly measured teacher characteristics have little correlation with student achievement, there is some evidence that principals recognize which teachers are most effective in their schools. One might still be concerned, however, that principals would be hesitant to deny tenure to many teachers or to fire underperforming teachers. One reason may be that it is difficult to hire high-quality replacements. It is also possible that principals are simply reluctant to incur the social and political costs associated with dismissal. In either case, it suggests that policies to raise the tenure bar must incorporate some system to ensure that these tough decisions are made.

Conclusion

The release of the Coleman Report in 1966 led to a wave of pessimism about the ability of schools to improve the life chances of poor children. The report found that observable school inputs such as teacher educational attainment were only weakly correlated with student test scores. Many subsequent evaluations of educational interventions found disappointing results. In the more than forty years since the Coleman Report was released, however, a number of promising reform strategies have come to light.

In this chapter, we have highlighted several promising avenues of educational interventions. Early childhood education for disadvantaged children can generate lasting benefits for schooling attainment and other important life outcomes. Changing what happens when the classroom door closes, whether through selected curricular interventions, changing the incentives facing teachers, or increasing the quality of the teacher in front of the classroom, also has the potential to improve student learning. Getting the design features right for these interventions is crucial. But appropriately crafted educational interventions along these lines have considerable promise in improving long-term outcomes for low-income children.

The educational interventions that serve as the focus of our review essay are themselves not free from political debates, and in fact politics seems like the most important explanation for why many of these promising educational approaches have not been implemented on a large scale. Even though expanded and intensified preschool education for disadvantaged children seems likely to generate benefits to society in excess of costs—also perhaps true for efforts to reduce class sizes in the early grades in a way that holds teacher quality constant—these interventions will nonetheless require additional government spending. Changes in how teacher labor markets operate, or how schools select their curricular approaches, require cooperation from teacher unions. And accountability reforms require teachers to change their behaviors and subject them to potentially substantial changes in their work environments. But at least education research has been able to illuminate the path forward. Policymakers interested in improving the schooling outcomes for disadvantaged children should focus their political efforts on enacting school policies that are contentious but promising as opposed to those that seem to be contentious but potentially not very helpful.

Chapter 4

Before or After the Bell?
School Context and Neighborhood Effects
on Student Achievement

Paul A. Jargowsky and Mohamed El Komi

Most of the debates over education reform focus, as they should, on direct inputs into the educational process, such as the quality of teachers, the financial resources available to schools, and the support students receive from their families. Nevertheless, the achievement of elementary school students may also be affected by the school environment, which depends in part on the abilities, attitudes, and performance of their classmates. Similarly, the neighborhood environment may affect school outcomes via positive or negative role models and local attitudes about the value of schooling relative to other pursuits. These two factors tend to reinforce each other because schools are often directly or indirectly neighborhood institutions.

Many previous studies have addressed school context effects and neighborhood effects on achievement. Researchers with good school data usually study school context effects, whereas researchers with good neighborhood-level data tend to study neighborhood effects. Given the high degree of correlation between school and neighborhood characteristics, any analysis that omits one of these factors runs the risk of overstating or misstating the effect of the other. These different groups of researchers may, in effect, be attributing the same variance in achievement to two different causes.

Few data sets have both types of data together with individual and family control variables. Moreover, a large sample is necessary to disentangle the relative contribution of school and neighborhood characteristics. This chapter addresses the limitations of earlier studies by using a longitudinal panel data set including nearly 10 million students from the state of Texas compiled by the Texas Schools Project (TSP). The

TSP recently completed geocoding all the schools in the state, providing a connection to the complete array of neighborhood-level census data, including poverty, employment, family structure, and housing characteristics.

We examine the relative impact of school context variables versus neighborhood characteristics on fifth through eighth grade math and reading scores. We also examine variations in these effects by race, ethnicity, and other factors.

School Context and Student Achievement

While students are graded individually, they participate in a group learning process in an interactive school environment (Manski 1993). For example, fellow students may indirectly affect a student's achievement level by his or her absorption of the prevailing attitudes toward the value of working hard in school. Classmates may also have a direct impact on a student's achievement if they study and work together. However, it is not just the cognitive abilities of classmates that may matter. Students with poor discipline or low morale may disrupt the classroom and slow the pace of instruction, resulting in poor achievement that in turn leads to dropping out.

A number of studies examine the effects of peers and school environment on student achievement and school completion. For example, Zimmer and Toma (2000) examined mathematics test score data from over 16,000 public and private schools in five countries (Belgium, Canada, France, New Zealand, and the United States). They analyzed the effects of the classroom average test score on a student's test score after controlling for the student's previous test score. This so-called value-added approach implicitly controls for the student's own ability level and prior achievement (Hanushek 1986). The analysis also controlled for mother's and father's occupations and education levels and other family characteristics, as well as a number of school characteristics.

Zimmer and Toma found that "the higher the mean test score of the classmates, ceteris paribus, the higher the achievement level of the student." The effect is nonlinear, with a decrease in the peer effect as the mean score of peers rises. This implies that the peer effect is greatest in low-performing schools such as those in poor neighborhoods. There is also a negative interaction between a student's pretest score and the mean level of peer achievement. Thus, students who are already struggling are those most likely to be negatively affected by having underperforming fellow students. The peer effects were not significantly different in the five countries in the study or between public and private schools, despite vast differences in school financing, student assignment policies, and pedagogy.

The Zimmer and Toma study is particularly strong because of the rich set of parental controls, but many other studies confirm these results. Hanushek et al. (2003), using public school data from Texas, took a different approach by using "fixed effects" to isolate the peer effect from other confounding influences. In a fixed effects model, the variation across statistical units is effectively removed from the data so that only variation within the units contributes to the estimated effects. Hanushek et al. (2003) included fixed effects for students and schools by grade. They found that average peer achievement has a highly significant effect on learning across the test score distribution. Further, a higher proportion of students eligible for reduced-price lunch significantly reduces math achievement gains in value-added models, although not in models with fixed effects for students, schools, or school-by-grade. To the extent that family income matters, it is presumably not the poverty of the students per se but unobserved characteristics of the students that are correlated with family income.

Summers and Wolfe (1977) analyzed sixth grade outcomes on the Iowa Test of Basic Skills, controlling for the third grade score from 627 students in 103 randomly selected Philadelphia elementary schools and for a wide variety of student, family, teacher, and school characteristics. They concluded that "high achievers are relatively unaffected by the variation in the percentage of top achievers. But, for the low achievers, the intellectual composition associated with other characteristics of the student body has a direct impact on learning" (p. 647). In contrast, Argys, Rhys, and Brewer (1996), analyzing the National Education Longitudinal Study (NELS) data, found that the gains lower-ability students experience when they share classes with higher-ability students are offset by nearly identical declines among the higher-ability students.

Neighborhood Effects on Achievement

Similarly, substantial support exists in the literature for a neighborhood effect on achievement. Wilson (1987) argued that many of the negative outcomes observed in high-poverty neighborhoods, including high levels of dropping out and low levels of student achievement, can be attributed to "concentration effects." Children in high-poverty neighborhoods "seldom interact on a sustained basis with people who are employed," and that causes students to question the value of education. In this social milieu, both students and teachers become discouraged and put in less effort, leading to a vicious downward cycle of low expectations and low achievement.

The empirical evidence, though far from consistent, certainly includes studies finding evidence of neighborhood effects on education outcomes. Datcher (1982), using the Panel Study of Income Dynamics (PSID), found that a $1,000 increase in the mean income at the zip-code level increased years of schooling by about one-tenth of a year. Corcoran et al. (1990), also using the PSID, found effects of zip-code-level measures of family structure and welfare receipt. Zip codes, however, are quite a bit larger than our mental conception of what constitutes a neighborhood. Crane (1991b) argued that high-poverty communities experience epidemics of social problems. Using a special tabulation of the 1970 census based on neighborhood units much smaller than zip codes, Crane found a sharply nonlinear effect of the percentage of neighborhood workers in professional or managerial jobs on the probability of dropping out. Crowder and South (2003) found that neighborhood effects on dropping out among African Americans have increased over the past quarter century, perhaps tied to increasing concentration of poverty (see also Vartanian and Gleason 1999).

Few studies actually look simultaneously at school and neighborhood variables. Gonzales et al. (1996) did report significant effects on gains in GPA for both "peer support" and "neighborhood risk" for a sample of African American high school students. However, the sample size was small (151), the sample was not randomly selected, and the peer and neighborhood variables were self-reported. Owens (2008) found that both relative and absolute neighborhood resources have effects on high-school graduation and graduation from college in models that control for school environments.

Studies of neighborhood effects must contend with selection bias (Tienda 1991). Because parents choose neighborhoods, the attributes of parents may be correlated with neighborhood and school characteristics even after controlling for observed parental variables. If this selection effect is present, the estimated effects of school and neighborhood variables may be biased by picking up the effect of the unmeasured parental characteristics. Experiments are a good way to deal with selection bias, because random assignment minimizes variation between the experimental and control groups. However, there are very few truly experimental studies of neighborhood effects, because it is both difficult and expensive to randomly assign families to neighborhoods and/or schools. The Moving to Opportunity (MTO) Program, however, did randomly assign families to a treatment consisting of a move from high-poverty public housing projects to housing rented with Section 8 vouchers in lower-poverty neighborhoods in five major cities. Early analyses indicated substantial gains in reading and math scores among young children in Baltimore, those between the ages of 5 and 12 at the time of random assignment (Ludwig, Ladd, and Duncan 2001). However, later studies on larger samples found no measurable effect on either reading or math test scores (Sanbonmatsu et al. 2006). Final evaluation studies of MTO are ongoing, focusing on children who were young at the time they moved to lower-poverty neighborhoods. Thus, the question posed in the title of this chapter remains unanswered: should we worry more about negative environments to which children are exposed *before* or *after* the school bell rings?

Data and Methods

Three types of data are used in this analysis. Data on students and schools are drawn from the Texas Schools Microdata Panel (TSMP) compiled by the Texas Schools Project at the University of Texas at Dallas. The TSMP contains individual-level data on students in Texas public schools from the 1989–1990 through the 2001–2002 school years. The data include basic demographic characteristics on the students and scores on a criterion-referenced test, the Texas Assessment of Academic Skills (TAAS). However, not all students were tested in all years, and no students were tested in 1989–1990, the date of the last census. Therefore, to align our school and neighborhood data, we focus on the fifth to eighth graders in 1999–2000 who were tested in math and/or reading.

Data on neighborhoods are drawn from the 2000 census, Summary File 3A, at the census tract level. Census tracts are small, relatively homogeneous administrative units delineated by the U.S. Bureau of the Census, in coordination with local authorities. In 2000, there were 4,388 census tracts in Texas with an average population of 4,742 and a standard deviation of 2430. Census tracts are commonly used in demographic research as proxies for neighborhoods (White 1987).

School addresses obtained from the Texas Education Agency and other public sources were used to geocode the schools by identifying the latitude and longitude of the school and linking that location to the corresponding census tract. While census tracts and elementary school attendance zones are similar in size, in practice they are unlikely to overlap exactly. Any given elementary or middle school's attendance zone is likely to include all or part of the census tract in which it is located and may contain all or part of neighboring census tracts. However, the sociodemographic characteristics of a school's census tract are likely to be highly correlated with the characteristic of the school's attendance

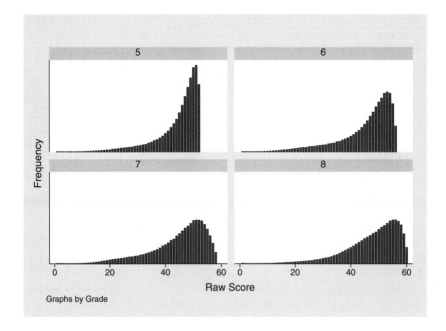

Figure 4.1. Raw 2000 TAAS Math Scores

zone, and in any event the tract variables reflect the actual local environment of the school itself.

The dependent variables in these analyses are test scores. Texas was an early adopter of a testing regime tied to school accountability. The TAAS test was administered statewide at various grade levels from 1991 until 2002, when it was replaced by a different testing system. The TAAS tests were not high stakes tests for students, but the passing rates (not average scores) were used to determine accountability ratings at the school and district levels.

We focused on the fifth to eighth grade TAAS test scores (both math and reading) in 2000 as our outcome variable and the corresponding fourth to seventh grade TAAS test scores in 1999 as controls for prior achievement and, implicitly, for the student's ability. Figure 4.1 shows the distributions of the 2000 TAAS raw math scores by grade, with a maximum score that varies by grade. The data actually include a huge spike of values at zero that for the most part do not indicate actual test scores but rather students who for various reasons did not take the test: they were absent, ill, exempted, and so forth. The lower tail, students scoring 9 or lower, is so thin that nothing is lost by excluding all zeros from the analysis, even though it is theoretically possible that a handful of them were actual scores.

Even with the zeros excluded, the frequency distribution of test scores is troubling. The scores are bunched up near the maximum value; the distribution is heavily skewed to the left. Converting the raw scores to z scores would only change the scale and not affect the shape of the distribution. Given the administrative focus on the use of TAAS passing rates for school accountability, the test was constructed to be more sensitive at the lower end of the scale. Very few questions differentiate students at the higher end of the achievement distribution, creating a ceiling effect (Clopton 2000). Vijverberg (2004) pointed out that the ceiling effect is not an example of censoring, which would be indicated by a spike in the histogram at the maximum score. Rather, the scale of the test is not constant, because a one-point increase in the raw score in the lower or middle of the distribution represents a smaller increase in actual achievement than a one-point increase near the top of the distribution. Linear regressions, as employed below, assume that a one-unit increase in the test score "represents the same amount of learning regardless of the students' initial level of achievement or the test year" (Harris 2009). Therefore, regression based on the raw scores or z scores are problematic.

The solution is to renormalize the scores to a scale such that a fixed increase represents the same increase in achievement at any score value. An assumption must be made about the actual distribution of achievement in the student population, since according to this argument the distribution is not accurately represented by the raw scores. The standard assumption is that most social psychological variables are normally distributed in the population (see Mayer 1960). In effect, we calculated the percentile score of the student in the raw score distribution and converted it back to a z score *as if* the distribution were normal.[1] A z score has a mean of zero and a standard deviation of one.

This procedure spreads out the scores at the upper end of the distributions, as shown in Figure 4.2. While the normalized score is still less precise at higher levels, a one unit change in the normalized score has the same meaning at any point in the scale, conditional on the normality assumption. Further, the normalization is done separately by grade, resulting in a consistent mean and standard deviation across grades, allowing the data to be pooled for analysis.

We analyzed the math test scores for all fifth to eighth grade students who took the test in 2000. Initially, there were slightly more than 1 million valid student scores across 4,755 schools. Since about 1.2 million students were enrolled in those grades in 2000, substantial numbers of students did not take the math test. Some students were exempt from

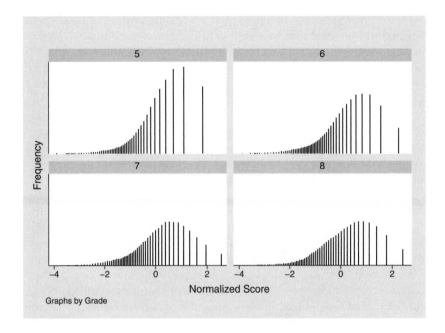

Figure 4.2. Normalized 2000 TAAS Math Scores

taking the test. Some students are given a Spanish version of the test, which we chose not to include in our analysis. Local school officials may have exempted some special education students and students not sufficiently proficient in English or Spanish to take one of those versions of the test. Finally, some students may have been ill or absent on the day of the test.

We attempted to match those students with valid 2000 scores to a corresponding test score in the previous grade in 1999, so that the prior year score could be used to control for prior achievement and ability. The identifier used to link the records across years is an encrypted version of the student's social security number. Twenty-two percent of the valid 2000 math scores could not be matched to previous grade test scores from 1999. In some cases, the students had temporary or mistyped identifiers in one of the years. In other cases, the students may have moved into Texas in 2000 from out of state or from private school. We also excluded students who, despite seeming to have a matching identifier, appear to be different students because of differences in race, gender, and/or birth date. Excluding the students who could not be reliably matched to a prior score drops the final analysis sample to 822,268 for math and 819,955 for reading. Of the students observed in both years, 62 percent were in the same school in both years, and 38 percent moved from one school to another between 1999 and 2000. The movements can occur either because the family moved or because the student moved to the next level of schooling, for example, from elementary to a middle school. The exact year of structural school transition varies from district to district in Texas.

The inability to find a previous test score for so many of the students is a cause for concern. Simple t-tests comparing students with prior year matches to those without matches found significant differences in race, ethnicity, poverty status, and gender. While we controlled for the observed differences in our analysis, the possibility remains that there may be unobserved differences between the students we could track and those that we could not track that are correlated with school and neighborhood characteristics. We attempted to control for these unobserved differences using a value-added model, as described below.

Student scores on a standardized test are a noisy measure of their skills and knowledge at a point in time, which in turn result from the confluence of several factors. Any given test score can be modeled as a function of individual and family characteristics, school characteristics, and neighborhood characteristics. Ideally, we should include variables for the entire history of the child's school and neighborhood experiences. In practice, we only have measures of these quantities at or near the time of test administration. Omitting past values of these variables is also problematic because students and their classmates often have experienced similar schools and neighborhoods over time, potentially inflating the estimated coefficients for the current observed school and neighborhood characteristics (Hanushek et al. 2003). Further, bias will be introduced if unmeasured individual or family characteristics that affect achievement are correlated with school and neighborhood characteristics as the result of geographic mobility and other parental choices that affect when and where a student goes to school.

One approach to this dilemma is to estimate value-added models, which include previous test scores for each student. The lagged test scores implicitly incorporate the influence of unmeasured factors in prior years. The prior test scores also implicitly incorporate individual student attributes for which we do not have good measures, such as native ability and motivation, so long as these attributes are constant over time. More than one prior test can be included; for example, in a model for the math score we included both a prior math score and a prior reading score, as these prior scores were included to capture a variety of past influences that may bear on the ability to learn a subject in the current period, not simply subject-specific knowledge. As a result, the coefficients in this analysis measure the current contribution of individual, school, and neighborhood factors to the *change* in the student's test score.

In addition to the lagged test scores, a number of individual-level control variables were included in the analysis. These include indicator variables for race and ethnicity: Black, Hispanic, Asian, and Native American; non-Hispanic White is the omitted category. Indicator variables for female and eligibility for free and reduced price lunch were also included. The latter indicates family income up to 185 percent of the federal poverty line. Several variables were included to indicate the academic classification of the student. These are gifted, special education, and limited English proficiency. These three variables were taken from the student's 1999 record, rather than 2000, to avoid the possibility that they are caused by, rather than the cause of, the student's current academic performance.

Several characteristics were included to capture the *school context*. These were computed at the school/grade level. Unfortunately, the TSP data do not identify the specific classroom and teacher of the student. If there are four eighth grade classes within one school, the data do not allow you to tell which students were in which classrooms. We computed the averages for all classes for a given grade within the school. The variables are percentage of students eligible for free and reduced price lunch; turnover, defined as the percentage of students in 2000 who attended a different school in the previous year; and the average math or reading score of the students in the school/grade. To avoid spurious correlations with the student's own test scores from 2000 and 1999, the average peer scores were based on the math test from two years in the past (1998), following Hanushek et al. (2003).

The *neighborhood* characteristics are the poverty rate in the school's census tract, the percentage of children in married couple families, and the percentage of adults who are college graduates. Of the many variables available in the census, these three were chosen to represent several of the causal mechanisms described in the neighborhood effects research: economic status, parenting styles and resources, and local attitudes toward education, respectively. The census data were collected on April 15, 2000, but the income question asks about income in the previous year. Thus the neighborhood poverty rate corresponds most closely to the neighborhood of the school attended in 1999. For the four in ten students who moved between the 1998–99 and 1999–2000 school years, this may be different from the neighborhood of the school attended in 1999–2000. Thus, we linked neighborhood data through the student's school in 1999.

Descriptive statistics for these variables can be found in Appendix

Table 4.1. Normalized 2000 TAAS Math and Reading Scores by Race/Ethnicity

	Math			Reading		
	Freq.	*Mean*	*Std. Dev.*	*Freq.*	*Mean*	*Std. Dev.*
All Students						
Native American	1,596	0.08	0.92	1,585	0.14	0.90
Asian	20,544	0.72	0.90	20,497	0.50	0.89
Black	110,781	−0.38	0.91	110,029	−0.28	0.92
Hispanic	274,253	−0.10	0.93	272,940	−0.19	0.91
Anglo	415,094	0.34	0.91	414,904	0.38	0.90
Total	822,268	0.10	0.96	819,955	0.11	0.96
Economically Disadvantaged						
Native American	609	−0.19	0.89	605	−0.15	0.91
Asian	5,593	0.50	0.91	5,579	0.18	0.89
Black	67,539	−0.49	0.90	66,913	−0.41	0.90
Hispanic	198,376	−0.17	0.92	197,264	−0.29	0.89
Anglo	71,620	−0.02	0.90	71,496	−0.01	0.90
Total	343,737	−0.19	0.93	341,857	−0.25	0.91
Not Economically Disadvantaged						
Native American	987	0.25	0.90	980	0.32	0.85
Asian	14,951	0.81	0.88	14,918	0.61	0.86
Black	43,242	−0.20	0.91	43,116	−0.07	0.91
Hispanic	75,877	0.07	0.92	75,676	0.08	0.91
Anglo	343,474	0.42	0.89	343,408	0.46	0.88
Total	478,531	0.32	0.92	478,098	0.36	0.91

Table 4.A, based on the math test sample. The figures for the reading test sample are virtually identical.

Results

Table 4.1 shows the 2000 normalized TAAS math and reading scores for the analysis sample by race and ethnicity. The normalization described above was computed using all students who took the test in a particular year (the full distribution of valid test scores), but the statistics in these tables only include those in our analysis sample, those who had a test in both 1999 and 2000 and could be linked over time via valid identifiers. This explains why the mean score is slightly greater than zero; the students whose scores could not be matched had lower scores on average than those who could be matched.

Mean math scores vary by race and ethnicity. Anglo students are about one-third of a standard deviation above the mean, while black students

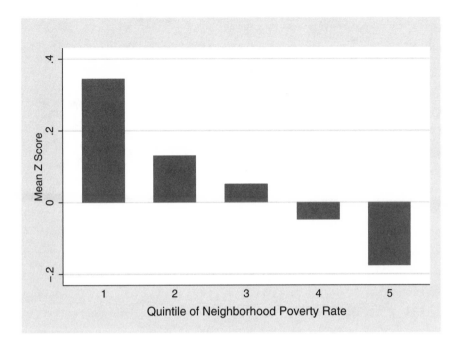

Figure 4.3. Math Scores and Neighborhood Poverty Rate

are about a third of a standard deviation below the mean. Hispanics are also slightly below the mean, while Asians and the small sample of Native Americans are above the mean. Lower-income students, those eligible for free and reduced price school lunches, score lower in every racial and ethnic group. Overall, low-income students are about one-half standard deviation lower than higher income students.

There is a clear and consistent relationship between student math test scores and the poverty rate of the neighborhood, as shown in Figure 4.3. Students in the lowest quintile of neighborhood poverty rates have an average math test score of 0.35. As neighborhood poverty increases, the average math score steadily declines. Students in the highest quintile of neighborhood poverty rates have an average math score of −0.18. Similarly, Figure 4.4 shows that the average math score is strongly positively correlated with the proportion of children in married couple families in the neighborhood.[2] While these graphs present prima facie evidence of neighborhood effect on student achievement, one cannot attribute a causal effect to neighborhood characteristics without controlling for student characteristics and school environment variables.

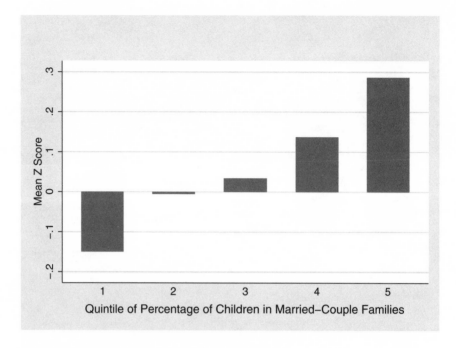

Figure 4.4. Math Scores and Percentage of Children in Married-Couple Families

Tables 4.2 and 4.3 show the results of value-added regressions for the 2000 TAAS math and reading scores with various combinations of explanatory variables. All regressions have robust standard errors allowing for correlation in the disturbance terms within a school. Model 1 includes only the student variables, Model 2 includes student and school variables, Model 3 includes student and neighborhood variables, and Model 4 includes all three sets of variables simultaneously. The coefficients can be read as multiples of a standard deviation, because the normalized test score scale has a mean of zero and a standard deviation of one. In other words, a coefficient of 0.10 would indicate an effect size equal to one tenth of a standard deviation in the test score, which would be considered a very large effect.

Both math and reading prior scores, from the 1999 TAAS, have large and highly significant effects on the math test scores in all models. As expected, the size of the coefficient on the prior math score is larger for the math test and vice versa, but both are less than one indicating some regression to the mean. In other words, students who performed very well or very badly in a given year tended to move back toward the mean in the following year, other things equal.

Table 4.2. Value-Added Regressions for Normalized 2000 TAAS Math Score

	(1)	(2)	(3)	(4)
Constant	0.0894***	0.0593***	−0.0511*	−0.0390
	(24.28)	(8.58)	(−2.38)	(−1.83)
Student Characteristics				
TAAS Math 1999	0.562***	0.558***	0.561***	0.558***
	(311.28)	(320.41)	(309.31)	(319.78)
TAAS Reading 1999	0.194***	0.192***	0.192***	0.191***
	(149.82)	(150.51)	(149.98)	(150.85)
Black	−0.131***	−0.122***	−0.120***	−0.117***
	(−22.03)	(−21.66)	(−20.52)	(−20.69)
Hispanic	−0.0264***	−0.0250***	−0.0264***	−0.0277***
	(−6.64)	(−6.59)	(−6.77)	(−7.42)
Asian	0.180***	0.178***	0.177***	0.176***
	(28.47)	(28.13)	(28.20)	(27.89)
Native Am.	−0.0640***	−0.0616***	−0.0624***	−0.0618***
	(−4.02)	(−3.87)	(−3.92)	(−3.86)
Female	0.00325*	0.00335*	0.00337*	0.00341*
	(2.12)	(2.19)	(2.20)	(2.23)
Econ. Disadvant.	−0.0437***	−0.0429***	−0.0383***	−0.0420***
	(−14.82)	(−20.12)	(−15.02)	(−19.70)
Gifted 1999	0.177***	0.180***	0.177***	0.179***
	(40.95)	(42.17)	(40.64)	(42.36)
Spec. Ed. 1999	−0.131***	−0.133***	−0.133***	−0.134***
	(−34.74)	(−35.59)	(−35.46)	(−35.93)
Lim. Eng. 1999	−0.0206***	−0.0197***	−0.0241***	−0.0224***
	(−3.68)	(−3.56)	(−4.37)	(−4.12)
Moved	−0.0752***	−0.0531***	−0.0746***	−0.0513***
	(−17.95)	(−15.26)	(−17.81)	(−14.84)
School/Grade Characteristics				
% Econ. Disadvant.		0.0611**		0.0830***
		(4.65)		(5.39)
Turnover		−0.0302***		−0.0323***
		(−4.50)		(−4.79)
Avg. Peer Math 1998		0.108**		0.0982***
		(10.35)		(9.15)
Neighborhood Characteristics				
Poverty Rate			0.100**	0.0273
			(3.11)	(0.78)
% Children in MCF			0.140***	0.0988***
			(5.80)	(4.08)
% College Graduates			0.0638**	0.0435*
			(3.29)	(2.23)
Observations	822268	822268	822268	822268
R-squared	0.5775	0.5783	0.5778	0.5785

Note. t statistics in parentheses. *$p < 0.05$ **$p < 0.01$ ***$p < 0.001$. Robust standard errors with clustering by school.

Table 4.3. Value-Added Regressions for Normalized 2000 TAAS Reading Score

	(1)	*(2)*	*(3)*	*(4)*
Constant	0.0989***	0.0545***	−0.00890	−0.0322
	(33.28)	(8.98)	(−0.48)	(−1.73)
Student Characteristics				
TAAS Math 1999	0.242***	0.239***	0.241***	0.239***
	(189.55)	(190.84)	(188.59)	(190.53)
TAAS Reading 1999	0.489***	0.486***	0.487***	0.485***
	(324.70)	(323.36)	(318.67)	(322.26)
Black	−0.0931***	−0.0850***	−0.0852***	−0.0856***
	(−17.03)	(−16.85)	(−15.26)	(−16.28)
Hispanic	−0.0764***	−0.0705***	−0.0700***	−0.0745***
	(−23.19)	(−22.07)	(−21.35)	(−23.57)
Asian	0.00625	0.00134	−0.00457	−0.00649
	(1.15)	(0.25)	(−0.84)	(−1.19)
Native Am.	−0.0407**	−0.0377**	−0.0382*	−0.0389*
	(−2.59)	(−2.40)	(−2.43)	(−2.47)
Female	0.0610***	0.0610***	0.0612***	0.0612***
	(39.17)	(39.25)	(39.32)	(39.36)
Econ. Disadvant.	−0.0971***	−0.0932***	−0.0836***	−0.0908***
	(−38.51)	(−43.71)	(−36.30)	(−42.87)
Gifted 1999	0.216***	0.218***	0.217***	0.216***
	(59.98)	(60.81)	(57.90)	(59.65)
Spec. Ed. 1999	−0.145***	−0.148***	−0.150***	−0.150***
	(−39.16)	(−40.58)	(−41.09)	(−41.55)
Lim. Eng. 1999	−0.150***	−0.148***	−0.151***	−0.151***
	(−28.27)	(−28.56)	(−29.02)	(−29.55)
Moved	−0.0566***	−0.0470***	−0.0557***	−0.0433***
	(−16.70)	(−14.08)	(−16.47)	(−13.02)
School/Grade Characteristics				
% Econ. Disadvant.		0.0793***		0.134***
		(6.79)		(10.23)
Turnover		−0.0115*		−0.0161**
		(−2.04)		(−2.87)
Avg. Peer Read 1998		0.127***		0.109***
		(13.46)		(11.27)
Neighborhood Characteristics				
Poverty Rate			0.0525*	−0.0292
			(2.00)	(−1.08)
% Children in MCF			0.0706**	0.0488*
			(3.19)	(2.25)
College Graduates			0.143***	0.122***
			(9.47)	(8.03)
Observations	819955	819955	819955	819955
R-squared	0.5749	0.5758	0.5755	0.5762

Note: t statistics in parentheses. *$p < 0.05$ **$p < 0.01$ ***$p < 0.001$. Robust standard errors with clustering by school.

Indicator variables for race and ethnicity are included because of the large and persistent gaps between groups discussed earlier, but ultimately the goal is to understand the process that drives these gaps by adding variables that reduce the dummy variable coefficients to zero. The coefficient for black students is negative and significant in all models, but it is much lower than the unconditional gaps shown in Table 4.1 that do not control for prior test scores or other variables. For example, in Model 1, the math score for a black student is 0.131 lower than for Anglo students, conditional on past scores and other student characteristics. The comparable figure for reading is somewhat smaller, -0.0931. This is a much smaller gap between black and white students than in Table 4.1.

The unconditional Hispanic/Anglo gap is more than 0.4 of a standard deviation, but it is quite small in the math value-added specifications shown here, about -0.026. The reading gap is about three times larger. Asian students score about one-fifth of a standard deviation better than Anglo students do in math, but not better in reading. The reduction in the racial gaps accomplished by including lagged test scores does not indicate that disparity between the race groups has been explained. It only indicates that the gap is somewhat persistent from year to year and was already reflected to a large extent in the 1999 test score.

Girls score higher than boys do on reading tests by about 0.06 in all models, even controlling for past scores. There is also a very slight advantage for girls in math, about 0.003. Economic disadvantage was measured by eligibility for the federal school lunch program, which is based on family income in relation to the poverty line. While limited, it is the only indicator of family socioeconomic status available statewide in Texas public school administrative data, at least for children in lower grades. Economic disadvantage is associated with a decrease in math and reading scores of about 0.04 and 0.09 in math and reading scores, respectively.

Assignment to certain educational categories, such as gifted and talented, special education, and limited English proficiency (LEP), may have consequences for how the student is taught and may also induce behavioral responses from the student. Gifted, special education, and limited English proficiency have signs in the expected direction and remain significant in all models. A student who changed schools between the 1999 and 2000 tests scored about 0.05 lower on the tests, other things equal.

The estimated effects of school characteristics are not sensitive to the inclusion of neighborhood variables. Contrary to expectations, the coefficient on the percentage of economically disadvantaged students in the same school and grade as the student is positive and significant. This finding is consistent with Hanushek et al. (2003), based on the same underlying data, who reported positive coefficients for federal school lunch program participation. They argued that school lunch is a noisy measure and that schools vary in their efforts to identify eligible children. However, simply omitting peer average math score (discussed below) from the model reverses the sign on classmates' school lunch participation. Thus, lower-income peers are not harmful, and possibly an advantage, controlling for the academic performance of those peers and the other variables, including the student's own school lunch status and prior performance. This is possibly a relative deprivation or "frog pond" effect, where a student may get more resources or have more confidence if he or she is relatively higher in the local social status ranking (Mayer and Jencks 1989; Owens 2008).

What is harmful, apparently, about having poor classmates is not that they are from low-income families but that on average they have lower academic performance. This is confirmed by the large and highly statistically significant coefficients on average performance of the student's peers in the school in the same subject (lagged two years), about one-tenth of a standard deviation in both reading and math. The effect of peer scores is only slightly diminished when neighborhood characteristics are added in Model 4. Despite controlling for a student's past test score, this coefficient may be biased upward by correlation between unmeasured factors that are common to the student and classmates, such as teacher quality; the two-year lag in the peer test scores mitigates this concern to a certain extent.

Another potential source of bias is the "reflection problem" (Manski 1993), which posits that cooperative and interdependent elements of teaching and learning lead to joint determination of student outcomes. Peers influence a student's performance, but by the same token the student influences the peers. For reasons stated earlier, the peer measure here is based not on the specific classmates of a student but on all students in the same grade within a school. The inability to identify classrooms is a disadvantage in terms of measuring the actual quality of a student's peer group, especially if there is nonrandom sorting into classrooms. However, it serves to slightly diminish concern over the reflection problem, because students are far less likely to jointly determine outcomes of students in different classrooms.

Turnover measures the proportion of students in the school and grade who attended a different school in the prior year. More turnover lowers academic performance, presumably by the disruptive effect of high turnover rates on the school and classroom environment. One potential problem in interpreting this coefficient is that school turnover is related to geographic mobility, given the geographic basis of school assignment. Therefore, school turnover is related to residential instability, which could also be construed as a neighborhood characteristic. We intend to introduce a residential instability measure in future models.

Neighborhood poverty is the key measure in the theoretical and empirical literature on neighborhood effects. While the census contains far more detailed measures of the income distribution than the poverty rate, it is the measure most comparable to the school lunch program eligibility variable. Recall that we are examining the relative contribution of school and neighborhood characteristics. If neighborhood socioeconomic status were measured with more precision than school socioeconomic status, we would tilt the playing field toward neighborhood effects.

Contrary to expectations, for both reading and math the neighborhood poverty rate is positive and significant in Model 3 (which does not include the school characteristics). The coefficients decline (and become negative in the case of reading) but lose statistical significance in Model 4, which includes the school/grade characteristics as well. In the absence of school controls, the neighborhood poverty rate is biased by the omission of the student poverty rate, which has a positive coefficient, as discussed earlier. In contrast, both the percentage of children in married-couple families and the percentage of college graduates in the neighborhood have the expected positive signs and are significant in both Models 3 and 4. All four of the coefficients are reduced by about one-third in Model 4, which includes the school/grade characteristics. Thus, while neighborhood effects on student achievement are overestimated when controls for school context are omitted, these social dimensions of the neighborhood appear to have an independent effect on student achievement. Moreover, while both neighborhood and school variables are measured with error, the school variables are likely to be more precisely measured because of the nature of the data. If anything, the neighborhood coefficients in these models are biased toward zero because the neighborhood data are based on the school's census tract, not the address of the child's residence.

There is little change in the R^2 when the neighborhood variables are added to the model that includes school variables. However, a joint test of the significance of the three variables rejects the null hypothesis that the coefficients are all zero.

The prior discussion gives evidence that neighborhood socioeconomic conditions affect student test scores. However, the models presented certainly do not include all of the ways in which schools might differ from one another. Given that variables concerning the school context are left out, and given that school context and neighborhood condi-

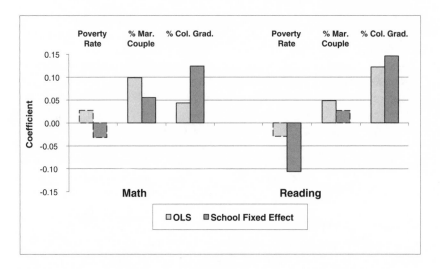

Figure 4.5. Neighborhood Coefficients with and Without School Fixed Effects

Note: Bars with solid outlines are statistically significant at the 0.05 level.

tions are clearly correlated, incompletely controlling for school context can easily bias the coefficients on neighborhood conditions. To overcome this issue and confirm the finding that neighborhoods have an independent effect, we employed a second strategy. We repeated the models of Tables 4.2 and 4.3, now including fixed effects for schools. The fixed-effect model essentially discards the variation *between* the schools in test scores and explanatory variables and uses the variation in those variables *within* schools to identify the effects on student achievement. Thus, the school fixed-effect models implicitly control for the influence of any school context variables that are common to all classes within the school.

The coefficients on the student characteristics were largely unaffected. However, the school/grade variables became minuscule and insignificant with the inclusion of school fixed effects. The reason for this is that these coefficients are only identified by variation across grade levels within a school. Apparently, the poverty, student turnover, and prior math scores of a student's peers vary much more across schools than across grades within schools.

The neighborhood variables performed differently in the school fixed effects model. The coefficients on neighborhood poverty became negative and, in the case of reading, statistically significant. As shown in Figure 4.5, the coefficients on percent of children in married couple

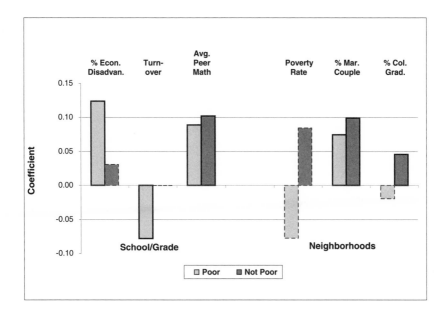

Figure 4.6. School and Neighborhood Effects for Poor vs. Not Poor Students
(Math)

Note: Bars with solid outlines are statistically significant at the 0.05 level.

families were reduced by half or more relative to the models in Tables
4.2 and 4.3 and, in the case of reading, the coefficient loses statistical
significance.[3] The effect of the percentage of college graduates in the
neighborhood remains positive and statistically significant in both reading and math, and the magnitude of the coefficient increases nearly
three-fold for math. When school context is maximally controlled by
the inclusion of school fixed effects, the most powerful neighborhood
variable turns out to be the higher education indicator. Taking this
result at face value, it suggests that neighborhood effects on student
achievement, after controlling for student and school characteristics,
operate more through aspirations and attitudes toward education than
through resources or parenting styles.

Given the particular interest in how disadvantaged students are
affected by living in poor neighborhoods and attending dysfunctional
schools, we also estimated separate regressions for poor and non-poor
students, again determined by their participation in the federal school
lunch program. As shown in Figures 4.6 and 4.7, school effects are larger
and more statistically significant for poor children than for nonpoor

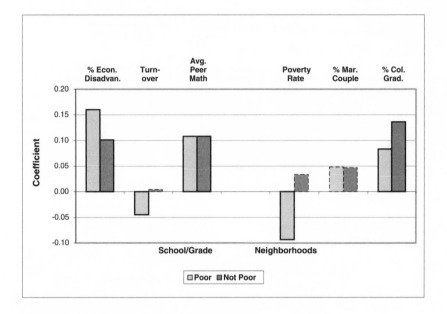

Figure 4.7. School and Neighborhood Effects for Poor vs. Not Poor Students (Reading)

Note: Bars with solid outlines are statistically significant at the 0.05 level.

children.[4] In contrast, the positive effect of married couple families and college graduates in the neighborhood is stronger and more statistically significant for nonpoor children in math. For reading, the percentage of college graduates has a larger positive effect for the nonpoor, and the neighborhood poverty rate, which has been insignificant in all the previous models that controlled for school/grade variables, has a negative and significant effect for poor children.

Conclusion

Looking at the results, several observations stand out. First, the school variables are more robust and explain a greater degree of the variance in test scores than the neighborhood characteristics. Little harm is done in estimating school context effects without considering neighborhood effects, at least if neighborhood characteristics are measured by census tract variables. On the other hand, we note that very different estimates of neighborhood effects are obtained if school context variables are omitted or if they are controlled via fixed effects. If researchers attempt to link significant coefficients to conclusions about causal mechanisms operating at the neighborhood level, perhaps through value formation, community role models, and so on, then the lack of control for school context can be misleading.

On the other hand, the neighborhood variables in this analysis are drawn from the census tract in which the school is located, which may or may not be a good approximation of the school's physical neighborhood or any given student's residential setting. Despite this measurement error, which would tend to bias the coefficients toward zero, the neighborhood-level variables as a group were statistically significant even in the presence of school variables. The particular pattern of effects varied by the way in which school context was modeled, by poverty status, move status, and location in the conditional achievement distribution. Nevertheless, neighborhood always mattered.

From a policy perspective, the question is slightly different. School environments and school context are shaped by many factors, but clearly the characteristics of the families in the neighborhood are a principal driving force. Even if neighborhood conditions are less robust than school context effects, concern about neighborhood conditions is still justified. Schools are largely formed as a geographic overlay on residential segregation. Reducing the concentration of poverty and economic segregation generally may be the easiest way to decrease the "savage inequalities" that exist between schools (Kozol 1991). Thus, we ought to be concerned about neighborhood effects on school achievement both by direct mechanisms and indirectly through their role in shaping school environments.

Appendix

Table 4.A. Descriptive Statistics for Fifth to Eighth Graders in the Regression Sample

	Mean	Std. Dev.	Min.	Max.
Ability-Normalized TAAS Scores				
Math, 2000	0.105	0.959	−3.897	2.558
Math, 1999	0.092	0.955	−3.960	2.383
Reading, 1999	0.078	0.959	−4.225	2.103
Demographic Characteristics, 2000				
Black	0.135	0.341	0	1
Hispanic	0.334	0.471	0	1
Asian	0.025	0.156	0	1
Native American	0.002	0.044	0	1
Female	0.509	0.500	0	1
Eligible for Free/Red. Lunch	0.418	0.493	0	1
Student Categorization, 1999				
Gifted	0.136	0.343	0	1
Special Education	0.056	0.230	0	1
Lim. English Prof.	0.060	0.237	0	1
Student Moved	0.382	0.486	0	1
School Context, by Grade				
Percent Free/Red. Lunch	0.445	0.275	0.000	1.000
Turnover	0.434	0.385	0.000	1.000
Avg Math (lagged 2 years)	0.052	0.318	−3.888	1.774
Neighborhood Characteristics				
Poverty Rate	0.151	0.116	0.000	1.000
% Children in Married Couple Families	0.745	0.121	0.000	1.000
% College Graduates	0.272	0.180	0.000	0.863

Source: Texas Schools Microdata Panel, calculations by the authors, except neighborhood characteristics. Neighborhood characteristics are from census tract-level data, based on the census tract of the school attended in 1999.
$N = 822,268$.

Chapter 5

Neighborhoods, Social Interactions, and Crime
What Does the Evidence Show?

Steven Raphael and Michael A. Stoll

Although national crime rates have fallen over the past several years from highs in the late 1980s, the impact of crime on society remains quite strong. By one estimate, the combination of direct monetary losses and costs of pain and suffering among crime victims in the United States is approximately 0.5–0.7 percent of GDP (Freeman 1996). However, there are substantial indirect costs regarding reducing the costs of crime as well. The Bureau of Justice estimates that in 1999, federal, state, and local government criminal justice expenditures amounted to $146.5 billion, or 1.6 percent of GDP (Bureau of Justice Statistics 2003). In addition, crime affects people at the household level. Not only are many people willing to pay higher costs to live in neighborhoods with lower crime rates, but they also purchase security devices and insurance to limit the impacts of crime and victimization.

Public policy responses to crime have been costly as well. Recent criminal justice reforms to address crime, such as lengthening prison sentences and setting mandatory minimum sentences, have led to growing populations of the incarcerated as well as those released from prison with criminal records (Raphael and Stoll 2009). The number of inmates in federal and state prisons grew from 300,000 in 1977 to 1.4 million in 2003, quadrupling the U.S. incarceration rate from 136 to 482 inmates per 100,000 residents.

While there has long existed a large body of research on both the individual decisions and the demographic characteristics that influence criminal involvement and victimization, recently a new body of literature on the influence of neighborhoods and social interactions on crime has emerged. In the 1980s and 1990s, a number of important scholars argued that growing up in poor neighborhoods matters with regard to criminal delinquency because of a variety of influences from collective socialization, peer-group influences, and institutional capacity (Wilson 1987; Jencks and Mayer 1990). Since then, a number of studies have emerged that have directly examined these propositions. This chapter critically examines this literature on the influence of neighborhoods and social interaction on criminal involvement.

Many of the ideas about the potential mechanisms by which neighborhoods and social interaction matter with respect to the crime question were reinvigorated by the seminal work of William Julius Wilson (1987). Wilson argued that the economic transformations in American cities in the 1970s and 1980s, such as decline in manufacturing employment, reinforced important social transformations that were already unfolding there. Between 1970 and 1990, the number of poor people living in high-poverty areas nearly doubled. Much of this growth occurred in predominantly black neighborhoods, with a vast majority located in central cities. These changes in the economic structure of cities influenced the growing social isolation and concentration of the poor.

Wilson warned that the growing social isolation of the poor, especially the black poor, was a cause for concern. The isolation of the poor coincided with their disconnection from strong social institutions such as active churches, functional schools, and strong middle-class role models, leading to the emergence of negative "concentration effects" in which antisocial activities such as criminal activity became more prevalent than would otherwise be the case. Moreover, Wilson argued, as criminal activity spread through these impoverished communities, it increasingly became accepted and, indeed, even a community norm.

Wilson's argument provides a framework for thinking about the neighborhood literature on the question of crime. That work suggests that the effect of neighborhoods on crime could operate through two mechanisms: neighborhood as place or neighborhood as arena for social interactions. Although we elaborate on this distinction below, here we note that these are rather different pathways through which neighborhoods could influence criminal involvement. One conceptualization emphasizes the physical amenities of a neighborhood, such as the availability of jobs, while the other emphasizes the social interactions that take place within it.

Defining Neighborhoods

The meaning of neighborhood varies a great deal across disciplines and other dimensions. To economists and, to a large extent, to urban planners and geographers, neighborhoods are spatially bound places that provide a locus of economic activity and amenities that in turn give value to areas. Sociologists, anthropologists, and other geographers, on the other hand, concentrate on the social relationships and community identities of neighborhoods.

Of course, the different meanings of neighborhoods are strongly related. Neighborhoods near good jobs or with other or nice amenities are also likely to have well-connected residents with good incomes who develop or maintain strong prosocial neighborhood institutions, and thus have lower levels of crime. Within the body of neighborhood research, a few broad conclusions point to descriptions of places within metropolitan areas. It is clear that there is considerable socioeconomic inequality and racial segregation among neighborhoods, with African Americans especially concentrated in disadvantaged areas. Similarly, there is a growing consensus that social problems are geographically correlated with social inequality, with poor neighborhoods showing higher levels of crime, school dropout rates, social and physical disorder, and single parent households. Finally, this ecological concentration of disadvantage has increased considerably during the recent decades, while the concentration of wealth has increased (Sampson, Morenoff, and Gannon-Rowley 2002; Jencks and Mayer 1990). What is still in question is the extent to which this concentration of disadvantage limits the social and economic life chances of individuals who experience these neighborhoods and whether this affects their criminal involvement and victimization.

Is There a Neighborhood-Crime Connection?

Of course, the question of whether neighborhoods affect crime outcomes is premised on the assumption that there is variation in both neighborhood and crime outcomes that moves in expected directions. To what extent is this true? Data on neighborhood characteristics and crime are largely nonexistent across metropolitan areas, so we use as a proxy for neighborhoods the characteristics of metropolitan areas. Raphael and Sills (2006) provided some data on this question by presenting average metropolitan area violent and property crime rates stratified along a number of metropolitan characteristics for more than 300 metro areas.[1] The crime rate data are tabulated from the FBI Uniform Crime Reports (UCR) for 2001. Although these data show cross-area patterns, they are likely to overlap to a large extent with submetropolitan areas (like neighborhoods) that share similar characteristics. That is, many neighborhoods within the metro area are likely to share similar characteristics of whole metropolitan areas with respect to size, poverty

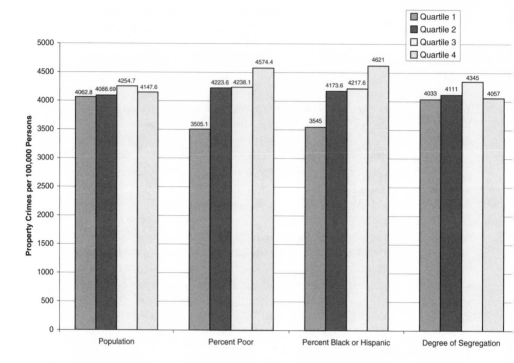

Figure 5.1. Average Property Crime Rate for MSAs Stratified by Population, Percentage Poor, Percentage Black or Hispanic, and the Degree of Black/White Segregation

Source: Raphael and Sills (2006)

rates, minority representation, and racial segregation. Figures 5.1 and 5.2 present crime rates for metropolitan areas separated into four population-size quartiles for the 300 metropolitan areas in the United States (i.e., the first bars on the left of the figures). The second set of bars presents crime rates by the percentage of the metropolitan area residents who are poor. The third set presents crime rates by the percentage of the metro area population that is black or Hispanic. And the final set presents crime rates by the degree of black-white segregation in these metropolitan areas. Figure 5.1 shows these for property crimes, while Figure 5.2 does so for violent crimes.

The data in Figure 5.1 show that metropolitan areas that are more heavily segregated or that are more black and Latino also report higher levels of property crime rates. Property crime is somewhat higher in larger, poorer, segregated, and predominantly black and Latino metro

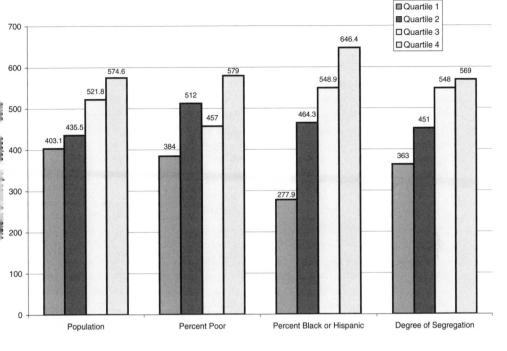

Figure 5.2. Average Violent Crime Rate for MSAs Stratified by Population, Percentage Poor, Percentage Black or Hispanic, and the Degree of Black-White Segregation

Source: Raphael and Sills (2006)

areas. Figure 5.2 shows these same patterns for violent crime, but they are much stronger than that for property crime. With respect to violent crime, low-poverty metro areas generally have lower crime rates than do high-poverty ones. While there could potentially be a number of factors that explain why violent crime rates are more strongly correlated with these metro area characteristics than are property crime rates, one prominent factor is that opportunities to commit property crimes are higher in areas that are more affluent, and thus less impoverished.

Neighborhoods as Place, and Crime

The neighborhood as place and its effect on crime is mostly premised on the economic model of criminal participation. In this model, the decision to participate in crime is based on the expected economic returns from crime relative to the risk of arrest and incarceration or of injury and possibly death. As Freeman (1996) noted, increases in criminal activity can occur if the economic rewards from crime rise relative to those from legitimate work and if individuals respond significantly to these relative rewards.

Thus, neighborhood economic conditions such as the number and availability and pay of jobs in the neighborhoods should affect an individual's decision to participate in crime. At a broad geographic level, the local labor market-crime nexus finds strong empirical support in several recent studies based on varying data sources and empirical methodologies (see, for example, Gould, Weinberg, and Mustard 2002; Raphael and Winter-Ebmer 2001; Freeman and Rodgers 2000; Grogger 1998). They all show statistically and quantitatively significant correlations between the extent of crime and the relevant labor market variables—either real wages (in which case the correlation is negative) or unemployment (in which case it is positive).

But an obvious question is whether these results reflect a truly causal relationship between crime and local labor market conditions, or whether they are merely spurious, evidence of other underlying factors. After all, individuals with very low skills and motivation are likely to be less employable and more prone to criminal activity and sort themselves into similar neighborhoods. Moreover, high concentrations of crime and criminals in inner cities could prompt employers to move from or avoid these places and thereby cause lower employment and wages of individuals there. Statistical techniques that control for these kinds of reciprocal links do exist; those researchers who employ them detect a strong economic effect on criminal activity (Gould, Weinberg, and Mustard 2002; Raphael and Winter-Ebmer 2001; Ihlanfeldt 2007; Lochner and Moretti 2004). Of course, the problem of sorting, or self-selection, is likely to be more of a problem in studies that use lower levels of geography such as a census tract as opposed to broader geographic definitions such urban/suburban. This is because locational (dis)amenities such as crime, lack of parks, and poor schools, which in part influence residential preferences are more identifiable at this level. Still, even in the latter case, selection could be a problem, since conventional wisdom still implies that (dis)amenities broadly correlate across broad geographic areas such as the cities and suburbs.

If we agree to the statistical significance of these findings, these empirical models should account for the actual quantitative changes in crime rates during the 1980s and 1990s. As shown in Figure 5.3, reported property and violent crime rates increased from the early 1980s until the early 1990s and then declined over the rest of the decade.[2] Drug arrest rates followed a similar course initially, but after a sharp drop in the

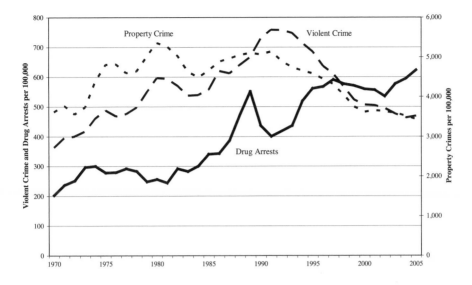

Figure 5.3. Property and Violent Crime Rates and Drug Arrests, 1970–2005

Source: Author's Calculations from the Bureau of Justice Statistics.

early 1990s they quickly rebounded by 1997 and then declined gradually until 2002.

Applying Grogger's (1998) estimate of the strength of the relationship between real wages and property crime, the decline in real wages over the 1980s more than explains the actual property crime increase over the period. Focusing on counties in metropolitan regions, Gould, Weinberg, and Mustard (2002) similarly found that declining real wages rather than rising unemployment rates spurred the increase in property crimes in the late 1980s. As further support for their economic model, they turned to the "high pressure" labor market of the late "Roaring Nineties" (Hines, Hoynes, and Krueger 2001; Freeman 2001). In this case they showed that the "rising tide" in the form of falling unemployment rates for less educated workers accounted for virtually the entire drop in property crime rates (appropriately adjusted for demographic shifts). Likewise, Raphael and Winter-Ebmer (2001) attributed 40 percent of the drop in property crimes to the economic boom.

Explaining the trends in violent and drug arrest rates is more complicated. Property and violent crimes are highly correlated, at least until the period associated with the War on Drugs. This result is not too surprising. Robbery and aggravated assault comprise the largest components of the total index and are directly motivated by or are often a means to pecuniary ends. As corroborating evidence, regression estimates of the economic model for these violent crimes but not others like murder or rape are "quite similar to those for property crimes" (Gould, Weinberg, and Mustard 2002; Raphael and Winter-Ebmer 2001).

Participation in the illicit drug trade no doubt depends on the same risk-reward calculus as that involved in property crimes. Still, it is difficult to square this simple economic logic with the divergent trends in drug arrest rates, which increased more sharply over the 1980s by 84 percent as compared to only 14 percent for property crime rates, and then barely fell in the late 1990s despite the rapid economic expansion. More striking but also more relevant to our analysis, drug arrest rates were more strongly correlated with violent crime, and in particular homicide, than with property crime rates.

We explain these empirical anomalies by external increases in the market for illegal drugs and hence drug violations, but also by adoption of tougher drug enforcement policies leading to more arrests per actual drug offense. Although changes in social norms increased the acceptability of illegal drug use and hence demand, the timing of the surge in drug arrests points to an innovation in the drug trade, namely, the spread of crack cocaine (see, for example, Golub and Johnson 1994; Grogger and Willis 2000; Fryer et al. 2005).

The real puzzle for the economic model is the late 1990s boom, when the crack market matured and then waned, at least among younger cohorts. In this case, the evidence points to declining legitimate employment opportunities for young, less skilled black males, not the increasing rewards for drug dealing. While the boom modestly increased the wages of those who were in the labor market, it did not stem the secular decline in their employment and labor force participation rates (Freeman and Rodgers 2000; Holzer, Offner, and Sorenson 2005; Raphael and Stoll 2002; Rosen, Kim, and Patel 2003). These downward trends, however, were not observed for comparable white or Latino men. Given this evidence of uneven expansion, it is likely that young black men's participation in the drug economy continued over the 1990s despite more robust national economic conditions.

The growth in drug arrest rates also depended on discretionary drug enforcement policies. As evidence, we point to the divergent trends in the share of African Americans among those arrested for property, violent, and drug crimes during the 1980s and 1990s (see Figure 5.4). By this measure, blacks were no more likely to participate in property and violent crimes offenses than whites. They accounted for a stable share of the arrests for property crimes over the period and a declining share of violent crime arrests in the 1990s. By contrast, the share of blacks in

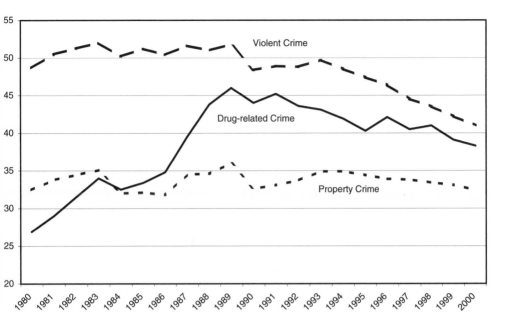

Figure 5.4. Blacks as a Percentage of Those Arrested for Major Crimes in U.S. Cities, 1980–2000

Source: Author's calculations using data from the Bureau of Justice Statistics.

drug arrests jumped from 27 to around 45 percent in the 1980s. According to survey evidence, African Americans were no more likely to use cocaine (or heroin) than whites but tended to buy drugs through local dealer networks in outdoor markets where they were more vulnerable to police sweeps (Johnson et al. 1996; Caulkins and Chandler 2006; Tonry 1995; Mauer 1999).

These trends in drug arrests were reinforced by racial disproportionality in the subsequent stages of the criminal justice system, which together account for increasing prevalence of incarceration among black men during the War on Drugs period. In the early 1990s black men accounted for 35 percent of drug-related arrests, but 55 percent of drug-related convictions and 74 percent of prison sentences for drug-related crimes. Put another way, the rise in the number of convictions, sentences, and prison commitments for drug offenses over the late 1980s and early 1990s accounted for 42 percent of total growth in the number of black inmates but only 26 percent of the growth in white inmates (Mauer and Huling 1996; Sampson and Laub 1993).

If economic conditions in the local economy affect criminal propensity, we should also detect this effect at even more local levels. Imbalances between people and jobs, especially for less-educated individuals, across neighborhoods should provide variation in economic rewards that identifies the effect. These imbalances are commonly referred to as spatial mismatch.

Ihlanfeldt (2002, 2007) has examined this question for neighborhood crime generally and for neighborhood drug crime more specifically. Ihlanfelt (2002) used unique data from Atlanta that draws on panels at the neighborhood level over a four-year period and with over 200 census tracts. Controlling for both differences in time and neighborhood-based characteristics, he found that job access, defined as a census tract-based weighted distance measure of individuals to local employment growth, matters. The results show that poor job accessibility is strongly associated with neighborhood crime and can explain 21 percent of the difference in property crime rates between black and white neighborhoods. Using a similar methodology, Ihlanfeldt (2007) asked whether having greater access to jobs would reduce drug crime in neighborhoods. He found that even modest improvement in job access can substantially reduce the amount of drug crime within poor inner city neighborhoods.

Of course, the major methodological concern in these types of studies is the problem of selection bias. The results for job accessibility and crime are consistent with the idea that less-educated individuals with possible low motivation either move to or live in areas with low job accessibility, thus causing a spurious relationship between employment opportunities and participation in crime.

Experimental methods, including random assignment, are a response to concerns of selection bias. In fact, these studies have found more mixed results. Most of this research uses data from the Moving to Opportunity (MTO) program to examine the impact of neighborhood quality on a host of adult and adolescent outcomes, including those related to crime and criminal propensity. The MTO housing mobility experiment was designed to analyze the effect of moving predominantly poor, minority, and female-headed households out of central city public housing projects located in high-poverty neighborhoods and into private rental housing in neighborhoods with lower poverty rates and greater socioeconomic diversity. The program enlisted a large group of public-housing households and randomly assigned each household to one of three groups: (1) a treatment group that was given a Section 8 housing voucher, which could be used to rent housing in the private market but could only be used in neighborhoods with a poverty rate lower than 10 percent; a (2) Section 8-only group that was given a rental voucher with no restrictions on where it could be used; and (3) a control group that was offered nothing in terms of housing assistance above and beyond what the household was already receiving.

The research suggests that living in low-poverty neighborhoods has some noticeable impacts on adolescents in the realm of crime, but mostly for girls, though with a number of caveats (Ludwig and Kling 2007; Clampet-Lundquist et al. 2006; Kling, Liebman, and Katz 2007a, 2007b; Kling, Ludwig, and Katz 2005; Ludwig, Duncan, and Hirschfield 2001; Katz, Kling, and Liebman 2001). In particular, girls in the experimental group had fewer arrests for property and violent crimes compared to those in the control group. On the other hand, boys in the experimental group had fewer arrests for violent crime but had higher arrest rates for property crime compared to the control group (Kling, Ludwig, and Katz 2005).

Continued research in this area is needed because the validity and generalization of MTO results can be called into question for several reasons. At the most basic level, the experimental group moved to areas not far from their original residential locations. Furthermore, only half of the experimental group ever moved, leaving the other half in their original place of residence. Thus, a significant share of the subjects did not experience a fundamental change in the nature of their place, electing to live in or near areas close to home that likely did not have appreciably different economic or social characteristics. In fact, Quigley and Raphael (2008) documented that the experiment, observed *ex-post* and accounting for additional moves by some experimental movers after the initial relocation to a low-poverty neighborhood, resulted in a reduction of the neighborhood poverty rate for the experimental movers from the 96th percentile of the poverty distribution in their respective metropolitan areas to the 88th percentile, a largely statistically insignificant change in the poverty condition of the neighborhood of residence. These problems cast some doubt on the MTO findings, probably leading to underestimates of the impacts of place on crime, and thus leave one unable to completely rule out the idea that place has a strong influence on criminal propensity. Moreover, even with improvements, given the research design of MTO it would be difficult to sort out the neighborhood mechanisms—"neighborhood as place" or "neighborhood as arena for social interactions"—that generate these results.

The idea of collective efficacy and its effect on crime in neighborhoods can also be conceptualized and categorized as "neighborhoods as place" when analyzing the mechanisms by which neighborhoods affect crime. Collective efficacy, as termed by Sampson (1997a), refers to the linkage of mutual trust and the shared willingness to intervene for the public good within the neighborhood context. Examples of neighborhoods with strong collective efficacy are those with neighborhood associations, crime watch councils, and volunteers to pick up trash and/or erase graffiti. According to this theory, residents are less likely to intervene in stopping crime in a neighborhood context where the rules are unclear and people mistrust or fear one another. This implies that neighborhoods with strong collective efficacy are likely to be better equipped to address social ills that might plague the neighborhood.

The theory can be treated as neighborhood as place because it fits well into the overall conceptual framework of crime as rational choice. Collective efficacy in a neighborhood is likely to affect potential offenders' probability of being caught, thereby affecting the risk-reward calculus of deciding to engage in crime by increasing risk. Neighborhoods that score high in collective efficacy are also likely those that share information within neighborhoods and are unafraid to summon these resources when crime occurs. These outcomes are likely to appear physically in neighborhoods through the visibility of neighborhood watch signs, of increased police patrols, and so on. The perceived odds of being caught would be higher than in other potentially socially dysfunctional neighborhoods. Accordingly, a series of papers exploring these relationships have shown that collective efficacy explains lower rates of crime, especially violent crime (Sampson, Morenoff, and Gannon-Rowley 2002; Wikstrom and Sampson 2003; Sampson and Raudenbush 1999).

Of course, a difficult methodological challenge is how to measure collective efficacy. Sampson and colleagues (1999, 2006) constructed a measure of collective efficacy by combining scales of the capacity for informal social control and social cohesion using unique data obtained in Chicago that included video surveillance of neighborhoods in action. Still, many of these indicators of neighborhood cohesion are themselves interrelated, raising questions about their independence and validity. Another challenge is whether a notion of social disorder is an explanatory mechanism of criminal involvement or victimization, or an outcome itself. Much of the research on this question was fueled by earlier work looking at the dynamics of "broken windows" (Wilson and Kelling 1982), a theory that suggests that physical sights of disorder such as broken windows and graffiti signal the unwillingness of residents to confront strangers, intervene in a crime, or call the police, thereby lowering the perceived risk of being caught. Others have presented evidence to suggest that the direct link between disorder and crime is not as strong as the broken windows theory would suggest, and that disorder is predicted by the same characteristics as crime itself (Sampson and Raudenbush 1999). This does not mean that disorder is not relevant. Such disorder may in fact trigger general apathy among residents because signs of disorder are visual reminders of neighborhood deterioration.

Other questions about collective efficacy, including whether it can develop in poor neighborhoods and whether it absolutely reduces crime or merely pushes it to neighboring areas, remain. Sampson and Morenoff (2006) demonstrated that persistent poverty and increases in poverty from 1970 to 1990 predict lower collective efficacy in neighborhoods, suggesting that collective efficacy may be strongly associated with income, which itself may influence crime in neighborhoods. Rankin and Quane (2000) demonstrated similar findings. They showed that poverty can inhibit social organization because resources in low-income neighborhoods are scarce. Thus, community institutions have less of an incentive to grow in areas where residents cannot provide resources to sustain them, thus influencing collective efficacy.

Neighborhoods as Peers, Families, and Networks, and Their Relation to Crime

A neighborhood can be conceptualized as a locus of places where individuals interact. While not all social interaction is neighborhood based, it is clear that neighborhoods are prime places where such interaction takes place, possibly because of proximity, community and perhaps even human nature. These interactions could occur through social networks, peers and other similar types of bodies. Neighborhoods, however, are not monolithic; they differ with respect to poverty concentration, racial mix, and other important social and economic demographics. These variations across neighborhoods also influence the types and qualities of individuals who reside there. Thus, the kinds of social networks and peers across these areas are likely to have varying influences on other residents. Unlike the conceptualization of neighborhood as physical place, neighborhood quality and its influence on individual behavior is a reflection of the extent, kind, and quality of social interactions.

This reasoning has been extended to examine the impact of social interaction on criminal propensity and victimization (Calvó-Armengol and Zenou 2004; Haynie 2001; Glaeser, Sacerdone, and Scheinkman 1996; Case and Katz 1991). In this paradigm, neighborhoods influence crime though social interactions and opportunities. Thus, residents are more likely to interact with criminals or potential criminals and also have greater opportunities to participate in illegal activities in neighborhoods with a high concentration of poverty that are also likely to have or to result in areas with high crime rates. Criminals in the area benefit from learning tricks of the trade from other criminals, thus fueling their criminal propensities, but they also must compete with others for illegal activities. Family members, peers, or neighbors who are criminals also increase the likelihood that someone will engage in criminal behavior. On the other hand, strong family structures or noncriminal-based social networks could reduce external peer influence to commit crimes.

Thus, in this model, an individual's peers can promote either positive or negative behavior with respect to crime, depending on the peer group's expectations and norms. When an individual has a dense peer network, as in a highly populated area, he or she will be exposed to more types of people, including those who are criminally prone. In a densely populated area, however, an individual will have less pressure to conform to behavioral norms, because he/she will not interact as frequently with the same peer group (Browning, Feinberg, and Dietz 2004; Haynie 2001). Structured, monitored activities may reduce the likelihood that individuals will become involved in criminal activities (Calvó-Armengol and Zenou 2004; Wikstrom and Sampson 2003).[3]

Networks refer to the tight or loose web of social interaction to which individuals belong and in which information and other resources are exchanged. It has by now been clearly established that a vast majority of those committing crimes, especially adolescents, do so in the company of others (Shaw and McKay 1942; Matsueda and Anderson 1998). Thus, it is reasonable to explore the role that social interactions play in influencing crime. The body of evidence points clearly to a strong relationship of peers, families, and networks with crime. There is uniform evidence that peer participation in crime correlates with youth criminal activity. Case and Katz (1991) suggested that "The direct effect of moving a youth with given family and personal characteristics to a neighborhood where 10% more of the youths are involved in crime than in his or her initial neighborhood is to raise the probability the youth will become involved in crime by 2.3%" (17). Of course, they assume that all youth in neighborhoods are peers, but this need not be the case. In more direct evidence of peer networks, others have shown that peer delinquency is directly correlated with an individual's delinquency and that peer influence predicts future delinquent behavior as well (Haynie 2001).

Family members could also play the role of peers and influence other members' orientation to criminality. Sampson (1997b) shows that family instability can decrease social control and increase the probability of crime. Likewise, strong families may prevent criminal behavior because they have more prosocial interaction (Glaeser, Sacerdone, and Scheinkman 1996). Family structure and involvement can also influence criminal activity. For example, children in two-parent families and married men are less likely to be criminals than those in female-headed families and men in common-law marriages, respectively (Laub, Sammpson, and Sweeten 2006; Williams and Sickles 2002).

Somewhat independent of the role of family, there is also a firmly established literature that examines the role of aging on crime. This life-course view focuses on the idea of desistence from crime, in which criminal propensity declines with age, especially for men. Life course events such as getting married or having children or general maturation affect the decision to participate in crime (Sampson and Laub 2003, 2005).

Of course, the key problem in these types of social interaction studies is the problem of selection bias or unobserved heterogeneity, the main theme of our chapter. And there are two types here. The first is that neighborhood sorting could influence these associations, resulting in a spurious relationship between peers, families, networks, and crime, as we have noted earlier in the chapter. That is, neighborhoods typically have strong correlations between neighborhood amenities such as the extent of crime and the quality of the residents, measured by such things as good incomes or high employment. To the extent that people choose their neighborhoods based on shared values and also choose their peers, networks, and family members with whom they associate, then these neighborhood preferences are likely to drive both their type of residence and their associations, all of which are spuriously correlated with crime.

The second is that many, but certainly not all, of these studies overlook the possibility that individuals have preferences that may be endogenous to the sorting of their peer and social networks, and perhaps even their family ties. Certainly, individuals have choices about with whom they may want to interact, even within families, although the immediate environmental context could impose constraints on the quality and kinds of peers, networks, and families with whom such individuals could choose to associate. But if individuals are choosing to interact with peers, networks, or families who are just like them, then these influences would be a reflection of the values and norms of that individual and not necessarily of the influence of these groups. In fact, these groups may just reinforce these values and behaviors. In this sense, the construction of an individual's peer groups, networks, and perhaps even some family ties may be an endogenous process, and the identified effects on behavior would be spurious to these internalized factors.

Conclusion

Even with all of the aforementioned caveats, the evidence points to strong support for the idea that neighborhoods and their social interactions influence crime. Still, it is difficult to draw firm conclusions that these effects are causal, even though more recent studies have used state-of-the-art statistical techniques and data to study these questions. Studies are still plagued by the problem of selection bias, the key identification problem in these areas of inquiry. That is, in many of these studies, there still remains the possibility that they are picking up a process of selection whereby individuals who are more prone to crime sort into neighborhoods where crime is extensive or more accepted by the community, or sort into social networks, peer groups, or even interactions with family members because their values and behaviors reflect their own preferences. The randomized MTO experiments help reduce this uncertainty, but problems with the implementation of the study design limit generalizations about the results.

A bigger issue that has yet to be addressed surrounds the question of sorting out the potential mechanisms through which neighborhoods could affect crime. It is very difficult in most of the studies of neighborhoods and crime to disentangle whether the physical or economic assets of neighborhoods are the mechanism generating the results, or whether the results reflect outcomes operating through social interactions that are taking place within neighborhoods. Of course, the real possibility is that both mechanisms are at play, but the methods and data that have been used heretofore have been unable to completely isolate their separate or unique effects or to examine their interactions. This is not simply an academic question. It is also a question of public policy, since the different mechanisms that might drive these results and problems have very different consequences for the types of public policy interventions that should be considered to address these problems. We also have very little insight into the conditions under which either conceptualization of neighborhood may be more important or how they would interact differently, given different conditions in neighborhoods. It is our strong belief, therefore, that before we can draw firm conclusions about the role of neighborhoods or social interactions in influencing crime, or before we can think hard about the appropriate role of public policy in confronting these questions, these research problems should be addressed.

Chapter 6

Daily Activities and Violence in Community Landscapes

Douglas J. Wiebe and Charles C. Branas

The social and physical attributes of communities have profound implications for health (Wilson and Kelling 1989; Cohen et al. 2000; Sampson 2003). Violence is one of the primary threats to health in urban communities, and within the urban landscape there are places where violence occurs with disproportionate frequency. This chapter describes two Philadelphia-based research projects investigating the health risks associated with specific places in urban communities, and how the things people do and the places they go relate to the likelihood of being the victim of violence. We are motivated by research that has sought to understand "how place matters" and that describes new approaches to understanding how older communities might be reinvented with places that foster safety and healthy living.

The "triangle of human ecology" provides a helpful framework for studying how place matters for violence (Meade and Earickson 2000). It describes the ability of a community to be in a healthy state as a function of the population's characteristics, people's behaviors, and the habitats in which people reside. The attributes of a population that relate to a community's health include age, gender, genetic susceptibility, nutritional status, resiliency, and psychological status. The behaviors that relate to health are the observable aspect of culture; they stem from cultural precepts, social norms, economic constraints, and individual psychology. And the habitat includes not only houses but also workplaces, settlement patterns, naturally occurring physical phenomena, health care services, transportation systems, schools, and government. These components each influence one another, in that through their behavior, people create habitat conditions, expose themselves to or protect themselves from conditions of the habitat that have positive or negative impacts on health, and move elements of the habitat from place to place. In this way, the health of a population is the result of fluid interconnections between the components of the triangle of human ecology.

This broad framework helps us to appreciate that the disease burden that is carried by any population (i.e., the incidence of disease, violence, or injury) will be a function of how many people are susceptible to a given disease and the extent to which those people are exposed to habitat conditions that produce the disease. In describing how people impact their habitat as well, the framework also draws attention to the importance of identifying those features within the community landscape that are driving the incidence of disease. Indeed, identifying place-based risk factors is a fundamental goal in the field of public health, given the potential to use land-use policies and zoning laws to make places safer if the attributes that compromise the health of a community can be identified (Maantay 2001).

The features of the urban landscape that promote violence are thought to include social disorder (Aneshensel and Sucoff 1996; Sampson et al. 1997), physical decay (e.g. dilapidated buildings) (LaGrange, Ferraro et al. 1992), and attributes that include alcohol outlets in particular (Scribner et al. 1995; Alaniz et al. 1998; Graham et al. 1998; Pernanen 1998; Speer et al. 1998; Livingston 2008). Communities that are socially disorganized are characterized by high residential turnover, social flux, and single-parent families, all of which lessen the likelihood that adults will be involved in informal networks of social control (Wilson 1987; Bursik and Grasmick 1993; Sampson et al. 1997). As a result, there is generally little adult supervision of the activities of teenagers, creating environments conducive to mischief and crime and creating a lack of guardians who, if present, could promote feelings of oversight and thus security for the adolescents in the area. The level of guardianship is low overall, which allows for interactions between potential offenders and victims to occur in locations where they otherwise might not (Felson 1986, 1987). Physical decay including dilapidated buildings, graffiti, vacant buildings and trash-filled lots are contextual features that play a role in the occurrence of violence, giving the impression that residents are not invested in the area and that incivilities and violence will be tolerated (Skogan and Maxfield 1981; LaGrange et al. 1992). Alcohol outlets, which increase the availability of alcohol and the likelihood of group intoxication in the immediate area, are a feature of the urban landscape that may play a unique role in creating situations conducive to assaults and violence (Scribner et al. 1995; Alaniz et al. 1998; Graham et al. 1998; Pernanen 1998; Speer et al. 1998; Livingston 2008).

If community characteristics, including social disorder, physical disorder, and alcohol outlets, put people at risk to be victims of violence, how do we determine the relative contribution that each of these factors makes to the burden of violence that is carried by a given community? If certain places within a community are thought to pose higher risks for violence than others, how do we measure the extent to which people spend time in those locations, and how do we quantify the risk of being the victim of violence that is associated with doing so?

A place to start is by taking accurate measurements of the attributes of communities that are thought to affect health. Social disorganization as described above is an example of a characteristic that affects health that is not measured at the individual level and instead is measured at a larger aggregation, such as neighborhood, county, or country. Collective efficacy is an example as well, in that collective efficacy is a quality that is measured among a group of individuals as a whole and is a feature of communities that appears to be protective against violence (Sampson et al. 1997). It is the neighborhood level at which attributes of things like social disorganization and collective efficacy are typically measured, despite the fact that no consensus exists over the issue of how "neighborhood" is operationally defined (O'Campo 2003). Because investigators often depend upon existing data to characterize population attributes of environmental conditions, we often rely on census data for our research. As a result, it is the boundaries of census tracts and block groups that are commonly used as proxies for "neighborhood."

A shortcoming of this approach is that a neighborhood defined according to an administrative unit has no meaning to an area's inhabitants (O'Campo 2003). In addition, there are methodological problems that stem from arbitrarily drawing neighborhood boundaries and using the conditions within those boundaries as a way to derive a best estimate of the extent to which people residing there are "exposed." The boundaries of these administrative geographic units were typically determined for purposes other than the specific relationships under study and as such may be awkwardly shaped, correspond poorly to lived space, have edge-effects (i.e., a subject assigned to a tract but located on its border may be more influenced by the neighboring tract), or impose a neighborhood scale that is inappropriate for the topic being studied (Openshaw 1984; Wong 1991; Wrigley 1995; Holt et al. 1996; Scribner 2000; Krieger et al. 2002; Geronimus 2006). By nesting subjects within solitary administrative geographic units (i.e., a single census tract or block group), research can generate misleading findings, including overestimating the effect of the hypothesized risk factor on the health outcome being studied (Openshaw 1984; Wong 1991; Wrigley 1995; Holt et al. 1996; Scribner 2000; Krieger et al. 2002; Geronimus 2006).

The work about to be described takes an epidemiologic approach to studying the features of communities that put people at risk to be a victim of violence, and it places special attention on measuring "exposure" based on the activity spaces where people spend time rather than based on the administrative area where their residence is located. These studies could not have been conducted without support from the National Institutes of Health (NIH), the largest public health research agency in the United States. This work is already pioneering with respect to firearm violence, the most prevalent form of fatal violence, and accounts for two-thirds of all the studies of firearm violence the NIH has ever funded. This is true despite the fact that firearm injuries have a far greater burden on health than many of the conditions for which NIH research dollars are much more heavily invested (Branas et al. 2005).

Thus through the NIH and other supporters, most notably the Chicago-based Joyce Foundation, our work seeks to advance the understanding of violence in Philadelphia and other urban communities. This work has included two major studies, both of which consider "how place matters" as they seek to better understand community violence: the Philadelphia Gun and Alcohol Study (NIH grants R01AA13119 and R01AA016187) and the Space-Time Adolescent Risk Study (NIH grant R01AA014944).

The Philadelphia Gun and Alcohol Study

The Philadelphia Gun and Alcohol Study (PGAS) is an epidemiologic investigation of the impact of factors related to the risk of being shot. These include personal factors, such as drinking alcohol or having a gun, and community factors, such as proximity to alcohol outlets or households with guns. Over thirty months, the PGAS enrolled more than 2,000 adult residents who were the victims of shootings in the city of Philadelphia along with residents with similar characteristics who had not been shot. This "case-control" approach is commonly used by epidemiologists to study diseases and is the same method that originally established the link between smoking and lung cancer.

The PGAS is a real-time research effort that has involved numerous academic, government, and industry partners. Daily, the locations and activities of recent shooting victims were sent to the University of Pennsylvania from the Philadelphia Police Department and Medical Examiner's Office. Each time this occurred, an age, race, and sex-matched adult Philadelphia resident who had not been shot was randomly selected as a control and interviewed over the telephone to establish their own location and activities at the time of the victim's shooting. As a testament to the seamless and invaluable cooperation of the study's municipal partners, these victims and their matching controls were typically enrolled within one to two days of each shooting. Additional victim and community data were later obtained from a dozen local, state, and federal data partners. Additional aspects of this effort have been described in detail elsewhere (Branas et al. 2008).

Because information about what each person in the study was doing (Were they drinking? Did they have a gun?) and where they were (Were they close to alcohol outlets or in an area where many people own guns?) was obtained at the time of each case's shooting, several new and (to the best of our knowledge) unique analyses were conducted. Most basically, this included the ability to determine if individuals were at greater risk of being shot by virtue of what they were doing or where they were at the time of a shooting.

The process of measuring the extent to which subjects were exposed to hypothesized risk factors began by geographically coding victims and their controls according to where they were located at the time of each shooting. We then compared these points to the point locations of various community factors around them, including access to alcohol outlets, household gun ownership, perceived safety, social capital, median age, racial diversity, ethnic diversity, education, unemployment, family structure, poverty, crowding, and household income. Many of these geographic factors also included the amount of exposure at each of their point locations, such as sales volume of alcohol per outlet or number of households that owned a gun. Point-to-point geographic exposure measures assigned each subject a unique neighborhood and were inversely weighted by distance, with more distant factors having less impact on the subject (Longley et al. 2005).

Statistical analyses were then conducted to account for the time-matched and geographic nature of our data (Breslow 1996). After adjusting for the personal characteristics of victims and controls (such as their education, occupation, marital status, prior arrests, etc.) and various geographic factors (such as those mentioned above), several key relationships became apparent. With respect to alcohol, heavy drinkers were at 2.7 times the risk of being shot when compared to nondrinkers ($p<0.10$), while light drinking did not put people at risk (Branas et al. 2009). Being near bars and taverns, businesses where patrons purchase and consume alcohol on-site, on average appeared to pose little if any risk of getting shot. However, being near so-called stop-and-go outlets, where patrons purchase and are supposed to consume alcohol off-site, was associated with a 2.0-fold increase in the risk of being shot ($p<0.05$). Additionally, the combination of drinking heavily while in an area of high off-premise alcohol outlet availability was associated with a 9.3-fold increase in the likelihood of being shot ($p<0.05$), possibly because there is much less monitoring of intoxicated patrons. With respect to firearms, individuals who were in possession of a gun were 4.5 times more likely to be shot than those who were not in possession of a gun ($p<0.05$); being in an area where more people report owning guns appeared to be neither a strong risk nor a protective factor (Branas et al., in press).

The Space-Time Adolescent Risk Study

Adolescents typically travel in and around their community in a manner consistent with their daily routines as students, employees, family members, and friends (Barker and Wright 1951; Anderson 1999). Their activity spaces are therefore defined by the locations of schools, jobs, homes, and places of recreation. Because daily routines influence the timing and locations of activities, they also have a large influence on time spent in places where adolescents might be exposed to factors affecting their health (e.g., Takahashi et al. 2001).

Obtaining accurate readings of adolescents' behaviors during the course of their daily activities is the primary goal of our Space-Time Adolescent Risk Study (STARS), a case-control study designed to better understand the influence of community factors on adolescents' risk of being assaulted. A study that motivated our interest in measuring adolescents' activities as accurately as possible was *One Boy's Day: A Specimen Record of Behavior.* This book, written by Barker and Wright in 1951, is a seminal work in the field of ecological psychology, the study of how people interact with and understand their environment. Eight trained observers, with the cooperation of parents, teachers, and citizens, took turns for fourteen consecutive hours to follow and document the travels of a 7-year-old research subject minute by minute throughout the course of his activities in a small Midwestern town. Their goal was to document the nature of the subject's interactions with people, places, and situations in the environment. The book includes photographs, maps, and sketches of environmental conditions; it reports in exceptional detail including minute-to-minute accounts of the subject over the course of his experiences. One account describes him encountering a pair of barking and snarling dogs as he approaches his school in the morning; another documents his walk along the peak of a steeply sloped garage roof during unsupervised time at play; and a third describes him as he idly pulls from his pants pocket a firearm shell casing that he has been saving. With our focus being injury epidemiology, here are examples of this youngster's day involving the potential for a dog bite, a fall from a height, and access to firearms, each of which can produce serious injuries.

We point to *One Boy's Day* as a way to convey the importance of studying people's behaviors in detail if we hope to measure with accuracy the time they spend in contact with factors in their community that have implications for their health. This example serves also to encourage consideration of the logistical and ethical challenges inherent in collecting the data that are necessary to complete scientific research designed to improve our understanding of how people function within the built and social environments of communities and the resulting implications for health. Interestingly, *One Boy's Day* was accomplished through funding from the National Institutes of Health, which is testament to the groundbreaking nature of this research at its time.

The approach taken in the STARS involves using geographic information systems (GIS) as a way to better understand how the nature and locations of daily routines create windows in space and time that place adolescents at risk of being violently assaulted. We are using a case-control study set in Philadelphia as a way to do this. The case subjects are adolescents requiring emergency room treatment for an assault-related injury (e.g., gunshot, stab wound), and the control subjects are adolescents recruited randomly from the community. Each subject participates in an in-person interview, sitting side-by-side with the interviewer and viewing a customized street-level map of the subject's neighborhood on a laptop computer. Starting at the time they woke up, the subject sequentially reports his or her daily activities by location and time on the day the injury occurred (or, for control subjects, on a recent day). Using the mouse and a stylus to draw a line on the neighborhood map, the interviewer creates a graphic that provides a minute-by-minute record of how, when, where, and with whom the subject spent time over the twenty-four hours he or she walked or otherwise traveled from location to location and from activity to activity. At the same time, the subject is asked to describe his or her activities that day (including use of alcohol and firearms) as well as those of other people in the vicinity. A street map and a satellite photograph can also be switched on and off as a way to help the subject identify locations and communicate them to the interviewer. As part of the data management process conducted later, the points along the path of each subject are linked to community information including characteristics of streets, buildings, and neighborhood populations. Empirical methods will then be used to analyze the data in an attempt to quantify the assault injury risk that is associated with specific places within the urban environment.

Figure 6.1 provides an example of how the activity pattern of a study subject is captured. This is a hypothetical 18-year-old case subject who woke up at home at 7 A.M. (denoted by the white circle), walked east (denoted by dashed line) to a street corner where he boarded a trolley (denoted by solid line), which traveled north and then east across the

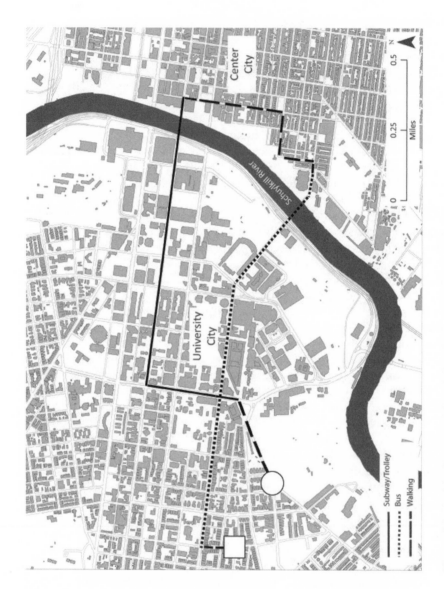

Figure 6.1. Activity Pattern of One Subject's Day in Philadelphia

river where he exited and walked to work. He reported staying at work from 7:45 A.M. to 3 P.M., and then leaving work and walking south and then west, where he arrived at a basketball court. He played basketball until 5 P.M., walked south, boarded a city bus (denoted by dotted line), traveled across the river and farther west, exited the bus, and then walked a short way south to a friend's house. He was there until 9:15 P.M., when he and his friend walked outside and south to a nearby convenience store to buy snacks. It was then at an intersection when the two were surprised from behind and robbed, during which time the subject was shot (denoted by white square).

In addition to enabling us to test our study hypotheses about activities, locations, and the risk of being assaulted, these activity pattern data in themselves are valuable for the insight they give into where and how adolescents spend time in their communities over the course of a day. By overlaying Figure 6.1 with a map of census tracts in Philadelphia, it is revealed that this subject spent time during this single day in ten distinct census tracts. There may be instances in which it is logical to classify this subject according to an attribute of the census tract where his residence is located, for example, as a way to assign baseline characteristics to the subject such as the median household income in the tract where he lives. However, this single-location assignment method will provide inaccurate information if the goal is to classify the subject according to the nature of the surroundings where his daily activities occur. Classifying the land area of his activity pattern according to its level of social stress, for example, may reveal that the subject was in an area of high social stress while he was at his friend's house as well as at the time of the shooting, whereas the hours he spent at work and playing basketball occurred in areas of low social stress.

This notion is conveyed nicely through time geography, a method that helps to characterize people's movements over time and the levels of location-based exposures that are experienced as a result (Hägerstrand 1970; Hägerstrand 1974; Löytönen 1998). The route in Figure 6.2 involves another hypothetical subject waking up at home at 7 A.M., arriving at school at 7:45 A.M., leaving school at 3 P.M. and spending time in several locations with friends until 5:15 P.M., and then returning home and going to bed at 10:15 P.M. The area boundaries correspond to the sixty-nine areas considered to be neighborhoods by Philadelphia municipal agencies, and darker shading is used to indicate neighborhoods with above-average levels of violent crime in recent years. (The shading in the figure is hypothetical, for purposes of the example only.) Through this method emerges a realization that this subject lives in a low-crime neighborhood, yet his in-school hours as well as a considerable amount of leisure time are spent in neighborhoods of high crime.

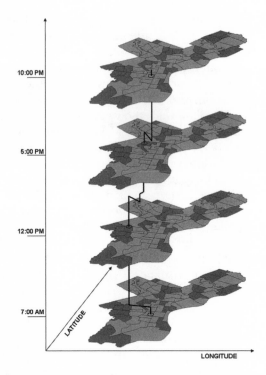

Figure 6.2. Route of One Subject Through Philadelphia Neighborhoods over the Course of One Day

For the analyses of the STARS it will be critical to have these exposure durations quantified, because it is this information that will let us test whether the likelihood of an assault is a function of conditions of the environment where the assault occurred or conditions of the environments experienced in different aspects of people's activities.

Although the STARS is still under way and thus results are not yet available, studying activity patterns in this way is likely to add considerably to our insight of whether activities, as a function of where they take place, serve to protect adolescents at certain times of the day and make adolescents vulnerable to assault at other times.

Conclusion

Violence is a threat to health in urban communities, and a better understanding of where people go, the things people do, and the nature of the places where people spend time will add considerably to our understanding of how communities influence whether violence occurs. Research that can add insight into the nature and health implications of the interplay between people and places will make it possible to capitalize on opportunities to make places safer. Projects that involve reinventing older communities are in an excellent position to take advantage of this opportunity to plan with a design aimed at facilitating safety and healthy living.

PART II

Geographies of Opportunity

Chapter 7

Exploring Changes in Low-Income Neighborhoods in the 1990s

Ingrid Gould Ellen and Katherine O'Regan

While there has been much talk of the resurgence of lower-income urban neighborhoods in the United States over the past ten to fifteen years, there has been surprisingly little empirical examination of the extent and nature of the phenomenon.[1] Were lower-income urban neighborhoods during the 1990s any more likely to experience gains in income than they were during the 1970s and 1980s? And to the extent that patterns in fact differed during the 1990s, we know even less about what may have driven those differences.

Our chapter aims to address these key questions. In the first half, we undertake a broad empirical investigation of income changes in low-income neighborhoods in U.S. cities during the 1990s, comparing them to the changes that occurred during the two previous decades. Our analysis relies on the Neighborhood Change Database, put together by Geolytics in conjunction with the Urban Institute, which offers a balanced panel of census tracts with consistent boundaries from 1970 to 2000 for all metropolitan areas in the United States.

In brief, we find a dramatic reversal in the frequency of income gain for our lowest-income urban neighborhoods during the 1990s. In the previous two decades, such neighborhoods were three times more likely to experience a large loss than a large gain. In the 1990s, this pattern was nearly reversed, with very low-income urban neighborhoods over two and a half times more likely to experience a large gain than a large loss.

In the second half of the chapter, we explore some reasons why the fortunes of lower-income urban neighborhoods improved during the 1990s. We focus on three possible explanations: income gains among lower-income households triggered by expansions of the Earned

Income Tax Credit and other poverty policies enacted during the 1990s; investments in place-based housing programs, such as the significant investments made by the Low Income Housing Tax Credit Program; and finally, reductions in urban crime.

Background

While many have asserted that economic gain among low-income neighborhoods became more common in cities during the 1990s, there is surprisingly little empirical work that supports (or refutes) this claim. Much of the work on neighborhood change examined earlier decades (Aaronson 1997; Bostic and Martin 2003; Fogarty 1977; Galster et al. 2003). Meanwhile, the papers that do include data from the 1990s aim to examine change over a longer time horizon rather than analyzing the patterns evident in the 1990s themselves (see Rosenthal 2006) or focus on changes in the concentration of poverty (see Jargowsky 2003; Kingsley and Pettit 2003).

The papers examining changes in the concentration of poverty have consistently found that poverty concentration declined during the 1990s. Jargowsky (2003) found that the number of people living in very high poverty neighborhoods (tracts with poverty rates of at least 40 percent) declined during the 1990s, reversing a trend of increasing poverty concentration that began in the 1970s. He also reported that the number of high-poverty neighborhoods declined at the same time. Kingsley and Pettit (2003) extended this work to consider a broader share of disadvantaged income tracts (tracts with poverty rates of 30 percent or higher) and confirmed the changes and patterns found by Jargowsky.

It is worth noting, however, that these papers focus on a very small share of census tracts—only 10 percent of all metropolitan census tracts in 2000 had poverty rates of over 30 percent, and even fewer had poverty rates of more than 40 percent. We focus on a broader share of neighborhoods—albeit those that are still low income. Unlike these other works, we also focus specifically on neighborhood change in central cities, since concern about neighborhood changes (whether neighborhood decline or gentrification) has typically focused on cities.

As for the determinants of neighborhood economic gain, Rosenthal (2006) nicely summarized the competing theories offered in the literature. The first theory follows from the filtering model, which posits that as a neighborhood's housing stock ages and deteriorates, higher-income residents exit, opting for neighborhoods with newer housing (Muth 1972; Sweeney 1974).[2] Eventually, however, after the housing stock reaches a certain threshold age, the housing—and the neighborhood more broadly—is likely to become a target for reinvestment and redevelopment. The key driver of neighborhood change in this model is the age of the housing stock.

An alternative theory focuses instead on social externalities—or essentially, racial or class preferences as drivers of neighborhood change (Bailey 1959). Schelling's tipping model represents the classic version of this hypothesis (Schelling 1971). His model shows that if households care about the composition of their neighbors, then small changes in demographic makeup can lead to the rapid tipping of a neighborhood from one group to another. Similarly, higher-income households may be attracted to low-income neighborhoods with greater shares of homeowners or more educated residents.

Few studies have empirically tested these alternative explanations. Fogarty (1977) studied neighborhood economic change in Pittsburgh during the 1960s, focusing on neighborhoods with median incomes below the city's overall median income. He divided neighborhoods into four income categories and found that the correlates or predictors of subsequent change varied quite a bit depending on the initial income. For example, while a higher percentage of black residents in 1960 was associated with greater gains for neighborhoods with initial incomes that were less than 60 percent of the city median, a higher black share was associated with income reductions for neighborhoods in which initial incomes were between 60 and 80 percent of the citywide median.

Brueckner (1977) studied the 1950s and 1960s in eight cities, with a specific focus on neighborhood succession, that is, reductions in mean family income over time. He explored the extent to which various housing stock and housing market characteristics are associated with a neighborhood's transitioning from high to low income. While he found large variation in effects across cities, a range of housing characteristics were consistently related to neighborhood decline. Specifically, higher homeownership rates were negatively correlated with succession, while older housing was positively correlated, as predicted by the filtering model.

Rosenthal (2006) explored the determinants of change for census tracts around the country and attempted to test the relative validity of the filtering and social externality theories. He found evidence to support both. Newly built homes are linked to gains in economic status, as are very old homes, which are presumably ripe for redevelopment. As for socioeconomic status, he found that initial homeownership rates and education levels are positively linked to income gains, while higher concentrations of minority residents are associated with losses. Brueckner and Rosenthal (2005) extended this paper to develop a simple theoretical model showing how age of the housing stock affects the residential location of rich and poor households. In their empirical work, they found further evidence that dwelling age affects residential location patterns.

Data and Measures

As noted, our key aim is to describe and better understand the economic changes that occurred in low-income central city neighborhoods during the 1990s. We use census tracts as a proxy for neighborhoods, relying on the Neighborhood Change Database (NCDB), which was constructed by Geolytics, in partnership with the Urban Institute. The key advantage of this data set is that it links census tract data from 1970, 1980, and 1990 to census tracts as they were defined in the 2000 census. This permits us to examine how neighborhoods' economic fortunes have changed over a three-decade period, with constant geographic units of analysis. We are, however, limited to the subset of data that are collected as part of the decennial census and are included in the NCDB.

We eliminated census tracts with very small populations (less than 200) and those with primarily institutionalized populations.[3] Given our focus on economic gain, we only included tracts for which measures of tract income are available for each year. As such, this work focuses on patterns of neighborhood change for census tracts that existed as part of a metropolitan area as of 1970. Our final balanced panel included more than 38,500 census tracts in 226 metropolitan areas.[4] While our panel included a constant number of tracts in each year, the share of all metro tracts included in our sample declined from census year to census year both because metro areas that existed in 1970 added tracts over time and because the total number of metro areas also grew.

As for capturing neighborhood economic status, we use a relative measure of income: the ratio of average household income in the census tract to that of the metropolitan area.[5] For example, if the mean household income in the tract is $35,000 and the mean income of the metropolitan area is $50,000, then the tract's relative income is 70 percent. Consistent with several other studies in the area, such a relative income approach permitted us to measure how a neighborhood is faring relative to the larger metropolitan area. Ratios are also easy to compare across different time periods.[6] To some extent, however, our approach may be a conservative measure of upgrading during periods of metropolitan growth and prosperity, since neighborhoods are only identified as gaining if their incomes are rising more rapidly than the mean income of the metropolitan area as a whole.

We created five categories of neighborhoods based on their relative income, from the lowest ratio to the highest (referred to as very low income, low income, moderate income, middle income, and upper income). Our very low-income tracts had an average household income relative to the surrounding Metropolitan Statistical Area (MSA) of 70 percent or less. Neighborhoods with relative incomes above 70 percent and less than 87 percent were considered low income; those with ratios of 87 percent through 100 percent are moderate income; those with ratios of up to 122 percent were middle income, while those with relative income ratios above 122 percent were upper income.[7]

We next considered how to measure economic gain or improvement. We relied on a measure of economic gain that is based on the change in a neighborhood's relative income in any decade. Specifically, assume a neighborhood starts a decade with an average household income relative to the surrounding MSA of 70 percent. If the neighborhood's relative income—or the ratio of the tract's mean income to the mean income in the metropolitan area—rises over the decade (say to 75 percent), then we would identify that tract as gaining economically in that decade. If the neighborhood's relative income rises by at least ten percentage points (which here would mean an increase to more than 80 percent), then we would consider the tract to have experienced a large economic gain.[8]

Since our focus was on central city neighborhoods, we also needed to identify the census tracts located in the central cities within their metropolitan areas. The NCDB does not include an explicit central city identifier, but we used a variable collected in 1990 that reports the percentage of the tract's population who reside in the central city. Because tract boundaries have been normalized, this variable can take on values between 0 and 100. We considered tracts to be located in the central city if a majority of its population resided in the central city in 1990. In fact, however, in virtually all the tracts in our sample, the share of the population residing in the central city was either very close to zero or very close to 100 percent. So a few of our central city tracts had a substantial noncentral city population. As this variable exists only in the 1990 data, our measure of central city location was determined by whether the census tract was within the central city boundaries in 1990. However, we do not expect that many of our tracts would have been classified differently in 1970, 1980, or 2000. Of the 38,552 census tracts in our data, 18,252 (47 percent) are classified as central city.

Among central city tracts in our sample, 39 percent fell into the lowest income category (mean household income in tract < 70 percent of MSA mean household income) in 1990. (Among all metropolitan census tracts in 1990, 23 percent fell into this lowest income category.)

Table 7.1.   Share of Central City Tracts with Gain/Loss in Relative Income Ratio

| | Share of Tracts | | | |
| | Panel A: Any Change in Income Ratio [a] | | Panel B: Large Change in Income Ratio | |
N type at start of decade	Gain	Loss	Large Gain[b]	Large Loss[b]
1990–2000				
Very low-income	0.56	0.44	0.19	0.07
Low income	0.34	0.66	0.10	0.22
Moderate income	0.30	0.70	0.11	0.33
Middle income	0.29	0.71	0.13	0.43
Upper income	0.29	0.71	0.19	0.55
ALL TRACTS	0.41	0.59	0.15	0.25
1980–1990				
Very low-income	0.29	0.71	0.08	0.26
Low income	0.23	0.77	0.07	0.34
Moderate income	0.25	0.75	0.10	0.39
Middle income	0.29	0.71	0.15	0.43
Upper income	0.43	0.57	0.28	0.39
ALL TRACTS	0.29	0.71	0.12	0.35
1970–1980				
Very low-income	0.29	0.71	0.07	0.23
Low income	0.28	0.72	0.08	0.27
Moderate income	0.31	0.69	0.12	0.31
Middle income	0.31	0.69	0.14	0.40
Upper income	0.28	0.72	0.16	0.55
ALL TRACTS	0.29	0.71	0.11	0.34

[a]It is highly unlikely for a neighborhood's income ratio to remain exactly the same across two decades.
[b]"Large" is defined as at least a 10 percentage point change in ratio of tract mean household income to MSA mean household income.

How Much Neighborhood Upgrading Occurred in Cities During the 1990s?

Table 7.1 shows the proportion of central city tracts in our sample undergoing various changes in their relative income ratio in each decade, grouped by their economic status at the start of the decade. Panel A shows the share of tracts experiencing economic gains and losses of any magnitude. Overall, the probabilities of gain and loss were identical during the 1970s and 1980s—29 percent of our central city census tracts experienced a gain in their relative income ratio, while 71 percent experienced a loss. During the 1990s, however, we see a significant shift—the proportion of central city neighborhoods experiencing an economic gain jumps to 41 percent. Of course, a majority of urban neighborhoods were still experiencing reductions in income relative to the larger metropolitan area during the 1990s.

That said, looking separately at the individual categories of neighborhoods shows that very low-income neighborhoods were actually more likely to experience an economic gain than an economic loss during the 1990s, with a full 56 percent undergoing economic gain. By contrast, the proportion of tracts that gained for the other four categories of neighborhoods ranged from just 29 to 34 percent.[9]

This pattern was unique to the 1990s. During the 1970s, we see very similar patterns across all neighborhood types. Each type of neighborhood was more than twice as likely to experience an economic loss as an economic gain. Further, the prevalence of economic gain was very similar across neighborhood classification. Just under a third of all neighborhoods in each category experienced a gain in economic status. The 1980s look very similar to the 1970s, with the exception of the highest income neighborhoods, which experienced a sizable increase in the likelihood of economic gain.

During the 1990s, the likelihood of economic gain for these high-income neighborhoods fell back to 29 percent, and meanwhile the likelihood of gain increased for the two lowest-income groups of neighborhoods. The change for the lowest-income neighborhoods is particularly striking. While these shifts in proportions are dramatic, the gains occurring in neighborhoods could have been quite small. Thus, Panel B of Table 7.1 examines the prevalence of *large* changes in economic status. We define large change, whether positive or negative, as a ten percentage point (or more) change in relative income.[10] The first column of Panel B reports the share of tracts in a particular neighborhood category that experienced a large economic gain, while the last column reports the share of tracts in that category experiencing a large loss. The magnitudes of the proportions naturally differ for large changes as compared to changes of any size, but the same general pattern holds. In the 1970s and 1980s, neighborhoods of all types were about twice (if not three times) more likely to experience large losses than they were large gains. Once again, the one exception was the highest-income neighborhoods in the 1980s, which were significantly more likely to experience a large gain. And once again, that increase was not maintained in the 1990s.

Turning to our lowest-income neighborhoods, while such neighborhoods were three times as likely to experience a large loss as a large gain during the 1970s and 1980s, this pattern was almost reversed in the 1990s. During the 1990s, very low-income neighborhoods were over two and a half times more likely to experience a large gain than a large loss. In short, the number of very low-income and low-income urban

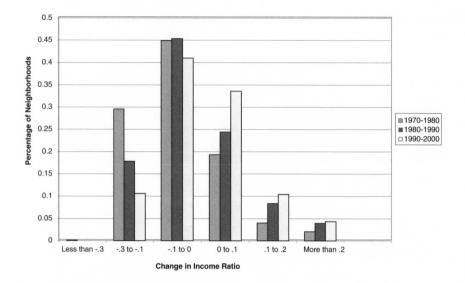

Figure 7.1. Change in Average Household Income Ratio, Very Low Income Neighborhoods, Northeast

Note: "Average (or mean) household income ratio" refers to the ratio of average household income in the census tract to average household income in the metropolitan area.

neighborhoods gaining economically was clearly significantly higher in the 1990s than during the 1970s and 1980s. That said, the neighborhoods that gained were not completely transformed. More than half of the tracts in the lowest-income category that experienced a large gain actually remained in the lowest-income category after their gain.[11]

Much of the attention paid to the revival of urban areas in the 1990s has focused on the Northeast and coastal cities, such as Boston, New York, and Washington, D.C. Contrary to the conventional wisdom, however, the gains in other regions of the country were, if anything, more dramatic; in addition, they were more concentrated in the 1990s. It appears that whatever happened to very low-income tracts in the 1990s happened in all four regions of the country (see Figures 7.1 through 7.4).

Explaining Neighborhood Economic Change

As a general matter, there are two potential reasons why the fortunes of lower income urban neighborhoods improved during the 1990s. The first is that the individual incomes of low-income households rose, whether through policies or market conditions. Given that low-income

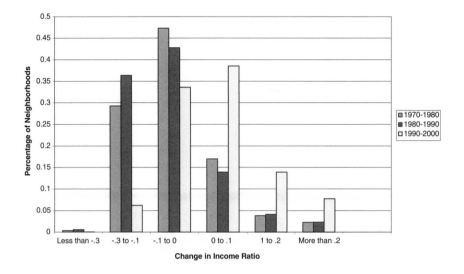

Figure 7.2. Change in Average Household Neighborhood Income Ratio, Very Low Income Neighborhoods, Midwest

Note: "Average (or mean) household income ratio" refers to the ratio of average household income in the census tract to average household income in the metropolitan area.

households disproportionately live in lower-income urban tracts, such a general increase in the economic status of households at the low end of the income spectrum would be felt particularly strongly in these tracts. The second concerns the spatial distribution of lower-income households. In particular, if the concentration (or spatial density) of low-income households decreased, the average household incomes in the lowest-income neighborhoods would have naturally increased.

The rest of this chapter explores these possible pathways. First, we consider whether the shift in the fortunes of lower-income urban neighborhoods could have been driven by increases in the incomes of lower-income households, as suggested above. Second, we appraise two possible reasons why the spatial distribution of households by income level might have changed during the 1990s: place-based housing investments, specifically the investments in housing made by the Low Income Housing Tax Credit (LIHTC) program, and reductions in central city crime. We take each of these possibilities in turn.

Income Gains Among Lower-Income Households

Perhaps the most obvious explanation for the resurgence of lower-income neighborhoods during the 1990s is the robust rate of growth

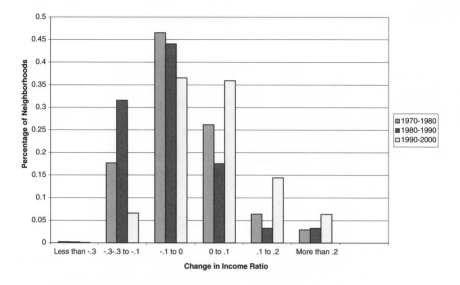

Figure 7.3. Change in Average Household Income Ratio, Very Low Income Neighborhoods, South

Note: "Average (or mean) household income ratio" refers to the ratio of average household income in the census tract to average household income in the metropolitan area.

in the overall economy. After peaking at around 7.5 percent in 1992, unemployment in the United States declined thereafter, hitting a low of 4 percent in 2000 (Bureau of Labor Statistics).[12] Economic growth, however, cannot fully explain our results. After all, *only* the lowest-income neighborhoods experienced a dramatic resurgence during the 1990s. This differential pattern of economic improvement remains even when metropolitan area fixed effects are included in the models; simply put, lowest-income neighborhoods did better than other neighborhoods, within the same economic boom and within the very same metropolitan areas.

A more plausible set of explanations relates to increases in income that were specific to lower-income households. During the 1990s, the Clinton administration enacted some fairly substantial changes in low-wage labor market policies. Most famously, in 1996, President Clinton signed the Personal Responsibility and Work Opportunity Reconciliation Act (PRWORA), which fundamentally restructured the federal system of cash assistance to families. Prior to the passage of this law, many states had already received federal waivers to experiment with reform efforts of their own. Many have pointed to the combined impact of the

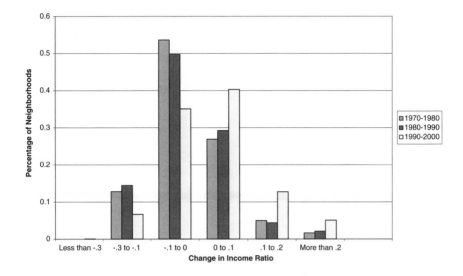

Figure 7.4. Change in Average Household Income Ratio, Very Low Income Neighborhoods, West

Note: "Average (or mean) household income ratio" refers to the ratio of average household income in the census tract to average household income in the metropolitan area.

welfare reform act and the earlier waivers in explaining the dramatic decline in welfare caseloads (which fell by over 50 percent between 1994 and 2000), the decreased spending on cash benefits (which also dropped by more than 50 percent), and the ten-percentage-point increase in labor force participation for single women with children (Blank 2002).

Another policy change enacted during the 1990s was the expansion of the Earned Income Tax Credit (EITC), a refundable federal income tax credit that targets the working poor (primarily those with children). The value of the federal credit increased substantially during this time period, surpassing federal and state welfare payments in 1996 and the federal food stamp program in 1998 (Ellwood 2001; U.S. House 2004). This program is generally credited as the primary driver (along with the economic boom) behind increased employment among working heads of poor families (Holt 2006; Grogger 2003).[13]

Many believe that the EITC expansion and welfare reform together helped to reduce poverty and increase the incomes of lower-income households. During the 1990s, poverty rates in metropolitan areas declined from 12 percent to 11.3 percent, suggesting an improvement in the economic status of many poor households. Given that poor households tend to be concentrated in lower-income central city neighborhoods, these reductions in poverty may have contributed to the income gains that occurred in lower-income urban neighborhoods during the 1990s. But while these poverty reductions likely played a part in explaining the reversal of fortunes of lower-income central city neighborhoods, these reductions are not large enough to fully explain the turnaround described above. Consider that if the poverty rate in the lowest-income neighborhoods had fallen at the same rate as the poverty rate in metropolitan areas as a whole during the 1990s, their poverty rates would have fallen from an average of 37.9 percent in 1990 to 35.6 percent in 2000. But poverty rates in the lowest-income neighborhoods fell far more dramatically. Among very low-income tracts that experienced large gains in income, the mean poverty rate fell from 37.9 percent to 29.5 percent during the 1990s.

Federal Housing Policy

A second possibility is that shifts in federal housing policy have helped to trigger neighborhood income gains through encouraging the deconcentration of poverty. In the past, federally subsidized rental housing developments clearly contributed to poverty concentration. Federal programs such as Section 8 New Construction and Public Housing exclusively targeted very low-income households and tended to be located in very poor urban neighborhoods (Newman and Schnare 1997). Moreover, the developments built through these programs gained a reputation for not only housing the poorest of the poor but also for being poorly built and poorly managed. As a result, higher-income households may have avoided neighborhoods with such developments, further concentrating disadvantage in the communities surrounding them.

There are reasons to think that these patterns may have changed during the 1990s, however. First, virtually no new public housing was constructed during the decade, and efforts were made to integrate the existing developments.[14] Second, tenant-based vouchers became more important as a source of federal housing assistance. And finally, the major source of new federally subsidized housing during the 1990s, the LIHTC Program, may have contributed, in a small way, to deconcentration. While place-based housing programs are typically not viewed as a means of deconcentrating poor households or improving neighborhoods, LIHTC developments were sited in higher-income neighborhoods than earlier subsidized housing.

Table 7.2 presents the distribution of LIHTC units built during the 1990s by the poverty rate of census tracts and shows that 36 percent of LIHTC units built during the decade were placed in low-poverty communities (tracts in which the poverty rate was lower than 10 percent),

Table 7.2. Distribution of Low-Income LIHTC Units Built During the 1990s, by Neighborhood Poverty Level

	Share of Units in Neighborhood Type
Low-Poverty (poverty rate < 10%)	36.4%
Moderate Poverty (pov rate, 10–30%)	40.4%
Medium Poverty (pov rate, 30–40%)	11.0%
High Poverty (poverty rate > 40%)	12.2%

while 12 percent were built in high-poverty neighborhoods (with poverty rates above 40 percent). These numbers suggest that the program's tenants are far more likely to reach low-poverty areas than recipients of other forms of federal housing assistance (see Newman and Schnare 1997; Cummings and Dipasquale 1999; Rohe and Freeman 2001). Newman and Schnare (1997), for example, reported that in the mid-1990s, only 7.5 percent of public housing units were located in census tracts with poverty rates below 10 percent. More surprisingly, McClure (2006) reports that 25 percent of voucher holders in 2002 lived in low-poverty census tracts, so even voucher holders appear to be less likely to reach low-poverty neighborhoods than LIHTC tenants. That said, voucher holders also appear less likely to live in the extremely high poverty tracts too—just 6 percent of voucher holders in 2002 were living in tracts with poverty rates of at least 40 percent (McClure 2006).

The LIHTC program also tends to serve a more moderate income population than traditional public housing or Section 8 vouchers. While there are few hard data on the income levels of tenants, there is some evidence that this is true (Cummings and DiPasquale 1999; General Accounting Office 1997; Stegman 1991). Moreover, in some cases, in fact, market-rate units are included in the developments. Thus, the construction of LIHTC developments in lower-income neighborhoods may have led to increases in average tract incomes.

Finally, there is some evidence to suggest that LIHTC developments generated positive spillovers in their surrounding community, at least when built in lower income communities (Ellen, O'Regan, and Voicu 2009; Ericksen and Rosenthal 2007; Rosenthal 2006). LIHTC investments, that is, might have actually made neighborhoods more attractive to higher-income households, perhaps because LIHTC units are often of higher quality than the housing in the surrounding neighborhood, or because they are built on previously blighted sites (Cummings and DiPasquale 1999).

In previous work, we have found that through some combination of these mechanisms, the completion of tax credit units does appear to be associated with reductions in poverty concentration at the metropolitan-area level (Ellen, O'Regan, and Voicu 2009). Thus, it seems reasonable that the completion of more tax credit units per capita in a metropolitan area might also be associated with greater income gains among its lower-income tracts.

Crime

During the 1990s, crime rates in the United States declined dramatically. From 1991 to 2000, aggregate crime rates dropped by 30 percent; violent crime declined by 33 percent; and homicide rates decreased by 44 percent (Uniform Crime Reports 2000). The decrease in crime was continuous over this time period, and pervasive. Reductions were seen in all major crime categories and in all regions of the country, though declines were particularly dramatic in urban areas and large cities.[15] While the proximate causes are under lively debate, the magnitude of the change is well documented.

Past research suggests that high and increasing crime rates prior to this decline contributed to population losses, at the level of both the city (Cullen and Levitt 1999) and the neighborhood (Morenoff and Sampson 1997). Therefore, it seems likely that dramatic reductions in crime would reverse or at least abate such losses and could make neighborhoods more attractive to higher-income households. Presumably the positive impact would be largest in those areas previously damaged the most by high crime rates: very low-income central city neighborhoods.

Empirical Analysis

To test the validity of these various explanations, we exploited the cross-sectional variation in the degree to which lower-income neighborhoods improved during the 1990s in different metropolitan areas. Specifically, we estimated a series of regression models of neighborhood income gain to see if tracts that were low-income in 1990 were more likely to gain in metropolitan areas that as a whole experienced larger overall declines in poverty, greater LIHTC construction per capita, and/or larger reductions in crime. The data, methods, and results are described in detail in the appendix.

Our regression models offer some preliminary evidence about all three of the hypotheses outlined above. First, we found that the likelihood that a very low-income tract upgraded between 1990 and 2000 was positively associated with the reduction in its metropolitan area's poverty rate between 1990 and 2000. The low-wage labor market policies that may have prompted these reductions in metropolitan area poverty rates, in other words, may have disproportionately affected low-income central city neighborhoods.

Second, we found weak evidence that very low-income tracts located in metropolitan areas with larger investments in LIHTC units were more likely to experience large gains in neighborhood income. Third, we found that low-income tracts in cities experiencing a reduction in crime were somewhat more likely to experience large income gains.

Conclusion

This chapter shows clearly that an urban resurgence *of sorts* did take place in low-income urban neighborhoods during the 1990s. We found a notable increase in the 1990s in the proportion of lower-income neighborhoods experiencing an increase in economic status (household income). Second, in terms of geographic patterns, we found that this type of upgrading occurred throughout the country, not just in selected regions or cities.

In the second half of the chapter, we describe how we tested some possible explanations for this shift in the fortunes of lower-income urban neighborhoods. Examining cross-sectional variation in the likelihood of income gains, we found some support for the notion that broad declines in poverty rates may help to explain the gains in neighborhood income at the low end of the distribution. We also found some support for the idea that the completion of LIHTC units was associated with an improvement in the incomes of at least very low-income census tracts. This association might be due to one of three pathways: LIHTC developments may have brought somewhat higher-income households into very low-income tracts; they may have brought very low-income households into higher-income tracts; or they may have helped to revitalize very low-income tracts through spillovers. Finally, when examining changes in city crime rates, we also found evidence that reductions in crime are associated with larger gains among lower-income neighborhoods. Thus, changes in crime rates may have been a part of the story too.

It is important to stress that these last sets of results are exploratory. We have not determined what drives these associations and cannot say with certainty that these policies actually led to changes in the likelihood that very low-income central city neighborhoods would experience gains. There are, however, some implications even from these tentative findings. First, there are several potential avenues through which the prospects of neighborhood trajectories may be affected. To the extent that it is the neighborhood's prospects in which we are interested, these avenues appear amenable to policy influence. Second, while not all of these avenues are place-based in nature, they may have spatial implications. Finally, it is worth underscoring that neighborhood gains do not imply individual gains. In future work, we will use data on individual households, linked to neighborhoods, to examine what happens to original residents as neighborhoods gain.

Appendix

To test our hypotheses about why the fortunes of lower income neighborhoods changed during the 1990s, we estimated a very simple model to explain income gains in low income neighborhoods as a function of relevant tract and metropolitan characteristics at the start of the decade. We then expanded this model to add in a series of city and metropolitan-area variables that help to capture changes in policies and conditions. Specifically, our basic empirical models are:

$$(1)\ \Pr(\text{Gain}_{ij}) = \alpha + \beta X_{ij} + \varphi \text{MSA}_j + \epsilon$$
$$(2)\ \Pr(\text{Gain}_{ij}) = \alpha + \beta X_{ij} + \varphi \text{MSA}_j + \gamma \Delta \text{Poverty}_j + \epsilon$$
$$(3)\ \Pr(\text{Gain}_{ij}) = \alpha + \beta X_{ij} + \varphi \text{MSA}_j + \gamma \Delta \text{LIHTC}_j + \epsilon$$
$$(4)\ \Pr(\text{Gain}_{ij}) = \alpha + \beta X_{ij} + \varphi \text{MSA}_j + \gamma \Delta \text{Crime}_j + \epsilon$$

where $\Pr(\text{Gain}_{ij})$ indicates the likelihood of a ten percentage point gain or more in the relative income ratio of tract i in MSA j over a decade.[16] As for the independent variables, X_{ij} is a vector of tract-level demographic and housing characteristics, and MSA_j is a set of MSA or city-level variables that measure economic conditions, while the three change variables capture changes between 1990 and 2000 at the city or MSA level in poverty rates, per capita LIHTC units, and crime rates.

Model 1 is a simple model that includes a series of neighborhood-level independent variables that may affect the likelihood that a tract experiences a gain in income. Following the filtering theory of neighborhood change, we included the share of very new housing in the neighborhood (since newer housing is generally more attractive to wealthier households) and the share of very old housing, since the filtering model also suggests that significant turnover and upgrading may occur when a large share of the stock is old enough to be prime for large-scale reinvestment (Rosenthal 2006).

Drawing on the theories of neighborhood change that emphasize preferences for neighborhood racial and/or socioeconomic composition, we also controlled for the proportion of blacks and Hispanics and the poverty rate. In addition, we controlled for homeownership rates and the share of residents with college degrees, since more educated residents and homeownership opportunities may help to attract and retain higher-income residents. The higher human capital these residents bring to the neighborhood may also benefit lower-income households and help them to prosper.[17]

All models included controls for baseline demographic and socioeconomic conditions in the larger metropolitan area. Specifically, we included regional dummy variables, the share of the MSA population that is black, the share that is Hispanic, the share foreign-born, the proportion under 18 and over 65, the poverty rate, and the percentage working in manufacturing.

In Models 2–4, we tested our key policy questions. In Model 2, we included the change in the MSA poverty rate between 1990 and 2000 to capture overall changes in labor market outcomes and income among lower-income households that may have been driven by welfare reform and the expansion of the EITC.

In Model 3, we examined whether the completion of more LIHTC units per capita in a metropolitan area is associated with a greater or lesser chance of income gain in its lower-income neighborhoods. Model 4 included the change in the central city crime rate. Many central cities experienced dramatic reductions in crime during the 1990s, reductions that may have been felt most dramatically in lower-income neighborhoods. Thus, one possibility is that reductions in crime rates made lower-income central city neighborhoods more attractive places to live.

Our sample for Models 1–3 included 7,610 very low-income, central city census tracts in over 300 metropolitan areas. (We restricted the sample to central city census tracts in which the mean household income was less than 70 percent of the mean income of the metropolitan area in 1990.) The sample size for Model 4 was somewhat smaller, because we only have data on city crime rates for 145 of our metropolitan areas.

Results

Table 7.3 shows results for all of our models. We found that several tract variables capturing racial, socioeconomic, and housing characteristics were significantly associated with the likelihood of neighborhood economic gain. Consistent with expectations based on social externalities, urban neighborhoods with greater shares of college graduates and higher rates of homeownership were generally more likely to gain, either because higher-status neighborhoods were more able to attract or retain higher-income residents or because they enabled original residents to thrive. As predicted by the filtering model, tracts with a larger share of both housing that is new and housing that is very old were also more likely to gain, suggesting that the age of the housing stock helps to shape neighborhood economic changes.

However, there are some surprises here. The share of the population that was Hispanic was positively correlated with economic gains. Perhaps more surprising still, poverty was positively associated with economic

Table 7.3. Logit Regression of Probability of Large Gain in Relative Income in Tract, 1990s Sample: Low-Income Central City Census Tracts, 304 MSAs

	(1)	(2)	(3)	(4)
TractPopulation	−0.261***	−0.260***	−0.261***	−0.261***
	(0.022)	(0.022)	(0.023)	(0.024)
Tract%Black	0.064	0.060	0.080	0.164
	(0.158)	(0.160)	(0.156)	(0.185)
Tract%Hispanic	0.960***	0.961**	0.978***	1.107**
	(0.276)	(0.280)	(0.271)	(0.320)
Tract%ForBorn	−0.748*	−0.751*	−0.724*	−0.740*
	(0.388)	(0.391)	(0.386)	(0.398)
Tract%College	1.286**	1.289**	1.325**	1.925***
	(0.444)	(0.445)	(0.443)	(0.480)
Tract%Homeown	0.744**	0.704**	0.732**	0.859**
	(0.283)	(0.278)	(0.282)	(0.328)
Tract%Oldhousing	0.781***	0.770***	0.804***	1.049***
	(0.215)	(0.211)	(0.211)	(0.228)
Tract%Newhousing	1.311*	1.398**	1.299*	1.452*
	(0.689)	(0.690)	(0.696)	(0.801)
TractPovertyrate	2.870***	2.838***	2.898***	3.276***
	(0.328)	(0.323)	(0.329)	(0.379)
MSA%Manufact	−2.323*	−2.753**	−1.829	−0.443
	(1.368)	(1.354)	(1.469)	(1.938)
MSA%Black	−0.033 0.044	−0.097	−0.314	
	(0.755)	(0.757)	(0.781)	(1.018)
MSA%ForBorn	4.690***	6.829***	4.738***	3.711**
	(1.335)	(1.495)	(1.305)	(1.658)
MSA%Hispanic	−1.804**	−2.279**	−1.598*	−2.093*
	(0.883)	(0.871)	(0.949)	(1.103)
MSA%College	−3.580*	−4.773**	−3.812*	−2.676
	(2.085)	(2.129)	(1.993)	(3.004)
MSA%Under18	1.259	1.419	1.474	−0.019
	(3.528)	(3.420)	(3.593)	(5.784)
MSA%Over65	−1.030	−1.326 0.436	−1.675	
	(3.599)	(3.516)	(3.957)	(6.295)
MSAPovertyrate	−2.363	−5.104**	−2.460	−0.019
	(2.002)	(2.320)	(2.052)	(3.080)
ChangeMSAPovrate		−11.824**		
		(4.160)		
PercapLIHTCunits			67.95*	
			(39.94)	
ChangeMSACrimerate				−6.408*
				(3.600)
Observations	7,610	7,610	7,610	6,181

Notes: Standard errors in parentheses. Standard errors clustered at MSA level. All models include regional dummies and a constant term.
Model 4 includes data for only 145 metropolitan areas.
* significant at 10% level; ** significant at 5% level; *** significant at 1% level.

gain. While counterintuitive, this result was robust to many other model specifications. To some degree higher poverty rates may imply a wider distribution of income within census tracts, since we were controlling for the percentage of residents with college degrees. But it appears true that even after controlling for other factors, the lower income census tracts with the highest rates of poverty in 1990 were the most likely to gain economically over the next decade.[18] These results are consistent with the pattern of poverty deconcentration that has been found in other work (Jargowsky 2003; Kingsley and Pettit 2003).

In terms of the broader context in which these neighborhoods are embedded, the coefficients on the regional dummies (not shown) provide some evidence that tracts in the Northeast were less likely to gain.[19] At the metropolitan level, only two variables were consistently significant. The percentage of the population in a metropolitan area that is Hispanic was negatively associated with the prevalence of neighborhood income gains, while the percentage of the population that is foreign-born was positively associated with gain.

In Model 2, we began to explore the broader changes that might be explaining the likelihood of neighborhood income gains. We tested whether there is any association between the change in a metropolitan area's poverty rate between 1990 and 2000 and the likelihood that its lower-income tracts upgraded between 1990 and 2000. The change in MSA poverty has a significantly negative coefficient, suggesting that low-income neighborhoods in the metropolitan areas where poverty was declining were more likely to experience large gains in income.

Note that once we controlled for the change in the MSA poverty rate, the negative coefficient on MSA poverty in 1990 increased in magnitude and became significant, suggesting that low-income neighborhoods in metropolitan areas with higher overall rates of poverty in 1990 were less likely to experience large gains. In Model 3, we tested whether the completion of additional LIHTC units per capita in a metropolitan area was associated with greater gains among that area's lower-income neighborhoods. We found a positive association, statistically significant at the 10 percent level.[20] Specifically, we found that very low-income tracts located in metropolitan areas with larger investments in LIHTC units were more likely to experience large gains in neighborhood income.[21]

In Model 4, we considered whether changes in city crime rates are associated with a low-income neighborhood's chances of experiencing large gains. (Due to data limitations, our sample for this model was limited to tracts located in central cities for which we had crime data available, or 145 cities in total.) The coefficient on changes in city crime rates was negative and statistically significant at the 10 percent level, suggesting that low-income tracts in cities experiencing a reduction in crime were somewhat more likely to experience large income gains.

Chapter 8

Reinventing Older Communities Through Mixed-Income Development
What Are We Learning from Chicago's Public Housing Transformation?

Mark L. Joseph

A prevailing challenge for those working to revitalize older U.S. cities in the twenty-first century is the enduring inequity of social and economic opportunity that is starkly defined by place. Without addressing the uneven geographies of opportunity that exist throughout metropolitan areas, the United States will continue to subject significant portions of its population, predominantly racial and ethnic minorities, to a future with limited access to educational, labor market and other resources that are critical for economic mobility (Briggs 2005; Galster and Killen 1995). Furthermore, our metropolitan areas and nation as a whole, by failing to put human and built environment resources to their most productive uses, will fail to maximize their potential and global competitiveness (Brookings Institution 2007; Dreier, Mollenkopf, and Swanstrom 2004).

The uneven geography of opportunity in urban America is most severely manifested in social and economically marginalized communities with high proportions of families in poverty (Jargowsky 1997). In these communities, not only do these families have to confront their own deprivation and social isolation, but they are also surrounded by other similarly challenged individuals and families (Wilson 1987, 1996). The most extreme concentrations of urban poverty in the United States are found in public housing developments, originally constructed as temporary housing for lower- and working-class families, which in the 1960s and 1970s become permanent enclaves of poverty and violence for generations of low-income, predominantly African American families (Bowly 1978; Hirsch 1998; Popkin et al. 2000a; Venkatesh 2000).

In the United States, the last decade of the twentieth century saw increased federal and local government implementation of two strategies to deconcentrate these most severe manifestations of concentrated poverty (Goetz 2003; Khadduri 2001). First, through dispersal strategies, such as the Gautreaux program in Chicago, the national Moving to Opportunity (MTO) demonstration program, and the increased allocation of housing choice (formerly Section 8) vouchers, families living in public housing have been provided with an opportunity to leave their high-poverty, racially segregated neighborhoods and move to (hopefully) less economically and racially segregated neighborhoods elsewhere in the metropolitan region (for research on dispersal strategies see, for example, Briggs 1997; Goering and Feins 2003; Rosenbaum 1995; Varady and Walker 2003; and chapters by Briggs et al., Clampet-Lundquist, Galster, and Gennetian et al. in this volume). Second, mixed-income development, a complementary poverty deconcentration strategy, seeks to attract middle-income families to the site of former public housing developments, while retaining a portion of the low-income population, by demolishing the buildings and rebuilding high-quality housing and investing in strong property management and local amenities (Joseph 2006a; Joseph, Chaskin, and Webber 2007; Kleit, 2005).

Through the $4.5 billion HOPE VI program (Housing Opportunities for People Everywhere) launched in 1992, the federal government has supported mixed-income development on public housing sites throughout the country (for reviews of the HOPE VI program, see, for example, Popkin 2007; Popkin et al. 2004; Sard and Staub 2008). Mixed-income housing has also been built independently of public housing redevelopment across the country (see, for example, Brophy and Smith 1997, Smith 2002). Several Western European countries have also implemented mixed-income housing strategies to revitalize their public housing estates and reintegrate marginalized poor and immigrant families into the broader population (see, for example, Bailey et al. 2006; Berube 2005; Musterd and Andersson 2005; Silverman, Lipton, and Fenton 2005)

What explains the wide-scale adoption of the mixed-income approach as a means of deconcentrating poverty? Dispersal strategies, such as housing choice vouchers, are a people-based strategy and address the poverty of place by trying to move people to neighborhoods of less deprivation and greater opportunity. Mixed-income development, on the other hand, is a people- and place-based strategy, seeking to improve the lives of low-income families at the same time that it improves the quality of urban neighborhoods and ultimately cities.

In terms of benefits to low-income families, a basic expectation is that compared to their previous public housing residences, which were

plagued by deteriorated buildings, crime, violence, and low-quality public services, their quality of life will be vastly improved by living in a new,
clean, well-managed development in the midst of a revitalizing neighborhood. However, policymakers, practitioners, and, as my research has
found, many residents themselves expect mixed-income development to
accomplish much more than just improved housing quality for low-
income families (Joseph 2006a, 2006b, 2008; Joseph, Chaskin, and Webber 2007; Kleit 2001b). First, there is the hope that through living in
proximity to more affluent families, low-income families can establish
social networks that would increase their access to information and
resources, such as jobs, beyond their own often-limited peer and familial
social space. Second, there is an expectation that the presence of more
affluent families, particularly homeowners, will lead to a greater degree
of informal social control and collective efficacy, with families taking
more responsibility for maintaining strong norms of local neighboring
and civic responsibility. Third, it is hoped that the opportunity to
observe and engage with residents who, it is presumed, may be more
likely to display productive behavior such as working and less likely to
be involved in delinquent or antisocial behavior would lead to a role
modeling effect on the behavior of low-income residents. Finally, more
pragmatically, it is expected that the higher-income residents will bring
greater levels of economic and political power that will enable them to
be more effective in generating and sustaining investments in local services and amenities.

Briggs (1997), Pattillo (2007), and Vale (2006) have argued particularly convincingly that policymakers should also consider the possible
downsides of mixed-income development and recognize some implicit
biases in this approach. Most fundamentally, redeveloping public housing sites for a mix of less densely constructed units requires reducing
the number of units available for low-income families at a time when
affordable housing is in short supply throughout the country. Furthermore, the mixed-income focus on the social and economic resources
to be imported with affluent families often leaves low-income families
characterized solely in a deficit perspective framed by the culture of
poverty (Pattillo 2007). Briggs (1997) cautioned that the new mixed
environments may mean an increased sense of relative deprivation,
increased stigma, and a loss of local power and influence for public
housing residents. Finally, the fundamental problems of structural inequity in America can be obscured by discussions of income mixing.
Clearly, physical integration alone will not be enough to counteract the
entrenched inequities and racial discrimination—in schools, labor market opportunities, and the criminal justice system—that are prevalent in
current U.S. society (Crump 2002; Joseph 2006a; Turner 2008).

Much of the policy discussion of mixed-income development focuses on its aspirations as a people-based strategy, but it is important to consider its potential impact on places, particularly given the political support for investment in this approach that is derived from this possibility (Abt Associates 2003; Turbov and Piper 2005; Zielenbach 2003). With the renewed taste for urban living in cities across the United States, particularly among the young, upwardly mobile and empty-nesters, there is an increased demand for central city housing that has increased gentrification pressures in most metropolitan areas. With the large tracts of land consolidated for public housing in the mid-twentieth century, city governments face an opportunity and a dilemma. Private developers, at least prior to the recent housing market woes, have been hungry for opportunities for market-rate residential development in locations with easy access to downtowns and other urban amenities. Affordable housing advocates have been increasing pressure for greater production of subsidized housing for the metropolitan workforce and low-income families. Mixed-income development represents a win-win proposition with its mix of market-rate and subsidized housing and its potential to anchor the physical revitalization of central city neighborhoods with new housing and infrastructure improvements, decrease pockets of poverty and the associated social challenges and public sector costs, attract and retain more city residents, and increase property values and property tax revenues.

This chapter reviews the insights and policy implications that are emerging from the early experiences of the nation's largest-scale effort at mixed-income development currently underway in Chicago. Launched in 1999, the Chicago Plan for Transformation (the Transformation) aims to completely remake the city's public housing landscape, demolishing 22,000 residential units, including all of the high rises that had become nationally renowned as symbols of the failure of large-scale public housing. While most of the residents of the former developments are being relocated into the private housing market with housing choice vouchers or into other rehabbed low-rise public housing developments, there will be over 6,000 units reserved for former public housing residents in the ten new mixed-income developments being built across the city (see Table 8.1 for more statistics).

For the first five years or so of the effort, the main story of the Transformation was about the political, strategic, logistical, social, and economic complexity of managing the massive relocation of low-income families, and the challenges of designing, financing, and constructing the new developments. As increasing numbers of units have come on line in the past two years and a critical mass of residents of all income levels has begun to settle in to several of the developments, the prevail-

Table 8.1. Chicago Mixed Income Developments: Planned Units

Development	CHA[a] #	%	Affordable[b] #	%	Market Rate[c] #	%	Total Planned
Cabrini Replacement Housing	700	25	303	11	1815	64	2,818
Hilliard Homes	305	47	349	53	0	0	654
Jazz on the Blvd	30	22	36	26	71	52	137
Lake Park Crescent	120	24	122	25	248	51	490
Legends South	851	32	1,013	38	832	31	2,696
Oakwood Shores	1,000	33	680	23	1320	44	3,000
Park Boulevard	439	33	438	33	439	33	1,316
Roosevelt Square	1,467	46	728	23	966	31	3,161
West End	264	31	265	31	326	38	855
Westhaven Park	824	63	133	10	360	27	1,317
Total	6,000	36	4,067	25	6,377	39	16,444

Source: CHA FY 2006 Annual Plan: Plan for Transformation Year 7.
[a] CHA: Units allocated for former residents of Chicago Housing Authority developments.
[b] Affordable: Subsidized rental and for-sale units for households meeting certain income criteria.
[c] Market rate: Units to be rented or sold at full market rates.

ing challenge (in addition to continuing the construction, sales, and leasing of ongoing phases of the developments in the midst of a debilitating housing market slowdown) has become facilitating the emergence of some degree of community and good neighboring among the broadly diverse range of residents of the newly constructed housing.

Besides a review of existing literature on mixed-income development (discussed in detail in Joseph 2006a and Joseph et al. 2007), the insights in this chapter are drawn from case study research under way at four new mixed-income developments in Chicago. My research method has been primarily qualitative, with the objective of generating a rich and grounded sense of the mixed-income development process and resident experience, which can inform future, more large-scale analyses that would enable more rigorous investigation of particular facets of this phenomenon. A case study at the Jazz on the Boulevard development on the south side of Chicago was initiated in 2004. Data collected included in-depth interviews with members of developer and social service provider teams, a convenience sample of residents in the midst of their move out of public housing, and interviews with residents of all income levels at the new development, as well as structured observations of resident and community meetings (Joseph 2006b, 2008, 2010). In addition, very preliminary observations are available from the first wave of data collection at three other, much larger, new mixed-income developments in Chicago: Oakwood Shores, Park Boulevard, and Westhaven Park. The data from these three sites are currently being more rigorously analyzed in specific areas of research investigation, but some early insights can be shared here.

In the remainder of this chapter, I will first briefly review the origins of mixed-income development as housing policy in the United States and findings from research on early efforts at mixed-income developments across the country. I then provide some background detail on the mixed-income strategy in Chicago and its current implementation status. I will then delve into emerging insights about progress, challenges, and early resident experiences and will conclude by discussing implications for policy and practice based on the Chicago experience thus far.

Place Matters: Deconcentrating Poverty Through Mixed-income Development

Mixed-income development is not a new strategy. Indeed as originally conceived and implemented in the 1930s and 1940s, public housing developments in the United States were home to a mix of very low-income and working-class families (Ceraso 1995). Renewed governmental efforts to promote housing developments that would include residents with a range socioeconomic backgrounds date back to at least the 1970s. Building on aggressive inclusionary zoning efforts that date back to 1974, the government in Montgomery County, Maryland, promoted the development of several mixed-income housing sites in the 1980s and early 1990s (Barnett 2003; Brophy and Smith 1997; Schubert and Thresher 1996). In 1990, the U.S. Congress approved the Mixed-Income New Communities Strategy demonstration program (MINCS) intended to pilot and promote this approach (Ceraso 1995). In Chicago, prior to the 1999 launch of the Plan for Transformation, the Chicago Housing Authority had completed the mixed-income developments Lake Parc Place and Orchard Park (Ceraso 1995; Rosenbaum, Stroh, and Flynn 1998).

The current large-scale federal and local government commitment to mixed-income development as a poverty deconcentration strategy was initiated with the launch of the $4.5 billion HOPE VI program. In its original 1992 form, the program was focused on rehabilitating developments exclusively as public housing, but by 1995 the philosophy of the program had shifted to promoting mixed-income redevelopment (for reviews of the HOPE VI program see Cisneros and Engdahl 2009; Popkin 2007; Popkin et al. 2004; Sard and Staub 2008). As of 2006, 149,000 units had been demolished and 61,545 had been constructed (Kingsley

2009; Sard and Staub 2008). The program has been strongly criticized for reducing the number of available affordable housing units, problems in the relocation of families, and delays in construction of new units. The Obama administration is planning to replace the HOPE VI program with a broader strategy called Choice Neighborhoods which combines public housing redevelopment with investments in transportation, education, and other urban revitalization.

Scholarly research has not kept up with the pace of mixed-income implementation, and there is limited in-depth evidence to draw on about the outcomes of various efforts across the country. A few general findings have been reported from several sites. It is clear that with high quality design and construction, prime location, a strong real estate market, and strong property management, middle-income residents can be successfully attracted to rent and purchase units at market rates in developments where a substantial proportion of units are reserved for former public housing residents (Brophy and Smith 1997). Little is known about rates of turnover. Several studies provide evidence of positive spillover effects on the broader neighborhood in terms of reduced crime and increased economic activity (Abt Associates 2003; Turbov and Piper 2005; Zielenbach 2003). These general levels of success have not been easy to come by. A major lesson learned has been the complexity of mixed-income financing, construction, and management. While presenting opportunities to generate profits on well-located property, these high-risk projects require multiple layers of public and private sector financing with varying time frames and requirements and institutional collaborations at several levels of government as well as with local civic and community partners. They also require private real estate developers to play a variety of roles including some, such as contracting with and overseeing social service provision, that are unfamiliar to them (Schubert and Thresher 1996; Turbov and Piper 2005).

In terms of resident satisfaction and experiences in the new developments, available research suggests that residents of all incomes are mostly satisfied with their units and the surrounding development, although they may emphasize different characteristics of the development (Holin and Amendolia 2001; Pader and Breitbardt 2003; Rosenbaum, Stroh, and Flynn 1998). Some research has pointed to some emerging frictions among residents, sometimes along income lines, but often between owners and renters, or families with children and those without (Pader and Breidbardt 2003; Varady et al. 2005). A key finding across several studies is that there are low levels of social interaction among residents of different backgrounds, particularly with engagement of a level that might lead to the social benefits suggested above

(Brophy and Smith 1997; Buron et al. 2002; Hogan 1996; Kleit 2001a, 2001b, 2005; Rosenbaum, Stroh, and Flynn 1998; Ryan et al. 1974).

The Chicago Plan for Transformation

Among public housing authorities across the country, Chicago has been most notorious for mismanagement, corruption, racial divisiveness, and the creation of thousands of units of isolated, crime-ridden, high-rise developments that segregated many of the city's poorest African American families from the rest of the population. The living conditions for residents became so dire that the U.S. Department of Housing and Urban Development took over the management of the Chicago Housing Authority (CHA) in 1995. Upon regaining control of the authority in 1998, Mayor Richard Daley announced his intention to completely remake the landscape of public housing in the city and to end the physical and social isolation of the city's public housing residents. The subsequent public housing transformation has unfolded in a highly politicized and contentious atmosphere, with high levels of criticism and distrust from public housing residents and their advocates, and two high-profile lawsuits (which have since been settled) against the CHA to delay and modify the process.

Announced in 1999 as a ten-year, $1.5 billion strategy and now slated to last at least fifteen years and cost considerably more, the CHA Plan for Transformation involves the demolition of about 22,000 units of public housing, the rehabbing of over 17,000 units, and new construction of about 7,700 public housing units in 10 new mixed-income developments with a total of about 17,000 units (CHA 2008). All of the developments are being built and managed through public/private partnerships with eight different private developers having lead responsibility at various sites for securing financing, overseeing design and construction, marketing to subsidized and unsubsidized residents, and contracting for property management and social service provision. The mix of units is negotiated among the developer, CHA, and local community stakeholders according to a rough guideline of one-third public housing, one-third subsidized, and one-third market-rate. Most of the developments include a mix of rental and for-sale housing (for more details on the developments, see Joseph 2010).

Residents of public housing in October 1999 were presented with several relocation options. They could elect to use a housing choice voucher to relocate into a rental unit in the private market and leave public housing permanently. Or, they could retain their right to return to a rehabbed family development or new mixed-income development.

If they retained their right to return, they selected whether they wanted to temporarily relocate to the private market with a housing choice voucher or to another public housing development and they identified their three top choices of developments to which they wanted to return. Residents who retained their right to return were entered into a lottery that randomly assigned the order in which families would be offered the new or rehabbed units as they came available.

Eight years into the Transformation, the CHA reports that almost 65 percent of the 25,000 replacement units have been completed. However, while this represents almost 80 percent of units to be rehabbed, only 32 percent of units to be newly constructed in mixed-income developments have been completed (CHA 2008). This is evidence of the complexity of the mixed-income financing and development process.

The most important question is the status of the public housing residents. Although almost 90 percent of the residents initially retained their right to return to a new or rehabbed unit, as residents have relocated to the private market with temporary housing choice vouchers, many are deciding not to return, even when units are made available (Metropolitan Planning Council 2003; Joseph 2010). The relocation process has proceeded steadily while being fraught with challenges (for more details about the relocation process, see, for example, P. Fischer 2002; Metropolitan Planning Council 2003; National Opinion Research Center 2006; Venkatesh et al. 2004; Williams, Fischer, and Russ 2003). Findings from the Urban Institute Hope VI Panel Study show that those residents who have relocated to the private market with vouchers have improved many facets of their quality of life, while many of those who are still in 100 percent public housing developments are actually faring worse (see Popkin 2007 and the research reports on the Urban Institute HOPE VI Panel Study available at www.urban.org).

Emerging Insights: Launching the Developments

With eight different development teams working on ten redevelopments in Chicago for the past five to seven years, much has been learned about the process of bringing a mixed-income development to life. I will highlight here what is being learned about levels of expectation regarding the developments, elements of the process that have gone quite well, and implementation challenges that have been encountered.

Expectations for Success

It is important to understand what those working and living in mixed-income developments actually expect for them to achieve. Like others who have spoken with those working on developments (Brophy and Smith 1997; Smith 2002), I have encountered a variety of definitions of "success" for these developments among the real estate developers, social service providers, public agency representatives, and other civic and community stakeholders with whom my research teams and I have spoken. All would agree that the basic goal is to end concentrated poverty on the public housing site and to reconnect the place and its residents with the area around it. Some talk specifically about the nature of the social and economic mix that is intended to be generated and sustained in that area, which adds the requirement of leveraging but managing gentrification pressures. Many would agree that beyond revitalizing the place, successful mixed-income development would also promote social mobility among the former public housing families, helping them to be not only safer and better-housed but also on a path toward greater economic self-sufficiency. Many reference the notions of role modeling, social networks, social control, and local influence that I discussed earlier. Some, who realize that most of the relocated public housing families will not return to their original sites, argue that success should include social mobility for those who do not return as well as those who do. Many would argue that mixed-income developers are not just building housing but, in fact, are building *community* and, to be successful, must intentionally invest in strategies to help generate strong social relations and neighboring among the new residents. This may be the most debated expectation for mixed-income developments, with many practitioners and observers wondering why the policy community has such high aspirations for levels of interaction among neighbors in these artificially integrated developments when there is so little interaction among residents in most neighborhoods across America. Finally, there are those who envision success not only as a well-functioning housing development but also as the promotion of broader revitalization in the neighborhood within which the development is located. Ideally, this broader revitalization would be planned and realized with the engagement and influence of low-income residents and with strategic attention to avoiding displacement as the neighborhood improves.

When interviewing residents of some of the new Chicago developments, it is interesting to hear these expectations for success echoed and questioned among those who have chosen to live there. Among public housing residents, opinions are divided between those who have high hopes for the differences that their move to a mixed-income development will make in their lives and those who simply see it as a nicer environment in which to live, without any expectation for specific changes in the opportunities for them and their families. Among those public housing residents my research teams and I have interviewed thus far, a substantial proportion subscribe to this latter point of view and indeed are quite vigilant in asserting that they have no expectations of their new community and neighbors and, in fact, plan to intentionally keep to themselves and maintain a low profile. A key factor generating these instincts of self-isolation may be the high degree of screening and monitoring in these developments, with a pervasive threat of eviction for residents who do not maintain the expected standards of behavior and compliance. However, among those residents with stated expectations that their new home is also a pathway to opportunity, it has been intriguing to hear them talk eloquently in their own terms about the possibility of making employment connections through their new neighbors, of learning about how their neighbors have achieved their social and economic status, and about the personal motivation for self-improvement that they are gaining from being around people with successful professional lives and being away from an environment in which they were surrounded by so much deviance and hopelessness.

The more affluent residents of the mixed-income developments with whom we have spoken have, for the most part, quite modest and pragmatic expectations for their new residential development. While there are many who express hopes for a sense of community and togetherness among neighbors, and even those few who describe having decided to live in a mixed-income development with an intention of personally building social bridges with low-income families, the vast majority appear to have primarily made their residential decision based on the basics of any real estate decision: location, price, and quality of design and construction. For most of the higher-income families, their strongest expectations for the developments are that they will be safe and well maintained, and that the investment in residential development will soon be matched by investments in the neighborhood amenities, such as stores and restaurants, which are sorely lacking in these historically economically isolated neighborhoods.

Implementation Successes and Challenges

As in HOPE VI redevelopments across the country, the demolition of the severely distressed public housing stock proceeded far more quickly than the subsequent building of the new developments. However the new physical landscape of public housing in Chicago is an achievement not to be diminished: many never thought they would see the day when every single one of the towers of poverty was either gone or slated for imminent demolition. However, that success quickly pales when compared with the controversies around the relocation of residents and the difficulties of bringing new units on line.

At one level, the city's level of ambition regarding the scale of the transformation is admirable, but, on another level, much of the complexity of the process and resultant impact on the lives of thousands of public housing residents is due to the city's commitment to embarking simultaneously on the depopulating, financing, construction, and repopulating of ten mixed-income developments. Each phase of each redevelopment requires multiple layers of financing; coordination among numerous public sector departments at the federal, state, and city level; newly formed public-private partnerships, including the meaningful inclusion of community stakeholders representing residents and the broader neighborhood; and contracts with social service providers and other agencies that help residents relocate and, in some cases, return. Most cities with HOPE VI grants have had to navigate the challenge of implementing the relocation and redevelopment tasks associated with a few hundred units. The city of Chicago has set itself the task of simultaneously redeveloping ten developments, seven of which will have at least 850 units each, four of which will have close to or over three thousand units each. While presenting an opportunity to permanently and thoroughly remake the urban landscape, this has greatly complicated the mixed-income effort in Chicago (for more details see Joseph 2008).

Looking to the engine of the private market to generate the economic resources to undergird the redevelopment also makes the progress of the Transformation completely dependent on the strength of the housing market. In the first years of redevelopment, market-rate for-sale units in the pipeline generated waiting lists and strong pre-sales. As the housing market crashed in Chicago and around the nation and lenders tightened their loan requirements, sales have slowed tremendously, putting severe stress on the progress and future of the entire initiative. One strategic response among some developers is to market the unit to investors who see it as a long-term investment and will use it as a rental property or are willing to assume the short-term risk and potential profit of reselling the unit themselves. This challenges theoretical assumptions about purchasers of market-rate units as concerned neighborhood stakeholders who may be more likely to become engaged in the community, contributing to greater informal social control through their active presence and exerting demands for local amenities on external actors.

Some of the best early news about the mixed-income effort in Chicago, prior to the housing market downturn, was the high levels of demand for the market-rate units. Just as in other developments around the country, it has been demonstrated that the advantageous locations in proximity to downtown, as well as anchor institutions such as universities, hospitals, and transportation arteries (and in the case of some Chicago developments, Lake Michigan) where public housing developments were historically sited, provide a market appeal that, when combined with high-quality design and strong property management, can outweigh concerns that prospective tenants and owners might have about living among former public housing residents. It should be no surprise that the units in the affordable middle tier have been in particularly high demand.

Emerging Insights: Early Resident Experiences

While it is still relatively early in the unfolding of each of the new developments, there is now enough of a critical mass of residents in the developments to begin to get a sense of what life is like for those who have been among the first wave to settle in. The most heartening findings are about the improvements for former public housing residents in their residential unit and its immediate surroundings. Residents speak enthusiastically about living in a quality of unit that they never imagined possible and strikingly compare the peace, quiet, and stability of their new environment with the constant activity and stress of their former residence. It will be much longer before strong conclusions can be drawn about the ultimate outcomes of their move on residents and their family members in terms of mental and emotional well-being, but from early impressions, it appears likely that there could be meaningful gains of the type rigorously documented in the MTO demonstration program (see, for example, Kling et al. 2004).

While it remains for now much more hypothetical than realized, there are certainly indications among some of the public housing residents that they expect to make substantial changes in their own lives as a result of living around their new neighbors. Although some speak about expectations of direct interactions and social exchanges with others, for many the effect is anticipated to be much more indirect, through observing the actions of others and as an impact of the general atmosphere that is being established in the development. On the other hand, as mentioned earlier, many of the public housing residents came to the development holding very limited expectations of interaction and benefits from those around them and they report that their early experiences have borne this out. Although obviously self-fulfilling to some extent, some of these residents have reported that the homeowners (the easiest way for them to verbally distinguish higher-income residents, even though several of the developments have market-rate rental units) have been standoffish and, in some cases, judgmental and demeaning.

Among higher-income residents, early impressions suggest that there is a relatively high level of general satisfaction with the new developments, with particularly strong enjoyment of the location's proximity to downtown and ease of transportation access to the rest of the city. The strongest dissatisfaction among this population regards broader neighborhood issues of safety and lack of amenities. Safety is emerging as the biggest shared concern among residents of all income levels. There have been instances of break-ins, burglaries, and car theft in the developments, prompting residents to express their concerns at community or resident meetings and, in at least one case, to create a community watch group. However, not only the former public housing residents but, according to my initial findings, also the more affluent residents were previously living in an urban environment and many express a level of comfort and savvy about the realities of city living and the need to be vigilant.

Overall, as in mixed-income developments across the country, there have been low levels of informal social interaction across income levels. While no major conflicts among residents have occurred, there have been ongoing challenges of minor neighboring annoyances: noise, misuse of parking spaces, unsupervised children, and, above all, different opinions about the acceptable use of public space. The issue of former public housing residents, their visitors, and their children spending extended time in entryways, building lobbies, front yards, or parking lots has generated the most intraneighbor tension in the new developments. While for some this is simply hanging out, for others it is loitering. This is particularly exacerbated in developments where the physical design did not create much public gathering space within the development.

An overriding dynamic that appears to shape the relations, or lack thereof, among residents in the new developments appears to be the perceptions and stereotypes held about neighbors from different backgrounds. In our interviews, residents of all income levels, races, and backgrounds acknowledge the expectation among many that the public housing residents will be the source of problems. In some cases, former public housing residents themselves talk about having selected a development in the hopes of minimizing the number of other public housing residents with whom they would have to interact. But, at the same time, there are residents of various income levels who express the hope that living in this proximity will provide a meaningful opportunity for individuals to have their stereotypes questioned and to learn not only that public housing residents are not always a source of problems and that more affluent residents often can be, but also that lower-income residents have much to offer as strong neighbors in the development.

An emerging and substantial challenge for the new developments will be establishing governance structures that can promote decision-making processes that are seen as legitimately representative and inclusive. At this early stage, the structures in place are in fact creating the opposite effect and exacerbating the sense of segregation among residents. Legally, the primary associational structures at the mixed-income developments are condominium or townhome associations to which the private developer cedes management authority once occupancy has reached a certain threshold. Those associations collect property assessments, hire a property management firm to maintain the property, set policy, and monitor compliance at the development. In some cases, owners of single-family homes in the development have formed homeowners' associations to perform an analogous function managing the shared common space and infrastructure. The rental units in the development remain the property of the developer. As the owner of those units, the developer holds a proportional number of seats on the condo or townhome association board. Therefore the renters themselves do not have any claims to direct representation on the entity with the power to make decisions that affect all residents in the development. Conceivably, the developer could make an arrangement whereby renters assume a more direct role using the seats controlled by the developer. But, to date, developers have felt strongly that it is their responsibility to maintain their direct control over that voting power in order to influence decisions that are in the best interest of the long-term success and viability of the development. Further heightening the social divide, at some developments other resident groups have been established which serve as convening and support mechanisms for the renters, often dominated by renters of public and subsidized housing. In addition, traditionally there have been elected resident councils at public housing developments and there is currently debate between the CHA and leaders of these councils as to whether these councils will continue to exist in the new developments.

As we are learning more about everyday life in these mixed-income developments, an important insight is that the most relevant category of "mix" may not be income, but other distinctions among residents that are proving to be more salient in terms of capturing differences in background, comportment, or outlook that give rise to potentially incongruent behaviors, priorities, or levels of stake in the development. Certainly the notion of class, with its reference to educational achievement, professional status, and associated lifestyles, more accurately captures the social gulfs to be bridged among residents of these developments (Pattillo 2007). Among other salient categories are housing tenure (ownership or renter status) and life stage (families with children, families without children, seniors, middle-aged empty-nesters, university students). Earlier I mentioned the important distinction emerging between live-in owners and absentee investors. At this stage, it is difficult to sort out the salience of race and ethnicity, but certainly the relative diversity of the more affluent residents compared to the predominantly African American population of public housing residents and the reality that race is an all-too-easy proxy for other characteristics makes race central to understanding emerging social relations. We have heard, for example, from African American residents in subsidized or even market-rate rental units who perceive that others at the development have assumed that they are former public housing residents due to their race.

Policy Implications

Perhaps the most important question that will be asked to assess the outcomes of mixed-income developments is: who benefits? While there are compelling benefits to high-poverty neighborhoods, the city as a whole, and other residents of the city who benefit from the high-quality, well-located housing, there can be little argument that ultimately these efforts should be judged in large part on the basis of their impact on the families who were living in the original public housing developments. By this measure, outcomes have been mixed—while many residents who have relocated with vouchers may have improved their quality of life, those in 100 percent public housing developments are often in much worse conditions, and there is a substantial population of families with multiple barriers to self-sufficiency who are not well-served by the current approach. And even those families that make an initially successful move with a voucher may fall prey to a unit that is poorly maintained or foreclosed and transferred due to the growing subprime crisis. The main focus of this essay is the new mixed-income developments, but my argument here is that the success of these developments in Chicago must be considered in the context of the broader public housing transformation, especially since so few of the original residents will return (for policy recommendations regarding the relocation process see, for example, Buron, Levy, and Gallagher 2007; Comey 2007; Popkin et al. 2000b; Popkin et al. 2007; Popkin, Cunningham, and Burt 2005; Venkatesh et al. 2004; Williams, Fischer, and Russ 2003). While the gleaming new mixed-income developments will draw an inordinate share of policy attention, it is critical that policy focus and investments are sustained and indeed increased on the challenge of providing appropriate supports and options for the estimated three-quarters or more of the original public housing families that will not return.

Turning to the mixed-income developments, the policy challenge is to motivate and help developers to achieve a set of objectives that include balancing resident mix, using screening and selection criteria for *all* residents that ensure a stable, well-maintained development, and including a high enough proportion of market-rate units to make the project financially feasible while maximizing the numbers of former public housing residents who are able to benefit from living in the newly-constructed developments. We have much more to learn to be able to strategize in an informed way about the appropriate balance and even then it will be dependent on the strength of the local housing market and other considerations. However, the initial market demand for mixed-income units in Chicago where most sites have in the range of 22 to 33 percent public housing units suggests that, in the context of a strong market, this is at least a lower bound of what can be achieved. Two sites in Chicago, with 46 and 63 percent public housing, should be closely watched for any implications from proportions that high. In terms of marketing to residents, developers and the housing authority must dedicate much greater creativity and attention to recruiting former public housing residents than originally anticipated. One Chicago developer reported that practically his entire marketing budget is now used to attract residents back to public housing units.

The mixed-income strategy requires strong partnerships across public, private, and nonprofit sectors due to the shrinking available public resources to fund revitalization of this scale as well as for the for-profit and non-profit expertise that can be leveraged. However, given that the primary social objective is to provide housing and a pathway to self-sufficiency for low-income families, over the longer term it may be worth considering ways to build the capacity of nonprofit developers to play a greater role in these projects. Certainly in Chicago, the nonprofit developers that have been engaged have brought to the table deep experience in housing and supporting low-income families.

Finally, given the preexisting prejudices and social distance between residents of the development, it may not be enough simply to maintain order in the development and keep residents in compliance with property rules. In order to avoid gradually increasing tensions based on misperceptions and lack of trust, it may be necessary for external entities, whether the developer, social service providers, or other community-based actors, to take intentional steps to move beyond the building of housing to promoting the building of community. Applying principles and lessons from other community-building initiatives, we know that this can be achieved in a variety of ways, including physical design with an attention to maximizing common space and shared entryways; social services and property management with expanded roles that encompass promotion of activities that appeal to a variety of residents; and investment in amenities on-site and nearby, such as schools, community centers, libraries, fitness centers, and grocery stores, which offer services that could attract residents of many different backgrounds. As we have seen, maintaining conventional governance structures—some for owners, some for other resident groups—will likely increase rather than decrease intraresident distrust and tension. Overarching, inclusive structures or smaller intergroup structures should be considered as alternatives which can promote rather than inhibit community building. Above all, while the task of constructing and populating these developments has proven to be complicated and resource-intensive, the subsequent process of building community and ensuring the sustainability of the developments will require just as much persistence and ingenuity.

Chapter 9

Reinventing Older Communities
Does Place Matter?

Janet Rothenberg Pack

Most discussions of place-based policy or "reinventing older communities" are concerned with discrete metropolitan areas, cities, neighborhoods, or occasionally larger regions, such as Appalachia or the Rust Belt.[1] In this chapter I take a broader approach to place-based policies by looking at the larger picture, that is, the major changes that have resulted in the reorganization of the urban landscape. Data are compared for all four major census regions (Northeast, Midwest, South, and West), as well as 250–277 metropolitan areas, and their cities and suburbs.[2]

U.S. history is replete with shifting locational forces. Although such change is always disruptive, here I show how substantial geographical shifts—from place to place, region to region, city to suburb—over the last four decades have, in general, been welfare improving. At the same time, it must be recognized that not all welfare-improving changes improve welfare for all (places or people). This overview provides the background for a more informed discussion of whether "distressed" communities would benefit from place-based policies. Rather than recommending or discouraging such policies, this chapter provides the context within which such policies need to be evaluated by examining geographical shifts and their welfare implications over the last four decades.[3]

Much of the recent focus on place-based policies stems from the major relocations of population and economic activity that have taken place in the post–World War II period, especially the movement from the Northeast and Midwest to the South and West, and from central cities to suburbs. Counterintuitively, welfare measures for the nation as a whole—looking at the four major census regions—have for the most part improved everywhere, albeit at different rates. Yet from the perspective of economic theory, these results are not counterintuitive, given that, barring market or policy impediments, people and firms would indeed "move to opportunity." Workers respond to vibrant labor markets and higher wages; firms respond to lower costs.

History

In thinking about reinventing older communities, it is useful to review the evolution of urban areas in response to the major historical shifts. Over the course of the eighteenth and nineteenth centuries, increased agricultural productivity and the industrial revolution transformed what had been a largely agricultural economy, causing massive relocations from rural to urban areas, particularly from the rural South to the manufacturing centers of the Northeast and Midwest. The advent of World War II accelerated this trend by moving civilian workers to the military production industries in the Northeast and Midwest, while production was devoted to war materiel, not consumer goods. After the war, there was a demand for the production of consumer goods of all types, including housing, and the resources available to fulfill it. This combination of pent-up resources and demand, along with the desire of many to leave overcrowded cities and to own their own homes, led to the first large wave of movement of families of modest means to the suburbs. Important public policies facilitated these movements; in particular, the Sixteenth Amendment to the Constitution establishing the income tax, along with associated federal tax code permitting the deduction of mortgage payments from gross income, and the establishment of the FHA in 1934 both facilitated the ability to move from renting to home ownership. Similarly, the Federal Highway Act of 1956 facilitated travel to areas on the periphery.

Suburbanization was a complex interaction of household relocation and changes in technology that affected the location decisions of firms, which in turn stimulated further household relocation. In addition to the demand and resources available to households after World War II, equally or perhaps more important were the technical innovations in manufacturing, which displaced vertical production processes by horizontal production processes (assembly lines). This new style of manufacturing required larger parcels of abundant, inexpensive land—the type to be found most commonly on the fringes or in the outer suburbs of older cities. The growth of trucking diminished the importance of locating factories near rail hubs, and the spread of automobile ownership made access to road networks (outside of congested cities) necessary and required even larger land parcels that could accommodate parking lots, further spurring the decentralization of employment. And this need for roads and road access was met in large part by public policy, namely the National Highway Act.

More recently, since the late 1960s, interregional movement has dominated locational change, as population and firms moved from the Northeast and Midwest to the South and West. The movement can be attributed to many phenomena: the relocation of manufacturing, for example, the textile industry, from the Northeast to the South in response to lower wages and less unionization; from the Northeast and Midwest, as the United States lost heavy industry to other countries, steel being the paradigmatic example; and to the West, as high-technology industries became increasingly important and clustered on the West Coast. In addition, the aging U.S. population has flocked to warmer climates in retirement, accounting for much of this shift. Immigration patterns have contributed to and reinforced many of the geographical shifts documented below.[4] And in all regions the suburbanization of the population, the movement from central cities to suburbs, continues.

Welfare Improvement

In considering urban policy—any public policy—the criterion for evaluation is whether it improves individuals' social welfare. Some of the obvious components of welfare improvement are increases in per capita income and improvements in educational achievement. Reductions in poverty rates and in unemployment are clearly welfare improvements for individuals/households but are clearly dependent upon the phase of the business cycle at any given time. They therefore cannot be easily compared with cumulative changes in per capita income and educational achievement, although they will be documented and discussed below.[5] Other increases in welfare that derive from community characteristics, such as decreasing crime and increasing community amenities, are not discussed here.

Given the large shifts outlined above, I turn now to the data and focus on several implications and aspects of these changes that should influence how we think about place-based policy: (a) the overall change in welfare of the population and its distribution; (b) the general tendencies, but somewhat erratic nature of shifts, over the decades; (c) the differences between and among regions, cities, and suburbs; and (d) the relationship between metropolitan areas and their central cities.

How have welfare indicators—educational achievement, per capita incomes, poverty rates, and unemployment rates—changed over the period 1970–2000, given the large shifts in population and employment

Table 9.1. Regional Distribution: Metropolitan Population, 1960–2000 (Percentage of Metropolitan Total)

	1960	*1970*	*1980*	*1990**	*2000**
Northeast	31	29	26	22	19
Midwest	28	28	27	25	23
South	24	25	28	32	34
West	17	19	21	22	24

Source: Tables are author's computations based upon data from the U.S. Decennial Census of Population for 1960, 1970, 1980, 1990, and 2000 for metropolitan areas, their cities, and their suburbs and the U.S. Department of Housing and Urban Development's State of the Cities Data System (SOCDS).
*250 metropolitan areas; other years based on 277 metropolitan areas.

Table 9.2. Regional Distribution of Total MSA Income, 1960–2000

Census Region	*1960*	*1970*	*1980*	*1990**	*2000**
Northeast	32	30	26	26	20
Midwest	30	28	26	23	23
South	20	22	26	27	32
West	18	19	22	24	25

Source: Tables are author's computations based upon data from the U.S. Decennial Census of Population for 1960, 1970, 1980, 1990, and 2000 for metropolitan areas, their cities, and their suburbs and the U.S. Department of Housing and Urban Development's State of the Cities Data System (SOCDS).
*250 metropolitan areas; other years based on 277 metropolitan areas.

sources experienced in recent decades? How do these changes differ across space, that is, the four major census regions? To begin, I consider changes within regions, across regions, and between cities and suburbs. I then turn to the more specific changes in individual metropolitan areas and cities and the relationship between them.

Shifting Population and Economic Activity: Welfare Implications

As will be demonstrated these substantial relocations among places have generally been welfare improving. As with all welfare-improving changes on such a scale, however, they are rarely Pareto improvements, that is, improvements that benefit everyone.

The relocation of population and economic activity (measured by total income) among regions over the four decades 1960–2000 (Tables 9.1 and 9.2) and between cities and suburbs (Tables 9.3 and 9.4) have been substantial. The largest decrease in proportion of the total U.S. metropolitan population (note: not absolute population) occurred in

Table 9.3. Percentage of U.S. Population in Cities and Suburbs, 1960–2000

	1960	1970	1980	1990*	2000*
Cities	44	40	36	34	33
Suburbs	56	59	64	65	67

Source: Tables are author's computations based upon data from the U.S. Decennial Census of Population for 1960, 1970, 1980, 1990, and 2000 for metropolitan areas, their cities, and their suburbs and the U.S. Department of Housing and Urban Development's State of the Cities Data System (SOCDS).
*250 metropolitan areas; other years based on 277 metropolitan areas.

Table 9.4. Percentage of Metropolitan Income in Cities and Suburbs, 1960–2000

	1960	1970	1980	1990*	2000*
Cities	45	39	33	30	29
Suburbs	55	61	67	70	71

Source: Tables are author's computations based upon data from the U.S. Decennial Census of Population for 1960, 1970, 1980, 1990, and 2000 for metropolitan areas, their cities, and their suburbs and the U.S. Department of Housing and Urban Development's State of the Cities Data System (SOCDS).
*250 metropolitan areas; other years based on 277 metropolitan areas.

the Northeast region, declining by 12 percentage points or about 40 percent. The largest proportional increase occurred in the South, by 10 percentage points, or about 40 percent. A smaller, albeit significant, relative decline occurred in the Midwest and a smaller relative increase took place in the Western region metropolitan areas.

The redistribution of population between cities and suburbs does not appear quite so great. By 1960, it was already the case that more than half of the metropolitan population lived in the suburbs. Nonetheless in the following four decades, the relative proportion of the metropolitan population that lived in the city declined by another 25 percent—from 44 percent to 33 percent (see Table 9.3). These changes varied substantially by region and within regions.

The regional changes in total income (Table 9.2) were substantially greater than the shifts in population—more than 50 percent loss in share in the Northeast and more than 50 percent gain in the South. The shifts in total income between cities and suburbs followed a similar pattern (Table 9.4).

A summary of the changes in welfare indicators by census region averaged (weighted by population) for metropolitan areas, their cities, and their suburbs can be seen in Table 9.5. Looking first at metropolitan areas, in each region, the two indicators most sensitive to overall economic conditions (poverty rates and unemployment rates) fluctuate

Table 9.5. Socioeconomic Indicators, Metros, Cities, and Suburbs, by Region and Decade

	Metros				Cities				Suburbs			
	1970	1980	1990	2000	1970	1980	1990	2000	1970	1980	1990	2000
Per Cap. Income ($)												
NE	8943	9093	12583	14126	8673	8162	11091	12110	9151	9645	13429	15294
MW	8782	9576	11331	13643	8256	8466	9502	11268	9211	10302	12396	14824
S	7765	8965	11150	13145	7681	8581	10084	11693	7789	9209	11728	13775
W	9088	9922	12059	13646	9240	9750	11627	13006	8973	10015	12293	13974
% College Grad.												
NE	11.13	17.33	23.13	27.85	9.30	15.33	20.84	24.80	12.36	18.42	24.28	29.53
MW	10.65	16.30	20.64	25.87	9.52	15.09	19.38	23.21	11.44	16.96	21.25	27.13
S	11.66	17.67	22.00	26.56	12.23	18.60	22.60	25.61	11.26	17.15	21.72	26.95
W	13.71	20.00	23.61	27.68	14.43	21.53	25.26	28.93	13.22	19.07	22.68	27.04
% < High School												
NE	47.90	33.62	24.53	19.43	54.62	41.01	32.06	27.37	43.39	29.61	20.75	15.06
MW	45.23	30.73	21.71	15.89	50.42	36.63	27.08	21.79	41.62	27.52	19.12	13.09
S	49.90	34.76	25.01	19.85	49.96	36.22	28.15	24.38	49.86	33.95	23.53	17.96
W	36.82	25.13	21.31	19.78	37.27	26.22	23.32	22.68	36.50	24.47	20.18	18.28
Poverty Rate												
NE	10.14	11.83	11.36	12.66	14.85	19.89	19.90	21.77	7.15	7.52	7.01	7.43
MW	9.15	9.88	11.45	10.17	13.02	16.14	19.82	17.94	6.56	6.50	7.33	6.36
S	15.72	13.39	13.85	12.83	18.28	17.97	20.46	19.38	13.91	10.80	10.71	10.04
W	10.80	11.05	12.22	12.85	12.65	13.69	15.80	16.83	9.59	9.52	10.26	10.82
Unemp. Rate												
NE	3.82	6.62	6.51	6.37	4.41	8.52	9.15	9.77	3.44	5.70	5.27	4.62
MW	4.11	7.36	6.18	5.15	4.72	8.94	8.81	7.75	3.68	6.54	4.95	3.94
S	3.46	5.00	5.82	5.51	3.85	5.60	7.60	7.63	3.18	4.66	4.99	4.62
W	5.88	6.23	6.23	6.21	6.26	6.58	7.01	7.02	5.61	6.02	5.79	5.79

Source: Tables are author's computations based upon data from the U.S. Decennial Census of Population for 1960, 1970, 1980, 1990, and 2000 for metropolitan areas, their cities, and their suburbs and the U.S. Department of Housing and Urban Development's State of the Cities Data System (SOCDS).

somewhat, but the other indicators (per capita income, percentage of college graduates, and percentage of adults with less than a high school education) all improve steadily throughout the period 1970–2000.

Looking at changes in cities and suburbs, however, yields a far more uneven picture. In each region, the proportion of poor persons in cities increases but changes little in the suburbs (with the exception of a decrease in percentage poor in the suburbs of the South). The unemployment rate gap between cities and suburbs also widened considerably between 1970 and 2000, with city unemployment rates double those of the suburbs in 2000 in the Northeast and Midwest and elevated in the South and West. This concentration of poverty and unemployment in cities substantially constrains city fiscal standing and the ability of cities to undertake remedial policies (Pack 1998). This, undoubtedly, is an important part of the impetus behind the interest in and adoption of place-based policies.

The other social indicators make clear several further distinguishing features between cities and suburbs. Per capita incomes in cities and suburbs were, with some regional differences, fairly similar in 1970. By 2000, they were substantially higher in the suburbs, with the exception of the West, where, on the average, they were higher by only about 7 percent. However, the small difference in the West should be compared to the fact that in 1970 per capita incomes in the cities of the West were somewhat higher, on average, than in the suburbs.

Differences Among Growing and Declining Regions

Beyond relative changes in welfare between cities and suburbs, there are substantial differences in the relationship between cities and suburbs in the older metropolitan areas (i.e., those that reached their peaks earlier) and the more recently expanding metropolitan areas. Across the census regions, there are major differences between those whose proportion of population and income has fallen and those where they have risen. Although welfare differences between cities and suburbs have widened everywhere in favor of suburbs, the differences are generally greatest in the Northeast and parts of the Midwest. There are many changes and numerous surprises in these data. For example, despite the population shifts away from the Northeast and Midwest, these census divisions had the lowest poverty rates in both 1970 and 2000 (Table 9.5). The West's metropolitan areas also had low poverty rates in 1970, but here the surprise is the increase in overall poverty rates in an area that experienced major increases in population and economic activity.[6] And while the Southern metropolitan areas have maintained the highest poverty rates in all four decades, the poverty rates, albeit still high, have been falling.

The education variables, which include the percentage of the adult population with college degrees and the percentage that did not complete high school, are the major distinguishing characteristics between places doing very well and those that are severely distressed. The figures here are relatively easily summarized: (a) educational achievement improved in all census regions, in metros, cities, and suburbs, whether measured by percentage of adults with a college degree or by those without a high school degree; (b) the comparison of cities and suburbs shows city adults substantially less well educated relative to suburban residents over the entire period in the Northeast and the Midwest; (c) the patterns are different in the South and West, the areas that experienced significant growth. In the South, the percentage of college graduates in the suburbs did not exceed that in the cities until 2000 and then only slightly; in the West, the proportion of college graduates in the city and the suburbs are more similar, although the proportions in the cities exceeds that in the suburbs throughout. Among the least educated parts of the population, those with less than a high school degree, cities and suburbs were very similar in 1970 in the South and West but began to diverge thereafter, with increasingly smaller proportions of non-high school graduates in the suburbs. Nonetheless, the city-suburb differences are far less in the South and West than they are in the Northeast and Midwest.

In sum, there have been general improvements in welfare in all regions despite very different rates of population and total income change, but these have been accompanied by generally widening gaps between cities and suburbs. This increasing concentration of problems in cities has increased the emphasis on cities—even neighborhoods—in urban policy for revitalization of places.

Metropolitan Areas and Central Cities: Doing Well Versus Severely Distressed

As indicated above, not all general welfare improvements are Pareto improvements.[7] Despite the overall regional improvements, some areas are doing substantially less well than others. I will define places—both metropolitan areas and central cities—as "severely distressed" if they have per capita incomes one-half a standard deviation below that of the average metropolitan area or central city, respectively, and unemployment and poverty rates one half a standard deviation above average for that year. The "well-off" areas are symmetrically defined—per capita incomes greater than one-half a standard deviation above average, and poverty and unemployment rates one-half a standard deviation below average.[8]

Distressed Metropolitan Areas

The first pattern that stands out in Table 9.6 is that there is relatively little persistence in the metropolitan areas that are severely depressed. Forty-eight of the 277 metropolitan areas in the sample are severely distressed in at least one of the four census years, but only six are distressed in all four years. An additional six appear in three of the four years. Fourteen metropolitan areas are recently distressed, that is, they show up in both 1990 and 2000; another twelve appear in 2000 only.[9]

In addition to the absence of persistence in the specific metropolitan areas characterized as distressed, it is also surprising, given the relocation of both population and total income from the older metropolitan areas of the Northeast and the Midwest to the South and West and the very substantial improvement in welfare measures in the South, that metropolitan areas in the South dominate the various categories of distressed metropolitan areas. This indicates substantial variation in the metropolitan areas of the South.

Well-Off Metropolitan Areas

We find that the number of metropolitan areas that have been well-off in at least one of the decades (Table 9.7) is substantially greater than those that have been distressed: 62, compared with 48. Of these, only about 15 percent were well-off either in all four census years (six MSAs) or the last three of the four years (three MSAs). Here, too, there is a lack of persistence even more pronounced than that found for distressed metropolitan areas.

In contrast to the distressed areas, the findings here are more mixed with respect to region. Of the six metropolitan areas well-off in all four years, four are in the Midwest, one in the South, and one in the West. However, the three well-off in the three most recent decades are all in the growing regions, with two in the South and one in the West. The regional picture is more mixed than might have been expected for the nine well-off metropolitan areas in the last two decades. Five of the metropolitan areas are in the South and West, but four are in the Northeast and Midwest. Less surprising, the thirteen well-off metropolitan areas in 1970 were all in the Midwest and Northeast. Thus, the overall pattern is somewhat consistent with the big interregional movement pattern: in 1970 all of the well-off metropolitan areas were in the Northeast and Midwest, but the picture is more mixed in subsequent decades. None-

Table 9.6. Severely Distressed Metropolitan Areas, 1970–2000

		2000	1990	1980	1970
Persistently Distressed (1)					
Brownsville, TX	South	X	X	X	X
Huntington-Ashland, WV-KY-OH	South	X	X	X	X
Las Cruces, NM	West	X	X	X	X
McAllen-Edinburgh-Mission, TX	South	X	X	X	X
Pine Bluff, AR	South	X	X	X	X
Yakima, WA	West	X	X	X	X
Persistently Distressed (2)					
Lafayette, LA	South	X	X	X	
Lake Charles, LA	South	X	X	X	
Laredo, TX	South	X	X	X	
Mobile, AL	South	X	X	X	
Texarkana, TX-AR	South	X	X	X	
Gadsden, AL	South		X	X	X
Recently Distressed (1)					
Albany, GA	South	X	X		
Alexandria, LA	South	X	X		
Bakersfield, CA	West	X	X		
Beaumont-Port Arthur, TX	South	X	X		
Corpus Christi, TX	South	X	X		
El Paso, TX	South	X	X		
Fresno, CA	West	X	X		
Longview-Marshall, TX	South	X	X		
Monroe, LA	South	X	X		
Odessa, TX	South	X	X		
San Angelo, TX	South	X	X		
Shreveport, LA	South	X	X		
Wheeling, WV-OH	Midwest	X	X		
Recently Distressed (2)					
Vineland-Milleville-Bridgeton, NJ	Northeast	X		X	
Athens, GA	South	X			
Bryan-College Station, TX	South	X			
Cumberland, MD-WV	South	X			
Danville, VA	South	X			
Gainesville, FL	South	X			
Miami-Hialeah, FL	South	X			
Modesto, CA	West	X			
Norfolk-Virginia Beach-Newport News, VA	South	X			
Riverside-San Bernardino, CA	West	X			
Stockton, CA	West	X			
Waco, TX	South	X			

Table 9.6. (Continued)

		2000	1990	1980	1970
Occasionally Distressed					
Anniston, AL	South			X	
Baton Rouge, LA	South		X		
Biloxi-Gulfport, MS	South		X		
Jersey City, NJ	Northeast			X	
Memphis, TN-AR-MS	South			X	
Muncie, IN	Midwest		X		X
New Orleans, LA	South		X		
Pueblo, CO	West		X		
San Antonio, TX	South		X		
Tuscaloosa, AL	South			X	

Note: "Severely distressed" is defined for the census years as follows:
2000: Per capita income < $11,253, poverty rate > 14.7%, unemployment rate > 6.6%.
1990: Per capita income < $9455, poverty rate > 16.2%, unemployment rate > 7.0%.
1980: Per capita income < $8081, poverty rate > 14.3%, unemployment rate > 7.5%.
1970: Per capita income < $7059, poverty rate > 16.6%, unemployment rate >5.0%.
Source: Tables are author's computations based upon data from the U.S. Decennial Census of Population for 1970, 1980, 1990, and 2000 for metropolitan areas, their cities, and their suburbs and the U.S. Department of Housing and Urban Development's State of the Cities Data System (SOCDS).

theless, the number of well-off metropolitan areas in the South and West remains small.

One of the questions prompted by these classifications of distressed and well-off metropolitan areas is whether those metropolitan areas that cease to appear in the distressed category appear over time on the well-off list, and vice versa. In other words, do places that are no longer well-off become distressed? Do distressed places become well-off? In fact, not one of the twelve severely distressed metropolitan areas that appear only on the list for the year 2000 appears on the well-off list in any of the three previous census years. Similarly, none of the recently well-off metropolitan areas appeared on the distressed list in earlier years. What this and the earlier discussion of lack of persistence indicate is that from decade to decade places become worse or better off but not radically so. When places move on or off the distressed or well-off lists, they move closer to average values.

The major characteristics that distinguish well-off and distressed metropolitan areas, aside from those that I have used to define these categories, are shown in Table 9.8. Education is clearly the major defining difference between the two groups (many other variables were examined, including industrial structure). Although education levels both for metropolitan areas classified as distressed and for those classified as well-off rise over successive decades, well-off metropolitan areas have popula-

Table 9.7. Well-off Metropolitan Areas, 1970–2000

		2000	*1990*	*1980*	*1970*
Persistently Well-off (1)					
Denver, CO	West	X	X	X	X
Des Moines, IA	Midwest	X	X	X	X
Madison, WI	Midwest	X	X	X	X
Minneapolis-St. Paul, MN-WIS	Midwest	X	X	X	X
Rochester, MN	Midwest	X	X	X	X
Washington, DC	South	X	X	X	X
Persistently Well-off (2)					
San Francisco, CA	West	X	X	X	
San Jose, CA	West	X	X	X	
Sarasota, FL	South	X	X	X	
Persistently Well-off (3)					
Springfield, IL	Midwest	X	X		X
Hartford-New Britton-Middletown-Bristol, CN	Northeast		X	X	X
Recently Well-off (1)					
Boulder-Longmont, CO	West	X	X		
Burlington, VT	Northeast	X	X		
Indianapolis, IN	Midwest	X	X		
Portland, ME	Northeast	X	X		
Raleigh-Durham, NC	South	X	X		
Richmond-Petersburg, VA	South	X	X		
Santa Rosa-Petaluma, CA	West	X	X		
Seattle, WA	West	X	X		
Recently Well-off (2)					
Boston, MA	Northeast	X		X	
Cedar Rapids, IA	Midwest	X		X	
New London-Norwich, CN	Northeast	X			X
Akron, OH	Midwest	X			
Boise City, ID	West	X			
Cincinnati, OH-KY-IN	Midwest	X			
Fort Collins-Loveland, CO	West	X			
Nashville, TN	South	X			
Recently Well-off (3)					
Albany-Schenectady-Troy, NY	Northeast	X			X
Allentown-Bethlehem, PA-NJ	Northeast	X			X
Reno, NV	West		X	X	
Trenton, NJ	Northeast		X		X
Ann Arbor, MI	Midwest		X		
Atlanta, GA	South		X		
Baltimore, MD	South		X		
Orlando, FL	South		X		
Portland, OR	West		X		

Table 9.7. (Continued)

		2000	1990	1980	1970
Rochester, NY	Northeast	X			
Santa Cruz, CA	West	X			
West Palm Beach-Boca Raton- Delray Beach, FL	South	X			
Wilmington, DE-NJ-MD	South	X			
Well-off Early-1970 and 1980					
New Haven-Waterbury-Meriden, CT	Northeast			X	X
Well-off Early-1980 Only					
Casper, WY	West			X	
Enid, OK	South			X	
Fort Worth-Arlington, TX	South			X	
Lincoln, NE	Midwest			X	
Fort Lauderdale-Hollywood- Pompano Beach, FL	South			X	
Topeka, KS	Midwest			X	
Wichita, KS	Midwest			X	
Well-off Early-1970 Only					
Bloomington-Normal, IL	Midwest				X
Champaign-Urbana-Rantoul, IL	Midwest				X
Chicago, IL	Midwest				X
Cleveland, OH	Midwest				X
Elkhart-Goshen, IN	Midwest				X
Fort Wayne, IN	Midwest				X
Harrisburg-Lebanon-Carlisle, PA	Northeast				X
Kansas City, MO	Midwest				X
Milwaukee, WIS	Midwest				X
Newark, NJ	Northeast				X
Peoria, IL	Midwest				X
Philadelphia, PA-NJ	Northeast				X
Reading, PA	Northeast				X

Note: "Well-off" is defined for the census years as follows:
2000: Per capita income > $13,321, poverty rate < 10.4%, unemployment rate < 4.9%.
1990: Per capita income > $11,223, poverty rate < 11.0%, unemployment rate < 5.3%.
1980: Per capita income > $9217, poverty rate < 10.1%, unemployment rate < 5.4%.
1970: Per capita income > $8199, poverty rate < 10.5%, unemployment rate <3.6%.
Source: Tables are author's computations based upon data from the U.S. Decennial Census of Population for 1970, 1980, 1990, and 2000 for metropolitan areas, their cities, and their suburbs and the U.S. Department of Housing and Urban Development's State of the Cities Data System (SOCDS).

Table 9.8. Educational Achievement: Severely Distressed and Well-Off Metropolitan Areas, 1970–2000

Educational Achievement	Distressed Metropolitan Areas (Percentage)	Well-Off Metropolitan Areas (Percentage)	All 250 Metropolitan Areas (Percentage)
< High School			
1970	58	42	46
1980	44	23	32
1990	32	18	24
2000	27	12	18
College Graduates			
1970	8	13	11
1980	12	21	16
1990	15	27	20
2000	18	34	24

Source: Tables are author's computations based upon data from the U.S. Decennial Census of Population for 1970, 1980, 1990, and 2000 for metropolitan areas, their cities, and their suburbs and the U.S. Department of Housing and Urban Development's State of the Cities Data System (SOCDS).

tions that are considerably better-educated in each decade. This distinction is an important consideration for policymakers in their formulation of urban policy to stimulate local economic development.

Distressed and Well-Off Cities

Tables 9.9 and 9.10 show severely distressed and central well-off cities by decade.[10] There is substantial similarity in the overall patterns of distress and well being between cities and metropolitan areas. However, the cities that are well-off or severely distressed are more consistently so than are the metropolitan areas. Although only 5 of the 65 well-off cities have been well-off in all four census years, an additional 18 have been well-off in the last two or three census years. Similarly, although only 2 of the 59 highly distressed cities have been so in all four years, an additional 20 of the 59 have been distressed in the last two or three census years.

In thinking about place-based policy or attempts to revitalize older areas, it is informative to look at the relationship between distress and well-being in metropolitan areas and their central cities. We see particular coincidence between cities and metropolitan areas that are severely distressed. Because neither the direction of causality nor the lags with which any relationship between central city and metropolitan distress or

Table 9.9.   Severely Distressed Central Cities, 1970–2000

		2000	*1990*	*1980*	*1970*
Persistently Distressed (1)					
Newark, NJ	Northeast	X	X	X	X
St. Louis, MO	Midwest	X	X	X	X
Birmingham, AL	South	X	X	X	
Buffalo, NY	Northeast	X	X	X	
Cleveland, OH	Midwest	X	X	X	
Dayton, OH	Midwest	X	X	X	
Detroit, MI	Midwest	X	X	X	
Gary, IN	Midwest	X	X	X	
Harrisburg, PA	Northeast	X	X	X	
Saginaw, MI	Midwest	X	X	X	
Persistently Depressed (2)					
Brownsville, TX	South	X	X		X
Pine Bluff, AR	South	X	X		X
Atlantic City, NJ	Northeast	X		X	X
Recently Depressed (1)					
Albany, GA	South	X	X		
Alexandria, LA	South	X	X		
Elmira, NY	Northeast	X	X		
Flint, MI	Midwest	X	X		
Hartford, CT	Northeast	X	X		
Johnstown, PA	Northeast	X	X		
Miami, FL	South	X	X		
Monroe, LA	South	X	X		
Muncie, IN	Midwest	X	X		
Youngstown, OH	Midwest	X	X		
Recently Depressed (2)					
Athens, GA	South	X			
Fresno, CA	West	X			
Gadsden, AL	South	X			X
Gainesville, FL	South	X			
Lima, OH	Midwest	X			
Macon, GA	South	X			
Reading, PA	Northeast	X			
Rochester, NY	Northeast	X			
Stockton, CA	West	X			
Syracuse, NY	Northeast	X			
Texarkana, TX-AR	South	X			
Waco, TX	South	X			
York, PA	Northeast	X			
Recently Depressed (3)					
Anniston, AL	South		X	X	
Augusta, GA	South		X	X	
Lake Charles, LA	South		X		X

Table 9.9. (Continued)

		2000	1990	1980	1970
Laredo, TX	South		X		X
New Orleans, LA	South		X		X
Cumberland, MD	South		X		
El Paso, TX	South		X		
Fort Pierce, FL	South		X		
Jackson, MI	Midwest		X		
Kankakee, IL	Midwest		X		
McAllen, TX	South		X		
Steubenville, OH	Midwest		X		
Intermittently Depressed					
New Haven, CT	Northeast	X		X	
Philadelphia, PA	Northeast	X		X	
Providence, RI	Northeast	X		X	
Depressed Early					
Las Cruces, NM	West				X
Mobile, AL	South				X
Provo, UT	West				X
Baltimore, MD	South			X	
Jersey City, NJ	Northeast			X	
Louisville, KY-IN	Midwest			X	
Trenton, NJ	Northeast			X	
Wilmington, DE	South			X	

Note: "Severely distressed" is defined for the census years as follows:
2000: Per capita income < $10,089, poverty rate > 21.5%, unemployment rate > 9.1%.
1990: Per capita income < $8863, poverty rate > 22.1%, unemployment rate > 9.0%.
1980: Per capita income < $7788, poverty rate > 18.6%, unemployment rate > 8.6%.
1970: Per capita income < $7217, poverty rate > 18.1%, unemployment rate > 5.3%.
Source: Tables are author's computations based upon data from the U.S. Decennial Census of Population for 1970, 1980, 1990, and 2000 for metropolitan areas, their cities, and their suburbs and the U.S. Department of Housing and Urban Development's State of the Cities Data System (SOCDS).

well-being occur are well established, we simply record here the number of cities that appear at least once on the distressed list that are in metropolitan areas that also appear on the distressed list in at least one of the years (they needn't be the same year), and do the same for the well-off cities and metropolitan areas.

Specifically, in 24 of 59 cases (41 percent) in which a central city appears on the distressed list in at least one of the four census years, its metropolitan area also appears on this list at least once. For the 63 cities that appear on the "well-off" list at least once, 34 (54 percent) are in metropolitan areas that also appear on this list at least once. Overall, then, there is a higher percentage of cities and metropolitan areas that

Table 9.10. Well-off Central Cities, 1970–2000

		2000	1990	1980	1970
Persistently Well-off (1)					
Bloomington, IL	Midwest	X	X	X	X
Lincoln, NE	Midwest	X	X	X	X
Madison, WI	Midwest	X	X	X	X
Omaha, NE	Midwest	X	X	X	X
Rochester, MN	Midwest	X	X	X	X
Springfield, IL	Midwest	X	X	X	X
Cedar Rapids, IA	Midwest	X	X		
Charlotte, NC	South	X	X	X	
Raleigh, NC	South	X	X	X	
Reno, NV	West	X	X	X	
San Jose, CA	West	X	X	X	
Santa Barbara, CA	West	X	X	X	
Tulsa, OK	South	X	X	X	
Persistently Well-off (2)					
Boise City, ID	West	X	X		X
Greensboro, NC	South		X	X	X
Recently Well-off (1)					
Albuquerque, NM	West	X	X		
Indianapolis, IN	Midwest	X			
Janesville, WI	Midwest	X	X		
Lexington, KY	South	X	X		
Little Rock, AR	South	X	X		
Nashville-Davidson, TN	South	X	X		
San Diego, CA	West	X	X		
San Francisco, CA	West	X	X		
Santa Rosa, CA	West	X	X		
Seattle, WA	West	X	X		
Recently Well-off (2)					
Bismarck, ND	Midwest	X		X	
Sioux Falls, SD	Midwest	X		X	
Austin, TX	South	X			
Colorado Springs, CO	West	X			
Denver, CO	West	X			
Dothan, AL	South	X			
Fargo, ND	Midwest	X			
Fort Collins, CO	West	X			
Kansas City, MO	Midwest	X			
New London, CT	Northeast	X			
Pittsfield, MA	Northeast	X			
Portland, ME	Northeast	X			
Salt Lake City, UT	West	X			

Table 9.10. (Continued)

		2000	1990	1980	1970
Recently Well-off (3)					
Wichita, KS	Midwest	X	X		
Orlando, FL	South	X			
Portland, OR	West	X			
Rockford, IL	Midwest	X			
Santa Cruz, CA	West	X			
Sarasota, FL	South	X			
Well-off Early (1)					
Des Moines, IA	Midwest			X	X
Phoenix, AZ	West			X	X
Topeka, KS	Midwest			X	X
Well-off Early (2)					
Bakersfield, CA	West			X	
Casper, WY	West			X	
Charleston, SC	South			X	
Davenport, IA	Midwest			X	
Enid, OK	South			X	
Houston, TX	South			X	
Longview, TX	South			X	
Odessa, TX	South			X	
Oklahoma City, OK	South			X	
Well-off Early (3)					
Allentown, PA	Northeast				X
Ann Arbor, MI	Midwest				X
Elkhart, IN	Midwest				X
Fort Lauderdale, FL	South				X
Fort Wayne, IN	Midwest				X
Kankakee, IL	Midwest				X
Minneapolis, MN	Midwest				X
Peoria, IL	Midwest				X

Note: "Well off" is defined for the census years as follows:
2000: Per capita income > $12,107, poverty rate < 15.9%, unemployment rate < 6.4%.
1990: Per capita income > $10,495, poverty rate < 16.1%, unemployment rate < 6.3%.
1980: Per capita income > $8974, poverty rate < 13.4%, unemployment rate < 5.8%.
1970: Per capita income > $8267, poverty rate < 12.4%, unemployment rate <3.9%.
Source: Tables are author's computations based upon data from the U.S. Decennial Census of Population for 1970, 1980, 1990, and 2000 for metropolitan areas, their cities, and their suburbs and the U.S. Department of Housing and Urban Development's State of the Cities Data System (SOCDS).

both appear on the well-off list than that both appear on the distressed list.

Despite the absence of a model of timing and relationship, that is, whether it takes a strong, vibrant central city to spill over and stimulate metropolitan well-being or a strong metro to bring along a strong city, I turn now to examine (1) whether cities that are well-off in a particular year are in metropolitan areas that are well-off or distressed in that year; and (2) whether cities that are distressed in a particular year are in metropolitan areas that are well-off or distressed in the same year.

The findings make clear that it is more likely to find an overlap between distressed cities and distressed metropolitan areas, and between well-off cities and metropolitan areas, than to observe distressed cities in well-off metropolitan areas or well-off cities in distressed metropolitan areas. The latter are virtually nonexistent.[11]

More specifically, in 3 of 4 census years, about a quarter of distressed cities are located in distressed metropolitan areas while the percentage of well-off cities that are located in well-off metropolitan areas is never less than one-third and rises as high as 50 percent. In contrast, across the 4 census years, the maximum percentage of distressed cities that are located in well-off metropolitan areas is 17 percent, and the percentage is considerably lower in other years; in the case of well-off cities, only in 1980 is such a city (one out of a total of 29 well-off cities that year) located in a depressed metropolitan area.

These relationships may be critical for place-based policies. The fact that there are hardly any distressed cities in well-off metropolitan areas, but that there are a number of well-off cities in well-off metropolitan areas—particularly in recent decades—suggests the need for further investigation of the dynamics of these relationships. Such investigations may suggest policies to stimulate cities that are distressed or not well-off (by the definitions used here) but are located in well-off metropolitan areas.

Conclusion

In addition to making the point—in numerous ways—that change is the rule when it comes to regions, metropolitan areas, and cities in the United States, and that change generally improves welfare, I have also tried to demonstrate that, using a strong definition of places that are severely distressed and well-off, there is substantial movement into and out of the distressed or well-off categories. This is the case not only over long periods of time but also from decade to decade. Moreover, despite the fact that there are numerous well-off cities in well-off metropolitan areas and virtually none in distressed metropolitan areas, other well-off cities are not in well-off metropolitan areas. Thus, it would be informative to further examine the characteristics of these pairings—what distinguishes cities that are linked to their metropolitan areas (both well-off or both distressed) from those that are decoupled (one well-off and the other distressed, or one well-off or distressed and the other not in either extreme category).

Constant change does not argue for or against place-based policies or for or against reinventing older communities. Rather, the major changes that have occurred and the responses to them pose a context within which it is necessary if one is to evaluate, to reject, or to structure place-based policies.

PART III

Moving People Out of Poverty

Chapter 10

An Overview of Moving to Opportunity
A Random Assignment Housing Mobility Study
in Five U.S. Cities

Lisa A. Gennetian, Lisa Sanbonmatsu, and Jens Ludwig

The U.S. Department of Housing and Urban Development's (HUD) Moving to Opportunity (MTO) experiment provides a unique opportunity to answer the question of whether moving from a high-poverty neighborhood to a lower-poverty community improves the social and economic prospects of low-income families. Authorized by the U.S. Congress in 1992, MTO made use of rental assistance vouchers, in combination with intensive housing search and counseling services, to assist low-income families to move from some of America's most distressed urban neighborhoods to lower-poverty communities.[1] The MTO demonstration has two broad research goals. The first, short-term, goal was to compare the costs and services of the MTO program with the routine implementation of the Section 8 tenant-based rental assistance program in existence at the time of MTO's implementation.[2] The second, longer-term, goal is to assess the impact of the demonstration on the well-being of families and their children, including their housing conditions, mental and physical health, employment and earnings, receipt of social program assistance and income, education, and delinquent or risky behavior of children.

A total of 4,608 families enrolled in the MTO demonstration and were randomly assigned between September 1994 and August 1998 to groups that received different opportunities to move to less disadvantaged neighborhood environments. The enrollment and randomization phase of MTO ended in February 1999, but MTO families continue to receive the housing vouchers that they were offered under the program as long as they continue to be eligible for them. Random assignment in MTO to different mobility "treatments" breaks the link between family preferences and neighborhood environments, and so provides us with the chance of overcoming the standard self-selection concern to identify the causal effects of neighborhoods on adult and child outcomes. The issue of self-selection will be discussed further in the following section.

This chapter provides a very brief introduction to the MTO demonstration and summarizes key findings from an interim evaluation that collected information from MTO families four to seven years after random assignment. We also briefly describe the MTO long-term evaluation that is currently in process. Research on the MTO demonstration by dozens of researchers has been ongoing for over a decade, and there have been several phases of research supported by HUD and other private and public entities to capture MTO impacts over time.[3] Interested readers should turn to these reports and papers to learn more about MTO and its effects on families and children.

The MTO Experimental Design in the Context of Neighborhood Research

The innovation of MTO over previous research on neighborhood effects—such as the large nonexperimental literature finding that neighborhood characteristics do appear to predict development outcomes and the quasi-experimental Gautreux program evaluated in the work of sociologist James Rosenbaum—stems from the randomized experimental assignment to MTO groups of families who subsequently have experienced very different long-term patterns of neighborhood environments.[4] At study entry these families had comparable characteristics. If random assignment was successfully implemented, then any difference in family and child outcomes across MTO groups at any point in time after study entry represents an unbiased estimate of MTO's impacts.[5] As such, random assignment studies like MTO provide a unique opportunity to study and isolate the effects of a housing mobility program from the myriad of other programs that families might be eligible for and participate in. Furthermore, because MTO families in the experimental group who move with the MTO housing voucher to areas with particular neighborhood characteristics that may be distinct from the neighborhood characteristics of comparable families who move in the control group, MTO also presents a unique opportunity to examine the role of neighborhood context separately from the factors that influence residential mobility decisions.

How did MTO work in practice? Local public housing authorities (PHAs) in each participating city recruited families living in public housing or privately owned, publicly subsidized developments, through fliers, tenant associations, and other means. All interested families had the chance to apply for the program. Families participated in a group orientation session to learn about the demonstration and the experimental design of the research study.

Before being formally accepted into the program, families were screened to determine if they met eligibility criteria for Section 8 rental assistance. Housing vouchers in MTO were administered comparable to the Section 8 Rental Voucher program, where an administering housing authority issues a voucher to an income-qualified household, which then finds a unit to rent. If the unit meets the Section 8 quality standards, the PHA then pays the landlord the amount equal to the difference between 30 percent of the tenant's adjusted income (or 10 percent of the gross income or the portion of welfare assistance designated for housing) and the PHA-determined payment standard for the area. Families in the experimental and Section 8 groups described in the next paragraph had four to six months to find qualified housing and move using a MTO voucher. MTO demonstration rules required that experimental group families sign one-year leases for the units they rented with MTO vouchers.

All families who signed up for MTO were randomly assigned to one of the following three groups.

1. The *MTO low-poverty voucher (LPV) group:* This group, also referred to as the "experimental group," received Section 8 certificates or vouchers usable only in low-poverty areas (areas with less than 10 percent of the population below the poverty line in 1990), along with extra counseling and assistance in finding a private unit to lease through a local nonprofit organization (NPO). These NPOs assisted the local PHA in the selection and assignment of experimental families who would move to low-poverty areas, recruited owners of rental property in low-poverty areas to make units available to MTO families, assisted MTO families in finding appropriate rental units in low-poverty areas, and provided short-term counseling assistance to help families adjust to their new housing locations.

2. The *traditional voucher group:* This group, also referred to as the "Section 8" group, received regular Section 8 certificates or vouchers (geographically unrestricted) and ordinary briefings and assistance from the PHAs.

3. The *control group:* This group received no certificates or vouchers but remained eligible for public or project-based housing and other social programs to which families would otherwise have had eligibility.

The baseline characteristics of the households are shown in Table 10.1. Over 90 percent of the households that signed up for MTO were

Table 10.1 Characteristics of Participants at Baseline

	Low-Poverty Voucher (LPV) Group	Traditional Voucher Group	Control Group
Characteristics of Sample Adult			
Age in years	39.7	40.1	39.6
Female	98	98	98
Race and ethnicity			
African-American, non-Hispanic	67	66	66
Other race	26	26	27
Hispanic ethnicity, any race	29	30	29
Marital status			
Never Married	62	62	62
Teen Parent	25	26	24
Education			
High school graduate	41	41	38
General equivalency diploma	18	19	21
Working	29	25	25
On AFDC	74	75	75
Characteristics of Household			
A member has a disability[a]	16	17	16
A member was victimized by crime[b]	42	43	41
Streets near home are very unsafe at night	48	49	49
Primary or secondary reason for moving is to get away from drugs and gangs	77	75	78

Source: Kling, Liebman, and Katz (2007).
Note: Data are percentages unless otherwise specified, weighted to account for changes in random assignment ratios. Percentages may not sum to 100% due to rounding. Surveys were completed in LPV, traditional voucher, and control groups with 1,729, 1,209, and 1,310 respondents, respectively, for a total sample size of 4,248 respondents.
[a]Disability is defined as a mental health or health problem that keeps the individual from normal activities.
[b]Victimization is defined as having been assaulted, threatened with a weapon, or having had purse, wallet, or jewelry snatched in the six months prior to baseline.

headed by a female, nearly two-thirds of whom were African-American (most of the rest were Hispanic). Three-quarters of household heads were on welfare at baseline and fewer than half had graduated from high school. On average these households had three children. The immigration status of MTO participants is unknown but most speak English. More than 40 percent of households reported that a household member was the victim of a crime in the preceding six months and more than half reported that their main reason for a move is to get away from drugs and gangs.

The control group is essential in order to correctly estimate the impacts of Section 8 rental assistance separate from the impacts of MTO assistance with counseling, providing a benchmark against which the outcomes of the other two groups can be measured. Over time, control group families remain eligible for public or project-based housing and other social programs and subsequently may move to neighborhoods that look similar to neighborhoods the MTO low-poverty and traditional voucher groups move to. This means that the counterfactual neighborhood conditions for families in the MTO low-poverty and regular voucher groups are no longer restricted to just the highest-poverty census tracts in which a relatively small set of public housing families reside. The postrandomization mobility of control families may change the effect of MTO's "treatment dose" on neighborhood characteristics. That is, if the MTO program did not alter the long-term future housing, neighborhood, and outcome trajectories of experimental group families as compared to control group families, then, over time, any initial or short-term differences in neighborhood characteristics between MTO experimental group families and control group families may diminish and hence will affect estimates of the long-term impact of MTO on family and child outcomes. However, these patterns may also make the MTO demonstration results somewhat more policy relevant.

It is also important to recognize that MTO is most informative about small-scale or incremental voluntary mobility programs serving families in very distressed areas. While studies with experimental designs such as MTO can derive unbiased estimates of neighborhood effects, such estimates may not be easily generalized to the effects of a similar housing program implemented during a very different time period or to a very different cohort of low-income families on housing assistance.

Key Findings from MTO Interim Evaluation

HUD sponsored an interim impact evaluation designed to measure MTO's effects on outcomes of participating families measured four to seven years after enrollment in the MTO demonstration. The key findings on outcomes for the LPV and control groups from the interim evaluation are summarized here, in Figures 10.1 to 10.5, and in Table 10.2. (Information allowing comparison across *all three* MTO groups, including the traditional voucher group, is provided in Table 10.2.)[6] We present the outcome level for all members of the LPV group (whether or not they moved in response to MTO) and the outcome level for all members of the control group. Because of MTO's random assignment research design, the difference in the outcome level for families and children in the LPV group versus the control group reflects the effect or impact of MTO.[7] This estimate is also called the intent-to-treat (ITT)

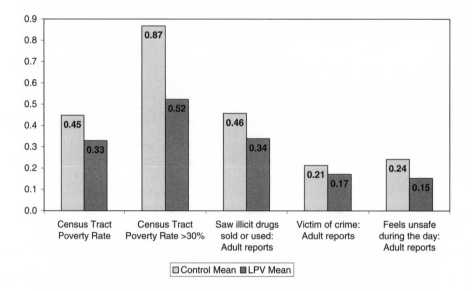

Figure 10.1. MTO's Effects on Selected Neighborhood Outcomes

Source: Kling, Liebman and Katz 2007a.
Note: Effects on census tract poverty rates presented in the figure reflect the situation one
year after random assignment. Other results presented in the figure reflect the situation
at the time of the interim evaluation.
All differences in outcome levels between the LPV group and the control group are
statistically significant at the p<0.05 level.

effect. The ITT represents the estimated impact of MTO on the assigned
group as a whole, including families who leased up and families who
never rented with a voucher obtained through MTO. For example, at
the time of the interim evaluation, 54.7 percent of the control group
and 52.8 percent of the LPV group were either not working or on Temporary Assistance for Needy Families (TANF), giving an ITT estimate of
− 1.9 percent. The ITT estimate removes the problem of self-selection
bias because it compares the entire experimental group to the entire
control group, two groups that differ only in their exposure to this program.

An alternative estimate is the treatment-on-treated (TOT) effect. The
TOT represents the effect of MTO on the program movers, that is, the
sample members who actually moved with the program vouchers, and
as such is not an experimental impact of MTO. The TOT estimate does
not remove the self-selection bias, since it compares the people in the
LPV group who leased up, a self-selected group, to the would-be movers
in the control group. One assumption of the TOT approach is that there

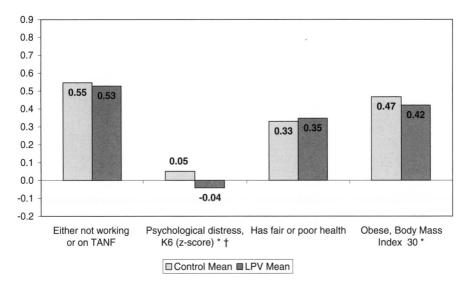

Figure 10.2. MTO's Effects on Selected Outcomes for Adults

Source: Kling, Liebman, and Katz 2007a.
*Indicates that the difference in outcome levels between the LPV group and the control group are statistically significant at the p<0.05 level.
†The K6 scale score ranges from 0 to 24. It was normalized to a z-score by subtracting the mean and dividing by the standard deviation.

is no average effect of being offered an MTO voucher on those who did not use an MTO voucher, which we believe is reasonable. Although the TOT estimates do not remove self-selection bias, the estimates are policy-relevant because they focus on the effects that a new neighborhood environment would have on the individuals who would be most likely to participate in a housing voucher program. The TOT estimates are calculated by dividing the ITT estimates for each group by the group's lease-up rate. As described next, because only 47 percent of the LPV group leased up, TOT estimates are substantially larger than ITT estimates. To continue the above example, the TOT estimated effect would be $[(-1.9 \text{ percent})/.47] = -4.04$ percent. That is, we estimate that LPV households who leased up were 4.04 percentage points less likely than controls either to be not working or on TANF.

MTO Moved Families to Less Economically Distressed Communities

Among the households assigned to the LPV group, 47 percent used an MTO voucher to relocate to a low-poverty census tract. (Sixty-two per-

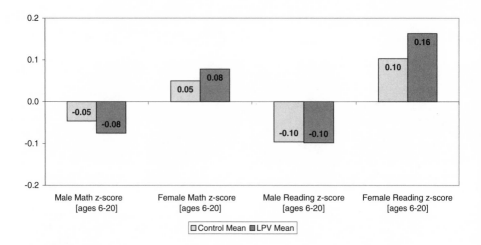

Figure 10.3. MTO's Effects on Children's Math and Reading Achievement

Source: Sanbonmatsu et al. 2006.
Figures reflect Woodcock-Johnson Revised (WJ-R) scale scores. Performance on the WJ-R can be reported using several different metrics. We use the WJ-R's "W" scale as our underlying metric because these scores reflect an absolute measure of performance and have the attractive property of being equalinterval. To facilitate interpretation of results, we transform the W scores to z-scores that have a mean of zero and standard deviation of one for the control group.

cent of those assigned to the traditional voucher group relocated through MTO. The relocation rates differed substantially by site from a low of 32 percent in the Chicago experimental group to a high of 77 percent in the Los Angeles Section 8 group.) The explicit goal of MTO was to help move families into less economically distressed communities, and by this measure MTO was successful. One year after random assignment, families in the LPV group lived in census tracts with an average poverty rate that was 12 percentage points (27 percent) below that of the control group (see Figure 10.1).[8] The gap declines over time in part because of subsequent mobility among all groups: after leasing up, approximately 66 percent of experimental group families made one or more additional moves. Even six years after random assignment, the experimental-control difference in tract poverty equals 8 percentage points (20 percent of the control mean), while the difference in cumulative exposure to neighborhood poverty (duration-weighted averages) are 10.6 percentage points (25 percent of the control mean) (Kling, Liebman, and Katz 2007a).

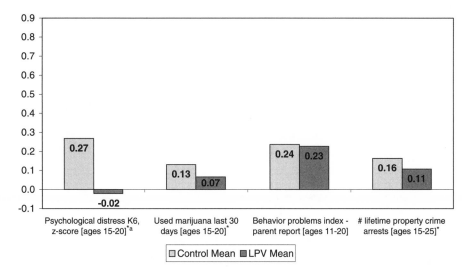

Figure 10.4. MTO's Effects on Outcomes for Female Youth

Sources: Kling, Liebman, and Katz 2007a; Kling, Ludwig, and Katz 2005; Sanbonmatsu et al. 2006.
*Indicates that the difference in outcome levels between the LPV group and the control group are statistically significant at the p<0.05 level.
[a]The K6 scale score ranges from 0 to 24. It was normalized to a z-score by subtracting the mean and dividing by the standard deviation.

Feelings of Safety and Satisfaction

Families in the MTO LPV group reported feeling safer and more satisfied with their housing and neighborhoods than families in the control group. Approximately 52 percent of households in the control group reported being unsatisfied or very unsatisfied with their neighborhoods, as compared with only 39 percent in the LPV group (Orr et al. 2003; Table 10.2). Figure 10.1 shows that 15 percent of LPV adults reported feeling unsafe as compared to 24 percent of adults in the control group. LPV adults were also 4 percentage points less likely to report being victims of crime and 9 percentage points less likely to report seeing illicit drugs sold or used compared to adults in the control group.

Effects on Labor Market Outcomes and Social Program Participation

MTO had no detectable effect on the labor market outcomes or social program participation of adults. However, MTO improved adults' men-

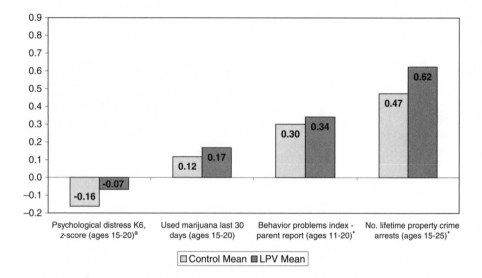

Figure 10.5. MTO's Effects on Outcomes for Male Youth

Sources: Kling, Liebman, and Katz 2007; Kling, Ludwig, and Katz 2005; and Sanbonmatsu et al. 2006.
*Indicates that the difference in outcome levels between the LPV group and the control group is statistically significant at the p<0.05 level.
[a]The K6 scale score ranges from 0 to 24. It was normalized to a z–score by subtracting the mean and dividing by the standard deviation.

tal health, as well as several important aspects of physical health such as obesity and health-risk behaviors including diet and exercise.

In Figure 10.2, similar proportions of LPV and control group adults were not working or on TANF (roughly 55 and 53 percent, respectively). As compared to adults in the control group, LPV adults were 5 percentage points, or 11 percent, less likely to be obese according to a body mass index (BMI) cutoff of 30 or higher. The interim evaluation collected a measure of psychological distress—an index that represents the fraction of six mental health outcomes that the adult reported feeling at least some of the time during the past thirty days—and a measure that captures episodes of major depression. Figure 10.2 shows lower levels of psychological distress among LPV adults compared to control group adults,[9] a finding that is equivalent to a one-fifth reduction in the incidence of psychological distress among LPV adults and comparable to effects found in some clinical and pharmacologic mental health interventions (see n. 29 in Kling, Liebman, and Katz 2007a for further discussion).

Table 10.2. Impact of MTO on Selected Neighborhood Outcomes, Interim Evaluation

	Control Mean	LPV vs. Control Intent-to-Treat	Traditional Voucher vs. Control Intent-to-Treat
Neighborhood Outcomes			
Census tract poverty rate[a]	.448	−.119* (.007)	−.097* (.006)
Census tract poverty rate[a] > 30%	.868	−.345* (.018)	−.242* (.020)
Saw illicit drugs sold or used[b]	.457	−.118* (.022)	−.104* (.024)
Victim of crime[b]	.213[b]	−.042* (.017)	−.055* (.018)
Feels unsafe during the day[b]	.242	−.090* (.018)	−.090* (.019)
Unsatisfied or very unsatisfied with neighborhood[b]	.524	−.136* (.022)	−.106* (.024)
Adult Outcomes			
Not working or on TANF	.547	−.019 (.020)	−.015 (.023)
Psychological distress, K6 (z-score)[c]	.050	−.092* (.046)	−.033 (.051)
Has fair or poor health	.330	.017 (.019)	.011 (.021)
Obese, body mass index ≤ 30	.468	−.048* (.022)	−.046 (.025)
Female Youth			
Math test scores [6–20]	.050	.028 (.041)	−.037 (.044)
Reading test scores [6–20]	.103	.060 (.038)	.012 (.043)
Psychological distress K6, z-score (15–20)[c]	.268	−.289* (.094)	−.145 (.106)
Used marijuana last 30 days (15–20)	.131	−.065* (.029)	−.072* (.032)
Behavior problems index—parent report (11–20)	.237	−.010 (.014)	−.007 (.015)
No. lifetime property crime arrests (15–25)	.164	−.057* (.026)	.031 (.039)
Male Youth			
Math test scores (6–20)	−.046	−.029 (.040)	−.038(.041)
Reading test scores (6–20)	−.096	−.002 (.045)	.033 (.046)
Psychological distress K6, z-score (15–20)[c]	−.162	.095 (.085)	.005 (.010)
Used marijuana last 30 days (15–20)	.118	.051 (.030)	.055 (.035)

Table 10.2. (Continued)

	Control Mean	LPV vs. Control, Intent-to-Treat	Traditional Voucher vs. Control, Intent-to-Treat
Behavior problems index—parent report (11–20)	.301	.041* (.014)	.025 (.016)
No. lifetime property crime arrests (15–25)	.474	.150* (.055)	.072 (.059)

Sources: Kling, Liebman, and Katz (2007a); Sanbonmatsu et al. (2006); and Kling, Ludwig, and Katz (2005).
* Indicates that the difference in outcome levels between the LPV group or traditional voucher group and the control group are statistically significant at the $p < 0.05$ level. Standard errors shown in parentheses.
For youth results, age range of analytic sample as of December 31, 2001 is reported in parentheses next to each variable.
[a]One year after random assignment
[b]Adult reports.
[c] The K6 scale score ranges from 0 to 24. It was normalized to a z-score by subtracting the mean and dividing by the standard deviation.

Effects of MTO on Reading and Math Achievement of Children

As shown in Figure 10.3, MTO had no detectable impacts for either male or female youth on academic achievement, as measured by Wood-cock-Johnson tests in reading and math, or on several schooling outcomes, including the likelihood of dropping out of secondary school (the latter effects are not shown; see Sanbonmatsu et al. 2006).

Effect of MTO on Male and Female Youth

The effects of MTO on youth outcomes in the interim evaluation differed for male as compared to female youth. For a wide range of measures of risky and delinquent behaviors as well as schooling outcomes, MTO improved outcomes for female youth but on balance had deleterious impacts on male youth. Figure 10.4 shows that compared to female youth in the control group, females in the LPV group had lower levels of psychological distress and were less likely to report using marijuana or be arrested for property crime. In comparison, Figure 10.5 shows that relative to their peers in the control group, male youth in the LPV group were slightly more likely to report using marijuana, scored higher on an index of behavioral problems (which includes acting out and aggressive behaviors) and were more likely to be arrested for property crime. Further analyses suggest that the disruption of moving per se does not appear to explain the gender differences in MTO effects for youth, as

MTO's deleterious impacts on male youth do not show up until a few years after random assignment (Kling, Liebman, and Katz 2007a, 2007b; Kling, Ludwig, and Katz 2005). The gender difference in impacts is also not due to families with boys versus girls moving to different types of neighborhoods, since moves are generally similar across families with boys and families with girls. Brothers and sisters within the same families also appear to respond differently to the MTO intervention. Qualitative interviews conducted after the interim survey data collection have helped deepen our understanding of MTO's differing effects on female as compared to male youth (for example, see Popkin, Leventhal, and Weismann 2008). This research suggests that the nature of how boys and girls interact socially with peers may enable girls to more successfully adapt to life in low-poverty areas. Girls were more likely to visit with friends on their porches or inside their homes, in part because some parents may place girls on a shorter leash than they do boys. Boys, on the other hand, often hang out in public spaces and this elevates the risk for conflict with neighbors and police, in addition to increasing their exposure to delinquent peer groups as well as opportunities to engage in delinquent activities themselves (Clampet-Lundquist et al. 2005; Popkin, Leventhal, and Weismann 2008).

Long-Term Evaluation of MTO

Sponsored by HUD and funded by several federal agencies and private foundations, the final MTO impact evaluation is currently under way and will provide an opportunity to learn more about the program's longer-term effects ten to twelve years after enrollment in the demonstration program and, in turn, the effects on families and children of living in varying neighborhood environments. The final impact evaluation is not only an opportunity to examine the set of outcomes studied at the interim point[10] but also a chance to expand on information collected about particular outcome domains, such as mental health, victimization, and criminal behavior, that showed effects at the interim follow-up point and that theory would predict continued effects over the long term. Investigating further whether differences in the effects of MTO on male and female youth hold up over the long term and better understanding why male and female youth responded so differently to changing neighborhoods is one example. Determining whether MTO impacts on basic screening indicators of adult mental health found in the interim MTO study translate into clinically important changes in mental health problems—which impose great costs to individuals and society at large—is another example. The final impact evaluation is designed to exploit the randomized experimental design of the MTO demonstration to best address the four key questions described below:

1. *What are the long-term effects of MTO on participating families, and how do these impacts evolve over time?* If differences in average neighborhood characteristics across MTO groups persist over time, MTO's effects on well-being and behavior may increase over time. Ties to old social networks will diminish over time, while social ties to new communities and use of new neighborhood institutional resources will increase. For example, the benefits of more exposure to more prosocial and affluent social networks may improve if families become more socially integrated into their new communities with time, more attuned to local social norms, and thus more responsive to the peer and adult social influences that play a central role in the epidemic and collective socialization models. Social integration itself might require families to learn new modes of dress, language, or interactions to fit in, and families may also learn how to fully utilize improved local services such as schools. Families may also learn over time how to better navigate the potential opportunities and pitfalls in low-poverty areas. On the other hand, "relative deprivation" models focus on the psychological impact on individuals' self-evaluations based on relative standing in the community (Luttmer 2005). These models suggest that poor families may actually fare better in low-income neighborhoods despite the poorer level of resources because they are not comparing their position to higher-income neighbors; such models predict that children in low-income families living in higher-income neighborhoods will exhibit worse outcomes, including low educational attainment, behavioral problems, and diminished mental health (Wood 1989; Marsh and Parker 1984; Collins 1996). To the extent to which exposure to the new resources and opportunities in low-poverty areas makes MTO adults and youth more competitive over time for prosocial rewards, any deleterious effects from competition or declines in relative position may diminish over time. Disruptions associated with the act of moving itself may exert independent effects on individual outcomes that may partially or wholly offset any benefits associated with moving to lower-poverty areas, though we would expect that any deleterious effects of moving may also attenuate over time. The increased integration of MTO participants into their new neighborhoods may lead to continued improvements in outcomes such as the mental health of participating adults.

2. *What are the long-term effects of MTO on those who were young children at baseline?* In some ways this is arguably the most important question to be answered by the MTO final impact evaluation. A growing body of research suggests that the malleability of behavior may decline with age (Becker and Murphy 2000; Shonkoff and Phillips 2000; Carniero and

Heckman 2003; Knudsen et al. 2006). The interim MTO data revealed little evidence for age differences in MTO impacts on educational achievement test scores. Like the interim evaluation, the MTO youth interview for the long-term evaluation will include forty-five-minute achievement assessments in math and reading designed for the fifth and eighth grade follow-up waves of the U.S. Department of Education's Early Childhood Longitudinal Study (ECLS), which have the advantage of more closely testing what youth are learning in school; the ECLS assessments have had extensive pretesting and piloting with national samples across a wide age range. MTO participants who were fairly young at randomization also were too young at the time of the interim study to provide developmentally meaningful measures for other key outcomes such as dropout rate, mental health status, or risky behavior which will be collected as part of the youth survey undertaken for the final impact evaluation.

3. *What explains the large gender difference found in the interim study in how youth respond to MTO moves?* Evidence on the source of the gender difference in MTO effects may help explain gender differences in the educational progress made over time in the United States as a whole among African American males and females. In the long-term evaluation we will collect mediating variables aimed at testing three general hypotheses for the gender difference in MTO impacts: (a) differences in the ability of schools to serve low-income minority male versus female youth, including the possibility of gender differences in within-school discipline, academic track or program assignments; (b) gender differences in how MTO moves affect the family learning environments and social interactions of youth; and (c) gender differences in how youth sort themselves into new peer groups and generally integrate into their new social environments. New research in behavioral economics also raises the possibility of gender differences in the effects of neighborhood mobility on basic decision-making processes, if whatever makes females better able than males to delay gratification more generally (for example, Silverman 2003) also makes decision-making by females more responsive to environmental influences.

4. *What are the mechanisms more generally through which neighborhood moves affect youth outcomes?* The interim MTO study examined the degree to which experiences with racial discrimination might hamper the ability of MTO youth to take advantage of new schooling or other opportunities. Yet MTO generated more pronounced changes in neighborhood economic than racial composition and so more attention will be paid in the long-term evaluation to the possibility of discrimination along class rather than race lines. As another way of understanding the role of social class discrimination, we plan to examine how MTO impacts lan-

guage patterns among program participants. Concern about crime was one of the most important reasons MTO families signed up for the MTO program. Because crime and concurrent feelings of being unsafe can manifest themselves through stress and poor mental health, the MTO long-term surveys include much more detailed items in order to measure several mental health disorders, drawing on diagnostic measures originally developed for the National Co-Morbidity Study. Finally, we hope to better understand MTO impacts on crime-related mediators like chronic stress by collecting biological samples (dried blood spots) to measure changes in the stress hormone cortisol as well as other long-term disease precursors.

Adult and youth outcomes for the long-term evaluation will be measured by both survey self-reports and administrative data. Administrative data on earnings, social assistance program participation, secondary and postsecondary education, and arrests will provide longitudinal outcome information for MTO participants,[11] are not susceptible to self-reporting problems, can in some cases be less susceptible to sample attrition compared to survey data, and are much less costly to obtain than surveys. Survey data complement administrative records by offering a richer and more detailed picture of well-being and perceptions of one's environment that is not possible to capture by existing administrative data systems.

Conclusion

The MTO study provides a significant opportunity to scientifically comprehend the causal effect of residence in distressed areas on the well-being and economic security of American adults and children. Understanding whether (and, if so, how) variation across neighborhoods in youth and parent outcomes reflects the effects of neighborhood context is crucial for housing policies that affect the concentration of poverty in America as well as for community development efforts, education policies, and many other social policies designed to improve the life chances of disadvantaged families. The final MTO impact evaluation will allow researchers and policymakers to more fully assess the long-term effects of location and to more specifically define those areas of life (health, education, economic position) on which location may have a bearing.

MTO is a relatively small demonstration program, and the lessons from it are most directly applicable to strategies to expand or revise current programs. Nonetheless, MTO represents a unique opportunity to uncover ways in which neighborhood characteristics affect families and children, and as such it stands out as an important contribution to neighborhood and housing research.

Chapter 11

How Does Leaving High-Poverty Neighborhoods Affect the Employment Prospects of Low-Income Mothers and Youth? Evidence from the Moving to Opportunity Experiment

Xavier de Souza Briggs, Elizabeth Cove, Cynthia Duarte, and Margery Austin Turner

Consider two very different cases of the role of relocation in the economic lives of low-income black women. Anique and her daughter Clara (all names used are pseudonyms) left public housing in a high-poverty, high-crime neighborhood of South Los Angeles seven years ago. Since then, Anique has struggled to line up steady work and child care while bouncing from apartment to apartment in L.A.'s sprawling housing market. At one point, her daily commute was seventy miles each way, from Long Beach, where her mother and sister provided child care, to her job in Riverside County. But Anique had considerable work experience, and the skills and confidence that often come with that experience, at the time of her move. As we completed our visits with her in 2005, she and Clara were living in a neighborhood that felt safe, across the street from Anique's steady new job as a child support investigator with county government.

Kimberlyn and her two teenaged boys also relocated from a public housing project in South Los Angeles to a much safer neighborhood in the San Fernando Valley. Kimberlyn credits that relocation—her "last chance," she recalls—with getting her away from an abusive relationship. Although the new neighborhood provided safer, better schools for her sons, which Kimberlyn prized, she experienced racial harassment from white neighbors in her apartment complex. Plus, Kimberlyn was on welfare when she moved and had almost no work experience or credentials. When she could not or would not secure, in the Valley, the job training and other resources she knew she needed, she moved her family back to South Los Angeles and put her sons back into the much more disruptive and dangerous schools there. Kimberlyn has been unable to line up steady work and is back on welfare after stints as a security officer and brief spells in training. The child care her sister had provided in South Los Angeles abruptly disappeared, and her mother's needs are a major burden.

For roughly half a century, policymakers and researchers have debated the impacts of place, and in particular of living in inner-city ghettos, on employment and self-sufficiency. Images of the welfare-dependent or socially isolated ghetto poor, together with evidence of a spatial mismatch between increasingly decentralized job locations and the neighborhoods where low-skilled people are concentrated, fueled an interest in housing policy as a tool for shifting the "geography of opportunity" (Abrams 1955; Briggs 2005; Downs 1973; Wilson 1987). Created in 1974, the federal rental housing voucher program allows low-income families to use government-provided housing subsidies to move away from poor and high-risk communities. Yet these families, minorities most of all, continue to face extraordinary barriers, such as racial discrimination, landlord refusal to accept the vouchers, the exclusion of affordable rental housing from more affluent and white communities, search costs, and more (Massey and Denton 1993; Pendall 2000; Turner 1998). Plus, some families have their own reasons for preferring poorer, more racially segregated areas to the unwelcome alternatives they perceive.

Yet research on the long-run effects of programs that seek to expand housing choice by *facilitating* access to better neighborhoods—an approach known as "assisted housing mobility"—has suggested that these efforts can improve the life outcomes of low-income, mostly minority adults and their children in several dimensions, including education, safety and security, mental health, employment, and self-sufficiency. Two programs, in particular, found their way to the headlines in the wake of Hurricane Katrina and the unprecedented relocation it forced. In 1994, encouraging results from the Gautreaux housing desegregation program (Rubinowitz and Rosenbaum 2000) spurred the federal government to invest $70 million in the randomized Moving to Opportunity experiment (MTO).

At baseline, only about one-quarter of MTO adults were working; most were on welfare (Goering and Feins 2003). Although MTO was not designed to directly address participants' employment status or employability—including the barriers to work that low-skill single mothers often face—the experiment had the research-based expectation that if families moved to low-poverty neighborhoods, adults could become employed or get better jobs by moving closer to employment centers, developing more useful job networks (as a form of social capital) with more advantaged neighbors, and/or gaining momentum from an environment with stronger work norms. Controversial or not, realistic or not, these expectations were real, *particularly in the minds of policymakers.*

Notwithstanding some encouraging evidence concerning early impacts of MTO on employment and welfare receipt at some sites, at the interim mark some four to seven years after random assignment, there were no generalized treatment effects on employment, earnings, or self-sufficiency (Orr et al. 2003). Significantly, though, more than twice as many MTO adults were working *in all groups* (Orr et al. 2003)—this over a period in which labor markets were tight and time limits on welfare assistance began to show effects—and many MTO families faced important barriers to work, in the form of chronic illnesses, lack of child care, and more (Popkin, Harris, and Cunningham 2001). So the market and entitlement reform effects may have swamped any treatment effect of MTO, at least in the short run. Moreover, by the interim point, many experimental-group families had moved on to somewhat poorer neighborhoods, for a range of reasons. Yet additional analyses of the interim impacts survey suggest that the employment picture may be more complex and mixed than initially thought, with positive effects for subgroups of adults or particular sites, and that interference and other challenges limit the experiment as a source of unbiased estimates of neighborhood effects, which are notoriously difficult to attribute.

In this chapter, rather than estimate MTO treatment effects, we use qualitative and quantitative analyses to analyze how and why the mixed patterns obtain for employment. The focus of our qualitative work is nonexperimental analyses of *causal mechanisms*, including social processes, that tie place of residence to economic opportunity. We employ a mixed-method approach that is particularly crucial for advancing our understanding of the role that structural factors as well as choice play in the lives of the poor in a changing society (see Newman and Massengill 2006).

Research and Policy Background

The study of context effects, including effects of neighborhoods, has a long history in the social sciences and, in particular, in sociology (Briggs 1997; Ellen and Turner 2003; Jencks and Mayer 1990; Small and Newman 2001; Tienda 1991). Prior research suggests several ways that residing in a particular neighborhood might affect employment specifically, whether directly or indirectly: via a spatial mismatch between job locations and workers' housing locations; through social networks; and through shifts in normative climate.

Spatial Mismatch

As economist John Kain's (1968) seminal work previewed, over the past generation, jobs have become increasingly decentralized in U.S. metropolitan areas—a pattern labeled "job sprawl"—while low-skill workers and low-cost housing have remained spatially concentrated in central city communities (Fernandez and Su 2004). Researchers generally conclude that spatial mismatch makes low-skill and minority workers (who have more limited housing choices in outlying areas) less likely to learn about job openings, more likely to face high commuting costs, more likely to quit when job locations shift significantly, and more likely to be rejected by employers based on residence in a stigmatized ghetto (reviews in Fernandez and Su 2004; Ihlanfeldt and Sjoquist 1998).

But since skill mismatches and other barriers also shape labor market outcomes, what might a shift in residence accomplish? In the nonexperimental Gautreaux desegregation program, which (in effect) assigned families to neighborhoods rather than to treatment groups, Popkin, Rosenbaum, and Meaden (1993) found that minority women who relocated from inner-city neighborhoods in Chicago to suburbs fifteen to thirty miles away were more likely to be employed, holding educational attainment and other factors equal, than counterparts who stayed within the city, though not at higher wages. Addressing the potential selection biases in those findings, more recent research has incorporated long-run administrative data on employment and welfare receipt and tested a variety of neighborhood traits rather than urbanicity alone; Keels et al. (2005) found that mothers who relocated to more racially integrated, nonpoor neighborhoods spent 7 percent less time on welfare, were employed at a rate 6 percent higher, and earned $2,200 more per year (on average) than women who relocated to poorer and more racially isolated areas. These results, while nonexperimental, strongly suggest that particular forms of relocation can positively affect the employment prospects of low-income, mostly low-skill mothers.

Social Networks

Networks can mediate both spatial matches and mismatches by shaping access to information, endorsements, and support. Many jobs are found through informal networks rather than more formal means (Granovetter 1974; Lin 2001), but the networks of the poor and disadvantaged tend to be more limited, strained, and insular than those of higher-income people (review in Briggs 1998). For example, in a study of public housing residents living near the Brooklyn waterfront, Kasinitz and Rosenberg (1996) found that physical proximity to the large concentration of high-wage jobs did little for the mostly African American poor in public housing who lacked social connections to the unions that brokered those jobs.

Relocation might enhance social resources, but for relocation to matter, one must be willing and able to make new contacts with usefully positioned individuals who are willing to provide aid (Briggs 1997; Smith 2005). One must also be willing to activate those ties to obtain such aid, yet there is some evidence that in the context of wary and often strained social relations, low-income blacks adopt an outlook of do-it-myself "defensive individualism," at least with nonkin contacts, which undermines such activation (see Rainwater 1970; Smith 2007). And movers might focus on their preexisting networks of kin, close friends, or other strong ties, as Stack's (1974) classic ethnography of mutual assistance networks among poor black mothers emphasized, rather than cast their social nets more widely in new neighborhoods.

Norms

Prior research suggests that high-poverty, racially isolated neighborhoods, particularly where joblessness is chronic and pervasive, may lose a strong culture of work—in the form of role models who demonstrate that work is viable and leads to a better life (Wilson 1987). Low-income black parents in the Gautreaux program reported new norms and capabilities for themselves and their children when they contrasted white, middle-income suburban neighborhoods with their former inner-city Chicago neighborhoods (Rosenbaum, DeLuca, and Tuck 2005). Some researchers have also suggested that living in stigmatized, socially isolated ghettos undermines the norms of interaction and the "soft skills" needed to succeed in mixed-race, lower-poverty employment contexts (Kirschenman and Neckerman 1991; Tilly et al. 2001)—that is, the cultural "toolkit" (Swidler 1986) or repertoire important for economic and social success.

Potential Losses and Barriers

Research suggests other reasons for caution as well. Relocated adults might lose contact with valuable coping resources—informal caregiving, small emergency loans, and other aid from social ties—that are particularly crucial for low-income people. Housing mobility might force a trade-off between one set of (familiar) social resources and another valuable-to-have-but-hard-to-come-by set (Briggs 1998). Also, those MTO adults who were working when they entered the program might lose valuable employment relationships and struggle to replace them, adding to the employment instability that the most disadvantaged appear to face as they enter or reenter the world of work (Herr and Wagner 2007). These risks, and the possible rewards of relocating as well, must be considered in the specific context in which low-skill, low-income single mothers look for work: safe, reliable, and inexpensive child care is hard to find; flexible transportation is critical and too often missing; and for many who live in public housing in high-poverty areas, which has become a housing of last resort for the ill and disabled poor, chronic illnesses—whether afflicting the job seeker or a family member or other loved one—represent particularly high barriers to work and overall life functioning (Popkin, Cunningham, and Burt 2005).

Exposure

One key necessary condition was taken for granted in launching MTO: that relocating to low-poverty areas would give families sufficient exposure to the "treatment" for measurable effects to register. But this exposure assumption included relatively stable residence in better locations. About one-third of U.S. renters move each year, and mobility rates have increased among low-skill workers in recent decades even as mobility has declined somewhat in the general population (C. Fischer 2002). Low-income people are also more likely than others to make what the Census Bureau terms involuntary moves, for example due to job loss or family emergency. Also, race, income, and life-cycle factors—but most of all race—shape the direction of these moves in important ways: blacks are far more likely than whites to fall back into a poor area after living in a nonpoor one (South and Crowder 1997). Over time, these differences add up to much longer spells of exposure to poor neighborhoods for blacks (Quillian 2003). This racialized dynamic appears to have persisted into the 1990s (Briggs and Keys 2005), in spite of the dramatic decline of extreme poverty concentration over the decade, suggesting that stable residence in low-poverty areas cannot be taken for granted, least of all for low-income minority renters.

Why Launch a Social Experiment?

Like other social experiments, MTO has evolved in the real world and not under controlled laboratory conditions (for an extended overview of MTO, see Gennetian et al. in this volume). First, about half of the experimental group did not successfully find private apartments in low-poverty areas, so discussions of the experiment's results may confound the question of how effective the treatment is *for those who received it* (the treatment-on-treated, or TOT effects) with that of *what shapes successful utilization* (which includes noncompliers, as reported in intent-to-treat or ITT effects). We report both TOT and ITT results in our quantitative component (see Gennetian et al. 2005). Second, per Sobel (2003), the conservative interpretation of MTO treatment effects, which employs ITT measures, is that they represent the difference between uneven treatment effects on the experimental group and *some* treatment effects, however modest, on the control group.[1] While Sobel presented methods of statistical adjustment, for example for bounding potential biases from interference, and recommended designing studies to randomize treatment only within groups that are isolated from one another, we do not aim to present unbiased estimates of treatment effects but rather to examine the causal mechanisms that plausibly underlie such effects.

Third, some MTO families who did successfully move to a low-poverty neighborhood moved on to poorer neighborhoods after the required year of residence, likely undermining many of the hoped-for social effects of "better" neighborhoods, which depend on exposure over time. Fourth, and in a related vein, about 70 percent of the control group had also moved out of public housing when an interim evaluation was conducted (see below), meaning that MTO controls do not serve as a fixed point of comparison for families who moved to low-poverty neighborhoods but rather as "cross-overs." Fifth, the geography of risk and opportunity shifted as the experiment evolved. Census data show, for example, that the MTO experiment group-complier neighborhoods became poorer in the 1990s even as the inner-city origin neighborhoods became generally safer and less poor (Orr et al. 2003). For these reasons, the treatment does not strictly conform to the stable unit treatment value assumption (SUTVA) of experimental science: the treatment has neither been stable over time nor perfectly standardized across participants (Rubin 1978). Instead, the MTO treatment experience reflects broad differences in observed residential exposure to particular kinds of neighborhoods over time.

Social experiments are imperfect, expensive, and challenging to implement according to *any* strict design, but they represent uncommon learning opportunities for society and for researchers. At the time of our fieldwork, and based on a wide range of measures, families in the MTO experimental group were still much more likely to be living in, and had lived for longer periods of time in, safer, lower-poverty areas, which they also perceived to be less disorderly, than families in the other treatment groups. MTO is a valuable mechanism for analyzing two important experiences for low-income, mostly minority families who previously lived in high-poverty public housing projects and who tend to be concentrated in poor and segregated places nationwide: (a) that of *living* in lower poverty neighborhoods for some period of time; and (b) that of *relocating*, after initial counseling and search assistance, to low-poverty neighborhoods, and then to a range of neighborhood types, while raising children and handling other life challenges.

MTO Employment Results So Far

Research on MTO has progressed over three distinct phases: site-specific, early-impact studies, conducted in the first few years after random assignment, using a variety of methodologies (see Goering and Feins 2003); an interim impacts evaluation, which included a large-scale qualitative interview study (Popkin, Harris, and Cunningham 2001), a structured survey and achievement testing of the program population, and collection of administrative data on this population at all five sites (Orr et al. 2003); and interim follow-on studies—quantitative, qualitative, and mixed method (our study and one other, focused on Baltimore and Chicago). In late 2006, HUD authorized a final impact evaluation to survey MTO participants in 2008–2009, about ten to twelve years after random assignment.

Early evidence concerning the experiment's employment effects was encouraging, if mixed. Within two to four years of random assignment, experimental-group compliers in Baltimore were 15 percent less likely than control-group families to be receiving welfare; using the ITT measure, the experimental group as a whole was significantly less likely than controls to be on welfare (Ludwig, Duncan, and Ladd 2003). However, comparable analysis for MTO families in Boston found no differences in either welfare recipiency or employment (Katz, Kling, and Leibman 2001).

Later, the interim evaluation found no significant impacts on employment, earnings, or receipt of public assistance across the five demonstration sites (see Table 11.1; Orr et al. 2003). Notably, about twice as many MTO adults were working in all three treatment groups. Researchers cautioned that market cycles and policy shifts—specifically, the strong job economy of the late 1990s and the shift from an entitlement-based welfare program to TANF—may have swamped any treatment effects of MTO at the interim mark.

Subsequent analyses have examined subgroup outcomes (by site, age, and other traits) and nonexperimental effects, for example the association between months residing in low-poverty areas (as a proxy for treatment intensity) and employment. These nonexperimental analyses highlight key predictors of higher employment rates and earnings for MTO adults, including age (younger is better), education, employment

Table 11.1. MTO Interim Impacts on Employment and Earnings

	Control Mean	Experimental vs. Control		Section 8 vs. Control	
		ITT	*TOT*	*ITT*	*TOT*
Adult employment and earnings (self-report)					
Currently employed (n = 3,517)	0.522	0.014 (0.021)	0.030 (0.044)	0.026 (0.023)	0.044 (0.039)
Currently employed full-time, i.e. 35 or more hours per week at all jobs (n = 3,488)	0.394	−0.001 (0.021)	−0.002 (0.044)	0.001 (0.023)	0.001 (0.044)
Currently employed with weekly earnings above poverty (n = 3,311)	0.329	−0.008 (0.020)	−0.017 (0.043)	0.016 (0.022)	0.026 (0.037)
Annual individual earnings in 2001 (n = 3,311)	$8,899	137 (449)	292 (957)	47 (495)	79 (829)
Adult employment and earnings (administrative data, n = 4,070)					
Annualized fraction of quarters employed, 1st through 4th years after random assignment	0.430	−0.017 (0.012)	−0.036 (0.025)	−0.001 (0.013)	−0.002 (0.021)
Annualized earnings, same period	$5,847	−215 (254)	−456 (539)	−55 (288)	−89 (470)
Youth employment and earnings, ages 14–19 (administrative data, n = 2,619)					
Fraction of quarters employed in 2001	0.222	0.006 (0.014)	0.014 (0.031)	0.018 (0.015)	0.029 (0.025)
Earnings during 2001	$1,366	77 (140)	173 (315)	170 (133)	277 (216)

Source: Orr et al. 2003, pp. 129, 130; adult survey and state unemployment insurance records (California, Illinois, Massachusetts, Maryland, New York). Includes adults randomly assigned through December 1, 1997.
Note: ITT = Intent-to-treat (includes compliers and noncompliers), TOT = Treatment-on-treated (compliers only). Control means and impact estimates are regression-adjusted with robust standard errors. (Standard errors are provided in parentheses.) None of the results reported here is statistically significant, using a standard of p < .05 on t-test.

status at program entry, disability status, and household composition (having teenagers in the household, who do not require adult supervision and who can provide it to younger siblings).

Using an alternative exposure-effects approach as well as a predicted-values simulation, Clampet-Lundquist and Massey (2006) presented nonexperimental analyses of the association between MTO employment outcomes and residence in neighborhoods that are both low in poverty and racially integrated. Emphasizing prior evidence that "non-poor black areas are not comparable socially or economically to the non-poor neighborhoods inhabited by other groups" (p. 8), the researchers noted that while Gautreaux achieved both economic and racial desegregation, MTO achieved only the former—and only for a time. Clampet-Lundquist and Massey found that 85 percent of the MTO population spent no time in an integrated (less than 30 percent minority), low-poverty census tract. We do not know whether those who are more likely to be employed and off welfare are simply more likely to live in more integrated, low-poverty areas or whether something about these areas contributed to their encouraging economic outcomes.[2] We strongly agree with these and other researchers, however, that the lack of strong treatment effects on employment in MTO cannot be reasonably interpreted as disconfirming neighborhood effects.

Data and Methods

The Three-City Study of Moving to Opportunity was designed to examine key questions about causal mechanisms and uneven treatment effects that emerged from the survey-based and largely statistical Interim Impacts Evaluation. We conducted our study in three of the five MTO metro areas: Boston, Los Angeles, and New York. To better understand why participants in social programs make the choices they do, as well as to understand variation within treatment groups, we employed mostly qualitative methods to focus on "how" and "why" questions. But as outlined below, quantitative analyses were also an important part of our work.

Our family-level data were collected in 2004 and 2005, about six to ten years after families' initial placement through the MTO program. We conducted 278 semi-structured, in-depth qualitative interviews with a stratified random sample of parents, adolescents, and young adults in 122 households. The sample included households from all three treatment groups, including compliers and noncompliers. We also launched "family-focused" ethnographic fieldwork (Burton 1997), visiting a subset of 39 control-group and experimental-group complier families an average of 10–12 times over a period of six to eight months. Both qualitative samples are quite representative of the much larger population of MTO families surveyed at the interim mark in terms of background traits, employment status, and a range of other social outcomes (Table 11.2). We modestly undersampled Hispanics and oversampled families on welfare. Based on refusal data for the ethnographic component, it appears likely that the latter were more available for repeat ethnographic visiting. They may also have been more motivated by the monetary incentives we offered for their participation. Consistent with our sampling strategy, the ethnographic sample overrepresents families still residing in low-poverty areas.

The qualitative interviews, which were conducted in English, Spanish, and Cambodian, let us cover a wide range of social outcomes (from very successful to highly distressed) for all three treatment groups, which is crucial for generating representative results. To enhance data validity and to extend our data, the ethnographic fieldwork added direct observation to what subjects report about their attitudes, choices, and outcomes. The ethnographic fieldwork also enabled us to ask key questions informally, as we built relationships with family members over months. This approach, combining informal interviewing and participant observation, provides a robust source of inferences about social processes and other causal mechanisms to complement formal interviews that are focused heavily on the outcomes themselves. Unlike more established traditions in ethnography, such as community, in-school, or peer-group studies, family-focused ethnography centers on developing rich, valid accounts of family-level decisions and outcomes, including efforts to support or advance children, elders, or other family members (Burton 1997).

Finally, we conducted what we call *scans* using census and administrative data to analyze the economic and social changes at the neighborhood, city, and metropolitan levels that are reshaping the geography of risks and resources for MTO families over time. To analyze spatial access to job growth and job creation, we integrated several data sets, following computational methods employed by Raphael (1998) and Mouw (2000). First, we estimated the number of new jobs paying less than $20,000 per year (as a proxy for skill-appropriateness) within five, ten, and twenty miles of MTO families in all three treatment groups. We computed two measures: total new jobs and net job growth as detailed below.

Data on business establishments come from Census Zip Business Patterns (BP), on earnings from the Census Transportation Planning Package (CTPP), Part 2, by place of work and industry, on overall turnover in the job type from Local Employment Dynamics (LED) data, and on MTO residential locations from Abt Associates tracking data for the pro-

Table 11.2. Descriptive Statistics: Three-City Interview and Ethnographic Samples Compared to Interim Evaluation Sample

	Interim Evaluation Sample (N = 2,720 households)	Qualitative Interview Sample (N = 122 households)	Ethnographic Sample (N = 39 households)
Demographic traits			
Adult female	98%	98%	95%
Children who are female	53%	53%	49%
Household head is black non-Hispanic	43%	54%	46%
Household head is Hispanic	46%	35%	39%
Family size: 2–4 children under 18	64%	68%	62%
Locational and social outcomes			
2000 Neighborhood poverty rate (2002 locations)			
Living in neighborhood less than 10% poor	8%	10%	14%
Living in neighborhood more than 30% poor	58%	50%	35%
Residential mobility: Moved 1 to 3 times	58%	61%	69%
Adult ever completed high school	37%	41%	36%
Adult employed	52%	55%	44%
Total household income (mean)	$16,703	$18,514	$16,278
Respondent or child receiving TANF	31%	40%	53%
Adult Body Mass Index (BMI, mean)	30	30	30
Adult psychological distress index (mean)	0.33	0.32	0.35
Child psychological distress index (mean)	0.27	0.21	0.22
Child ever arrested	12%	16%	28%
Youth risky behavior index (mean)	0.40	0.36	0.38

Note: The Interim Evaluation Sample here includes three of the five sites: Boston, Los Angeles, and New York. Column headers indicate total sizes for each sample; cell sizes vary somewhat due to missing data. Locations are as of the 2002 Interim Impacts Survey (Orr et al. 2003). TANF is Temporary Assistance to Needy Families. BMI of 30 or higher indicates obesity.

gram population. The LED data were not available for metro Boston or New York, so we limited these analyses to metro Los Angeles and, for comparison, Chicago (though we did no qualitative field work in the latter).

We conducted the analysis separately for four industries known to be major sources of entry-level jobs for low-skill workers (Newman 1999): retail trade, transportation and warehousing, healthcare and social assistance, and accommodation and food services, and then for the four industries combined. We calculated a low-wage net job growth indicator, by industry, for each MTO participant's zip code at the time of the interim survey as follows:

$$J_{mk} = \sum_{Z=1}^{N} T_p e_c l_p g_c, \; if \; d_{mp} < k,$$

where J_{mk} is the net growth in low-wage jobs within k distance of the MTO participant's interim survey zip code m, T_p is the number of establishments in zip code p, N is the number of zip codes, e_c is the ratio of employees to establishments in county c, l_p is the ratio of workers earning more than zero but less than \$20,000 per year (about twice the minimum-wage rate) to all workers with earnings in zip code p, g_c is the ratio of the net number of jobs gained to the number of workers who were employed by the same employer in both the current and previous year in county c, zip code p is in county c, and d is distance from the centroid of zip code m to the centroid of job location zip code p. For counties more than sixty miles from MTO baseline zip codes (i.e. zip codes at time or random assignment), g_c is a proxy value calculated as the ratio of the median difference between the current and previous employment of the counties within sixty miles of MTO baseline zip codes, to the median number of workers who were employed by the same employer in both the current and previous year of the counties within sixty miles of MTO baseline zip codes. A similar approach is used to calculate the number of new, low-wage jobs, for each industry, within k distance of the MTO participant's interim survey zip code.

To convert the tract-level Census Transportation Planning Package (CTPP) data (used to calculate l_p) to the zip code level, we applied a transformation to estimate the portion of a tract that is within a zip code, then weighted the tract-level data accordingly. Therefore, the zip code-level number of workers is equal to the sum of the number of workers in all overlapping tracts, weighted by the portions of the tracts that fall within the zip code. Next, we applied a distance equation to calculate the distance between the MTO residential zip code centroids and that of each job-location zip code, and then we summed the new, low-wage jobs in all zip codes within the specified distance to produce a single low-wage job growth indicator for each MTO participant. We report single-site ITT and TOT results for Los Angeles and Chicago.[3]

The integration of distinct types of data is crucial for generating richer, more valid results and actionable specifics to guide decision makers. Mixed-method approaches are also crucial for building better theory, over time, from a base of complex and mixed results (Rossman and Wilson 1994), including those that emerge in social experiments (Michalopoulos 2005).

Results

Spatial Mismatch

In the two study sites that were traditionally monocentric metro areas with dense central business districts, greater Boston and New York City, the assisted relocation made by experimental compliers was typically to a moderate-income neighborhood in the outer ring of the central city (e.g., the northeast Bronx) or an inner suburb proximate to the city (e.g., along Boston's south and north shores, which include many working-class and lower middle-class neighborhoods), not to more distant or affluent suburbs. In sprawling and polycentric Los Angeles, patterns were more mixed: compliers moved to moderate-income neighborhoods in nearby southern suburbs, as well as the San Fernando Valley (to the north), Long Beach to the southwest, and more distant, rapidly expanding eastern suburbs and satellite cities, mainly in Riverside and San Bernardino counties, where racial diversity is growing rapidly. Relocating generally meant leaving behind a denser concentration of low-wage jobs—in Boston and New York, areas with strong transit access, too—for low job density, more car-reliant areas served by a few bus lines.

Table 11.3 shows our results for Los Angeles and Chicago (the two sites with data available for this spatial analysis). The experimental group in Los Angeles lived in neighborhoods with fewer low-wage jobs, less net job growth, and less job creation within 5 and 10 miles of their housing locations than their control group counterparts. There was no significant difference in job concentrations within one mile in Los Angeles, however, and no apparent impact at all in Chicago, where the volume of low-wage jobs and job growth are dramatically lower overall. Section 8 compliers moved to locations with essentially the same number of low-wage job opportunities as control-group counterparts. As for spatial mismatch, these results confirm that relocating to a low-poverty census tract outside the inner city through the MTO program did not,

Table 11.3. MTO Interim Impacts on Spatial Access to Low-wage Jobs and Job Openings, as of Most Recent Residential Location

	Control *mean*	*Experimental* *vs. control*		*Section 8* *vs. control*	
		ITT	TOT	ITT	TOT
Los Angeles					
Net job growth within 5 miles of residence	7,900 485	−3,306* 588	−5,166* 919	−998 671	−1,313 883
New jobs within 5 miles of residence	21,208 1,301	−8,890* 1,578	−13,891* 2,466	−2,699 1,800	−3,551 2,368
Jobs within 5 miles of residence[a]	324,240 19,874	−135,855* 24,108	−212,273* 37,669	−41,178 27,494	−54,182 36,176
Net job growth within 10 miles of residence	13,196 482	−1,387* 653	−2,167* 1,020	−300 671	−395 883
New jobs within 10 miles of residence	35,398 1,296	−3,731* 1,757	−5,830* 2,745	−829 1,806	−1,091 2,376
Jobs within 10 miles of residence[a]	541,833 19,834	−57,232* 26,892	−89,425* 42,019	−12,631 27,643	−16,620 36,372
Chicago					
Net job growth within 5 miles of residence	107 4	−4 5	−12 15	−6 6	−9 9
New jobs within 5 miles of residence	882 33	−43 43	−126 126	−44 45	−66 67
Jobs within 5 miles of residence[a]	18,804 679	−936 894	−2,753 2,629	−801 935	−1,196 1,396
Net job growth within 10 miles of residence	392 10	−8 15	−24 44	−16 14	−24 21
New jobs within 10 miles of residence	3,176 82	−85 116	−250 341	−128 113	−191 169
Jobs within 10 miles of residence[a]	66,656 1,731	−1,741 2,453	−5,121 7,215	−2,674 2,376	−3,991 3,546

Sources: Census Zip Business Patterns (1998, 2002), Census Transportation Planning Package (2000), Local Employment Dynamics (2001, 2003). Abt Associates geocoded tracking data for MTO households.
* $p < .05$ on t-test. In each number pair, the standard error is provided directly below the measure of interest.
[a] Figures for jobs within 5 and 10 miles are observed measures, not estimates.
Note: ITT = Intent-to-treat (includes compliers and noncompliers), TOT = Treatment-on-treated (compliers only).

in fact, mean relocating to a job-rich zone, at least not on average, and that starting points and changes in the spatial organization of low-wage jobs are highly context (metro) specific.

Interview Findings on Spatial Mismatch

MTO mothers in the experimental group balanced competing concerns about safety, access to employment, and access to child care in different ways, and each factor had important implications for the quality of their housing locations as platforms for employment success. In effect, the challenge for these low-income, low-skill parents, most of them single mothers, was lining up spatial matches that included jobs, housing, and vital job *support*, especially reliable child care that was generally obtained within networks of reciprocal, but often unstable, support (see Henly 2002).

About one in seven mothers in the experimental group specifically identified the loss of convenient access to public transit as a price they paid to get out of the projects to safer neighborhoods. For example, when we asked Nicole, a mother in the Boston experimental complier group, how her current, low-poverty neighborhood compared to the one left behind in terms of worries and stress, she replied, "The stress here is more just transportation issues. How am I going to get from here to the doctor's today? . . . I don't have money for a bus, which is an hour-and-a-half walk. And if it's pouring rain and cold, with two babies, you can't walk an hour to a bus stop anyway. In South Boston and Dorchester, I didn't have worries like that. Um, but it was just more concern for my kid's safety." While most cited safety and security, not better job or school opportunities, as their top reasons for moving, a handful of MTO adults (about one in ten), when asked why they had chosen their current neighborhood, specifically mentioned relocating to be closer to jobs they already had. In New York, where participants in the experimental group did realize a significant gain in earnings over their control group counterparts, working participants had somewhat higher skill levels and more work experience. They held jobs that appear to offer more upward mobility as well. They are certified child care providers, paraprofessionals, retail managers, teachers, and even graduate students; some have left housing assistance altogether. Rhadiya, for example, a mother in the New York experimental group who used her voucher to reduce her commute time, found she could earn more:

Rhadiya: I started while I was in Manhattan and then I moved here where I was closer to work, which was a plus for me. Yeah, it's like now 10 minutes [away].

Interviewer:	How far was it when you were in Manhattan? How long did it take you?
R:	It took me like an hour and fifteen minutes.
I:	Oh, so it must be a big relief.
R:	Yes, definitely. Yeah, and I also do a lot of overtime. Like my annual salary was like 24, 26, but that year I made close to $40,000.

Although these women were indeed more likely than others in the program to succeed "on their own," the assisted relocation accelerated their mobility prospects and helped them achieve work-related strategies in which place was one key element among several.

However, the balancing acts these women sustain are extraordinary, and progress is generally in stutter steps, as the innovative Project Match in Chicago has long found (Herr and Wagner 2007). For example, Sabrina, a mother of two in the Boston experimental complier group, left public housing in the inner-city neighborhood of Roxbury, moved to Quincy, an inner suburb to the south of Boston, moved back to the inner city near her old "project" neighborhood, and finally returned to Quincy, where she has lived using a housing voucher ever since. She described the effect of the lower-poverty Quincy environment on her life as a single mother: "It gives you a sense of confidence. It's a better area and it's up to you to decide what you want to change. I don't feel like my life is in any danger, I never had that feeling here. Safety was a big worry there [in the projects]." Sabrina emphasized the importance of her living environment for setting out to work; her case emphasizes place as an enabler, though not a guarantor, of job prospects.

Anique, a mother in the Los Angeles experimental complier group whom we introduced at the beginning of this chapter, had more trouble aligning steady work, affordable housing, and child care, though her rental voucher and relocations helped. Her pre-move employment as a telemarketer and bill collector helped her find better work as she moved, but in a turbulent labor market, she suffered repeated spells of unemployment and financial hardship, including the loss of her housing voucher (when her attempt to purchase a small home failed) and bankruptcy. After eventually landing a job in Riverside County, some forty miles east of Compton, Anique moved to Perris, where she had an aunt and uncle to help look after her children. But when her relatives left the state, Anique and her daughter Clara had to move to Long Beach to live with Anique's mother. Then Anique was laid off from her job, thanks to company relocation, and so they stayed put for almost two years. "It was hard to even get a place," she says. "Everything just went downhill, downhill." Based on her work experience, she was hired as a child support investigator in Riverside County, but her daily commute from Long Beach was about seventy miles each way, which often meant leaving the house before 5 A.M. and having very little time with her daughter each day. Anique gradually saved enough to rent an apartment in Riverside, right across the street from her job. However, because they were now far from the social support Anique's mother and sister had provided, Clara, now eleven, was home alone after school each day. Anique has found some support services nearby and feels her apartment complex is quiet and safe, but she also reports experiencing racial harassment in the neighborhood. Anique is a revelatory case: a mother whose job, housing, and support locations remained unstable for a long period of time, challenging her to bring them into alignment, although she was an instant success at the narrow task of completing the program-assisted relocation.

Kimberlyn, the second Los Angeles experimental complier we introduced early on, faced one set of struggles in her low-poverty neighborhood in the San Fernando Valley: lacking credentials, work experience, and confidence in herself and feeling isolated and unwelcome. Moving back to the inner city led to a different set of struggles, as the child care her sister provided abruptly disappeared, and Kimberlyn could not manage to complete training and find steady work. She inquired widely about jobs and training opportunities, and she began, but never completed, training in cosmetology and other fields, as well as an associate's degree program. Constantly needy family members, now near at hand, and her son's dangerous school added to her stress and anxiety.

In general, this range of patterns underscores the role of neighborhoods as locations, important sometimes for what they allow one to access from the neighborhood (including child care and after-school programs, a reasonable commute to work or training, etc.), not as social worlds (significant as ecologies for human development through social interaction or influence through observation). In the range of balancing acts outlined above, while neighborhood locations were sometimes important, neighbors were not, at least for MTO adults—whether as working role models, sources of job referral, or providers of child care or other supports for work. We turn to these and other functions of networks next.

Social Networks

At the interim point, only 16 percent of experimental compliers reported that they got their current or most recent job through a referral provided by a friend, relative, or acquaintance in the current neighborhood. Networks are just one method of job search, of course. Like others in the market, MTO job seekers also used newspaper ads, the internet, and walk-in applications to find their jobs. But where networks did play a role, MTO adults in our qualitative samples were more likely to get useful referrals from job training program staff or fellow job seekers they met in those programs, and from friends or co-workers, than from neighbors. Here again, those who entered MTO with some work history, and the confidence and contacts that come with a history of job holding, were at an advantage. Some adults also got useful referrals from kin or from another trusted source, such as a pastor. The lack of neighbor-sourced job referrals in low-poverty areas, meanwhile, reflected a wariness about forming meaningful ties to neighbors, a lack of structural opportunities to form more ties, and a lack of willingness to activate ties to neighbors for help. As for hoped-for but largely unrealized gains in social capital, those who relocated rarely converted their lower-poverty address, even if they managed to keep it for years, into significant new social resources.

Like suburbanites across the country, MTO parents reported that their low-poverty neighborhoods were quieter and safer than the inner city. The gains in safety and mental health cannot be overstated, as they contributed significantly to participants' life satisfaction. But without formal institutions to connect them to neighbors and given ongoing mobility, which undercuts the formation of relationships in new places, interactions were fleeting. In general, however, there was little to encourage neighboring. Mothers described neighbors left behind (in public housing) as social but often untrustworthy, whereas neighbors in low-poverty areas were trustworthy but not social. MTO families attributed this to their new neighbors' busier, work-oriented lifestyles or their preferences for keeping to themselves.

Furthermore, preestablished networks, kin ties in particular, dominated the social lives of MTO adults and their children. And these were overwhelmingly disadvantaged networks, with adults that were often poorly educated, unstably employed, and, in the case of many male contacts, struggling to overcome the employment effects of a criminal record and incarceration.

Norms

Wilson's (1987) influential hypotheses about social isolation and ghetto poverty emphasized the importance of normative attachment to the labor force and the habits of regular work. Other researchers have emphasized the importance of noncognitive skills and routines, which are often socially learned—that is, cultural. Beyond gains in neighborhood safety and feelings of security and calm, a number of experimental compliers who made it to low-poverty areas—like counterparts in the suburban Gautreaux group (Rosenbaum, DeLuca, and Tuck 2005)—took great pride in their neighbors' working. Parents in the ethnographic sample who stressed this specifically emphasized the importance of this climate of working people for their children's healthy development. A few explicitly complained about the lack of commitment to getting ahead among those able to work in the projects and about the discouragement to working. For example, when we asked Jackie, an experimental complier in Los Angeles, whether she believed that most of her neighbors worked, she replied as follows, emphasizing the contrast with the social environment in which she had grown up in the Jordan Downs public housing project,

> Yeah. I see people leaving out, because I used to go to work, construction for security, at like five in the morning. And I see people leaving out 4:00, 4:30. And then you can hear the gates opening and close, the cars just going in and out, or walking through the hallways, the aisle-ways. I think mostly everybody get up and go to work. Except the older people . . . [Whereas in the projects] I think that's what really made me get a job. Because I grew up seeing everybody that *don't* work. And all I used to say is, "I want a check with my name on it." And everybody used to say, "You want a check?" I say, "Watch. When I grow up, I'm going to get me a check with my name on it." Nobody believed me.

In this instance, the individual considered her prior neighbors' disbelief a motivator. That is, she wanted to prove them wrong. Like about one-quarter of movers, Jackie differentiated herself from those whom she perceived to lack the right values or get-ahead attitude and motivation—a logic that the ethnography of low-wage work and community life in poor neighborhoods has uncovered since the 1960s (Hannerz 1969; Newman 1999).

Not all MTO movers described their public housing neighborhoods as hostile to work. A handful of MTO parents specifically argued that, in the post-welfare reform era, everybody "has to work" regardless of neighborhood environment. This underscores the notion that cultures are not static or monolithic—with regard to work or other life domains —in even the poorest neighborhoods (Small and Newman 2001). MTO families, who are overwhelmingly renters still (90 percent as of the interim survey), commonly move on within a few years or less. As we noted in the previous section, frequent moving is hardly a recipe for forming useful social ties in new neighborhoods. Demonstration effects alone may be a boon to the next generation, however. The interim survey found that adolescent girls in the experimental group were 22 percent more likely to be in school and 16 percent less likely to be idle than counterparts in the control group. When asked about the positive influences of their low-poverty neighborhood on girls, some mothers in the ethnographic sample, which we visited repeatedly to understand attitudes toward childrearing and perceptions of neighborhood, specifically emphasized the climate of work. Jackie, for example, told us that "It gives the kids a different atmosphere, because it's a lot of working people out here. And everybody's always busy. If they're not in school [or] working, they're doing something. So you never really just see anybody just hanging around." Brianna, also a mother in the Los Angeles experimental complier group, put it this way, emphasizing what she and her daughter notice about neighbors: "Well because she sees like our neighbors to go to work, come home. Just seeing, I think a lot of people [work] . . . that's why you see the people leave and go to work, you know. I see a lot of that, and I think she look up to that. You know, she watch that. She's very observant."

Two young adults in the experimental complier group show how relocation *can* dramatically expand young people's everyday experiences of cultural expectations and with them a cultural repertoire, including class manners and other "soft skills" to enhance employment prospects and upward mobility. These cases also reflect the strains of acculturating to new expectations. We cannot know how prevalent these patterns are in the MTO population, but we believe fine-grained data on social processes are important as researchers seek a better grasp of neighborhood effects, and relocation effects specifically, on young people.

Kaliyan is an 18-year-old freshman in the California State University system. Born to Cambodian refugee parents living in public housing, she has moved often since childhood, from the projects in South Los Angeles to a series of communities in the San Fernando and San Gabriel Valleys that ranged from middle-income, predominantly white to ethnically and economically diverse. Her peer relationships, formed mostly in school, ranged from middle- and upper-income teens driven (in her view) by brand-name consumption to gangs of low-income Asian youth she turned to, in the poorer Valley communities, to help her fit it. Kaliyan has had to recognize and respond to varied social boundaries. Though she still struggles with being different, Kaliyan has developed racially diverse friendships, skills at fitting in, and valuable knowledge about the power of attainment networks. She has held several jobs in retail and appears to confidently use her budding jobnetworks to get better jobs. Kaliyan has even pledged a sorority, because she heard that "they're good for networks and life-long connections." She has come quite a social distance from the South L.A. projects.

Esperanza is a 23-year-old Latina whose family left the South L.A. projects for Canoga Park, a middle-income area in the San Fernando Valley. She remembers learning a different "way to be" in the Valley: how to be "proper" rather than "ghetto." There was "less drama" and less picking fights in the Valley, she recalls, teachers took more of an interest in her, and she learned how to behave around "people who are more upper class," including "sitting up straight." She believes that this helped her when she decided to enter the Marines and had to deal with its strict demands. In the Valley, Esperanza had a diverse group of friends and she speculates that her exposure to racial diversity there also made her military experience easier. After completing her Marine service, Esperanza moved to a southern suburb about a half-hour drive from her family, now back in L.A. She marks her move there, initially to live with a boyfriend while she holds down several part-time jobs, as a step up from her family's life in L.A. "I'm not going backwards," she says.

Finally, the normative dimension of employment includes the "rightful" place of work in our lives. A small minority of the experimental compliers—about one in ten—who were not working at the time of our in-depth qualitative interviews emphasized this normative belief about work: their desire to focus on their children and the security of public assistance income compared to an insecure paycheck with no benefits. In this view, which other researchers have documented (Edin and Lein 1997), work is associated with insecurity and shortchanging one's children, not with advancement or self-respect. And while discussions of pro-work norms generally assume *readiness* to work, about a fifth of MTO families highlighted major barriers that made them, in effect, not ready at all.

Job Readiness

Many MTO adults face major barriers to work that were not directly addressed by the intervention. It is not clear that changes in spatial access to jobs, jobs networks, or normative support for work *could* have significantly benefited those who were not job ready. Nor is it clear that changes experienced through a relocation-only intervention could make them more job ready. Almost 40 percent of MTO participants were not in the labor force (neither working nor looking for work) at the time of the interim survey (Orr et al. 2003). These patterns reflect the severe disadvantage that characterized families living in high-poverty public housing—in some of the toughest neighborhoods of the target cities—by the early 1990s (Popkin, Cunningham, and Burt 2005). About 23 percent of MTO participants received SSI at the interim mark, a benefit primarily granted to individuals who are unable to work because of chronic health problems. Although experimental movers did experience reductions in depression and obesity over the study period, just under a fifth of these adults reported that problems such as depression, asthma, diabetes, heart problems, and obesity continued to interfere with their ability to look for work or keep a job after their initial move.

Conclusion

Our findings document key mechanisms through which relocation from high- to low-poverty areas can contribute to economic advancement while challenging still-prevailing notions about neighborhood effects and segregation. These findings also underscore the range of challenges facing families at the bottom of two markets—housing and labor—in America, as well as how shifting place of residence fits into broader strategies to line up "matches" in both domains and to needed social supports as well. In part for this reason, low-poverty areas, while less risky in a variety of ways, are not clearly advantageous for poor people across the board, as influential work on concentrated poverty has emphasized (Wilson 1987).

First, lining up viable jobs-housing matches was difficult for the mostly low-skill single mothers in the MTO experiment because basic *supports* for work, such as geographically accessible child care at low or no cost, were often unstable and sometimes far-flung, not just because both the low-wage job market and low-rent housing market were so bruising and so much in flux for those with few skills and other resources. Perhaps it is not surprising that prior research on the spatial mismatch hypothesis, dominated by a more static conception of housing location and generally ignoring the geography of informal social support for the poor altogether, has failed to uncover the importance of (a) the jobs-housing-support triangle and (b) the instability of each of its nodes. But in our view, this is a much more powerful way of conceptualizing spatial access to economic opportunity for low-skill single parents than the extant model. The latter focuses more narrowly on the commute from home to work and the location of job referral networks.

Second, assisted relocation actually led to significant loss as measured by the number of proximate entry-level jobs and net job growth in key employment sectors, at least in greater Los Angeles between 1998 and 2002. L.A.'s much greater job growth than Chicago over that period probably factors into the treatment effects observed for the former. We cannot rule out the possibility that moving farther away from large concentrations of low-skill competitors for those jobs had a countervailing effect. But our spatial results underscore how context-specific and cyclical spatial matches may be for those who move out of inner-city areas as entry-level job centers expand and contract around the metro area.

Third, we detected no social capital gains linked to moving outside the ghetto. Even where MTO movers were comparatively successful in the job market, a lack of joining (participation in area associations), along with very limited neighboring—both to be expected of very low-income renters who move about and express a general wariness about closer involvement with neighbors—truncated any social capital that might have been built through having more advantaged neighbors. Losses for some families, meanwhile, were in the form of lost or reduced child care from kin, although kin remained at the center of most of these families' social lives. Those lives remained insular in large part because MTO families' most important preestablished contacts (their relatives) remained so disadvantaged and often so needy. The persistence of these ties, the low rates of group joining, and the lack of localism (to the neighborhood of residence) in active ties dominated the picture.

Fourth, and conversely, there is some evidence that higher rates of employment and lower rates of idleness in low-poverty neighborhoods could be a source of demonstration effects for MTO children and that some MTO youth who moved as teens or preteens developed broader social networks and cultural repertoires, with positive effects on their soft skills through exposure to racial and economic diversity along with new expectations, in new neighborhoods and schools. But acculturating to new expectations posed strains and dilemmas that remained with these young people into adulthood. These findings are consistent with interview evidence on Gautreaux parents' perceptions of expectations in their advantaged neighborhoods (Rosenbaum, DeLuca, and Tuck 2005), and add young people's perceptions about the informal rules for fitting in and how those rules have served them in the transition to college or the world of work. Our findings underline how a given location may be an effective economic platform for children but *not* their adult single parents. This specific distinction has not been examined in earlier research on the importance of life stage for neighborhood effects—research that tends to emphasize the resource richness of higher-income areas across the board.

We see important lessons here for policy, beginning with *targeting* and extending to the *content* of interventions that include housing mobility. First, the evidence suggests that a family's capacity to take advantage of opportunities that relocation offers depends on critical attributes and circumstances, some of which may require intensive assessment up front. For those who began with advantages, there is evidence of relocation accelerating a family's exit from a more disadvantaged state. This underscores the value of strategies that help families move up a stepladder of successes and avoid the downward spirals caused by a single setback—such as the loss of free child care, a spike in rent forcing an onerous commute or cohabiting with a burdensome relative.

Second, relocation assistance alone is clearly insufficient to promote many disadvantaged families, particularly those headed by low-skill single mothers, forward toward greater economic security or self-sufficiency. In the future, assisted housing mobility programs could expand on MTO's positive but limited employment effects by improving participants' access to job-related resources, including job centers, training, and supports, including child care and transportation. Interventions could also target job-growth zones, not to mention high-performing school districts, directly. The least job-ready and those poised for upward mobility clearly need quite different supports. The most severely disadvantaged of the roughly one million very low-income households in public housing may be ill served by relocation strategies, no matter what they include; that group may need service-rich supportive housing or similar in-place approaches.

Third, to help the "move-ready" participants stay in better neighborhoods once they get to them, mobility programs could extend counseling services beyond the first year and expand the supply of stable, affordable housing in strong locations, including areas where jobs are growing. The tight housing markets in which MTO unfolded have not offered most of the motivated low-income families the real prospect of long-run residence outside ghetto neighborhoods. Fourth and finally, assisted housing mobility programs should offer participants active connections to institutions in their new neighborhoods that can link the movers to more and better jobs, whether directly (through job matching) or indirectly (by brokering ties to useful social contacts).

Some post-Katrina relocation brokered such connections, and we need more systematic evidence on these and other efforts to help poor people move *and* succeed. Assisted housing mobility is no cure-all for ghetto poverty, and it is not for everyone. But some gains were impressive, and research has now reality-tested MTO's "great expectations." The limits of this particular relocation-only demonstration program for the inner-city poor should not dissuade policymakers and practitioners from building on the gains and making bolder, more savvy efforts in the future.

Chapter 12

Teens, Mental Health, and Moving to Opportunity

Susan Clampet-Lundquist

Place matters. It affects job opportunities, public school quality, social networks, and housing value. Researchers have explored the relationship between residence and these outcomes while conducting community studies and while calculating the consequences of racial residential segregation in the United States. Placing individuals in their spatial context also allows us to consider the role of community influences on mental health (Bronfenbrenner 1986). The focus of this chapter is the relationship between neighborhoods and the mental health of adolescents.

Young people living in low-income urban neighborhoods face a number of stressors in their environments, including exposure to violence and disorder. Past research suggests the possibility of a link between such stress and mental health. Researchers have found a positive association between neighborhood-related stress and depression (D'Imperio, Dubow, and Ippolito 2000), ecological risk and depressive symptoms (Prelow et al. 2004), neighborhood violence and aggression (Guerra et al. 1995; Attar, Guerra, and Tolan 1994), and neighborhood hazards and antisocial behavior (Seidman et al. 1998). Aneshensel and Sucoff (1996) found that youth in Los Angeles who perceived their neighborhood context as filled with physical and social disorder were significantly more likely to score higher on depression, anxiety, oppositional defiant disorder, and conduct disorder measures.

In this chapter, I analyze survey and interview data for adolescents who participated in the Moving to Opportunity (MTO) demonstration, a federal housing mobility initiative that provided an opportunity for families to move from public housing into a low-poverty neighborhood. My research replicates the finding of previous MTO studies which found a different experimental effect on teen mental health by gender. However, the mixed-methods approach in this paper generates a more complicated story for a sample of MTO teenagers in one of the five MTO sites, Baltimore. In the in-depth interviews, those teens whose families moved to low-poverty neighborhoods ("experimental complier families") reported much less serious levels of family conflict, including abuse, compared to teens in the control group, and were less likely to discuss drug trafficking and gun violence in their neighborhoods. Perhaps most important, the analysis of qualitative data uncovered a potential mental health benefit for boys who moved to low-poverty neighborhoods. Forty percent of the boys in the control group discussed serious problems with anger, compared to none of the boys in the experimental complier group. Given the reduced conflict in the family and neighborhood contexts, this finding is not surprising, but it points to a critical area where we may explore benefits for teen boys from housing mobility programs.

MTO and Mental Health: Findings from the Interim Evaluation

Four to seven years after MTO, experimental group families (those families receiving vouchers which could only be used for an initial move to a neighborhood with a poverty rate below 10 percent) were living in neighborhoods with significantly lower poverty rates, on average, than families in the control group (31 percent vs. 39 percent). (For an extended overview of MTO and the interim evaluation, see Gennetian et al. in this volume.) Adults in the experimental group reported feeling safer and seeing less neighborhood disorder, compared to their control counterparts. Thus, given the relationship between community disorder and mental health, one would expect to see a relationship between increased neighborhood safety, decreased incivilities, and improved mental health among teens. However, while there were positive mental health effects for the experimental group girls, who scored significantly lower than control girls on scales of psychological distress and generalized anxiety, there were no significant differences between boys in the experimental and control groups. Analysis of the survey also revealed differences in risk behavior, as experimental girls were less likely to report certain risk behaviors than control girls, but the opposite was true for experimental boys (Orr et al. 2003).

These findings compare the experimental group as a whole to the control group as a whole, using intent-to-treat estimates, which are described in more detail in the methods section. Across all five sites, however, less than half (47 percent) of the experimental group actually used their voucher to move (compliers). Most of these movers had subsequently moved back to poorer neighborhoods, though not the high-poverty neighborhoods they lived in at baseline. Furthermore, 70 percent of the control group had moved in the years since signing up for MTO. Therefore, it is important to understand that we are not comparing an experimental group whose members all moved to and remained in low-poverty neighborhoods with a control group whose members all remained in their initial neighborhoods. One must be cautious in interpreting MTO findings as evidence of the presence or absence of neighborhood effects associated with movement from high- to low-poverty neighborhoods. Rather, these findings tell us what we can expect from a housing mobility initiative of the MTO type. From the results cited above, we know such an initiative can dramatically improve the neighborhood context for those who have the chance to move to a low-poverty neighborhood and can positively affect mental health and risk behaviors for some more than others.

Methods Used in This Study

I take a mixed-methods approach in examining mental health and stressors among teens in Baltimore. Quantitative data from the MTO Interim Survey were analyzed within an experimental design and with a standardized survey instrument. Qualitative interview data, on the other hand, offer richly detailed narratives from a small sample of teens, from which we can derive a deeper understanding of the processes that may have taken place as a result of this housing mobility initiative.

Quantitative Analysis

All families who participated in MTO were surveyed at baseline, before random assignment. Four to seven years after random assignment, researchers with the MTO Interim Survey fielded in-person surveys with adults and children (8–19 years old) (see Orr et al. 2003 for a detailed description of the data collection and analysis). The overall effective response rate for the youth survey, given to individuals 12 to 19 years old, was 89 percent. The survey data for individuals 14–19 years old in Baltimore were used in this analysis.[1] I focus on the experimental treatment effect of MTO, so I have not included teens in the traditional voucher group. My sample size is 283.[2]

Comparing average outcomes of all teenagers whose families were assigned to the experimental and control groups yields what are called intent-to-treat (ITT) estimates, which identify the causal effect of offering families the vouchers and residential mobility services made available through the experimental treatment. Not all families in the

Table 12.1. Comparison of Psychological Distress Levels of Experimental and Control Youth
(14–19), by Gender for Baltimore

	Females		Males		
	(1) *Average score, controls*	*(2)* *Difference in experimental/ control scores E-C*	*(3)* *Average score, controls*	*(4)* *Difference in experimental/ control scores E-C*	*(5)* *Difference in treatment effect between males and females*
Psychological distress index	.374	−.041 (.066)	.192	.111* (.058)	.153* (.091)

Source: MTO Interim Survey Data.
* $p < 10$.
$N = 185$.
Robust standard errors in parentheses.

experimental group took up the offer, so ITT estimates average together the impacts of those who moved with those who did not. Because of random assignment, we can presume that the control group would have exhibited similar take-up behavior had they been offered the voucher.[3]

I calculated the ITT effect of the MTO treatment on the psychological distress index using ordinary least squares regression, controlling for a set of covariates representing pre-random assignment (baseline) characteristics.[4] The psychological distress index is the fraction of six questions to which an individual provides a "yes" answer. Youth were asked if they had felt the following at least some of the time in the past thirty days: so depressed nothing could cheer you up, nervous, restless or fidgety, hopeless, like everything was an effort, or worthless.

Table 12.1 displays the results. There is no statistically significant difference in psychological distress for females in the experimental and control groups (column 2). However, males in the experimental group scored higher on the psychological distress index ($p<.10$) than males in the control group (column 4). The last column (5) in the table shows a significant difference in treatment effect by gender.

The basic premise of MTO and other housing mobility initiatives is that moving from high-poverty and into low-poverty neighborhoods can improve the well-being of families. This dramatic change in neighborhoods was experienced by the experimental compliers, the group I focus on in the qualitative analysis. Table 12.2 shows unweighted means on the psychological distress index scale for the experimental group, broken down by complier status, and the control group in Baltimore.

Table 12.2. Mean of Psychological Distress Index at Interim Survey for Experimental and Control Group Adolescents (14–19), Baltimore, Unweighted

	Experimental Group		*Control Group*
	Complier	*Noncomplier*	
Female	.314	.346	.348
Male	.258	.312	.220

$N = 218$.
Source: MTO Interim Survey data.

This table differs from Table 12.1 in that the complier status is separated, the means are not regression-adjusted (no baseline covariates are included as controls), nor are the means adjusted for siblings from the same households. Both of the experimental noncomplier groups (male and female), which had neighborhood poverty rates similar to the control groups at the time of the Interim Survey, have higher mean levels of psychological distress than the complier groups. This could certainly be related to household differences at baseline, but it could also be associated with continuing to live in higher-poverty communities.

What is unusual in this table is that the control male mean is so low. This may be related to an issue that Kling, Liebman, and Katz (2007a) found in their analysis of the MTO Interim Survey data for all five sites, which should serve as a caveat in interpreting findings. Rates of such outcomes as substance use and injuries were much lower for males in the control group than for males in a nationally representative survey, the National Longitudinal Survey of Youth 1997, whereas there was not a similar divergence for females in the control group. Furthermore, males in the experimental group who participated in the MTO Interim Survey had a higher level of behavior and other problems at baseline than males in the control group. This difference in the male experimental group appears to have been an artifact of sampling at the time of the Interim Survey, rather than a difference at the time of random assignment (Kling, Liebman, and Katz 2007a). Regardless, the lower than average incidence of problems for control males, and higher baseline incidence of problems for males in the experimental group may affect the findings in this analysis. Furthermore, differences found in the qualitative analysis may be underestimating the impact of a move to a low-poverty neighborhood, given the already lower level of distress for control males.

Qualitative Data Analysis

Interview data were collected as part of a qualitative study in Baltimore six to nine years after random assignment, from July 2003 to June 2004.[5]

We took a stratified random subsample of 149 families across the three MTO program groups. Heads of household were interviewed, and in households containing at least one teenager between 14 and 19, we attempted to interview a teen as well. For households with more than one teen, we randomly selected a "focal youth." Seventy-four percent of those teens sampled participated, for a total of 83 adolescent respondents.

In Baltimore, 58 percent of the experimental group used their vouchers to move to a low-poverty neighborhood, though almost all have since moved on to other neighborhoods. The qualitative analysis uses in-depth interview data from teens in the experimental complier group—those whose families used their vouchers—and the control group in Baltimore to explore the differences in mental health and stressors, six to nine years after random assignment. Thus, the analysis omits teens from the experimental noncomplier group. This analysis is not a direct replication of the survey analysis of psychological distress, as different measures were used. Moreover, this analysis is not experimental since, with the omission of the experimental noncomplier teens, the two groups being compared would not necessarily be expected to have a similar distribution of characteristics except for the voucher treatment. Although there were no significant differences on key behavior measures at baseline between experimental Baltimore teens whose families used their vouchers to move and experimental teens whose families did not,[6] there were observed differences at baseline between adults in these two groups, and there may have been differences in unobserved factors also.[7] This raises the possibility that differences in qualitative findings for experimental and control teens may reflect, in part, differences in underlying family characteristics rather than moves to low-poverty areas. Regardless of these considerations, the qualitative data offer us a window into the details of teens' feelings, including the cause of their distress or the seriousness of it.

The sample size for this analysis—between experimental compliers and controls—is 54, with 18 experimental compliers and 36 controls. Although the qualitative sample is small, the findings from the in-depth interviews provide background for understanding processes in the larger sample. In this qualitative sample, the median length of time at their current residence is the same for the controls and experimental compliers.[8] The mean age of each group is 16 years old.

Interviewers followed a standard in-depth interview guide with open-ended questions. Our goal was to elicit narrative responses in order to get the whole story on a topic. Interviewers were trained to use the guide in a flexible way, based on the flow of the interview and the particulars of the person's story. Interviews were taped and usually took one and a half to two hours to complete. Each individual was paid $35 for participating in the study. To protect confidentiality, each participant was asked to choose a pseudonym. After the tapes were transcribed, we coded the interviews.[9]

Findings

Sadness

The following section uses in-depth interview data to analyze the teens' narratives about sadness, anger, and stressors at the family level and neighborhood level in order to explore the underlying differences in these areas across four subgroups: control females and males and experimental complier females and males. Though these last two groups are referred to as just "experimentals" for the sake of brevity, they come from the subset of the experimental group whose families used the voucher to move.

We asked the teens about feeling "depressed" in several ways. First, we asked them whether there had been any time in the past month that they felt so sad that nothing could cheer them up. Later, we asked them to tell us what kinds of things get them "down." Sometimes a young person's feelings of sadness would come out in other parts of the interview, such as talking about a parent's or a friend's death. Measured in a quantitative way, experimental girls were the most likely to talk about feeling sad (91 percent), followed by experimental boys and control girls (71 percent each) and control boys (63 percent). But when one analyzes what makes them sad and the level of distress, it is clear that the control group teens are experiencing much more serious stressors that can affect their mental health. Respondents listed several different causes, but I focus on family conflict and death.

Family conflict. Family conflict was a frequently cited cause for sadness among this sample of teens. Though this conflict was cited across all four groups, in general it appeared to be of a more frequent and serious nature for the control group teens than their experimental counterparts. Three experimental females and one male reported becoming sad from basic conflict around issues such as chores or shopping. Another 18-year-old experimental male, Ron, had a somewhat more serious conflict with his mother, as they argued all the time. They have lived in the Baltimore suburbs for several years since the MTO move, but previous to this move, Ron was raised in a house frequented by drug addicts, including his mother, perhaps planting the seeds for this present conflict.

Three control females mentioned minor family conflict issues, like those above, as a source of sadness. However, five other girls from the control group were experiencing or had experienced more difficult circumstances. Fourteen-year-old Sherika painfully described how her mother's mental illness has affected her life. Her mother told the interviewer that Sherika and her brother were in foster care for a few months at one point due to her (the mother's) mental illness and physically abusive parenting. Sherika is now on medication and regularly sees a therapist. Her mother calls the therapist on a regular basis to complain about her, and Sherika believes that she is exaggerating what is happening and making it appear that Sherika has more severe mental health problems than she actually has. Moreover, Sherika notes that "Mommy always saying she gonna put me away. [I: What do you mean?] In foster care or whatever, because I'm getting on her nerves and all this stuff."

Mental illness and substance use by parents can co-occur to create an unhealthy living situation for children. This has been the situation for Candace, a 17-year-old control female. Her mother, Asia, told the interviewer that though she had been clean for several years, she had been a drug addict for over a decade. During the interview, Asia switched in and out of different voices and personalities. Similarly, Candace described herself as having many personalities: "I got 365 different personalities for each day of the year . . . sometimes I'm happy, sometimes I'm glad, sometimes I'm mad, sometimes I'm sad, sometimes I hate you, sometimes I don't want to look at you . . . sometimes I wish I'd die, sometimes I wish you would die, stuff like that."

None of the experimental teens reported witnessing abuse or experience with abuse. This is not to say that none existed, just that it was not reported in these interviews. In contrast, five of the control females reported witnessing abuse or being physically abused themselves. Eighteen-year-old Emily lived with her mother and her uncle during part of her childhood. Emily's mother told the interviewer (separately) that her (the mother's) boyfriend had physically abused her and had raped Emily. In addition, Emily reported that her uncle, now in prison for other offenses, physically beat her, and her mother did not believe her: "He was hitting me . . . he really tried to hurt me. [I: Did your mom know about this fight?] Yes, she did. [I: What did she do?] Nothing . . . It has been . . . a couple times she didn't believe what I had to say. She choose other people's sides over her own child." When 17-year-old Talia was 6 years old, she was removed from her mother due to the constant fighting in her household, and she stayed in foster care for eight years. Fast forward several years, and now Talia is in the process of leaving an abusive relationship with the father of her child. She describes the physical abuse he delivered when she was living with him and his mother while pregnant. His mother did not intervene and suggested that Talia had provoked the attacks: "[I: Did you get hurt when he hit you?] I ain't really get hurt as far as the baby-wise because I try holding myself in different positions. But this last time when he hit me, I just figured that was enough because he had . . . blackened my eye. So I'm just not there anymore."

Just over one-third of control males listed some type of family conflict that triggered their sadness. Three of the males described "minor" issues such as sibling squabbles. Juvon's situation was more serious. He is a 17-year-old in the control group and lives in a high-poverty neighborhood. He experienced the divorce of his mother and stepfather at the same time as breaking up with his girlfriend. The two events pushed him into a deep depression and he hinted that he had considered suicide during that time, though no longer. Unlike most of the male teenagers we interviewed, Juvon had attended one of the city's selective high schools and loved to write poetry. He told us, "I relied heavily on my poetry to help me vent some of my feelings." Unfortunately, the depression affected his grades in tenth grade, and when we met him, he was back at a chaotic high school in his neighborhood, after having lost his place in his first school.

Three of the more serious cases of family conflict were tied to substance use. Fourteen-year-old Kevin has lived with his grandmother his whole life because of his mother's drug addiction. When asked what makes him sad, he answered, "Like when my, like when my mother, my grandmother asks my mother to do something, she don't like never come do it. And that be like making her mad. I just hate to see her down and stuff." He then confessed that this constant disappointment of broken promises made him sad. Marcus is 16 years old and lives with his mother, sister, and a series of his mother's boyfriends. Marcus described how difficult it was watching his mother: "Yeah, I'll be feeling sad seeing my mother go through the things she go through . . . I don't like when she drink because she don't know what she be saying out of her mouth when she's drunk, and stuff like that. Cause it's so much stuff that my mother going through, and what I'm trying to do is help her ease the pain away." Two of the control males reported watching either their father or their mother's boyfriend beating their mother. Marcus has also seen his mother be physically abused by a series of men: "Like there was this man named [Robert], my mother husband, he kept abusing her. So I was only like 12 and stuff, and I ain't like it. The one time I had grabbed a knife, I was about to cut him—I'm like, man, you hit my mother, cause he had hit my mother with a gun." He and his cousins jumped in and beat the husband up.

Death. Another oft-cited factor for the teens' depression or sadness was the death of someone close to them. No experimental males brought up death, but two experimental females did, neither of which was of a violent nature. One girl's mother had passed away from pneumonia a year earlier, and the other girl felt sad about her grandmother's death, which occurred in third grade. The teens in the control group were much more likely to mention death, and the deaths were usually from violent causes.

Three control females cited death as a factor, and two of these had experienced someone dying a violent death. Ashanti is 16 years old and had survived a traumatic car accident a few months before the interview, leaving her arm severely damaged. She had gone out with Star, their mother's closest friend who had lived with them for several years, helping to raise Ashanti and her brothers. Star and Ashanti were out late one night and they caught a ride with a man Star had known only briefly. He crashed the car, killing himself and Star. Ashanti not only mourns the loss of Star but also blames herself for the extra trouble her mother has now that Star cannot babysit the children while she is at work. She said, "I just felt like [God] should of took me instead of her." In their interviews, Ashanti and her mother both recounted how Star haunted the house after her death and it wasn't until they moved to their current rowhouse that they were able to be more at peace. Candace, described earlier, told the story of the brutal death of her younger brothers' father. Hearing them cry for their father made her feel sad. He died of a drug overdose with a telephone cord wrapped around his neck, and it was also suspected that he was beaten severely. Candace also mentioned being visited by spirits after his death.

Death was a source of sadness for three of the control males. Sixteen-year-old Ray said "I just was hurting" when he found out that a friend had been shot and killed coming out of a bar one night. John, also 16 years old, lost his father in a car accident when he was 12 years old. His mother claimed that this loss launched John into a severe depression which landed him in a residential treatment facility for one and a half years. "The Kid" (a self-given nickname), 15 years old, had lost his mother a few months before our interview. She had just climbed out of years of drug addiction only to be diagnosed with a terminal illness. When asked when was the last time he was sad, he said, "On my birthday . . . cause my mother wasn't here." He felt a strong attachment to his mother, and he had used his earnings from drug dealing to move them out of a high-poverty neighborhood into the suburbs a couple of years earlier, but then had to witness her wasting away from another disease.

The qualitative analysis of the themes of sadness and its potential causes highlights clearer differences between the experimental and control groups than it does between males and females in the experimental group. While experimental girls were more likely than boys to report feeling sad in the interviews, this may very well be related to females' elevated level of depression in the general population, as well as to gender-specific socialization, which encourages females to discuss their feelings more than males. But the causes of sadness that emerged from the teens' narratives appeared to be quite similar for the males and females in the experimental group, especially in contrast to the control group.

Anger

The research literature suggests that anger and aggression—externalizing behaviors—are a more common response to depression among males than females. Moreover, Stevenson (1997) discussed how institutionalized racism and regular experience with discrimination can affect young African American men in particular, and result in anger issues. This may certainly be the larger context for the experience of these young men, who have grown up in racially segregated, high-poverty neighborhoods. Indeed, a recent court decision (*Thompson v. HUD*) found that the Department of Housing and Urban Development, along with the Baltimore Housing Authority, had created a racially segregated system of public housing in Baltimore. Unfortunately, it is difficult to measure how racism has affected the anger of the young men interviewed in this study.[10]

While the more extreme stories of death and family conflict set apart the experiences of control youth compared to experimental mover youth, another mental health outcome, anger—not measured comprehensively in the MTO Interim Survey—also sets them apart. Significantly, no experimental teen reported having problems with anger. On the other hand, one control female did so, and 40 percent of the control males admitted to having anger issues. This was not a question that was asked systematically in the qualitative interview; rather it was an issue that was spontaneously raised by the respondents.

Three of the control males had been placed in residential treatment facilities or psychiatric hospitals because of their anger problems (at times, it was explicitly tied to depression as well), and though Greg was not admitted to a facility, he received Ritalin to deal with his violent rages.[11] Jay, 16 years old, explained that he had been to the psychiatric hospital "eight or nine times" because of anger problems, and this does not include other time spent at a group home. When asked why he got angry, he simply stated, "'cause people always start with me." He has not been fighting recently and he is on four types of medicine for "anger management."

In the interview narratives, there are some hints as to causes of the anger that the young men describe, and in other situations it is left unsaid. For example, Greg's mother suggested that his fighting was related to ADHD; and Carl had been hospitalized with a lead paint poisoning level of 45 when he was a young child.[12] Two people tied their anger issues to the absence of their father. For example, when talking about his anger, James brought up his father, who has rarely been around because of drugs and incarceration: "It was like a little stuff like mainly stuff I, I think I was doing stuff because I was kind of mad at him. And trying to get back at other people. Just, like I say over the years just probably just holding a lot of stuff in. . . . But it's like I'm kind of like mad at him 'cause I'm like why couldn't he be there and why he couldn't do these certain things."

Community Violence and Disorder

These young people have grown up in a particular urban space; their participation in MTO is related to changing that space through mobility. In this analysis, I focus on the aspect of community violence and disorder, since improved safety has been one of the suggested mediators for the improvements we see in mental health for adults and teen girls. Though experience in previous neighborhoods certainly can have an impact on subsequent mental health (Wheaton and Clarke 2003), I focus on the context of the current neighborhood. (Eighty-six percent of the control teens in this qualitative sample moved from their original public housing development; thus for most of them, they are not describing their baseline neighborhoods.)

Safety. We asked the respondents whether they felt safe in their neighborhoods, or if anything had happened in the last six months to make them feel unsafe. We also asked them to tell us about their neighborhoods. Some youth attributed their feeling of safety to being "known" in their neighborhood. Bart, a 16-year-old high school dropout, had moved back into a high-poverty neighborhood—where several of his cousins live—after living for a while in the suburbs with the family's experimental voucher. He explained that "stuff happens, but I know a whole bunch of people so I feel safe wherever I go." After describing drug selling and fights in her East Baltimore neighborhood, Nikki, a 17-year-old dropout in the control group, explained, "Well, I already know it's safe for me and my sisters. Cause everybody already know who my mother is and mostly everybody around here knew me. . . . Not too many problems around here."

Several youths could not answer whether or not they felt safe in a simple dichotomous way, often giving mixed responses. This was particularly true with the control group. Reggie was a 16-year-old control whose family lived in an East Baltimore rowhouse with a rental subsidy from the Section 8 program. When asked whether he felt safe, he confessed: "I don't even know what a safe neighborhood is. What does [it] mean? . . . I don't think there's such a thing as a safe neighborhood . . . Because you could kill or somebody could do anything to you anywhere, but it may happen more places than another. And you can say that around here, you might wind up getting involved. Not to say it happens a lot, but it does happen."

Drugs. When teens talked about what makes their neighborhood feel unsafe, they focused on drug trafficking and shootings. Accounts of these events separate the controls from the experimentals, though such reports are not completely absent from experimental neighborhoods. Four experimental females and three experimental males report drug selling in their neighborhoods; however, two of the young women describe this taking place on another street near them, rather than on their block. Ron, eighteen years old, still lives in the same suburb where his family moved with the voucher. When the interviewer asked him if there were drugs in his neighborhood, he replied, "Not really, it's like a little bit but that's everywhere." The other two males describe more constant drug trafficking in their neighborhoods, although in one case, the neighborhood referred to is not the neighborhood he initially moved to with the experimental voucher but is the result of a subsequent move. Sixteen-year-old Kelly has lived in her current neighborhood for three years and claims that it is less safe than where her family had originally moved with the experimental voucher. She stated, "I don't think it's safe, I don't think it's safe for little kids definitely cause the drug dealers and things like that."

Control group members were more likely to report neighborhood drug activity, and their stories were of much more intense trafficking and visibility. Tasha, a 14-year-old control who lives in an East Baltimore rowhouse, smells weed as she's walking through her neighborhood, and sees "crackheads." She has also been a regular witness to drug exchanges at her local corner store, whose shelves are surrounded by bullet-proof glass so that she has to request items rather than choose them off the shelf herself: "And like I'm ordering something from the store and I just see somebody put something [on the floor] and I'm like, what is that, and I see what it is and then somebody else come and pick it up and stuff like they had it all planned out. . . . It's like them . . . little skinny holders and they got drugs or something in there." Clifton is a 16-year-old control male whose family now lives in a house in West Baltimore where it receives a subsidy through the Section 8 program. We interviewed him on a cold Sunday afternoon, and there were several men standing on the corner across the street from his house, tussling with each other and shouting as snow was drifting down. When asked to compare this neighborhood to his former, HOPE VI-redeveloped public housing, he admitted that he wished he was back in his old neighborhood because "around here nothing much but drugs, daily shooting." He suspects that a house across the street is a crack house, as he'll watch groups of people enter and not leave for hours at a time. The cold weather does not deter the dealers either: "They run like clockwork over there. That's why they're in the snow. They be out there with their big coats on, freezing [makes shivering sounds and pantomimes rubbing hands together]." Similarly, across town in a public housing development, Candace describes the constant presence of the dealers: "The young boys . . . starting at 16 to 20, they be on the corner selling drugs. It can be from sunrise to sunset. It can be rain, snow, hail, sleet . . . when they be selling drugs, they be at the basketball court and playground. . . . It can be any type of people [buying drugs], older people, crackhead people, junkies, white people." As if to prove her point, a young man pulled drugs from his sock and gave them to an older man as the interviewer walked past the playground after leaving Candace's house.

Violence. Four teens (two female, two male) in the experimental group discussed shooting in their neighborhoods, but only two described it at a level similar to the control group. Ralph, who had subsequently moved to a poorer neighborhood after the initial move made with the experimental voucher, described a man who was shot in his chest: "Me and my mother was out there in the backyard cooking on the grill, and my brothers and then, they just now got their new bikes. So they started riding around, and we heard like 12 gunshots in the summertime . . . [they] ran all the way towards [Market], and that's when we seen the man crawling up to the door right there on [Market] Street, all bloodied up." The narratives of control teens suggest that shootings occur more frequently in their neighborhoods. Marcus, whose friend was killed as he was coming out of a corner store in their neighborhood, said that it was "somewhat dangerous" there because "they'll just come up out of the blue and somebody might start shooting for no apparent reason." Ashanti witnessed a recent shooting in front of her house: "We saw him walk past us, but I don't know if he was arguing or they said he was trying to buy something but the man didn't have nothing so he just shot him in the face. Everybody was screaming and hollering, trying to get in their house, while we was just sitting there . . . and the boy walked, after he shot him he walked back toward us." Out of fear of retribution, Ashanti's mother ordered them to not say anything to the police, and she told the police she had not seen anything. Ashanti saw the shooter the other day walking on the street.

Other Aspects of Community Disorder. Popkin, Leventhal, and Weismann

(2006) have suggested that the improvement in MTO experimental girls' mental health may be related to reduced sexual predation in the low-poverty neighborhoods. These stories were rare in the Baltimore sample, but Tasha, a 14-year-old who lives in a drug-infested neighborhood, describes activity such as this when asked what she doesn't like about her neighborhood: "The people who, um, the men who mess with me. That's about it. When I walk to the store. [I: Has anybody ever tried to put their hands on you?] Yes, somebody did. Um, like tried to, um, reach out and touch me before, but I pulled away, you know, I didn't, I don't like that."

Research suggests that the experience of depression, anxiety, and aggression among children may be related to exposure to community violence (Prelow et al. 2004; D'Imperio, Dubow, and Ippolito 2000; Guerra et al. 1995; Attar, Guerra, and Tolan 1994). Interview data make it clear that control teens are still living in neighborhoods that expose them to more drug trafficking and shooting than teens whose families used the experimental voucher, which may have consequences for their mental health. However, these data do not address why boys in the Baltimore experimental group as a whole showed higher levels of psychological distress compared to control boys in the survey, while this was not the case for experimental girls compared to control girls.

Conclusion

Traumatic stories of young people growing up in high-poverty neighborhoods are, unfortunately, not rare. The MTO demonstration gave families the chance to move out of this high-poverty context. Findings from survey data suggest, however, that boys do not experience an improvement in psychological distress from this experiment—this holds across the MTO sites as a whole and in Baltimore, the focus of this study.

The qualitative interviews, however, complicate this picture. This analysis suggests that the stressors at the family and neighborhood level are more extreme for teens in the control group than those in the experimental complier group for both males and females. The experience of violent death, serious family conflict, abuse, and high-crime neighborhoods was consistently worse for control group members than experimental compliers. So while a teen may state that he/she has felt "down" in a survey, the likelihood is that the familial and neighborhood stressors that a teen from the experimental group is facing are less severe than what a teen from the control group is facing. MTO provided the opportunity for families to move from neighborhoods where crime and violent death were more common to those where these stressors were less frequent. It is surprising, then, that the quantitative analysis found that experimental boys had higher scores of psychological distress than their control counterparts.

In contrast to the quantitative analysis, gender differences in the experimental group were not salient in the qualitative analysis. Although nearly all (91 percent) of the girls in the experimental group talked about feeling sad in their interviews, compared to 71 percent of the boys, this is not surprising, given what we know about girls being socialized to express their emotions more and talk about their feelings. Digging deeper in order to look at the stressors that the young people linked to their sadness, girls and boys looked remarkably similar, particularly in contrast to the control group.

How might one interpret the difference in gender patterns between the survey and interview data? While the survey finding may be an artifact of the sampling, discussed earlier, it may also be related to issues that the boys did not tie to their mental health in the interviews. In another analysis of the interview data (Clampet-Lundquist et al. 2006), we found that experimental complier boys were not able to take advantage of lower-poverty neighborhoods in the way that girls did. Experimental boys were more likely to have friends involved in illegal activities compared to control boys, and they reported more hassles by police and neighbors. Their routine activities, including hanging out on the corner, were more at odds with the norms in the new neighborhoods than the girls' style of hanging out with friends. Moreover, control boys were more likely than experimental boys to have a nonbiological father figure in their lives.[13] One study of a similar population of male adolescents in single parent families found that the presence of a male family member in boys' lives was associated with less aggression (Florsheim, Tolan, and Gorman-Smith 1998). Perhaps the same factors that contribute to higher levels of risky behavior among experimental boys compared to control boys also contribute to slightly higher scores of psychological distress.

Nevertheless, this analysis uncovered a pattern that may point to a benefit for boys whose families made an experimental move. Forty percent of control group males in Baltimore discussed having a problem with anger—including some who were hospitalized or medicated for it—compared to no experimental group males. While this may be an artifact of small sample size, it may also be linked to living in a high-poverty neighborhood for a longer length of time.

What this analysis suggests, then, is that despite survey findings, which show no improvement for boys on mental health, the difference in the degree of stressors between the experimental and control groups may bode well for the future mental health of the experimental compliers, especially if the finding on anger is confirmed in further survey research. It also points to the importance of families remaining within low-poverty neighborhoods as part of a housing mobility initiative, as the few teens in the experimental group who discussed high levels of drug trafficking and shooting were those who had moved back to poorer neighborhoods. Services that make it easier for low-income families to remain in resource-rich neighborhoods can increase the odds that children and adolescents will continue to grow up in an environment without significant neighborhood disorder.

The combination of quantitative and qualitative methodology in this analysis built on the strengths of both approaches. The analysis of the survey data took advantage of MTO's experimental design and a larger sample and pointed to the difference in treatment effect by gender. The in-depth interview data provided rich detail about the stressors that underlie the survey results. The qualitative analysis is by no means definitive, given the small sample size. But the findings suggest two important directions for future survey and qualitative research with housing mobility studies. First, we need to probe more deeply—whether in survey or in-depth interviews—into how teens talk about their feelings, so as to better measure the severity and causes of stress that they experience. We may not be capturing the extent of the benefits of a move to a low-poverty neighborhood if we stick with asking about "feeling nervous." As found in this analysis, that answer could be "yes" for two teens, but stem from qualitatively different stressors. Being nervous about a test in high school is different from being nervous about one's chances of getting shot coming home from school. Second, more explicit items about anger should be included in survey research, in order to measure a potential benefit for boys in the experimental group. In addition to these two directions for research, it is also crucial to include parents in future analyses, as a parent's emotional well-being can affect the child. Since findings from the MTO survey indicate that adults in the experimental group showed improvement in depression and psychological distress, this is clearly an important mediator to explore.

Chapter 13

Changing the Geography of Opportunity by Helping Poor Households Move Out of Concentrated Poverty Neighborhood Effects and Policy Design

George Galster

Since the term "geography of opportunity" was introduced (Galster and Killen 1995) and amplified (Briggs 2005), there has been a groundswell of policy-oriented research related to the many facets of this issue. From the particular perspective of policies that help disadvantaged families move out of concentrated poverty neighborhoods, we must apply this body of research to addressing one overarching and four subsidiary scientific questions:

> Does moving out of a concentrated-poverty neighborhood substantially improve outcomes for the poor who move?

If so:

> What mechanism(s) of neighborhood effect are at work?
> How long does the neighborhood effect take?
> Which "neighborhood" matters?
> Which poor / which outcomes are affected?

Having addressed these questions it is then appropriate to address three key policy design questions:

> How can we best help the poor move into opportunity-rich neighborhoods?
> How can we best help the poor remain in and get the most out of opportunity-rich neighborhoods?

How can we best help opportunity-rich neighborhoods remain so as the poor move in?

In this chapter I will briefly address each of these questions, summarizing the state of science regarding each and placing the findings in this volume in broader context.

Does Moving Out of a Concentrated-Poverty Neighborhood Substantially Improve Outcomes for the Poor?

This question has been the subject of numerous scholarly reviews; see Gephart (1997), van Kempen (1997), Friedrichs (1998), Leventhal and Brooks-Gunn (2000); Sampson, Morenoff, and Gannon-Rowley (2002), Friedrichs, Galster, and Musterd (2003), Ellen and Turner (2003) and Galster (2005). Though most multivariate studies have observed correlations between neighborhood indicators and a variety of outcomes for adults and children, critiques have rightly questioned these findings on methodological grounds. The central methodological challenge in providing an unbiased estimate of the magnitude of neighborhood effects has been selection bias. The most basic selection issue is that certain types of individuals who have certain (unmeasured) characteristics will move from/to certain types of neighborhoods. Any observed relationship between neighborhood conditions and outcomes for such individuals or their children may therefore be biased because of this systematic spatial selection process, *even if all the observable characteristics of the individual are controlled* for (Manski 1995, 2000; Duncan, Connell, and Klebanov 1997). These biases can be substantial enough to seriously distort conclusions about the magnitude and direction of neighborhood effects.

There have been three general approaches adopted in response to the challenge of selection bias. The most common approach consists of a variety of econometric techniques applied to nonexperimentally generated data. The other two use natural or experimental designs to generate quasi-random or random assignments of households to neighborhoods.

Econometric Models Based on Nonexperimental Data

Most studies of neighborhood effects have used cross-sectional or longitudinal data collected from surveys of individual households residing in a variety of neighborhoods as a result of mundane factors associated with normal market transactions. They employ multiple regression or other multivariate analysis techniques to control for observed individual characteristics in order to ascertain the relationship between neighborhood characteristics and a variety of outcomes for these individuals.[1]

Quasi-Random Assignment, Natural Experiments

It is sometimes possible to observe nonmarket interventions into households' residential locations that mimic random assignment. In this way they may be viewed as second-best options for removing selection effects. The Gautreaux (Chicago) and Yonkers (N.Y.) court-ordered, public housing racial-ethnic desegregation programs (Rosenbaum, 1995; Rubinowitz and Rosenbaum 2000; Briggs 1997, 1998; Fauth, Leventhal, and Brooks-Gunn 2003a, 2003b; DeLuca et al. 2010) are illustrative. Evaluations of these programs revealed generally strong effects of neighborhoods in several dimensions. Recent evaluations of long-term impacts on Gautreaux (black) mothers found, for example, that residence in neighborhoods with the highest percentages of black and low-income residents was associated with significantly greater welfare usage, lower employment rates, and lower earnings. Sons of Gautreaux participants who moved far from their original, high-crime neighborhoods were less likely to run afoul of the criminal justice system, especially in matters related to drug offenses (DeLuca et al. 2010).

However, although these natural experiments may indeed provide some exogenous variation in neighborhood locations, the selection problems are unlikely to be avoided completely. There typically is selection involved in who chooses to participate in these programs and who succeeds in locating rental vacancies in qualifying locations. In some cases (Gautreaux, e.g.), participants have some nontrivial latitude in which locations they choose, both initially and subsequent to original placement. These selection processes raise the possibility that those who succeed in living in low-poverty neighborhoods are especially motivated, resourceful, and, perhaps, courageous—traits poorly measured by researchers but likely ones that would help their children succeed. So, is it these good parents or their good neighborhoods that yielded the outcomes observed for their children?[2]

Random Assignment Experiments

Many researchers advocate a random assignment experimental approach for best avoiding biases from selection. Data on outcomes that can be produced by an experimental design whereby individuals or households are randomly assigned to different neighborhoods is indeed, in theory, the preferred method. In this regard, the Moving to Opportunity (MTO) demonstration has been touted conventionally as *the* study from which to draw conclusions about the magnitude of neighborhood effects. As explained below, however, MTO proves to be a better experimental design for evaluating voucher-based housing policy impacts than for measuring neighborhood effects. In fact, many investigations of MTO data claimed to uncover no substantial neighborhood effects on educational and labor market outcomes (e.g., Ludwig, Duncan and Pinkston 2000; Katz, Kling, and Liebman 2001; Ludwig, Ladd, and Duncan 2001; Ludwig, Duncan, and Hirschfield 2001; Orr et al. 2003; Goering and Feins 2003; Kling et al. 2004; Kling, Leibman, and Katz 2007a; Ludwig et al. 2008). Based on this, it has been claimed both that "MTO is the gold standard . . . [and that] its results . . . have proven discouraging," seeming to indicate that "neighborhood quality . . . [has] little effect on desirable and measurable outcomes" (Smolensky 2007: 1016).

Such a sweeping conclusion is unsupportable for five main reasons. First, although MTO *started* with random assignment of participants to groups, it did not randomly assign initial neighborhoods. Moreover, it did not control the self-selection of neighborhood characteristics by *any* of the three comparison groups, and thus did not purge the relationship between neighborhood characteristics and unmeasured individual characteristics (Sampson, Morenoff, and Gannon-Rowley 2002; Clampet-Lundquist, and Massey 2008; Sampson 2008). The "control" group was not constrained to live perpetually in disadvantaged neighborhoods; indeed, many MTO controls have moved to better neighborhoods on their own. The group that receives only a rental subsidy with no mobility counseling and no geographic restrictions could (and did) freely select from a wide range of neighborhoods. The treatment group receiving intensive mobility counseling and assistance, though constrained to move initially to a neighborhood with a less than 10 percent poverty rate, had the ability nevertheless to choose neighborhoods varying in their school quality, home ownership rates, racial composition, local institutional resources, proximity to jobs, etc. That is, they could select many aspects of neighborhood opportunity structure within the poverty rate constraint. Moreover, subsequent to the initial move to a low-poverty location they were free after one year to move to different, higher-poverty neighborhoods should they choose; indeed, 85 percent have done so (Kingsley and Pettit 2007). As Ludwig et al. (2008) explain, this selection problem within MTO ultimately can be addressed through instrumental variables techniques. But the adjustment remains imprecise, because the neighborhood poverty instrument is measured as the average across the observed family's trajectory of moves. Thus, MTO's reputed benefit of "random assignment" is lost when it comes to measuring neighborhood effects; the imperfect instrumental variables approach remains only a second-best strategy here.

Second, MTO has failed to ensure adequate exposure to neighborhood conditions by any group at any location.[3] As amplified below, some neighborhood effects are likely to yield outcomes only after long-term exposure to the neighborhood context (Clampet-Lundquist and Massey 2008). Unfortunately, all three comparison groups in MTO evinced significant residential mobility (typical of low-income households), thus minimizing the chance to observe neighborhood effects that require substantial duration of exposure. Clampet-Lundquist and Massey (2008) analyzed MTO data from the perspective of only those who resided for substantial spells in low-poverty neighborhoods and found evidence that they experienced a variety of improved labor market outcomes. Though this evidence is subject to potential selection bias, it nevertheless is suggestive of the import of exposure duration effects.

Third, MTO failed to consider the potential lasting developmental effects upon children who spent their childhoods in disadvantaged neighborhoods before their families participated in the MTO experimental group. As Sampson (2008) points out, if the cumulative impacts of such environments created some durable disadvantages for these children, their (relatively short) exposure to low-poverty environments due to MTO might have been insufficient to observe many changes in their outcomes in these domains.

Fourth, it appears that even experimental MTO movers rarely moved out of predominantly black-occupied neighborhoods near those of concentrated disadvantage (Sampson 2008). Thus, they may not have experienced sizable enhancements in their opportunity structures. Put differently, the overall bundle of neighborhood attributes constituting racialized spaces in U.S. cities changed little for MTO experimental households, even thought the initial neighborhood poverty rate may have (Clampet-Lundquist and Massey 2008; Sampson 2008). This was especially true when it came to moving nearer job concentrations (Briggs et al., this volume).[4]

Fifth, many participants in MTO would not have been expected to evince much labor market activity in any neighborhood context, without additional assistance. About one-quarter of the MTO families were headed by an adult unable to work because of disabling, chronic illness, while many more needed childcare and transportation that were not in the package of supports offered in the experiment (Briggs et al., this volume).

Despite these weaknesses, one should not lose sight of the fact that many important neighborhood effects nevertheless *can* be observed from MTO data, as Goering and Feins (2003) and Gennetian et al. (this volume) summarize. Analysts have observed substantial improvements in mental health of mothers and daughters, rates of risky behaviors, perceptions of safety, and overall life satisfaction in lower-poverty neighborhoods. The picture for boys appears more complex, however, as they evinced reductions in violent crime but increases in property crime offenses in lower-poverty neighborhoods.

A Provisional Conclusion

A substantial number of studies (employing sophisticated econometric methods with nonexperimental data, natural quasi-experimental designs, and experimental designs for overcoming selection bias) have identified nontrivial correlations between various aspects of the neighborhood and several dimensions of the well-being of disadvantaged children and adults, controlling for other characteristics of individuals and their households. Many of these effects appear to be nonlinear, such that certain neighborhood characteristics only appear to affect outcomes after a threshold has been exceeded (Galster 2002).

But how does this evidence relate to the core question: Does moving out of a concentrated-poverty neighborhood substantially improve outcomes for the poor? Because in concentrated-poverty neighborhoods so many aspects of the social, economic, physical, and institutional environments take on extreme values, there is little doubt that substantial harmful effects accrue for most families residing there. But answering the question depends on the specification of a multidimensional counterfactual: moving out of a concentrated-poverty neighborhood to what alternative place? How long will the poor remain in that place? What are the gender, age, and racial-ethnic characteristics of the poor who move? And how do these neighborhood effects transpire?

What Mechanism(s) of Neighborhood Effect Are at Work?

There have been several comprehensive reviews of the potential theoretical links between neighborhood processes and individual outcomes. One set of studies has focused upon the social relationships among low-income households who are located among predominantly higher-income neighbors, often as the result of some sort of innovation, experiment, or court-mandated modification of an assisted housing program. The programs included racial desegregation rental housing vouchers (Rosenbaum 1991, 1995; Rosenbaum et al. 1991; Rosenbaum, Reynolds, and DeLuca 2002; Mendenhall 2004), MTO vouchers (Popkin, Harris, and Cunningham 2002; Rosenbaum, Harris, and Denton 2003), scattered-site public housing (Briggs 1997, 1998; Kleit 2001a, 2001b, 2002, 2005), and mixed-income public or private developments (Schill 1997;

Clampet-Lundquist 2004). These studies consistently show that the social relationships among neighbors of different economic groups are quite limited. Members of the lower-status group often do not take advantage of propinquity to broaden their social connections with higher-status neighbors and thereby enhance the resource-producing potential of their networks; instead, they often restrict their networks to nearby members of their own group or to those remaining in the "old neighborhood." This suggests that social networking may be a powerful neighborhood force *among* members of a given group but less so in an intergroup context. Even with minimal social interaction, however, the role model and social control mechanisms apparently operate strongly (Rosenbaum, 1991; Briggs et al., this volume). In these cases, neighborhood effects arise endogenously as residents shape each others' behaviors through social interactions and observations of various sorts. These studies also are noteworthy for what they did *not* find: evidence of substantial relative deprivation or competition that led to worse outcomes for the less-advantaged neighbors

A second set of studies establishes support for a variety of correlated neighborhood effects mechanisms. Numerous studies (see reviews by Kain 1992; Ihlanfeldt, 1999) have investigated the issue of differential accessibility to work (the "spatial mismatch" hypothesis) in the U.S. context. This literature generally suggests that mismatch can be an important aspect of opportunity differentials in at least some American metropolitan areas, though it seems of less importance than the social conditions of neighborhoods (O'Regan and Quigley 1996; Weinberg et al. 2004). Other studies have documented the differences in both public services and private institutional resources serving different U.S. neighborhoods (e.g., Kozol 1991; Card and Krueger 1992; Drier, Mollenkopf and Swanstrom 2004). Still others have shown how the internal workings of institutions serving poor communities shape expectations and life chances of their clientele (Rasmussen 1994; Bauder 2001). Although the evidence linking these differences to various outcomes for children has been subject to challenge (e.g., Burtless 1996; Morenoff, Sampson, and Raudenbush 2001; Popkin, Harris, and Cunningham 2002), there is increasing evidentiary prominence of some institutions, such as the public schools, serving as important mediators of neighborhood effects in the United States (Ennett et al. 1997; Teitler and Weiss 1996). For example, school may intensify collective norms that otherwise may not dominate in an individual student's neighborhood. These norms may, of course, enhance or retard educational achievements.

Other literature, both qualitative and quantitative, has documented how exposure to violence may produce serious and long-lasting emotional trauma for young children (e.g., Martinez and Richters 1993;

Richters and Martinez 1993; Aneshensel and Sucoff 1996). The Yonkers (N.Y.) Family and Community Survey and the MTO demonstration also provided strong support for the perceived importance of this factor, since safety concerns were cited by most public housing families as a prime reason for participating in these mobility programs (Briggs 1997; Goering and Feins 2003). Clampet-Lundquist (this volume) adds more evidence here in the context of mental health outcomes for teens.

My provisional conclusion to this section is that there is support for the socialization (i.e., role model and social control) endogenous neighborhood mechanisms as improving the well-being of the poor in opportunity-rich areas. By contrast, social networking may be a powerful neighborhood force *among* low-income residents' given group, but appear less important in an interclass context in providing new resources to the poor. Relative deprivation and intergroup competition do not seem to be operative to a worrisome degree. Several correlated effect mechanisms, especially spatial mismatch and institutional resources, are likely also operating, though their precise influences have been difficult to quantify. Finally, reduced exposure to crime and violence is likely an important source of benefits to the poor in opportunity-rich areas.

How Long Does the Neighborhood Effect Take to Work?

Researchers can readily identify the neighborhoods in which subjects reside, but it is a far greater challenge to identify the degree to which they are exposed to the processes thought to convey neighborhood effects, whether these processes work instantaneously to generate outcomes for individuals or with substantial lag or cumulative impact. As is the case with so much of research design in the context of neighborhood effects, the appropriate time frame for consideration depends on which underlying process is assumed to operate.

If, for example, stigmatization of an area based on its residents were the predominant mechanism through which neighborhood effects transpired, one could reasonably posit that the effect would apply equally to all residents of the popularly demarcated place that is stigmatized and that the effect would occur immediately upon a new resident's arrival. If socialization via role models were the predominant mechanism, however, the intensity of exposure to such an influence would depend on the degree to which the individual's social networks were contained within the neighborhood. Moreover, the degree to which such a socialization process would change the individual's behavior would be directly related to the duration of the individual's exposure to these role models.

Thus, within the context of the socialization mechanism we would expect neighborhood effects to be strongest for those who have only intraneighborhood social relationships and who have lived there an extended time during which these role models were observed. The empirical challenge is to operationalize these exposures and duration effects and allow for the measured neighborhood effect to be contingent upon them.

There have been a few attempts to measure neighborhood duration effects.[5] My provisional conclusion is that little empirical work has investigated exposure/duration effects of neighborhoods. It is strongly suggested by theory, however, that for many of the likely candidates for primary endogenous and correlated neighborhood effect mechanisms (see above) these effects are important. This implies that past studies may have failed to observe substantial neighborhood effects because individuals did not have sufficiently sustained exposures to the neighborhoods in question.

Which "Neighborhood" Matters?

This question has two dimensions: the scale of the space and the characteristics within that space that reputedly generate an effect. In an earlier survey, I noted the multiplicity of conceptualizations of neighborhood (Galster 2001). Many scholars have employed a purely geographic perspective: neighborhoods are delineated by boundaries unambiguously defined by administrative fiat. Others have attempted to integrate social and ecological perspectives in an attempt to incorporate residents' perceptions and patterns of social interactions into the formulation of boundaries. Suttles (1972) provided a seminal synthesis of these positions by positing that households perceived four distinct spatial scales of "neighborhood," each having its own functions. Moreover, different neighborhood effects operate at different spatial scales. Role model processes may, for example, extend over the block-face, but stigmatization may extend over a much wider area. The upshot is that, whatever "neighborhood" is, it undoubtedly has distinct social, economic, and psychological meanings and consequences at various geographic scales (Suttles 1972; Birch et al. 1979; Galster 1987). The challenge for empirical researchers of neighborhood effects that logically follows from the above is daunting: what is measured for neighborhood should be operationalized at *multiple scales.*

The most direct way of answering the question "what scale(s) of neighborhood matter in generating individual outcomes?" is to conduct parallel analyses of a particular outcome where neighborhood is measured at different scales and estimates of impact are compared. Several studies have taken this tack: Buck (2001), Bolster et al. (2004) and Knies (2007). All find statistically significant relationships at various scales, but stronger correlations between outcomes and neighborhood variables when the latter are measured at smaller spatial scales.

Another response has been to develop proxy measures for neighborhood mechanisms involving only prosaic, publicly available data. Prototype efforts to find such proxies in census-based indicators collapsed into a "neighborhood disadvantage index" by the use of factor analysis have proven only partially successful; see Sampson and Groves (1989); Elliott et al. (1996); Sampson, Raudenbush, and Earls (1997); Cook et al. (1997); Sampson, Morenoff, and Earls (1999); Coulton, Korbin, and Su (1999); Sampson, Morenoff and Gannon-Rowley (2002); and Kohen et al. (2002).

My provisional conclusion to this section is that "neighborhood" can be conceptualized (and indeed may perform different functions and have different effects) at different spatial scales. Research has typically used whichever scale was conveniently coded with the available data. The few studies that have systematically explored variations in neighborhood effects according to scale find stronger correlations between outcomes and neighborhood variables when the latter are measured at smaller spatial scales. Rarely have the potential mechanisms of neighborhood effect been measured directly. However, it is clear that both the appropriate scale of neighborhood and the characteristics of the space to measure differ depending on the potential neighborhood effect mechanism(s) being investigated.

Which Poor, Which Outcomes?

A holistic examination of prior work on measuring the magnitude of a neighborhood effect upon an outcome in question (regardless of methodological approach) makes one thing clear: the magnitude is contextualized by gender, ethnicity, and developmental stage of the low-income population being studied. Although it is beyond the scope of this work to provide a metaanalysis of the literature on this point, the apparent effects of neighborhood on a particular outcome typically are not the same for both adults and children, across children of different ages, across genders of the same age, across different racial-ethnic groups, or across all types of host neighborhoods. The chapters in this volume by Briggs et al., Clampet-Lundquist, and Gennetian et al. provide further convincing evidence of the multidimensional contextuality involved.

Interrelationships Among the Questions

Even though the foregoing considered four key questions related to measuring neighborhood effects as if they were independent, it is readily apparent that they are closely interrelated in numerous complex ways. Different mechanisms through which neighborhood effects transpire are likely associated with distinct differences in (1) the geographic scale over which they operate; (2) how they are appropriately measured; (3) the degree to which residents are equally exposed; (4) the speed at which exposure affects outcomes; and (5) how responses to exposure vary by gender, ethnicity, and developmental stage. An illustration: if area-based stigmatization were the dominant neighborhood mechanism, all adult residents of an externally defined "neighborhood" would find their opportunities immediately constricted the moment they moved into the area and external parties became aware of this fact. By contrast, if role modeling dominated, only adults and youths who had regular visual or verbal interaction with the role models would be affected, but probably only cumulatively over an extended period. Moreover, different neighborhood processes are likely to yield differential consequences over a variety of interesting outcomes. For example, peers probably have increasing influence on educational achievement as children age from preschool to high school years. Spatial mismatch, however, tends to affect the job prospects only of those of working age and has little impact on their health outcomes. Unfortunately, in most cases our theory is insufficiently developed to permit us to know with any certainty which mechanisms generate which outcomes over what exposure duration for which poor over what spatial scales. The upshot is that researchers are challenged to investigate, for any given outcome of interest, a wide set of potential causal mechanisms, each holding an associated suite of sobering implications for measurement, including scale, exposure, and duration.

Key Issues in the Design of Strategies for Deconcentrating Poverty

The foregoing review of key research questions related to neighborhood effects may be summarized as follows. Yes, living in concentrated poverty neighborhoods is undoubtedly harmful for low-income adults and children. However, how well-off they will be in a different type of neighborhood as the result of some sort of policy intervention that helps them move out is much more difficult to ascertain because of the multidimensional contextuality involved. This sets the stage for addressing three key policy design questions.

How Can We Help the Poor Move into Opportunity-Rich Neighborhoods?

Given the high degree of contextuality discussed above, it seems clear that one implication for designers of housing mobility strategies is that designating destination neighborhoods merely in terms of their poverty rate is foolish; "low-poverty" does not equally imply "opportunity-rich" (Briggs et al., this volume). For instance, Clampet-Lundquist (this volume) shows how proximity of a low-poverty to a high-poverty neighborhood may still allow youths who moved to the former to continue to participate in gang activities taking place in the latter. They may also continue to attend their original schools, as was discovered in MTO (Goering and Feins 2003). As another illustration, a low-poverty neighborhood may provide little improved access to employment opportunities if it is not serviced by public transit. A final (and potentially contentious) aspect of this issue is whether achieving racial and economic integration (as in the case of Gautreaux, but not MTO) is an important aspect of opportunity (Clampet-Lundquist and Massey 2008). Clearly, more work needs to be done in operationally defining and mapping opportunity-rich neighborhoods.

Other implications are that once such opportunity-rich areas have been identified, accessing them through housing subsidies must be achieved. Unfortunately, housing that is affordable to low-income households, even those with housing vouchers, is rare in such areas, and efforts such as inclusionary zoning have made little headway. Additionally, low-income households must be helped to locate and move into opportunity-rich neighborhoods, if we are to expect many to do so rather than move into neighborhoods with intermediate ranges of poverty that are unlikely to be places where their opportunities are maximized (Hartung and Henig 1997).

How Can We Help the Poor Remain in and Get the Most out of Opportunity-Rich Neighborhoods?

Experience from the Gautreaux and MTO programs shows that many poor households move to considerably higher-poverty neighborhoods after their initial experience in a low-poverty one (Rubinowitz and Rosenbaum 2000; Goering and Feins 2003; Orr et al. 2003). Often this is due to their need for reliable, proximate childcare, informal social supports, and institutional connections; other times it is due to friction between themselves and their new neighbors. This suggests that the ability to provide access to transportation, childcare, and other formal and informal supports within low-poverty neighborhoods should be seen as an important component of any mobility strategy, as Briggs et al. (this volume) argue.

How Can We Help Opportunity-Rich Neighborhoods Remain So as the Poor Move In?

A last issue relates to how the destination neighborhoods for poor households will respond over time. Will they remain opportunity-rich places, or will middle-class flight, property disinvestment, and upsurges in crime eventually re-create the conditions that the poor were trying originally to escape? Fortunately, in this realm we have a good deal of evidence (summarized in Galster 2004). There is no negative influence on crime or property values near assisted housing or housing voucher holders so long as the concentration of assisted households does not exceed certain thresholds and these thresholds are directly related to the strength of the neighborhood's investment flows. Unfortunately, in the absence of idiosyncratic court-ordered desegregation decrees (Popkin, Rosenbaum, and Meaden 2003) or local ordinances enforcing minimum separation requirements on assisted housing developments (Galster et al. 2003), there are few institutional vehicles for avoiding overconcentration of the poor in their destination neighborhoods. The problems may be especially acute with the housing voucher programs, where there are clear (perverse) market incentives for landlords to actively recruit such tenants in weak neighborhoods where market rents are lower than what they can get from the voucher program (Galster et al. 2003). The danger is that public policies aimed at deconcentrating the poor may unwittingly push destination neighborhoods past poverty-rate thresholds (generally estimated in the range of 10 to 20 percent; Galster, Cutsinger, and Malega 2008), after which they will quickly experience substantial declines in their property values as they transition to opportunity-poor places.

Conclusion

Identifying neighborhood effects—their magnitude, transmission mechanism(s), exposure duration properties, and spatial extent—is full of daunting empirical challenges. Further complicating the investigation is the likelihood that neighborhood effects are different across individuals categorized by developmental stage, gender, and race-ethnicity. Nevertheless, researchers have discovered a great deal about neighborhood effects—enough, I believe, to justify a public policy aimed at helping poor families move out of concentrated poverty neighborhoods. However, the degree to which the outcomes for these mover families will be substantially better in their destination neighborhoods will depend on a host of contingencies. Unfortunately, our current system for delivering affordable housing (either site-based or tenant-based) does an inadequate job of meeting them. This delivery system needs to be reformed in a variety of fundamental ways and better integrated within the broader social welfare delivery system in order to align the various contingencies that must be met to provide the maximum short- and long-term opportunities for the poor.

PART IV

Segregation

The Power of Place

Chapter 14

Are Mixed Neighborhoods Always Unstable?
Two-Sided and One-Sided Tipping

David Card, Alexandre Mas, and Jesse Rothstein

Racial segregation is a defining feature of urban neighborhoods in the United States. A large body of social science research has established that black children raised in more segregated areas have worse outcomes, including lower levels of completed education, lower test scores, lower marriage rates, lower employment and earnings, and higher crime rates (e.g., Massey and Denton 1993; Cutler and Glaeser 1997). Though researchers still do not agree about the extent to which the observed correlations between segregation and these outcomes are causal, a major goal of public policy over the past four decades has been to reduce racial segregation in neighborhoods, schools, and workplaces.

The efficacy of integration policies depends critically on the underlying forces that have led to and sustained segregation. While institutional and legal forces played an important part in enforcing segregation in the Jim Crow era, many analysts have argued that the preferences of white families for neighborhoods with a lower fraction of minority residents are the driving force in explaining segregation today (e.g., Cutler and Glaeser 1997). In a highly influential contribution, Schelling (1971) showed that even when most whites have relatively weak preferences for lower minority shares, social interactions in preferences are likely to lead to a fully segregated equilibrium. In Schelling's model (and in more recent theoretical studies, including Brock and Durlauf 2001 and Glaeser and Scheinkman 2003), a given neighborhood can have multiple equilibria. Holding constant conditions in the rest of the city, the neighborhood could either be (nearly) 100 percent white, nearly 100 percent minority, or a mixture. Importantly, however, in Schelling's formulation the mixed equilibrium is inherently unstable: adding a few extra minority families sets off a chain of departures by whites that only

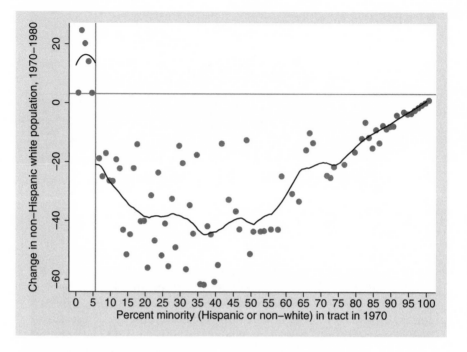

Figure 14.1. Neighborhood Change in Chicago, 1970–1980

ends once all the white families have left. Likewise, adding a few white families sets off a chain of departures by minority families that ultimately lead to an all-white neighborhood.

In this chapter we use data on the evolution of census tracts from 1970 until 2000 to investigate whether integrated neighborhoods are sustainable in the long run, or whether they are inherently unstable and destined to become either 100 percent minority or 100 percent white. Our analysis builds on a companion paper (Card, Mas, and Rothstein 2008b; hereafter CMR), in which we found that most major metropolitan areas are characterized by a city-specific "tipping point," a level of the minority share in a neighborhood that once exceeded sets off a rapid exodus of the white population. To illustrate this finding, Figure 14.1 plots mean percentage changes in the white population of Chicago census tracts from 1970 to 1980 against the tract's minority share in 1970.[1] The graph shows clear evidence of a critical threshold at around a 5 percent minority share: neighborhoods with 1970 minority shares below this threshold experienced gains in their white populations over the next decade, while those with initial shares above the threshold experienced substantial outflows. These patterns hold on average for a broad sample of U.S. cities in each of the past three decades.

Most common understandings of neighborhood tipping envision a transition from virtually all-white composition to virtually 100 percent minority. This is certainly the historical experience. Northern cities had relatively low numbers of racial minorities in 1940, but as African Americans migrated from the South, many neighborhoods within these cities tipped from all-white to nearly all-black. This process has been interpreted by many analysts as evidence of the inherent instability in integrated neighborhoods predicted by Schelling's model. According to this interpretation, the mixed neighborhoods observed today (say with a 10 or 15% minority share) are in the process of transitioning to an all-minority status. Nevertheless, a class of alternative models—including the one developed in CMR—suggests that mixed neighborhoods *can* survive in the long run, so long as the minority share does not exceed a critical tipping point. In these alternative models, the tipping point is not a "knife edge" temporary equilibrium that is destined to fail. Rather, the tipping point represents a boundary point. Neighborhoods with minority shares below this level can remain integrated; but once the tipping point is exceeded, the neighborhood will quickly move to a nearly 100% minority equilibrium.

The distinction between these views of tipping is quite important for policy purposes. Under Schelling's model, planners hoping to create and maintain vital integrated neighborhoods must fight continuously against market forces, which are always pulling the neighborhood toward complete segregation. By contrast, under the alternative models, a neighborhood can remain stable with a moderate minority share. The alternative models provide a justification for policies meant to encourage racial and ethnic diversity in neighborhoods. If integrated neighborhoods are inherently unstable, however, these efforts are likely to have little long run effect on the degree of racial segregation in a city.

We attempt to distinguish between alternative models of tipping by investigating whether integrated neighborhoods with minority shares *below* the tipping point tend to experience rapid minority flight (as predicted by Schelling's original model) or whether they can remain integrated over several decades. The answer to this question is of growing importance because tipping points appear to have risen. If neighborhoods below the tipping point are stable, increases in the tipping point can lead to increasingly integrated neighborhoods, all else equal. CMR documented average tipping points in the range of a 13 percent minority share over the 1970—1990 period, with slight increases over time. This contrasts sharply with earlier experience, where neighborhoods in many cities seemed prone to tip in response to even a small (1 or 2

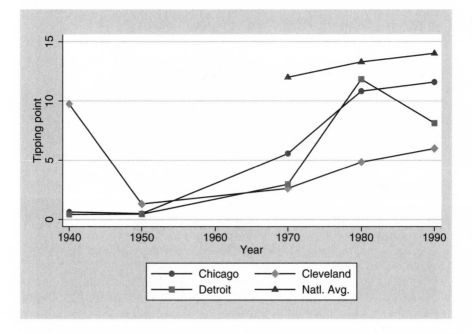

Figure 14.2. Tipping Points in Chicago, Cleveland, and Detroit 1940–1990

Note: Tipping points are unavailable in 1960.

percent) minority presence. Applying the same methods as in CMR, we estimated the tipping points for three large Midwestern cities (Chicago, Cleveland, and Detroit) for the 1940–1970 period. Figure 14.2 shows the evolution of the tipping points in these cities since 1940.[2]

In two of the three cities, the tipping point was near zero in 1940 and 1950 (in the third, Cleveland, it was near 10 percent in 1940 but fell to near zero in 1950), and in each case it rose substantially by 1970 and farther in the later years. Although 1940 and 1950 tipping points are not available for other cities, the figure also shows that the average tipping point across all large cities in the country was around 12 percent in 1970 and rose somewhat over the next two decades.

Changes in tipping points have been accompanied by dramatic changes in the cross-sectional distribution of minority shares across census tracts. Figure 14.3 shows the distribution of tract minority shares for the pooled sample of tracts from the three cities in 1950, 1970, 1980, and 1990. In 1950, this distribution is highly bimodal, with many all-white neighborhoods, a few all-minority (almost entirely black) neighborhoods, and essentially no integrated neighborhoods. This distribu-

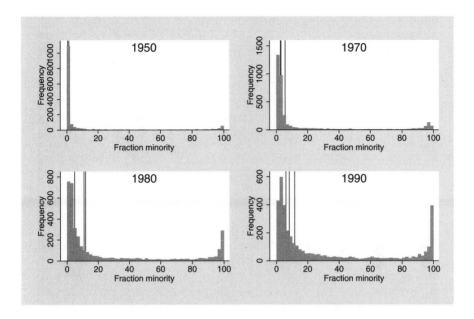

Figure 14.3. Pooled Histogram of Tract Minority Shares in Chicago, Cleveland, and Detroit, 1950–1990

Note: Vertical lines indicate the three cities' tipping points in the relevant years.

tion would be expected from a tipping point at a very low minority share. In more recent decades, we see two key changes. First, there are more neighborhoods with very high minority shares, as each city's black (and more recently Hispanic) population expanded over the second half of the twentieth century. Second, we increasingly see neighborhoods with intermediate minority shares, neither all-white nor all-minority. Many of these integrated neighborhoods have minority shares below the (now higher) tipping points. The histograms suggest the possibility that neighborhoods below the tipping points might be stable, though because they represent only cross-sections they are also consistent with instability of integrated tracts.

In what follows we present a series of tests for the stability of neighborhoods with minority shares below the tipping points identified by CMR. We focus on the 1970 tipping point. As indicated in Figure 14.2, 1970 seems to represent the beginning of the modern era for this sort of analysis, with tipping points that resemble those seen in the 1980s and 1990s more closely than they do the lower tipping points observed in the 1940s and 1950s.[3] Importantly for our purposes, a focus on 1970 allows us to observe neighborhoods' outcomes over a thirty-year period. We examine the racial/ethnic composition of census tracts in 1980, 1990, and 2000, relating this to a tract's location relative to the 1970 tipping point. Overall, we conclude that tipping is one-sided: while neighborhoods with minority shares above the 1970 tipping point appear to move toward high minority concentrations in later decades, those that remain below the tipping point are more stable, and show no indication of substantial minority flight.

Theoretical Framework

We consider a neighborhood with a fixed, homogeneous housing stock and two groups of potential buyers: whites (w) and minorities (m). Our analysis focuses on the properties of the so-called bid (or "inverse demand") function for housing in the neighborhood, which gives the highest price at which a specified number of families would be willing to purchase homes in this neighborhood rather than in some alternative.[4] In other words, for any given number n, the bid function describes the price that would have to prevail in order to get exactly n families to buy houses in the neighborhood.

We distinguish between the bid functions of white and minority families. Let $b^w(n^w, m)$ be the white bid function. We assume that this function depends on n^w, the number of units to be purchased by whites, and on m, the minority share in the neighborhood. Similarly, the bid function for minority buyers, $b^m(n^m, m)$, depends on the number of units held by minorities and on the minority share.

The two arguments of the bid functions reflect two distinct forces: the *specificity of demand* for homes in the neighborhood (reflected in the amount that prices have to fall to induce more members of a given group to purchase homes); and *social interaction effects* (reflected in the sensitivity of demand to the minority share in the neighborhood). Assuming that potential buyers have individual-specific valuations for a given neighborhood—due to local amenities that are valued differently by different buyers, for example—both groups' bid functions will be downward sloping in their first arguments: the more homes that must be bought by members of a particular group, the lower the price that the last buyer will be willing to pay.[5] Only if all families in a given race group value the neighborhood equally will the bid functions not depend on the number of homes occupied by the group. In this case, demand is perfectly elastic: any number of homes can be sold if the price is below the group's willingness to pay, but none will be purchased if the price is just above that point.[6]

Now turn to the second argument of the bid functions. If white buyers prefer neighborhoods with lower minority shares, then white bids will be declining in the neighborhood minority share, since in order to attract the same number of white families to a neighborhood with a high minority share as to one with fewer minorities, the price in the former will have to be lower than in the latter. Of course, if white buyers are indifferent to the neighborhood's minority share—that is, if there are no social interaction effects—bids will not depend directly on the minority share and the white bid function will be invariant to m, holding n^w fixed. Likewise, if minority buyers prefer a higher minority share, then minority bids will increase with the minority share, while in the absence of such effects the bid of any particular minority family will not depend on the neighborhood's minority share and the minority bid function will be invariant to m.

In an integrated equilibrium, the price paid by white and minority families for homes in the neighborhood must be the same; that is, the bid functions must coincide when evaluated at the needed numbers of white and minority buyers and at the minority share that would result from those numbers. But there may also be fully segregated (or "corner") equilibria. At an all-white neighborhood equilibrium, enough whites must be willing to pay more than even the highest-bidding minority for homes in the neighborhood to fill all of the homes, whereas at an all-minority equilibrium, the reverse is true.[7]

Four types of equilibrium are shown in panels A–D of Figure 14.4, depending on whether buyers have neighborhood-specific valuations and whether social interactions play a role in white buyers' demands. In each panel, the horizontal axis is the minority share in the neighborhood, while the vertical axis represents the price of homes in the neighborhood. The minority bid function should be read as a conventional inverse demand curve, from the left (corresponding to an all-white neighborhood, $m = 0$) to the right (an all-minority neighborhood, $m = 1$). The white bid function should be read as an inverse demand function that depends on $1 - m$ rather than m: reading from right (where white demand is zero) to left (where minority demand is zero), an increase in the number of white buyers corresponds to a decrease in the number of minority buyers and therefore a decrease in the minority share.

Panel A shows the benchmark case where there is no neighborhood specificity in demand and social interactions are unimportant. In this case the two bid functions are simply horizontal lines. As drawn here, white buyers value the neighborhood more than minority buyers, and the neighborhood will be all-white. On the other hand, if the minority

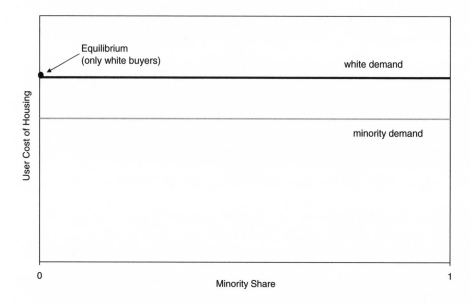

Figure 14.4.A. No Neighborhood-specific Valuations or Social Interactions

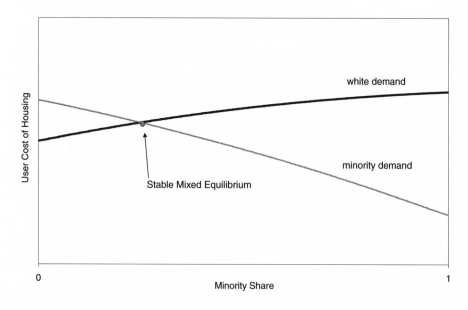

Figure 14.4.B. Neighborhood-specific Valuations, No Social Interaction

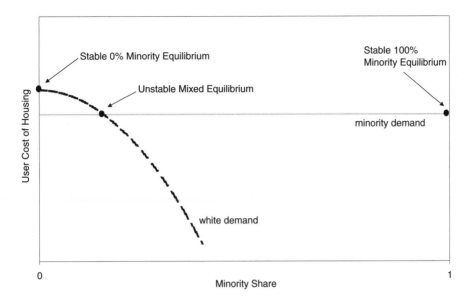

Figure 14.4.C. No Neighborhood-specific Valuation, Social Interaction in White Demand

demand curve for a neighborhood lies above the white demand curve, the neighborhood will be all-minority.

Panel B shows the case where the demand for the neighborhood from each group is less than perfectly elastic but there are no social interactions. In this situation, the number of families from either group choosing to purchase homes in the neighborhood can be increased only by lowering the price that they must pay. In other words, the minority bid function is downward sloping as a function of the neighborhood minority share, whereas the white bid function—which is downward-sloping in *1 − m*—*increases* with the minority share. If the two groups' bid curves intersect, as is shown in Panel B, there is an integrated equilibrium, though segregated equilibria are also possible if the bid curves are non-intersecting. Importantly, in the absence of social interaction effects, any integrated equilibrium is unique and stable.[8] A small increase in the fraction of minority homeowners means that the next white family's bid to purchase a home in the neighborhood exceeds that of the last minority family, leading to a transaction that restores the equilibrium.

Panel C shows the case that was considered by Schelling (1971): no specificity in the demand for the neighborhood, but negative social interaction effects in white demand.[9] Here, assuming that in the absence

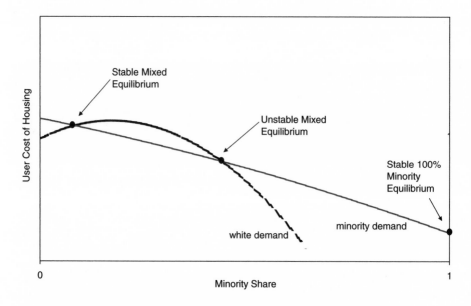

Figure 14.4.D. Neighborhood-specific Valuations and Social Interaction in White Demand

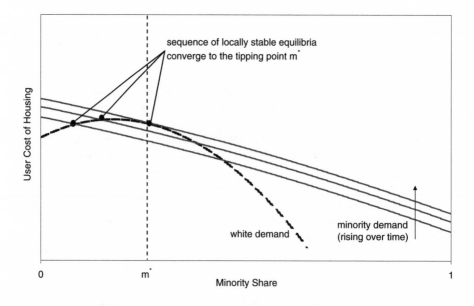

Figure 14.4.E. Tipping Point in Neighborhood Minority Share

of the interaction effect whites would bid more for homes in the neighborhood than minorities, there are three possible equilibria: an all-white equilibrium; an all-minority equilibrium; and a mixed equilibrium. The two segregated equilibria are stable whereas the integrated equilibrium is not: starting from the integrated equilibrium, a small increase in the fraction of minority owners would lead to a positive gap between the willingness to pay of minorities and whites, stimulating further sales that lead to white flight and ending at the all-minority equilibrium. Alternatively, again starting from the integrated equilibrium, a small increase in the fraction of white owners would lead to an opposite gap in willingness to pay, initiating a cascade of minority flight that culminates in the all-white equilibrium.

Panel D shows the more general case where there is both specificity in the neighborhood demand functions and a social interaction effect in white demand. In this case the inverse-demand function for whites can be nonmonotonic, reflecting two countervailing forces: (1) the downward sloping demand for housing with minority share fixed, which in isolation causes the white bid function to be upward sloping in the minority share; and (2) the social interaction effect, which produces a negative effect of the neighborhood minority share on white bids. The overall slope of the bid function will depend on the relative strength of these two forces, which may vary with the minority share. As the graph shows, at low minority shares the demand effect dominates, and, as the minority share rises from zero, the move up the demand curve yields a rise in the marginal willingness to pay by white buyers. At higher levels of the minority share, however, the social interaction effect dominates and further increases in the minority share lead to reductions in the marginal white bid. As drawn, there are three equilibria: two mixed and one all-minority. The first mixed equilibrium, at a relatively low minority share, is locally stable. A small increase in the minority share would raise white bids relative to those of minorities, while a small reduction would reduce the white relative bid. In each case, the resulting transactions would bring the minority share back toward the equilibrium point. By contrast, the second mixed equilibrium, at a higher minority share, is unstable, like the one in Panel C.

The comparison between Panel C (with a single unstable mixed equilibrium) and Panel D (with two mixed equilibria, one stable) suggests that some specificity in white demand is necessary to support a stable integrated equilibrium when whites treat a higher minority share as a pure disamenity.[10] Specificity might arise from locational features—individuals whose jobs are located nearby may have a particular demand to live in the neighborhood, but once all of these individuals have purchased houses, the marginal buyer must work farther away—or from fixed local amenities, like cultural institutions, that appeal more to some potential buyers than to others. The key feature is that, holding the minority share fixed, the white demand curve for the neighborhood is downward sloping, rather than horizontal (corresponding to perfectly elastic demand), as it would be if the neighborhood were perfectly substitutable with many others. In the presence of specificity, some whites will have high bids for housing in a neighborhood, even if the minority share is positive. In the absence of specificity, white demand is *monotonically decreasing* in the minority share, eliminating the stable integrated equilibrium shown in Figure 14.4D and leaving only the unstable equilibrium, as in 14.4C.

In CMR, we defined the tipping point for a model like the one shown in Panel D as the maximum minority share at which a neighborhood can be in stable equilibrium, assuming that the white and minority demand curves are subject to vertical displacements over time.[11] As shown in Panel E of Figure 14.4, this is the point of tangency between the white and minority demand curves, marked as m^* in the figure. When a neighborhood is at this point, any relative increase in minority demand for the neighborhood eliminates the integrated equilibrium, leaving only the all-minority equilibrium. The process may be irreversible once it has begun: once a neighborhood has begun tipping and has a minority share in excess of m^*, even a downward relative shift in the minority demand function may leave the integrated equilibria to the left of the neighborhood's position. If so, the neighborhood will continue its transition toward the all-minority equilibrium.

In contrast to this definition, Schelling (1971) and others have defined a tipping point as an unstable integrated equilibrium, such as that shown in Panel C or the rightmost mixed equilibrium in Panel D. By this definition, tipping is the movement away from an unstable equilibrium and is two-sided.

It is worth emphasizing the very different nature of the integrated equilibria and the tipping process in these different models. In the original Schelling model, an integrated neighborhood in equilibrium is like a marble placed precisely at the peak of a ridge. The marble is stable only so long as it does not move to either side. If it is perturbed even slightly via a random shock, it will inevitably roll off the ridge and will wind up either in the all-white or the all-minority valley. In the class of models illustrated by Figures 14.4D and 14.4E, however, dynamic behavior is analogous to a marble on an elevated plateau. The marble's position is stable so long as it is not too close to the edge of the plateau. Once it reaches the edge, however, it will roll down to the all-minority valley.

This analogy illustrates the nature of our test for the distinction between two-sided and one-sided tipping (or, phrased differently, between unstable and semi-stable understandings of the tipping point equilibrium). If integrated neighborhoods are inherently unstable, as in Figure 14.4C, then they will tend to experience either rapid losses of white residents or rapid losses of minority residents, depending on whether they are to the left or the right of the tipping point. If integrated neighborhoods are stable so long as their minority shares remain below the tipping point, however, then a neighborhood with a minority share less than m^* in a base year will not typically experience large losses of minority residents (or gains of white residents) in the following years.

We implement this test by focusing on the dynamics of neighborhoods with minority shares that are close to the set of city- and decade-specific tipping points identified in CMR. These tipping points are identified by searching for "break points" in the relation between the minority share in a neighborhood in some base year (the census years 1970, 1980, or 1990) and the subsequent change in the *white* population of the neighborhood over the next ten years. Although one-sided and two-sided tipping models both predict a sharp, discontinuous decrease in the number of white residents once a neighborhood is beyond either definition of a tipping point, they differ in their implications for the behavior of the *minority share*, and the *number of minority residents*, to the left of the tipping point. Two-sided models imply sharp losses in the number of minority residents and a sharp decline in the minority share for neighborhoods just to the left of the tipping point. One-sided models suggest that neighborhoods with a minority share below the tipping point can have stable minority shares and total minority population.

Data and Methodology

CMR estimated tipping points for each large metropolitan statistical area in 1970, 1980, and 1990. They documented a discontinuity in neighborhood evolution at these tipping points. In each decade, the tracts with minority shares just above the city- and decade-specific tipping point saw large declines in their white populations relative to tracts that began just below the tipping point. CMR did not investigate, however, whether this reflects symmetric movements away from the tipping point on each side or simply a contrast between rapid losses of white residents in tracts beyond the tipping point and approximate stability in tracts to the left of it. They also discussed only briefly the dynamics of *minority* populations around the tipping point. A closer investigation of these dynamics is important for distinguishing between the semistable and unstable models of tipping points, as in the latter model neighborhoods just to the left of the tipping point will experience minority flight and in the former they are likely to remain approximately stable.

The models above, for purposes of analytical simplicity, treat neighborhood size as fixed. This is a major obstacle in taking these models directly to the data, as many metropolitan neighborhoods see rapid changes in their populations and housing stocks over time. CMR documented that the neighborhood growth rate changes discontinuously at the tipping point, with tracts to the right of the tipping point seeing relatively slower growth over the next decade than those to the left of it, at least in the subset of neighborhoods in which there is remaining undeveloped land. To abstract from this differential neighborhood growth, CMR focused on the implications of tipping for the rate of growth in the white population of a neighborhood rather than for the neighborhood minority share. They documented rapid growth of the white population in tracts to the left of the tipping point and rapid declines in tracts to the right. The former would seem to support the two-sided tipping model. However, because minority populations may also be growing at a similar rate, the facts in CMR are also consistent with stable minority shares for tracts with minority shares just below the tipping point.

We consider alternative measures of neighborhood evolution—the growth rate of the tract minority population or the change in the tract minority share—to differentiate between the alternative accounts of tipping, focusing on the question of whether tracts that are below the tipping point trend quickly toward 100 percent white. As in CMR, we use census tract data for the 1970–2000 censuses from the Urban Institute's Neighborhood Change Database (NCDB) as our source of data on neighborhoods. We treat metropolitan statistical areas (MSAs) and primary metropolitan statistical areas (PMSAs) as defined in 1999 as "cities," and we define our sample identically to that used in CMR. We define minorities as nonwhite and Hispanics. We refer the reader to CMR for further details on the sample and variable construction.

We also follow CMR in the definition and estimation of a tipping point. That paper used two different methods to estimate candidate tipping points. In this chapter, we focus on the "fixed point" definition, corresponding to the minority share at which we predict that a neighborhood's composition will evolve in step with the city as a whole.[12] To identify this point, we fit a flexible model of racial dynamics in each city and find the initial minority share at which the predicted rate of change of the white share equals the city-level average. Details are available in CMR. Because this approach involves intensive "data mining," CMR adopted a split-sample approach, using a random subsample of tracts in a city to identify the potential tipping points and using only the remain-

Table 14.1. Overview of Candidate Tipping Points

	1970	*1980*	*1990*
Mean	11.87	13.53	14.46
Standard deviation	9.51	10.19	9.00
No. of MSAs in sample	104	113	114
Correlations			
1970	1.00		
1980	0.46	1.00	
1990	0.50	0.59	1.00

Source: Card, Mas, and Rothstein (2008b).

ing tracts to examine racial dynamics around those points. As we found evidence in CMR that most cities exhibit true tipping, the fact that the tipping points are estimated is not likely to induce bias in estimates of the city dynamics. Accordingly, here we use the full sample of tracts to estimate the tipping points and for our remaining analysis.

Table 14.1 presents summary measures of the estimated tipping points using the procedure from CMR. Tipping points vary by city, averaging 13 percent, with a standard deviation of approximately 10 percent. In CMR we found evidence that cities with more racially tolerant whites have higher tipping points.

Testing for the Stability of Tracts Below the 1970 Tipping Point

In order to distinguish between one-sided and two-sided tipping we examined the evolution of racial/ethnic composition in tracts on either side of the 1970 tipping point. Specifically, we examined the racial/ethnic composition of census tracts in 1980, 1990, and 2000, relating this to a tract's location relative to the 1970 tipping point. By focusing on the 1970 tipping point, we allowed for a relatively long time horizon over which we could follow the tract's evolution.

We began by selecting census tracts that are within three percentage points of their MSA tipping point in 1970. That is, for a city with a 1970 tipping point of 8 percent minority, we took all tracts with 1970 minority shares between 5 percent and 11 percent. From this subset of tracts we subdivided the sample between tracts at or above the tipping point in 1970 (in our example, between 8 and 11 percent minority) and those below it (5–8 percent). Hereafter, these groups will be referred to as the "$\geq m^*$ group" and the "$< m^*$ group," respectively. We compare the distributions of the minority share relative to the 1970 tipping point in these two samples between 1970 and 2000.

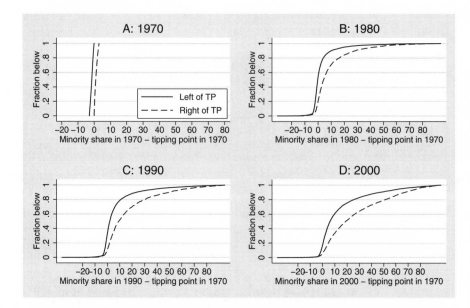

Figure 14.5. Cumulative Distribution Functions of Minority Shares of Tracts near the 1970 Tipping Point in 1970, 1980, 1990, and 2000. Sample includes tracts with $-3<m<m^*$ and with $m^* \leq m<3$ in 1970.

In Figure 14-5 we show the distributions of these deviations in 1970, 1980, 1990, and 2000, comparing the $\geq m^*$ and $<m^*$ samples. Points on the figure indicate the fraction of tracts in a city with minority shares in the indicated year, relative to the 1970 tipping point, that are lower than the corresponding value on the horizontal axis. For example, the solid line in Panel B has Y value of roughly 0.4 when the X value is 0. This indicates that 40 percent of tracts in the $<m^*$ sample had 1980 minority shares below the 1970 tippint point, while 60 percent of tracts in the sample had 1980 shares above that point.

The compression seen in the distributions of Panel A is an artifact of the sample selection criteria: In both the $\geq m^*$ and $<m^*$ samples all tracts are within three percentage points of the MSA-specific tipping point in 1970, so the latter sample is merely shifted to the left three percentage points relative to the former sample.

The panels corresponding to years 1980–2000 are more interesting. If tipping points are unstable rather than merely semistable, we expect to see that the $<m^*$ group will spread to the left of the 1970 tipping point over the following decades, indicating rapidly declining minority shares in many neighborhoods from this group. Panel B shows 1980.

Between 1970 and 1980, both tracts that began to the left and tracts that began to the right of the 1970 tipping point tended to gain minorities: as noted above, 60 percent of the tracts from the $<m^*$ group—tracts that were just to the left of the 1970 tipping point—had minority shares above the threshold by 1980. While it is surprising that such a large number of tracts below the tipping point eventually tip, this pattern is consistent with the semistable, or "plateau" view of tipping points. If indeed tracts just below the tipping point are approximately stable but are subject to random shocks, a fraction will eventually be shocked above the tipping point, off the edge of the plateau. Nevertheless, consistent with the tipping phenomenon, the minority share tended to rise by more in the $\geq m^*$ ("tipping") group than in the $<m^*$ ("non-tipping") group: The plot for the $\geq m^*$ group is everywhere below and to the right of that for the $<m^*$ group.[13]

Not all tracts in the $\geq m^*$ group tip immediately. In this group the median deviation in 1980 from the 1970 tipping point is close to the median deviation in 1970, though differences at upper percentiles are substantial, with the 75th percentile of relative minority shares in 1980 about 10 percentage points larger that in 1970. The tipping process becomes more pronounced in 1990 and 2000, with tracts in the $\geq m^*$ group showing increases in minority share at all points in the distribution. Nevertheless, while tipping is present, the rate of tipping (toward 100 percent minority) varies quite a bit and can be very slow in some tracts.

There is no evidence in Figure 14.5 of "minority flight" from the $<m^*$ group. There is no leftward spread in the distribution of minority share (deviated from the 1970 tipping point) in any of the decades. Most tracts, even in the $<m^*$ group, saw rising rather than falling minority shares, and essentially no tracts had minority shares more than 5 percentage points below the 1970 tipping point at any point in the three decades.

A possible concern with this analysis is that there is limited potential for declines in minority share if tipping points are small. For example, in a city with a tipping point at 5 percent minority, no tract can ever have a minority share relative to the tipping point lower than -5. To assess whether the absence of leftward spread in relative minority shares is due to cities with low tipping points, we limited the sample to MSAs where the tipping point in 1970 exceeds 10 percent. This excludes approximately half of the MSAs in the sample. We present the distributions of minority shares relative to the 1970 tipping point for this restricted sample in Figure 14.6. Among the higher-tipping point MSAs, the rightward shift in relative shares in the $<m^*$ sample is somewhat attenuated, though there remains a divergence between the $\geq m^*$ and

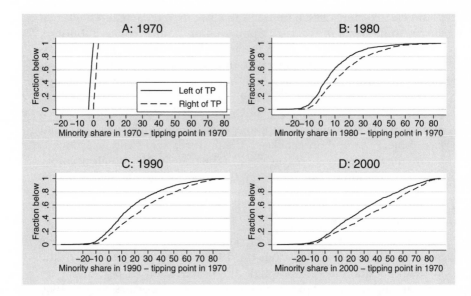

Figure 14.6. Cumulative Distribution Functions of Minority Shares of Tracts near the 1970 Tipping Point in 1970, 1980, 1990, and 2000, for MSAs with tipping points above 10 percent. Sample includes tracts with $-3 < m < m^*$ vs. tracts with $m^* \leq m < 3$ in 1970.

$< m^*$ samples in the growth of minority share.[14] As we would expect, there is now more leftward spread of relative shares, as compared to Figure 14.5. However, this leftward spread is almost identical in the $\geq m^*$ and $< m^*$ groups—the difference between the two distributions at the 10th percentile is less than 5 percentage points in 1980 and 1990, and close to zero by 2000. Only a relatively small fraction of tracts lose minority share—about 40 percent in 1980, 20 percent in 1990, and 10 percent in 2000. Moreover, the reduction in minority share tends to be small. Even in 1980, only about 10 percent of tracts in the $< m^*$ group had lost more than 5 percentage points in minority share since 1970.

From this analysis there is little indication that tracts to the left of the 1970 tipping point are tending quickly—or at all—toward an all-white equilibrium. However, changes in the tract minority share reflect both changes in the numerator—the number of minority residents—and changes in the denominator—the total number of tract residents. As a consequence, changes in minority share need not reflect changes in minority populations.

Figure 14.7 provides another look at the data that helps resolve this ambiguity. Here, we examine the tract's minority population in year t as

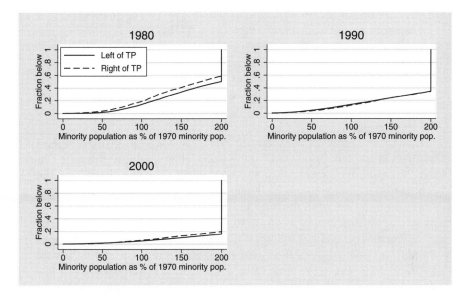

Figure 14.7. Cumulative Distribution Functions of Tract Minority Population in 1980, 1990, and 2000 as a Share of the 1970 Minority Population, Tracts near the 1970 Tipping Point. Sample includes tracts with $-3 <$ m $<$ m* vs. tracts with m* $\leq$ m < 3 in 1970.

Note: Both series are censored at 200% of 1970 minority population.

a percentage of the tract's minority population in 1970. A tract that is hemorrhaging minority residents will tend to have values well under 100, while one with a growing minority population will have a value in excess of 100. To focus attention on the relevant portion of the distribution, we censor the ratio at 200, corresponding to a doubling of the tract's 1970 minority population. A large fraction of tracts in both the $\geq m*$ and $<m*$ groups are censored, about half in 1980 and rising to 80 percent in 2000. This is not surprising for the $\geq m*$ group—a tract that begins with a minority share around 10 percent and begins transiting quickly toward an all-minority equilibrium will certainly double its minority population over thirty years. It is somewhat more surprising to see large increases in the number of minorities in the $<m*$ group. This pattern is consistent, however, with the semistable view of tipping points. As noted earlier, if indeed tracts just below the tipping point are approximately stable but are subject to random shocks, a fraction will eventually be shocked above the tipping point, off the edge of the plateau. This appears to have happened to at least half of the tracts in the $<m*$ group by 1980, and to much larger shares by 2000.

The density of the two groups to the left of 100 is of even greater interest for our purpose. Only a very small fraction of tracts lose minority residents on net in the years after 1970, never more than 20 percent of either group. Of those that do lose minority residents, most lose only a fairly small portion of their initial populations; essentially none lose more than half of their 1970 minority populations. There is thus no evidence whatsoever for rapid minority flight from tracts to the left of the tipping point.

Indeed, the contrast between the $<m^*$ and the $\geq m^*$ groups, at least in 1980, shows the opposite of the pattern that would be predicted by the "unstable equilibrium" model of tipping. The distribution of the proportional change in minority populations in the $<m^*$ group stochastically dominates that in the $\geq m^*$ group. Rather than losing their minority communities, tracts to the left of the tipping point seem to be *attracting* new minority residents at a *faster* rate than those to the right of the tipping point. The evidence for tipping seen in CMR and in Figures 14.5 and 14.6 here apparently reflects substantial differences in population growth rates, with relative inflows of white residents into $<m^*$ tracts that are even larger in proportion to the initial white population than are the minority inflows in proportion to the initial minority population.

Conclusion

Tipping points remain an important feature of the dynamic evolution of racially mixed urban neighborhoods. Neighborhoods with minority shares in excess of the tipping point tend to experience rapid white flight, transitioning quickly toward being 100 percent minority. By contrast, neighborhoods with significant minority populations but with minority shares below the tipping point appear to be relatively stable, gaining minority residents but at a much slower pace than do tracts that have tipped. There is no evidence of the minority flight that is predicted by Schelling's original model and other related models of tipping.

Our conclusion is that tipping points are "semi-stable", and that neighborhoods can retain an integrated character so long as they remain below the tipping point. Policies that are oriented toward maintaining stable neighborhoods can derive some justification from this result; these efforts need not contend forever against market forces that are pushing neighborhoods toward complete segregation.

Chapter 15

Preferences for Hispanic Neighborhoods

Fernando Ferreira

Hispanics officially became the largest minority group in the United States in 2005 according to the Census Bureau. Nurtured by immigration and natural population growth, the expansion of this segment of the population is becoming a very salient feature of the American demographic landscape. As with the African American migration to urban centers from the late nineteenth to the mid-twentieth centuries, the growth of the Hispanic population in a number of major American cities is having a major impact on neighborhood dynamics and segregation.

In this chapter I examine how variation in the number of local Hispanic residents affects housing markets, specifically focusing on the estimation of marginal willingness to pay (MWTP) for Hispanic neighbors. A vast literature has demonstrated the existence of capitalization of local public goods on housing values (Tiebout 1956; Oates 1969) as well as the applicability of the hedonic model (Rosen 1974) in estimating the market valuation of neighborhood characteristics, such as the share of Hispanics living on a block. In practice, the impact of an increase in the share of Hispanic neighbors on the house prices of the marginal homebuyer or home renter corresponds to the MWTP for Hispanic neighbors.

In addition to estimating this valuation parameter, I also test whether non-Hispanics display ethnic-based residential preferences, and thus avoid living in Hispanic neighborhoods. The estimation of heterogeneity in preferences by ethnicity is crucial for the interpretation of the results—there is a concern that estimating the average effect of Hispanics on the housing market may provide limited information, since differences in preferences based on ethnicity may be prevalent. For example, many whites may have strong preferences to live among whites and many Hispanics may have strong preferences to live among Hispanics, but the average marginal effect may be negligible if there are enough mixed neighborhoods where individuals of both groups derive a positive utility from that mix. (In this essay, "white" refers to non-Hispanic white.)

Previous literature related to the subject has used housing price differentials between African and European American neighborhoods to measure the extent of "decentralized racism" (Cutler, Glaeser, and Vigdor 1999). The main goal of this literature is to distinguish between discrimination against blacks in the housing market—which implies higher housing prices in black areas—and decentralized racism, where white flight is the product of white preferences for racial segregation which in turn implies lower housing prices in black areas. The results in this chapter present information on white preferences for segregation from Hispanics through direct estimation of preferences for change in share of Hispanic neighbors. (Other papers that have explored these issues include Bailey 1966; Berry 1976; Chambers 1992; Follain and Malpezzi 1981; Galster 1977; King and Mieszkowski 1973; Laurenti 1960; and Yinger 1978.)

However, there are several empirical challenges to estimating marginal willingness to pay for sociodemographic characteristics of neighborhoods using hedonic models. First, there is limited availability of micro data at any neighborhood level, which is the first requirement for estimating the impact of Hispanic neighbors on house prices. Second, even with the best data in hand, economists do not observe all of a neighborhood's features. Inevitably, the share of Hispanic households in a neighborhood is correlated with other unobserved characteristics of the neighborhood. This omitted variable bias problem may invalidate any estimation of the impact of Hispanics on the housing market.

I will review two approaches for dealing with these issues. The first method is based on Bayer, Ferreira, and McMillan (2007), who estimated a demand model of residential location decisions. Their discrete choice model is based on the following trio: (1) a detailed cross-sectional census data set, in which the exact location of every single household in the 15 percent long form database is known; (2) a discrete choice model that uses revealed preferences to recover MWTP in equilibrium; and (3) a regression discontinuity design approach based on school district boundaries to deal with the omitted variable bias. These instruments allowed Bayer, Ferreira, and McMillan to estimate both the mean marginal willingness to pay for ethnic composition of neighborhoods and the heterogeneity in ethnic-based residential preferences.

The second approach is based on the work of Ferreira and Saiz (2008), and it uses a panel of data on all housing transactions in a metropolitan area over a seventeen-year period. Their estimation strategy is also based on three pillars: (1) observed Hispanic ethnicity of all buyers and sellers—based on their reported surnames—in a sample of more than 1.2 million transactions; (2) the panel structure of the data, which allows the identification of the effect of small changes in the share of Hispanics on house prices; and (3) detailed geographic information about each house that allows neighborhoods to be defined at several levels—blocks, block groups, and census tracts.

The strengths of the first approach are based on its structural model. When this model is applied to detailed cross-sectional data, it allows for precise estimates of mean preferences and preferences that vary by ethnicity. The second approach relies on the quality of the transactions data, which permits the estimation of marginal preferences for Hispanic neighbors, even in small geographies such as a street block.

Estimates from both approaches provide remarkably similar results. First, Hispanic origin is not capitalized directly into housing prices at the margin; instead, the negative cross-sectional correlation between the share of Hispanics in a neighborhood and housing prices is due mostly to the fact that Hispanics live in lower-quality neighborhoods. The use of alternative strategies to control for omitted variable bias is crucial for reaching this result. Second, there is strong heterogeneity in preferences for neighbors of Hispanic origin. Specifically, Hispanics tend to present positive preferences to live with other households of Hispanic origin (relative to households of other races or ethnicities). Since other racial/ethnic groups present similar patterns, this heterogeneity in preferences leads to self-segregation, even in the absence of redlining or other discriminatory practices. Such a result is important for policy, since incentives to create mixed neighborhoods may backfire or be ineffective when households have low mobility costs and underlying preferences for self-segregation are strong.

Finally, these estimates are also consistent with Saiz and Wachter (2006), who focused on the growth in the immigrant population in the United States. Their results show that there is a negative association between growth in immigrant density and changes in housing prices but that the negative association is concentrated in neighborhoods with previously white majorities.

Residential Location Decisions Model

The first approach to estimating MWTP for Hispanic neighbors is based on the work of Bayer, Ferreira, and McMillan (2007)—henceforth BFM. BFM models the residential location decision of each household as a discrete choice of a single residence. The utility households derive from living in a certain house and neighborhood is based on the model developed by McFadden (1973, 1978) and Berry, Levinsohn, and Pakes (1995), which includes a term that estimates the impact of unobservable characteristics of the neighborhood. The model consists of two key elements: the household residential location decision problem and a market-clearing condition. While maintaining this simple structure, the model is quite powerful, allowing households to have heterogeneous preferences defined over housing and neighborhood attributes in a very flexible way; it also allows for housing prices and neighborhood sociodemographic compositions to be determined in equilibrium.

In the BFM model, each household chooses its residence to maximize utility, which is a function of prices and observed and unobserved housing features. Observed features include characteristics of the house itself (e.g., size, age, and type), its tenure status (rented vs. owned), and the characteristics of the surrounding neighborhood (e.g., school, crime, population density, and topography). Unobserved features refer to the unobserved quality of the house, taking into account the impact of the surrounding neighborhood. In addition, the model accounts for the effects of the distance from a residence to the primary work location of a household and, most importantly for the purposes of this study, the percentage of Hispanic households in the neighborhood. In sum, utility is a function of the house's price, its observable characteristics, its distance from place of employment, and the surrounding neighborhood's Hispanic share; both a common and a household-specific error term are also included. The common error term is important, in that it captures the aforementioned unobserved characteristics.

A household's utility is ultimately determined by its relative valuation of each of the above factors. These valuation parameters each have a component that is common across all homeowners (the mean component), as well as one that is based on the individual household's own characteristics (the heterogeneity component); these characteristics include education, income, race/ethnicity, employment status, and household composition. Our goal is to estimate the valuation parameter for the Hispanic factor. We will be particularly interested in how the average valuation of Hispanic neighbors varies according to the race/ethnicity of the household. As explained earlier, this type of heterogeneity in preferences is crucial to understanding the potential effectiveness of policies that give incentives for the creation of mixed neighborhoods.

Given the household's problem described above, each household chooses a residence only if the utility that it receives from this choice exceeds the utility that it receives from all other possible choices. Therefore, the probability that a household chooses any particular house depends in general on the characteristics of the full set of possible housing choices. This revealed preference argument is the main rationale behind the estimation of choice models.

Estimation of the model follows a standard two-step procedure similar to the one employed in Berry, Levinsohn, and Pakes (1995). The first step in the procedure is a maximum likelihood (ML) estimator, which estimates the impact of household-specific characteristics on each of the valuation parameters, as well as the mean indirect utilities, captured by the common error term, for each house. The ML estimator is based on maximizing the probability that the model correctly matches each household with its actual housing choice. After estimating the vector of mean indirect utilities in the first step, the second step of the estimation approach involves decomposing them into observable and unobservable components. This second step is particularly similar to a hedonic price regression, but with an important caveat: it provides a measure of mean preferences for each attribute of the model, including mean preferences for Hispanic neighborhoods. A fuller discussion of model and estimation can be found in BFM.

Data

Access to restricted census microdata for 1990 played a crucial role in obtaining the estimates in BFM. In addition to detailed individual, household, and housing unit variables found in the public-use versions, these restricted census files also include information on the location of individual residences and workplaces at a very disaggregated level of geography. In particular, while the public-use data specify the PUMA (Public User Microdata Area, a census region with approximately 100,000 individuals) in which a household is located, the restricted data can be used to identify a household location up to the census block level (a census geographic unit with approximately 100 individuals). This higher precision makes it possible to identify the local neighborhood that each individual inhabits, as well as the characteristics of each neighborhood, far more accurately than has been previously possible with public large-scale data.

Data from six contiguous counties in the San Francisco Bay Area were used: Alameda, Contra Costa, Marin, San Mateo, San Francisco, and Santa Clara. The focus on this area is justified for two main reasons. First, it is reasonably self-contained. Examination of Bay Area commuting patterns in 1990 reveals that a very small proportion of commutes originating within these six counties ended up at work locations outside the area; and similarly, a relatively small number of commutes to jobs within the six counties originated outside their boundaries. Second, the area is sizable along a number of dimensions. It includes over 1,100 census tracts and almost 10,000 census block groups, the smallest unit of aggregation used in the analysis. The sample consisted of about 650,000 people in just under 244,000 households.

The census provided a wealth of data on the individuals in the sample—race and ethnicity, age, educational attainment, income from various sources, household size and structure, occupation, and employment location. Throughout the analysis, the household was treated as the decision-making agent; each household's racial/ethnic status was characterized as that of the "householder"—typically the household's primary earner. The census data also provided a variety of housing characteristics: whether the unit is owned or rented, the corresponding rent or owner-reported value, property tax payment, number of rooms, number of bedrooms, type of structure, and the age of the building. The construction of neighborhood characteristics started with characterizing the stock of housing in the neighborhood surrounding each house. Using the census data, the neighborhood racial/ethnic, educational, and income distributions were also constructed based on the households within the same census block group, a census region containing approximately 500 housing units. Additional data describing local conditions were merged with each house record, including variables related to crime rates, land use, local schools, topography, and urban density. Finally, all homeowners and renters were included in the estimation, and house values are converted to monthly rents according to a weighted procedure outlined in BFM.

Instrumental Variables

The choice model alone does not provide a method to solve for the endogeneity of neighborhood sociodemographics, that is, the correlation between neighborhood sociodemographics and unobserved neighborhood quality. It is still necessary to apply a research design to deal with this type of omitted variable bias. The design is based on instrumental variables. The specific instrumental variable was a set of school attendance zone boundaries, a setup that is typical of a regression discontinuity design. Identification came in three steps. First, it was shown that housing characteristics were continuous around these boundaries, so we considered them exogenous. Second, since there is a noticeable discontinuity in school quality across those boundaries (that is, each boundary divided a relatively good from a relatively bad school within a district), we assumed that sorting around those boundaries is fundamentally driven by differences in school quality. Therefore, variation in sociodemographics, such as the percentage of Hispanics, is not endogenous but caused by an observed variable: school quality. Since we could control for school quality (by using test scores for example), we were in fact purging the estimates of the main endogeneity problem.

Results

Standard hedonic regressions that use the BFM data set show that marginal WTP is zero for Hispanic neighborhoods. This means that ethnicity is not capitalized at the margin, and that all negative correlation between house prices and minority share found in other studies may be due just to the fact that minorities tend to sort into areas with lower-quality amenities. However, marginal valuation may be quite different from mean valuation for Hispanic neighbors. It may be that such a zero result is driven by a few mixed neighborhoods whose residents are really indifferent to either an increase or a reduction in the proportion of Hispanic neighbors. Mean preferences, on the other hand, are a combination of preferences for all individuals in the sample. Since most individuals in the metropolitan area are of "white" descent, we can interpret mean preferences as being the same as those of a representative white household.

BFM model estimates of mean preferences for percentage of Hispanics in a neighborhood indicate that an increase of 10 percent in the Hispanic makeup of a neighborhood would decrease the value of a monthly rental by $8.80, or approximately −$1 per month in rents for every 1 percent change in the share of Hispanic neighbors. Since the baseline monthly rent is approximately $1,000, the 10 percent increase in Hispanic share would cause a decline in housing rents of approximately 1 percentage point. This first estimate does not include the instrumental variable strategy, though, and therefore its magnitude may be upward biased due to omitted variable bias.

In fact, when boundary fixed effects are included in the analysis, the estimated MWTP for the percentage of Hispanics in the block group is reduced to almost zero. In practice, the inclusion of boundary fixed effects substantially reduces the magnitude of the estimated MWTP of all of the neighborhood sociodemographic characteristics. For comparison purposes, BFM also show results from the sorting model with black neighbors. Here, even when boundary fixed effects are included, the estimated MWTP from the sorting model for black neighbors remains significantly negative, -$104 per month, and statistically significant; this result is noticeably different from the mean preference for Hispanic neighbors. Since the mean household in the Bay Area is probably a white household, this indicates that white households have stronger negative preferences for blacks than for Hispanics.

In addition to mean preferences, the BFM structural approach also allows the estimation of heterogeneity in WTP for neighborhood sociodemographic characteristics. The full model includes 135 interactions between nine household characteristics and fifteen housing and neighborhood characteristics—here we focus only on the parameters related to racial or ethnic status. While all households prefer to live in higher-income neighborhoods, *conditional on neighborhood income and education,* households prefer to self-segregate on the basis of race/ethnicity. In particular, the estimates imply that Hispanics are willing to pay $86 more per month than whites to live in a neighborhood that has 10 percent more Hispanics. The MWTP of whites for such an increase is -$0.35 per month. Thus $86 is the difference between the *positive* WTP of Hispanic households for this change and the *zero* WTP of white households (which are the majority of the population and also the representative mean household), indicating that households have strong self-segregating preferences based on ethnicity.

Taken together, estimates of the heterogeneous model of household sorting reveal a coherent story regarding the role of Hispanic ethnicity in the housing market. In particular, they suggest that (1) neighborhood ethnic composition is strongly correlated with unobserved housing and neighborhood quality, so that one really needs to control for these in order to estimate preferences for neighborhood ethnic composition; (2) households have strong self-segregating preferences; (3) neighborhood ethnic composition may not be directly capitalized into housing prices, as neighborhood price differences are not required to clear the market, and (4) mean preferences for an increase in the share of black neighbors seems more negative than mean preferences for an increase in the Hispanic share.

Estimating Preferences from Housing Transactions

This section reviews the results from Ferreira and Saiz (2008). Their study is unique in that they were able to pin down the ethnic group identity of all new home buyers and sellers in the San Francisco Bay area. Overall, the data set consists of over 1.2 million housing transactions over a period of 17 years (1988–2004) and includes data on the exact location of each house. All previous studies, mainly focusing on black-white price differentials, had to contend with cross-sectional data, with very small sample sizes, or with data aggregated at higher levels of geography. In addition, most conventional data sources do not identify the ethnicity/race of each new home buyer and seller.

Ferreira and Saiz derived Hispanic identity from using the surname of the buyer and seller of each home in the population of transactions. As it will be demonstrated in the following section, Hispanic self-identification corresponds very closely to possessing a Hispanic surname. With this information one can use a standard hedonic regression framework to estimate whether housing prices are affected by the share of Hispanics in the census tract (a geographic unit that corresponds to about 1,000 households), the same share at the block group level (an even smaller geographic unit with about 250 households), and, more important, changes in the Hispanic share at the block level.

This second approach to estimating MWTP for Hispanic neighbors also controlled for block fixed effects, relying effectively on the variance contained in the changes in the Hispanic share, and therefore controlling for quality attributes that may account for housing prices and be correlated with geographic patterns of Hispanic settlement. The richness of the data also allowed for the inclusion of a number of housing attributes (as recorded by the county assessors for local taxation purposes in each transaction) in the hedonic framework and for quarter-year fixed effects—effectively soaking up nonparametrically all time trends that are common to all neighborhoods in the San Francisco area. The Hispanic-ethnicity identity of the previous homeowner—no data on renters were available in this research—of each house was also included to control for additional unobserved features that arise from heterogeneous preferences for housing styles and certain types of renovation and maintenance.

Data

Ferreira and Saiz obtained a comprehensive data set of all housing transactions from the same six contiguous counties in the San Francisco Bay Area used in the BFM study—Alameda, Contra Costa, Marin, San Mateo, San Francisco, and Santa Clara—between the years 1988 and 2004. Relevant to this project, the data contained the names of the buyers and sellers, the transaction value, a number of structural quality and transaction characteristics, the exact date of the transaction, and the latitude and longitude coordinates of each property's location. Based on the entry for each buyer and seller, surnames were extracted and entities were categorized as organizations (company, institution, etc.), trusts, estates, and/or individuals. These classifications are not all mutually exclusive; a trust could be an organization or an individual, for example.

To determine the likelihood that a given surname was Hispanic, a data set was borrowed from Word and Perkins (1996), who compiled the Spanish Origin Record (SOR) file. The Census Bureau appended names to over seven million individual records from the 1990 census, initially for the purpose of estimating undercount. The SOR file was created by tabulating each individual's response to the Hispanic origin question under their surname, thus giving a frequency of positive responses to the question for each surname in the sample. Importantly, only surnames for which at least one person claimed Hispanic ethnicity are included in the SOR.

There are 25,266 unique Hispanic and non-Hispanic surnames in the SOR data that represent a wide range of Hispanic occurrences per surname. The surnames in the transactions data were then merged with the observed probabilities of Hispanic origin. Almost exactly half of all surnames matched a surname from the SOR file for both buyer and seller surnames. For surnames in the transactions data that did not match any SOR surname, a conservative value of zero likelihood of Hispanic ethnicity was assumed in order to minimize any possible Type II error. From these probabilities based on Hispanic surnames, a dummy variable indicating the Hispanic ethnicity of buyers and sellers was then created. A cutoff value of 60 percent likelihood of being Hispanic in the SOR data was chosen; non-Hispanic ethnicity was assumed for those surnames not on the SOR list. Because there are seldom values for likelihood of Hispanic ethnicity in the midranges—only 5 percent of buyer and 4 percent of seller surnames have a 10 to 90 percent probability of being Hispanic based on the SOR surname-ethnicity distribution—60 percent was chosen with reasonable expectation that there would not be an overly large number of false positive assignments of Hispanic ethnicity (the final results are robust to different cutoff points).

In addition to the impact of a single Hispanic buyer or Hispanic seller on housing values, it is important to capture the effect of the overall share of Hispanic owners in the neighborhood. By using exact latitude and longitude coordinates, 1990 census tract, block group, and block identifiers were assigned to each property. Ferreira and Saiz used tracts, block groups, and blocks to capture local effects at, respectively, broader and narrower neighborhood levels and in the immediate surroundings of the house under consideration. The data allow for the tabulation (at the time of each transaction) of the total number of owners and whether or not they were Hispanic, and therefore the neighborhood share of Hispanic residents at all neighborhood levels and at any single point in time.

To assess the quality of the data, we compared the changes between the 1990 and 2000 census in total homeownership, Hispanic homeownership, and the share of movers in the last year, to our predicted values based on the SOR data. For Hispanic homeownership comparisons, the differences between the two measures are not off by more than 2 percent except for Santa Clara, and the directions are the same except for Marin County (using observed "likelihood Hispanic"). Both measures of total transactions agree in direction except for Santa Clara, and the data estimates tend to be lower than the census estimates. In a sense, these comparisons are actually testing the quality of the census (sample) estimates, since the transactions data represent the entire population of transactions in these counties. Finally, the correlation of the running sum of total and Hispanic homeowners that purchased houses in 1999 at the tract level with the same measure based on the 2000 census data is a very high 0.962.

Results

First, it is important to give a sense of the strength of the association between the Hispanic owner share (as measured using the surnames involved in sales transactions) and transaction-based housing values. In practice, this is accomplished by running a hedonic regression of the log of housing values for all properties that transacted in 2000 on the Hispanic share in a census block. No other controls are added. The estimates imply that, on average, one can expect housing values to be about 1.2 percentage points lower with each increase of one percentage point in the Hispanic share. Of course, no causal statement can be inferred from that correlation, since, for instance, physical quality attributes can be different in Hispanic neighborhoods.

This basic association weakens when covariates are added for several quality attributes of the home in the transaction. One of the major advantages of using transactions records is that they contain a host of variables about the house and some information about individual sellers. Individual controls that are used throughout the paper include whether the seller is Hispanic (to allay any concerns that Hispanics invest lower amounts in renovation or maintenance and that, therefore, the quality of their homes is lower), whether the buyer and/or seller are individuals, and whether the buyer and/or seller are in a trust. Structural quality control variables include year of construction, lot size, square footage, size of additions, presence and size of basement, number of bathrooms, number of bedrooms, number of other rooms, number of stories, whether there is a fireplace, whether there is any garage and its size, details on heating and cooling devices, whether there is a pool, whether the property is multi-unit, whether there is a view, dummies for the shape of the building and construction quality (as defined by county assessors), whether it is a full sale (as opposed to a partial sale), and whether the sale is for a subdivision (as opposed to a resale).

These controls reduce by half the original association between Hispanic share and housing prices, suggesting that Hispanics live in homes that are observably of lower quality—a conclusion similar to that reached by BFM. Controls for the median household income on the block, a proxy for the social and environmental perceived "quality" of the neighborhood, further weaken the association between Hispanic density and prices. Covariates for the share of Hispanic owners at the block group and census tract levels are also added. Each upper geographic level excludes data from the lower levels of aggregation. The alternative measures at different levels of aggregation are important for understanding whether ethnic preferences operate at very localized levels or whether, on the contrary, people consider the ethnic composition at the broader neighborhood scale. Hispanic shares at all levels of aggregation seem to correlate negatively with prices. In general, however, the preferred focus of the analysis will be on the coefficient for Hispanic share at the block level. Any findings at the block level will be considered as stronger evidence of the existence of preferences for the ethnic makeup of a locale.

However, even after including all these observed covariates, one cannot take these cross-sectional correlations as prima facie evidence that the willingness-to-pay of the marginal buyer in these neighborhoods is lower because of higher shares of Hispanic residents. Many unobserved neighborhood attributes may still account for the remaining correlation. To account for this issue, Ferreira and Saiz used changes in housing prices and Hispanic resident shares, holding constant the neighborhood location, in order to identify changes in the willingness-to-pay of the marginal buyer. They ran a hedonic regression specification that includes block fixed effects (perhaps the most detailed neighborhood characteristic control) and also dummies for each quarter and year in the sample. These time-dummies therefore capture the general evolution of prices in the San Francisco metropolitan area. In order to account for spatial correlation of the error terms, all specifications cluster standard errors by census block and year.

The final estimates suggest a *zero* impact of the growth of the Hispanic resident share on housing values. Even when the Hispanic owner shares at the block group and tract levels are added to the model, there is still no evidence that new Hispanic move-ins have an impact on average at the block level. As a robustness test, the sample of transactions was restricted to the set of tracts with homeownership rates of at least 60 percent, so the results are not primarily driven by other potential changes in the rental market that are not observed in these data. Again, there is no impact of the growth in the Hispanic owner share at the block group level when one restricts the sample to blocks with high homeownership rates.

Do these results indicate the absence of ethnic-based residential preferences with regards to Hispanics in the San Francisco metropolitan area? As in the BFM approach presented earlier in this chapter, they do not. There is evidence that is consistent with the existence of heterogeneous preferences to live with Hispanic neighbors. When limiting the sample to blocks for which the initial share of whites was above 60 percent in the initial year (1990), the growth of Hispanic densities was in fact associated with price declines, that is, white neighborhoods have negative MWTP for positive changes in the Hispanic share. Focusing on the block effects, the elasticity of prices with respect to Hispanic shares is estimated to be approximately -0.1. For instance, if a mostly white neighborhood sees a transition of the Hispanic share from 0 to 10 percent, prices can be expected to decline by 1 percent.

Overall, these estimates are consistent with the existence of heterogeneous preferences for the ethnic composition of a neighborhood, as in the BFM approach. Minorities (blacks, Asians, and Hispanics) and whites living in mixed areas seem not to change their willingness-to-pay for a location with the growth of Hispanic population. Since in 2000 (1990) the share of minorities in San Francisco was 50 percent (40 percent) the impact on prices in many areas where Hispanics clustered is nonexistent. However, whites living in predominantly white areas seem to display decreasing willingness-to-pay for increasing Hispanic shares.

Conclusion

In this chapter I ask whether non-Hispanics display ethnic-based residential preferences and avoid living in Hispanic neighborhoods. If non-Hispanics exhibit negative preferences toward interacting with Hispanics, we may be able to capture this effect through housing market dynamics and its effects on housing prices.

Reviewing two alternative methods of dealing with the endogeneity of sociodemographic characteristics of the neighborhood, I find that both approaches lead to remarkably similar results. First, there is a strong correlation between the share of Hispanic households in the neighborhood and negative unobserved neighborhood quality. However, when controlling for these unobserved features, the impact of Hispanic share on price is negligible. Second, this does not imply that different groups of individuals have homogeneous preferences for Hispanic neighbors. In fact, there is strong heterogeneity in preferences, more specifically, strong preferences of individuals of the same racial or ethnic group to live with each other. This result indicates that such heterogeneous preferences may lead to self-segregation in the housing market, which is evidenced by the clusters of Hispanics in certain neighborhoods.

The results I reviewed for the Hispanic minority are also somewhat similar to more recent empirical results observed for the black minority, although it seems that an increase in the Hispanic share does not affect house prices in predominantly white neighborhoods as much as an increase in the percentage of blacks does.

Finally, caution should be used when enacting policies that try to mitigate observed housing segregation—to the extent that parameters estimated in this chapter can be thought of as primitive preferences, constraints to segregation may be bound to fail if households have low mobility costs. Given these patterns, future research could focus on the implications of this self-segregation, such as lower access to certain public goods like well-funded public schools.

Chapter 16

Increasing Diversity and the Future of U.S. Housing Segregation

Robert DeFina and Lance Hannon

Racial and ethnic diversity has increased markedly in the United States during the past two decades, mainly as a result of Hispanic and Asian immigration. Between 1990 and 2000, for example, the Hispanic and Asian populations in metropolitan areas grew 5 percent per year and 4.5 percent per year, respectively. Non-Hispanic blacks, Hispanics, and Asians now account for about 33 percent of metropolitan area residents, up from about 26.5 percent in 1990.

Growing diversity carries with it a number of potentially important challenges for communities that are experiencing the demographic change. A central issue is how increasing diversity will affect the ability of individual minority groups to successfully integrate themselves and comfortably share neighborhoods and other common resources with the majority white population.

Overall, trends in housing segregation of whites from minority populations have varied over the past twenty years, depending on the particular minority group in question. Segregation of non-Hispanic blacks from non-Hispanic whites has trended downward modestly, although still remains at relatively high levels. Segregation of both Hispanics and Asians from non-Hispanic whites has risen, by contrast, and by some measures of segregation, substantially so.

This chapter examines one way that rising diversity might have influenced these segregation trends; namely, that diversity has moderated an established empirical regularity whereby increases in an area's minority population share are associated with higher levels of segregation (e.g., Logan, Stults, and Farley 2004; Blanchard 2007; DeFina and Hannon 2009). The relationship between an area's percent minority and its degree of segregation has been called the "racial threat effect." The effect is thought to arise from reactions by white residents to perceived threats to their dominant political, economic, and social position that accompany growing minority populations (Blalock 1967). These reactions might include neighborhood flight and the imposition of social control measures, such as discriminatory housing practices. As will be discussed later, increased diversity could either strengthen or diminish the racial threat effect. The range of possibilities thus motivates an empirical study of the actual effects.

Using census data for 1990 and 2000 in a series of regression analyses, we examined how the effects of percent Hispanic and percent black on metropolitan housing segregation are contingent on the level of multiethnic diversity. We measured segregation by means of the well-known isolation index (Massey and Denton 1988). Given recent evidence pointing to the dynamic nature of both segregation patterns and racial and ethnic diversity in the United States, we employed a longitudinal research design in which we focused on explaining the sources of change in metropolitan segregation between 1990 and 2000.

Recent Trends in Housing Segregation and Diversity

There are a variety of indexes that researchers use to measure the degree of segregation in a metropolitan statistical area (MSA), as a metropolitan area is designated in the census. Two of the most popular and easily computed gauges are the dissimilarity index and the isolation index. In an earlier analysis (DeFina and Hannon 2009), we analyzed changes in the dissimilarity index over time. Here, we focus on the isolation index. The isolation index captures a different dimension of segregation than does the dissimilarity index, and it is important to see whether diversity affects different dimensions in similar ways.[1]

The isolation index measures the extent to which members of a minority group live in neighborhoods in which they are exposed only to other members of the group.[2] The index essentially gives the probability that when an African American who is picked at random from the MSA goes for a walk in his or her neighborhood, the first person encountered would also be African American. It has a minimum value of zero, which occurs when a member of a minority group has no neighbors of the same minority group. It has a maximum value of one, in which case a minority group member has neighbors who are all in the same minority group.

The average MSA index values, weighed by the size of the relevant minority population, for three racial and ethnic pairs are shown in Figure 16.1 for the years 1980, 1990, and 2000. Calculation of the index

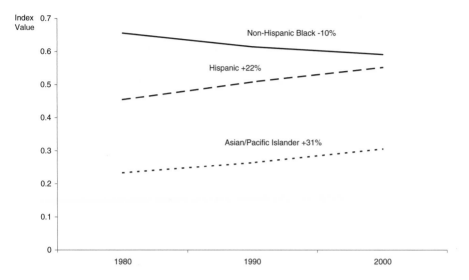

Figure 16.1. Trends in Segregation from Non-Hispanic Whites (weighted average MSA isolation index)

Note: The MSA average value for each minority group is weighted by the population of that group.

values requires detailed information from the decennial censuses, so a snapshot of segregation levels is available only for the years shown. The comparison group for each racial and ethnic category is composed of non-Hispanic whites.

Two points regarding African American segregation can be noted.[3] First, the level of African American isolation from non-Hispanic whites has fallen modestly during the past twenty years, about 10 percent. The decline decelerated slightly from the 1980s to the 1990s. Second, despite the decline, African American segregation remains relatively high. Researchers use a rule of thumb that an index value greater than 0.6 indicates a "highly segregated" area. The 2000 MSA average value, weighted by non-Hispanic black population, is roughly 0.6. In some cities, such as New York and Detroit, the index exceeds 0.8, a remarkably high degree of isolation.

In contrast to trends in African American segregation, Hispanic segregation has risen markedly during the past two decades, by 22 percent. The rising levels of isolation could reflect the ongoing influx of new Hispanic immigrants into limited ports of entry and their continued reliance on existing ethnic enclaves. Examples might include immigrant crowding in southern California and in parts of Texas that occur both because of the proximity to the border and because the established communities make it easer for new arrivals to find jobs, housing, and services. More complex dynamics could also be at work (Farley and Frey 1994). Hispanic isolation levels are somewhat less than those for African Americans (the weighted average MSA equals 0.55), but nonetheless would be considered "moderate to high" using typical standards. Finally, segregation of Asians and Pacific Islanders is lowest of all, although, like Hispanic segregation, it has risen sharply during the past twenty years, by 31 percent.

Coinciding with these trends in isolation has been a noticeable rise in metro area racial and ethnic diversity. As mentioned, this has occurred mainly due to the influx of Hispanics and Asians. Recent census data indicate that racial and ethnic minorities now constitute a majority of the population in one out of ten U.S. counties.

One way to summarize the extent of overall diversity in a metro area is with an entropy score (Massey and Denton 1988; Iceland 2004).[4] The entropy score is essentially a weighted average of the population shares of mutually exclusive racial and ethnic groups. The diversity index differs from the isolation index in that it simply measures the extent to which various groups are represented in the population of an MSA. It says nothing about the spatial distribution of the groups across the MSA. A given amount of diversity could be consistent with either high or low residential isolation, depending on how the various racial and ethnic groups are arranged spatially.

Figure 16.2 shows the population-weighted average metro area values of the diversity index.[5] Index values are calculated using six mutually exclusive groups: non-Hispanic whites, non-Hispanic blacks, Hispanics, non-Hispanic Asians and Pacific Islanders, non-Hispanic Native Americans and Alaska natives, and non-Hispanic other races. Index values can range from 0 (no diversity) to a maximum value that depends on the number of groups used in the calculation. In our calculations, the maximum value is 1.79 and occurs when all six groups are equally represented. As can be seen in Figure 16.2, the average diversity in metro areas has been rising throughout the last twenty years, with the pace accelerating in the 1990s. Overall, diversity rose almost 40 percent between 1980 and 2000.

The Racial Threat Hypothesis

The initial formulation of the racial threat hypothesis is largely credited to Blalock (1956, 1957, 1967), who argued that an increasing minority

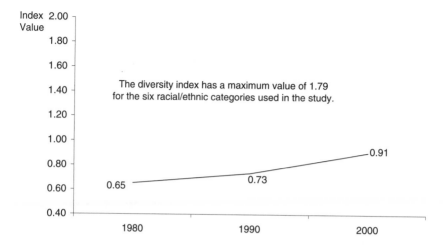

Figure 16.2. An Index of Racial and Ethnic Diversity (Population-weighted MSA average)

presence can threaten three aspects of a dominant group's position—its economic, political, and social status advantages.[6] Consequently, and consistent with general conflict theories of social control, a growing minority fraction is likely to elicit an increase in repressive measures from whites as they work to stanch the erosion of their privileges.

As noted earlier, researchers have found a positive link between percent minority and housing segregation, a relationship consistent with a racial threat effect. Housing segregation might function as a social control mechanism for various reasons. One is a possible desire by whites to limit competition for jobs. Segregation can be used, for example, to create a spatial mismatch between minority workers and jobs. Physically isolating minority populations can both remove them from job information networks and increase commuting difficulties, thereby limiting access to jobs. Segregation can also serve to help deny minority populations valued public goods. Because of their geographic isolation from each other, minority and white populations will have fewer common political goals. Whites, for instance, have less incentive to vote for community programs, parks, and cleaner streets in minority neighborhoods if they have no personal stake in these outcomes.

Blalock elaborated on the basic idea of racial threat, hypothesizing that the rate at which additional repressive actions are implemented will differ depending on which aspect of privilege is under attack. When the threat is political, Blalock believed that efforts toward social control will increase at an increasing rate.[7] That is, as the minority presence increases, the dominant group generally will have to intensify its actions to counter the minority's growing political influence.

By contrast, when the threat is considered economic, say, increased competition for jobs, the growth of repressive actions would decelerate as minority population increased. Blalock opined that the dominant group usually can reduce minority competition using some strong initial measures. In essence, the success of these strong initial measures helps relieve the dominant group's anxiety about the extent of racial threat. Blalock further suggested that the intensity of control measures might lessen based on a decreased ability of whites to assess changes in the size of minority populations (and therefore changes in threat level). By this logic, whites will be most sensitive to increases in the minority population when the minority population initially is small.

Formulated mostly before the civil rights and black power social movements of the late 1960s and early 1970s, Blalock's theory of racial threat and economic competition implies that nonlinearity in the minority share–social control relationship is almost exclusively a product of the perceptions and actions of whites. Alternatively, it is possible that increases in the minority share of the population are less likely to lead to increases in social control actions in places with a strong minority presence because in such areas, minorities are better able to collectively mobilize to mitigate them.

The prospect of a racial threat effect and its possible nonlinear form has been used to comprehend an array of social phenomena. One such line of research has explored the role of racial threat in incidents of southern lynching roughly between 1880 and 1930. Reed (1972) and Corzine, Creech, and Corzine (1983) found that the incidence of lynchings increased at an accelerating rate as the share of blacks in the population rose. Tolnay, Beck, and Massey (1989) offered somewhat different evidence, finding that lynching displayed a positive but decelerating relationship to percent black in counties of the Deep South. Similarly, Tolnay and Beck (1995) concluded that "A positive relationship exists between percent black in the county and black lynchings, but it grows weaker as black concentration increases" (p. 111).

The racial threat effect has also been explored in studies of school segregation. Examining the relationship between the percent black and school integration for North Carolina counties, Cochran and Uhlman (1973) found that as the percent black increased, so too did the amount of school segregation, although at a decreasing rate. A few studies of social control via criminal justice policy have also explored the relevance of Blalock's racial threat hypotheses (e.g., Carmichael 2005; D'Alessio, Eitle, and Stolzenberg 2005; Stucky 2005). For example, in his study of local politics and municipal police force size, Stucky (2005) reported positive relationships between both the percent Hispanic and percent black and the number of police per capita. The effects for both the percent black and the percent Hispanic were nonlinear, with the size of the positive effect on police per capita declining as either black or Hispanic share of the population grew.

McCreary, England, and Farkas (1989) examined the link between race and the probability of employment and found a negative but nonlinear decelerating relationship between percent black and the probability of employment for young black men. Additionally, Tolnay (2001) tested Blalock's theory using data on the occupational standing of blacks and immigrants in the United States in 1920. Inconsistent with Blalock's racial threat hypothesis, he found no evidence of a negative relationship between percent black and occupational standing for blacks. Interestingly, however, Tolnay's research suggested that the nature of the relationship between the size of the immigrant population and occupational standing for immigrants was contingent on the presence of other racial/ethnic groups in the area.

In sum, a fair amount of empirical evidence exists that documents a positive relationship between percent minority and various social control measures. These findings are consistent with a racial threat effect. The link has generally been found to be nonlinear, although the form of the nonlinearity appears to depend on the particular social control mechanism under study.

The Complex Impact of Diversity on Racial Threat Effects

Much of the theoretical and empirical research on racial threat effects mentions little about the context in which the effects supposedly arise. That is, the sizes of the effects are presumed to be independent of the social, economic, and demographic milieu in which whites and minorities interact. We suggest here that those effects might indeed be contextual as they concern housing segregation, specifically depending on the extent of racial and ethnic diversity in a metro area.

Precisely how the increased multiethnic diversity over the last decade affects the relationship between the size of a given minority population and whites' perceptions of racial threat is theoretically ambiguous and likely complex. For example, Krivo and Kaufman (1999:105) argued that "a relatively large presence of other racial and ethnic groups places substantial additional constraints on the potential for black-white desegregation. . . . In essence, whites want to live in neighborhoods in which *all* other racial ethnic groups have only a minimal presence."

Thus, whites might have a set tolerance level for non-whites of all racial and ethnic backgrounds, but additional contact with any nonwhites beyond some threshold could cause a desire for more segregation. Moreover, increased diversity might accentuate cultural distinctions, such as language and clothing differences, and obscure shared experiences and expectations. With a single minority group, whites may hope for eventual assimilation, but with high levels of multiethnic diversity whites may question the practical feasibility of social integration for so many different groups.

Along these lines, Putnam's (2007) analysis of survey data for U.S. metropolitan areas led him to conclude that

> inhabitants of diverse communities tend to withdraw from collective life, to distrust their neighbours, regardless of the colour of their skin, to withdraw even from close friends, to expect the worst from their community and its leaders, to volunteer less, give less to charity and work on community projects less often, to register to vote less, to agitate for social reform more, but have less faith that they can actually make a difference, and to huddle unhappily in front of the television. . . . Diversity, at least in the short run, seems to bring out the turtle in all of us.

Thus, on the surface, Putnam's results seem to imply that increased diversity will ultimately increase racial and ethnic segregation by weakening the desire for social integration among both whites and minorities and by eroding a community's willingness and ability to work toward common goals. The higher levels of social mistrust in diverse communities suggested by Putnam's results imply that white perceptions of racial threat for any particular minority population will be heightened when combined with the presence of multiethnic diversity.

Still, a close reading of Putnam's results suggests that the role of diversity in conditioning racial threat effects is probably complex. According to Putnam, diversity not only affects trust *between* racial and ethnic groups but *within* them as well. That is, he found that increased neighborhood diversity decreases trust among whites in addition to trust between whites and, say, Hispanics. Interestingly, diversity appeared to decrease trust within a racial and ethnic group more than between groups. Furthermore, Putnam (2007:154) noted that the deleterious "impact of diversity is definitely greater among whites." This finding is relevant here because it suggests that diversity may limit the ability of whites to collectively promote segregation more than it limits the ability of minority groups to collectively resist segregation. A more nuanced interpretation of Putnam's results consequently would suggest that diversity might ultimately reduce segregation by constraining the ability

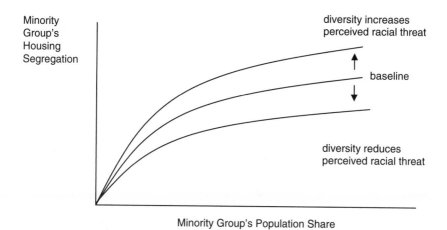

Figure 16.3. Diversity and the Racial Threat Hypothesis

of whites to act on any perception of growing racial threats, rather than ultimately increasing segregation by exacerbating racial threat effects.

It is also quite possible that increased positive interactions between whites and members of one minority group could translate into more positive attitudes toward members of other groups as well. That is, one minority group could serve as a social bridge between whites and another minority group. For example, white-Hispanic interactions might increase the likelihood of whites knowing blacks as "friends of a friend."

Another way in which diversity might alter white attitudes is suggested by the literature on "defended neighborhoods" (Suttles 1972; Reider 1985; De Sena 1990). In this view, the fraction of same-race neighbors determines whites' psycho-social attachment to a neighborhood and their desire and ability to keep it racially homogeneous. As areas become more diverse, "whites adapt to the notion that non-whites are an expected feature of the neighborhood while those most hostile to minority encroachment quit the neighborhood" (Green, Strolovitch, and Wong 1998:376). Thus, as neighborhoods become more diverse, a given share of a specific minority group will elicit less of an exclusionary response, such as segregation. Additionally, Frey and Farley (1996:42) argued that the presence of multiple minority groups can disrupt a "single minority vs. White majority" mentality that facilitates discriminatory real estate marketing.

Figure 16.3 summarizes the complexity of predictions regarding diversity's mitigating or aggravating impact on the relationship between a particular minority's population growth and its degree of housing segregation. The "baseline" relationship between the minority's share and segregation is positive, indicating that higher fractions of a minority population are associated with greater levels of segregation. This is the basic racial threat hypothesis. The relationship is presented as nonlinear consistent with some theoretical models and empirical evidence relating racial threat and other forms of social control, such as increased policing. The potential conditioning effects of diversity are shown as rotations in the baseline curve up or down. Should diversity exacerbate segregation, as argued by Krivo and Kaufman (1999), the curve would rotate upward, indicating that diversity causes greater segregation at a specified level of a minority's share. Should diversity mitigate segregation, consistent with the thinking of Frey and Farley (1996), the curve would rotate downward, so that less segregation would arise at each level of the minority's share.

Data and Methods

We examined whether diversity is consistent with mitigation or exacerbation of racial threat effects on segregation by incorporating interaction terms into standard multivariate regression models of segregation. Models were estimated for the changes in MSA isolation index scores between 1990 and 2000. Separate analyses were done for non-Hispanic black/non-Hispanic white and for Hispanic/non-Hispanic white isolation index scores. We distinguished between different minority groups because the strength with which a given determinant affects segregation could well differ from one group to the next. Some studies have found, for example, that differences in income matter more for white-Hispanic segregation than for white-black segregation.

The use of MSAs as our unit of analysis is consistent with the bulk of macro research in the area (Farley and Frey 1994; Iceland 2004; Logan, Stults, and Farley 2004; Krivo and Kaufman 1999; Massey and Denton 1988). To ensure reliable estimates given our sample size we used a robust regression procedure that downweights the influence of outlying observations. This procedure reduced the sample size from a total of 331 to 301 MSAs for both analyses. All variables apart from the isolation and entropy scores measuring segregation and diversity, respectively, were constructed using U.S. census data from Geolytics's (2004) Neighborhood Change Database. The isolation indexes and entropy scores for each MSA are taken from the Census Bureau Web site (www.census.gov/hhes/www/housing/housing_patterns/housing_patterns.html).

The variable to be explained in each change regression is the 1990 isolation score minus the 2000 value. To incorporate the basic racial threat hypothesis in the change regressions, we included the change in percent black or percent Hispanic from 1990 to 2000 as an independent variable, also measured as the 1990 value minus the 2000 value. If racial threat has a nonlinear effect, then changes in percent black or percent Hispanic should have an impact that varies systematically with the initial level of minority share of the population. Suppose, for example, that the slope of the relationship between the level of minority share and the level of segregation is positive but diminishes as minority share rises, as in Figure 16.3. Then, a given change in percent black should lead to a smaller change in segregation at higher initial levels of percent black than at lower initial levels. The possibility of a nonlinear effect is incorporated by including a separate variable equal to the change in percent black or percent Hispanic multiplied by the level of percent black or percent Hispanic in 1990.

The central empirical issue addressed here is whether the effects of a change in the minority's share of the population are significantly affected by overall metropolitan diversity. The possible conditioning effect of diversity is captured using a variable equal to the change in percent black or percent Hispanic times the level of diversity in 1990 as measured by the entropy score. If diversity plays a moderating role, then higher levels of diversity reduce the size of the positive relationship between changes in a minority's share of the population and changes in its segregation. The reverse would be true if diversity exacerbates racial threat effects.

In order to better isolate the racial threat effect and the potentially moderating effect of diversity, the models also controlled for various MSA-level attributes found to be significant predictors of segregation in previous studies (e.g., Massey and Gross 1991; Farley and Frey 1994; Frey and Farley 1996; Krivo and Kaufman 1999; Logan, Stults, and Farley 2004). These variables include separate indicators of whether an MSA's economic base is characterized by a pronounced military, retirement community, or university presence. Additionally, we controlled for changes in the income of a minority group relative to that of whites, changes in the amount of new housing in an MSA, the region in which an MSA is located, an MSA's population size, the initial level of the isolation index, and the minority's initial share of the population.

Results

We used multivariate iteratively reweighted least squares regression to test for a conditioning effect of diversity on the percent minority-segregation relationship. This robust regression procedure minimizes the least squares estimation problems that frequently occur when the sam-

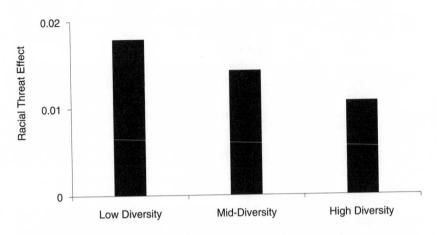

Figure 16.4. Magnitude of Racial Threat Effect for Change in Percentage Black, 1990–2000, by 1990 Level of Diversity

ple size is less than 500, as it is in the current analysis (301 metro areas). A table containing the full results is in an appendix to the chapter.

Central to the focus of the current study, and consistent with the results reported in other studies investigating racial threat effects (e.g., Cochran and Uhlman 1973), increases in the minority share of the population were significantly associated with increases in racial and ethnic isolation. The relationship appears to be nonlinear in that it depends on the starting level of percent minority; that is, the change in percent minority was found to have a smaller impact in areas that had a higher percent minority in 1990.

Consistent with important theorizing in this area (e.g., Frey and Farley 1996) and central to the chapter, the diversity score in 1990 moderated the positive effect of change in the minority group's share of the population on change in isolation. More specifically, the results suggested that the isolation-inducing impact of an increase in the percent black or percent Hispanic was relatively weak in areas that started off with high levels of diversity and relatively strong in areas that started off with low levels of diversity. Interestingly, these core results imply that, other things being equal, as the United States becomes increasingly diverse, increases in the minority share of the population will matter less for determining amounts of residential isolation.

Figures 16.4 and 16.5 illustrate how changes in percent minority affect changes in the black and Hispanic isolation indexes at different starting levels of diversity. The sensitivity of changes in the isolation indexes to changes in the relevant percent minority is referred to as the racial

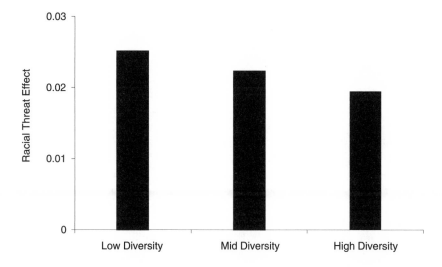

Figure 16.5. Magnitude of Racial Threat Effect for Change in Percentage Hispanic, 1990–2000, by 1990 Level of Diversity

threat effect in the graphs. It was measured using the estimated coefficients in the black and Hispanic regressions,[8] and represents the amount by which the change in the isolation index rises as the change in percent minority increases by one unit. The estimated sensitivity captures both the linear and nonlinear effects from changes in the minority's share.

Figure 16.4 demonstrates the racial threat effect associated with percent black changes across MSAs with three different levels of diversity: those that have diversity scores that are 1 standard deviation below the average level of diversity (Low); those that have diversity scores that are 1 standard deviation above the average level of diversity (High); and, those that have diversity scores at the average level of diversity (Mid). In general, our estimates show that the racial threat effect diminishes as an MSA's diversity scores increase. The estimated racial threat effect associated with an increase in the percent black is 67 percent greater in areas that start off with a low level of diversity (.0179) than in areas that start off with a high level of diversity (.0107).

Along the same lines, Figure 16.5 shows the varying magnitude of the effect of changes in the percent Hispanic on changes in Hispanic-white isolation. Consistent with the results for blacks, the estimates in Figure 16.5 demonstrate that the racial threat effect associated with an increase in the percent Hispanic is 29 percent greater in areas that start off with a low level of diversity (.0251) than in areas that start off with a high level of diversity (.0195). Thus, consistent with the racial threat hypothesis, increases in the minority share of the population are typically associated with increases in isolation. However, the strength of this relationship is contingent on the amount of preexisting multiethnic diversity. As a whole, the results suggest that solidly white areas are particularly likely to see a pronounced increase in minority isolation in response to an influx of Hispanics or blacks.

In terms of relevant theory, the results support Frey and Farley's (1996) contention that multiethnic diversity disrupts a type of binary thinking that underlies discriminatory real estate marketing practices. Furthermore, the results are consistent with the notion that increased positive interactions between whites and members of one minority group could translate into more positive attitudes toward members of other minority groups as well. From the defended neighborhoods perspective (Green, Strolovitch, and Wong 1998), the results are in line with the idea that whites are most defensive about minority encroachment when their neighborhoods are overwhelmingly white.

In addition, the results are congruent with at least one interpretation of Putnam's (2007) theory regarding diversity's impact on social trust and collective action. In particular, diversity may put greater limits on whites' ability to collectively discriminate than it does on the ability of Hispanics and blacks to collectively counter attempts at discrimination.

The results of the present analysis were arguably most inconsistent with Krivo and Kaufman's (1999) contention that whites have a certain threshold level of tolerance for nonwhites generally, and thus existing diversity increases the likelihood that a rise in the percent black or percent Hispanic will cause that threshold to be crossed and invoke a discriminatory response. Still, housing segregation is only one type of discriminatory response to perceived racial threats. Others may include increases in occupational segregation and wage inequality, use of harsh criminal justice policies, use of private security firms, attempts at political disenfranchisement, and anti-immigrant legislation. A potentially fruitful area for future research would be to explore whether diversity also exerts a moderating influence on the relationship between changes in the percent minority and these other forms of social control.

Policy Implications

The moderating effect that diversity appears to have on racial and ethnic isolation is certainly good news, given recent and likely continued demographic trends in the United States. As the population becomes increasingly diverse in the coming decades, segregation is likely to be lower than levels that otherwise would occur, since racial threat effects will probably diminish in magnitude.

A natural question to ask is, are there ways that concerted policy actions can make these demographic trends even more effective in promoting the goal of a more racially and ethnically integrated society? We believe that the answer is yes. Putnam (2007), for example, argued that even if diversity leads to increased social isolation and decreased trust in the near term, the long-term effects are unclear and hinge on various contextual factors. Some of these factors are subject to policy influence.

The ability to speak English has long been recognized as an obvious and key element in immigrant assimilation. Inability to speak the native language creates social distance and the lack of trust highlighted in Putnam's work. Policymakers thus might devote resources to community language-acquisition programs, especially ones that accommodate work schedules and childcare responsibilities.

Diversity driven by immigration can also cause problems and mistrust when immigrants gravitate toward a relatively limited number of jurisdictions. Over time, localities can become overwhelmed with increasing pressures on schools, housing, and health care and other social service needs. This type of dramatic influx can lead to resentment and increasing calls for social control of racial and ethnic minorities, and eventually to segregated housing patterns.

One possible response to this issue is to limit the overall number of immigrants arriving in the United States each year. Such a policy would, however, be counterproductive, given the documented economic benefits associated with immigration. A better option would be for policymakers to create programs that help disperse immigrants throughout wider areas. Such efforts would likely be most effective and defensible at the national level. Since immigration has been shown to create a net economic gain for the country as a whole, spreading the costs of adjustment and acculturation nationally via federal financing is sensible.

Finally, policymakers can help to create environments in which diverse populations can meet and interact in positive ways. Parks, community projects, and improved schools that are specifically designed to handle a diverse population are but a few possible initiatives that can emphasize the benefits of diversity and point the way toward socially richer, more productive, and closer-knit communities.

It is also important for policymakers to pursue initiatives that more generally help to promote integrated neighborhoods, beyond supporting the helpful roles that diversity might play. Doing so will yield additional benefits and could well enhance any impacts from increased diversity.

One set of ideas that is relevant comes from work by Ingrid Ellen (2000, 2008), who explored factors that underpin stability in racially integrated neighborhoods. The research of Ellen and others suggests that one facet of whites' aversion to integration is their concern that their homes will become part of a mythical "black neighborhood" infested with crime and drugs and lacking in social organization, public services, and serviceable infrastructure. In essence, as the share of minorities increases, whites increasingly come to expect the worst outcomes, with associated declines in housing values.

To the extent that such fears develop and can lead to white flight or other drivers of segregation, then policy actions can try to counteract them by dispelling stereotypes and highlighting successful examples of stably integrated areas. This can be accomplished through statements by political and community leaders, neighborhood events that showcase effective organizational strategies, and, of course, media coverage.

Policymakers can also be attentive to early signs of neighborhood decay and decreases in public services that can spur fears of neighborhood instability. Here, local governments might develop offices whose function is reliable information gathering about emerging neighborhood problems and the rapid handling of such issues. Such approaches have been put in place in various localities, such as Baltimore and Philadelphia, although it is too early to assess their achievements.

Policymakers can also think strategically about promoting integrated neighborhoods near anchoring institutions. Libraries, universities, and hospitals, for instance, provide longstanding structures and work forces that support both the appearance and the reality of vital and viable neighborhoods. They also constitute public spaces in which a sense of communal solidarity and social organization can develop, ingredients that are important for a stably integrated neighborhood.

Appendix

Table 16.1. Robust Regression for Changes in Metropolitan Isolation for Non-Hispanic Whites, 1990–2000

Independent Variable	Black/White Segregation		Hispanic/White Segregation	
	b	t-ratio	b	t-ratio
Isolation Index 1990	.1667***	13.78	.2540***	11.74
Total Population 1990 (ln)	−.0046***	−2.79	−.0098***	−6.49
Minority Population Share 1990 (either % Black or % Hispanic)	−.0024***	−8.49	−.0020***	−5.37
Minority Share Change	.0143***	9.47	.0231***	30.60
Diversity Index 1990	−.0079***	−3.51	−.0053**	−2.33
Diversity × Minority Share Change	−.0036**	−2.56	−.0028***	−4.33
Minority Share 1990 × Change in Minority Share	−.0003***	−3.32	−.0003***	−5.06
Minority/White Income Change	.0055	0.53	.0012	0.16
New Construction Change	.0007***	2.64	.00010	.48
Retirement Area 1990	.0047	1.04	.0064	1.38
University Area 1990	−.0009	−0.20	.0082	1.85
Military Area 1990	.0014	0.34	.0036	0.80
Northeast Region	−.0268***	−4.89	−.0344***	−6.24
Midwest Region	−.0075	−1.30	−.0168***	−3.44
West Region	−.0029	−0.54	−.009**	2.17
Intercept	.0117	0.57	.0353	1.83
Adjusted R^2	.5693		.8026	
N	301		301	

Note: The robust regression method used here is the iteratively reweighted least squares procedure in Stata 10.
Observations with a Cook's D greater than one were excluded from the analyses.
** $p < .05$, *** $p < .01$.

Chapter 17

Understanding Racial Segregation
What Is Known About the Effect of Housing
Discrimination?

Stephen L. Ross

My research experience in the area of housing discrimination began as a graduate student working on data from the 1989 Housing Discrimination Study (HDS 1989) and expanded dramatically when I had the opportunity to work as the lead researcher on the team that conducted the 2000 Housing Discrimination Study (HDS 2000) (Turner et al. 2002; Turner and Ross 2003a; Turner and Ross 2004). Since the completion of HDS 2000, I have had numerous opportunities to speak about the findings of the study at public events, often presenting as part of broader panels that contain fair housing advocates and officers of community groups involved in fair housing enforcement. Such individuals usually give presentations that provide compelling evidence concerning the existence of discrimination in housing markets and illustrate the real harm experienced by minority home seekers.

However, the compelling evidence on housing discrimination and its impacts is invariably followed by the assertion "and of course housing discrimination causes residential segregation and segregation causes . . ." Such assertions are assumed to be self-evident, and challenges to this conventional wisdom are received skeptically at best and often with disbelief. Our society's ability to craft policies that seriously address racial segregation is limited by the adherence to the view that current housing discrimination must be a key factor behind the persistence of racial segregation.

Therefore, a central purpose of this chapter is to consider the empirical evidence available and assess whether the evidence supports the view that current housing discrimination is a significant contributor to residential segregation in U.S. cities and metropolitan areas. The empirical patterns of racial segregation in the United States are often inconsistent with the available evidence on housing discrimination. This review offers evidence in support of alternative theories for why segregation persists today, especially emphasizing the important role of racial and neighborhood stereotypes that were created and maintained by residential segregation itself.

Admittedly, strong evidence exists both that housing discrimination exists today and that housing discrimination throughout much of the twentieth century was central to creating the high levels of segregation that we observe in U.S. metropolitan areas. The appropriate policy responses, however, may differ dramatically depending upon how these two phenomena are interrelated.

History of Racial Segregation

One of the major demographic events in the twentieth century was the great migration of African Americans primarily from the rural south to cities in the Northeast and Midwest. Cutler, Glaeser, and Vigdor (1999) demonstrated the strong empirical correlation between this migration and the patterns of segregation in U.S. cities. In 1890, the population of African Americans in U.S. cities was quite small, but it grew rapidly between 1890 and 1970. In a group of cities for which population data are available over the whole period, the African American population grew from under a million in 1890 to almost fourteen million in 1970. During this same period, segregation grew steadily from initially moderate levels, from a dissimilarity index near 0.50, to an index between 0.70 and 0.80.[1]

These increases in segregation appear to have been the result of quite rigid neighborhood barriers that were developed in the early twentieth century (Fischer 2007) and explicitly maintained by real estate agents (Yinger 1995). As the African American population increased, densities and housing prices in the limited number of African American neighborhoods increased substantially. These price premiums in African-American neighborhoods and high levels of segregation remained through 1970 (Cutler, Glaeser, and Vigdor 1999). During the 1960s, real estate agents actively exploited the price difference between white and African American neighborhoods by using an approach commonly referred to as "block busting." For example, Yinger (1995) describes the process by which real estate agents conspired to sell one home in the Mattapan neighborhood of Boston to an African American family and then encouraged panic selling among whites in that neighborhood. The same real estate agents bought these homes at deep discounts only to later sell the homes at a substantial premium to African American families. In this way, a predominantly white neighborhood or block was busted, creating room for new, racially segregated neighborhoods.

Recent Evidence of Racial Segregation in America

The last few decades represent a period of gradual improvements for minorities in U.S. housing markets. Segregation has declined moderately for African Americans while the lower levels of segregation faced by Asians and Hispanics remained steady or only increased slightly (Iceland 2004), though these levels might have been expected to increase substantially due to the large increases in the total Asian and Hispanic populations (Massey, 2001). In fact, Clapp and Ross (2004) found that Hispanic segregation in Connecticut would have declined substantially if the size of the Hispanic population had not increased. In addition, Bostic and Martin (2005) found a substantial shift of African American homeowners in the 1980s from central city neighborhoods toward higher-income suburban neighborhoods, while no such shift occurred for white households during this period.

Meanwhile, attitudes concerning integration with African Americans have also improved substantially during the last few decades (Schuman et al. 1997; Farley and Frey 1994), suggesting that white aversion to African American neighbors may play a decreasing role in housing segregation (Patterson 1997; Thernstrom and Thernstrom 1997). Bobo (2001) observed, however, that negative racial stereotypes persist and may have substantial negative impacts on African Americans in spite of broad improvements in the general attitudes of whites concerning racial equality.[2] Farley et al. (1994), Zubrinski and Bobo (1996), and Krysan (2002) found that the holding of negative stereotypes was a strong predictor of unwillingness to live with African Americans. In addition, Emerson, Chai, and Yancy (2001) found that a neighborhood's share of African American residents influences the willingness of whites to live in that neighborhood, even after controlling for school quality, crime, and housing prices. They found no such effect from the presence of Hispanics or Asians in a neighborhood. Alternatively, Ellen (2000) observed that white willingness to move into a neighborhood is affected by the presence of African Americans, but that white willingness to remain in their current neighborhood is unaffected by African Americans moving to the neighborhood. She concluded that whites must be using racial composition to stereotype neighborhoods, as opposed to having preferences for residing in all-white neighborhoods.[3]

Finally, many studies have examined whether housing segregation can be explained by economic factors. Massey and Denton (1993), Rosenbaum (1996), Bayer, McMillan, and Ruben (2004), and Ihlanfeldt and Scafidi (2004) all found that the majority of segregation faced by African Americans cannot be explained by racial differences in household characteristics. In general, Hispanics and Asians face much lower levels of segregation than African Americans, and a large share of the segregation faced by Hispanics and Asians can be explained by economic factors and the slow assimilation of immigrant groups.

Evidence of Housing Discrimination

Indirect Evidence from Housing Prices

Naturally, if African American segregation cannot be explained by economic and demographic factors and attitudes are improving more quickly than segregation is declining, a reasonable question to ask is whether housing discrimination plays a significant role in maintaining the level of racial segregation in U.S. metropolitan areas. The traditional approach for answering this question is based on the premise that housing discrimination will only influence racial segregation if it limits and constrains the residential location decisions of African Americans and that the effect of these constraints can be seen in housing prices.

A large number of studies have examined whether African Americans pay more for housing than whites in U.S. cities and metropolitan areas. Studies from the 1960s tended to find evidence that African Americans pay more for equivalent housing (King and Mieszkowski 1973; Yinger 1978), while studies from the 1970s (Schnare 1976; Follain and Malpezzie 1981) tended to find little or no evidence of a housing price premium. Cutler, Glaeser, and Vigdor (1999) confirmed this pattern, finding a large African American rent premium in the first half of the twentieth century that fell substantially between 1950 and 1970 and had reversed entirely by 1990. They concluded that the high prices today in predominantly white neighborhoods are consistent with "a decentralized racism," whereby whites pay a premium to live in segregated neighborhoods.

Of course, the decline in the African American price premium could have arisen because the neighborhoods available to African Americans were expanded while effective barriers were maintained for other predominantly white neighborhoods. Clapp and Ross (2004), however, examined housing sales in Connecticut during the 1990s, a period when there was a large in-migration of Hispanics, as well as substantial losses of white population. They found no evidence of any price premiums associated with these demographic changes. In their sample, housing prices appeared to adjust fairly quickly (over only one or two years) and to rise uniformly for all housing units throughout the affected metropolitan areas. One would expect to find price premiums in Hispanic neighborhoods if the growing population had their residential options artificially constrained. The rapid speed of adjustment found by Clapp and Ross (2004) is suggestive of a fairly free market for housing rather than a market characterized by rigid barriers.

Direct Evidence of Housing Discrimination

The second significant approach for examining housing discrimination is essentially an experimental examination of the behavior of real estate and rental agents. Specifically, two testers, one white and one minority, are sent to the same agency or apartment complex to inquire about available housing following a common protocol or script. After visiting an agency, the testers fill out detailed surveys recording their treatment on factors such as whether the unit advertised in the newspapers was available, whether they were able to visit or inspect the housing unit, whether they were shown additional housing units, and the address of the housing units recommended or visited. If the unit was available to or inspected by the white tester but not the minority tester, the test is coded on that treatment as being a white-favored test, while tests where the minority received positive treatment and the white did not are coded as minority-favored. Typically, if the experiment or testing effort finds more white-favored than minority-favored tests on a particular treatment (a net difference in treatment), this finding is interpreted as direct evidence of discrimination by real estate or rental agents.

Three major paired testing studies of housing discrimination were conducted in 1977, 1989, and 2000. The first major study, in 1977, performed a national set of tests for African American and white pairs and piloted tests involving Anglo-Hispanic pairs. Both the 1989 and 2000 studies conducted full-scale national testing programs for both African Americans and Hispanics.[4] All three studies found evidence of housing discrimination in both rental and sales markets. The 1989 study found high levels of adverse treatment discrimination against African American and Hispanic homebuyers and renters across a variety of measures of treatment intended to capture availability of housing, access to housing for inspections, encouragement, price and terms in rental, and financing assistance in sales (Yinger 1995). The 2000 study continued to find statistically significant levels of discrimination against both African Americans and Hispanics in both markets. However, in comparing the results from 1989 and 2000, we found that the levels of discrimination had declined substantially over the decade for both groups in one or both markets.[5] For example, the overall net difference between the fraction of white- and African American-favored tests was 13.4 percentage points in 1989 and 8.1 in 2000 for rental tests, and 19.9 percentage points in 1989 and 6.7 in 2000 for sales tests, using a composite of a broad set of treatment measures.[6] Similarly, adverse treatment against Hispanics fell from 16.8 percentage points in 1989 to 4.3 in 2000 in the sales market (Turner et al. 2002; Ross and Turner 2005).[7]

Two major exceptions existed to the general improvement between 1989 and 2000 in the treatment observed in the rental and owner-occupied housing markets. Most significantly, net adverse treatment against Hispanics in the rental market was high and persistent, rising from 13.4 to 15.6 percentage points. Second, the frequency of racial steering of African American homebuyers increased over the decade. Racial steering occurs when African Americans are more likely than whites to be shown units in neighborhoods that have a substantial African American population. The net measure of adverse treatment on racial steering increased from African Americans being six percentage points less likely to see units in integrated or minority neighborhoods to being five percentage points more likely to see units in those neighborhoods. This change appeared to be associated with an overall increase in the number of units in minority neighborhoods being shown by real estate agents (Turner et al. 2002; Ross and Turner 2005).[8]

Later phases of HDS 2000 examined discrimination against previously untested groups. In phase II, the national estimates of overall adverse treatment discrimination for Asians were 4.3 and 19.6 percentage points for rental and sales markets, respectively, suggesting much higher levels of adverse treatment against Asian Americans in the sales market than seen with other minority groups (Turner and Ross 2003). Phase III examined the treatment of Native Americans, primarily focusing on the rental market and finding net differences of 7.7, 21.3, and 19.0 percentage points in the states of Montana, Minnesota, and New Mexico (Turner and Ross 2004). Phase IV identified very high levels of discrimination against people with disabilities (Turner et al. 2005).

It is important to place these results in context with the recent report issued by the National Fair Housing Alliance (NFHA 2006). The NFHA report describes high levels of discrimination in the sales market against both African Americans and Hispanics. The first thing to realize is that NFHA focused their efforts on real estate agencies and markets where a variety of sources including HDS 2000 identified unusually high levels of adverse treatment. Therefore, while their findings document the existence of discrimination, they are likely to overstate the average incidence of discrimination among real estate agents in the United States.[9]

In addition, many of the results presented by NFHA represent the frequency of white-favored tests—referred to as the gross measure of discrimination—rather than the net difference in treatment. A comparison of gross measures from NFHA and HDS 2000 yields fairly similar results,[10] and the gross measures presented by NFHA can dramatically overestimate discrimination because sometimes a minority tester is treated unfavorably for reasons that have nothing to do with race.[11]

In the case of steering, however, the NFHA report and the results from HDS 2000 are far less consistent, with the NFHA report finding that steering took place in 87 percent of tests when testers were given an opportunity to see homes. One explanation may again arise from the reliance of NFHA on gross measures of adverse treatment. In addition, the NFHA report never mentions requiring that differences in neighborhood composition exceed a reasonable threshold in order to count as steering. Without a threshold, the gross measure in the presence of no steering is likely to be near 50 percent just due to random variation.

Another important area of discrimination is the role of agent editorializing concerning neighborhoods, schools, and communities. While HDS 2000 found only low levels of steering based on units recommended and inspected, the black-white tests in HDS 2000 indicated much larger differences in the comments made by real estate agents, with agents being 12–14 percent more likely to editorialize about neighborhoods in ways that would encourage segregation of African Americans rather than reduce segregation (Galster and Godfrey, 2005). Further, Galster and Godfrey (2005) found that agents offered more comments to whites and that 70 percent of those comments provided information about the racial or ethnic makeup of the neighborhood.[12] The HDS 2000 methodology, which instructs testers to focus on inspecting the advertised and similar units, quite likely reduces the influence of agent commentary on the type of units observed relative to either the NFHA testers or typical homebuyers.

Does Current Housing Discrimination Cause Residential Segregation?

While I am convinced that housing discrimination exists and does substantial harm to minority renters and homebuyers, I do not believe that housing market discrimination by real estate and rental agents is a major factor behind the persistent racial segregation found in U.S. metropolitan areas today. First, the pattern of housing prices in U.S. metropolitan areas is not consistent with the existence of major barriers to the neighborhood choices of one or more large minority populations. Second, the pattern of racial segregation observed in U.S. metropolitan areas is quite inconsistent with the direct evidence on housing discrimination from paired testing studies.

While Cutler, Glaeser, and Vigdor (1999) provide a compelling story of growing segregation during the twentieth century based on the increasing urbanization of African Americans and fairly rigid discriminatory barriers in housing markets, they also documented a dramatic decline and reversal of the price premium paid by African Americans between 1950 and 1990, and concluded that by 1990 segregation was the result of the preferences of white homeowners rather than housing discrimination. In fact, not a single study has found evidence that African Americans paid more for housing during the 1980s or 1990s. Similarly, Clapp and Ross (2002) found that housing prices adjust fairly quickly across communities and that prices increased across all Connecticut towns in growing urban areas, even though the population increases were driven entirely by in-migration of Hispanics who tended to settle in predominantly Hispanic communities. These findings suggest that the rigid barriers to minority neighborhood choice that were once enforced by real estate agents are no longer in place.

The evidence discussed earlier also implies that the racial segregation experienced by African Americans is different and dramatically more severe than the segregation experienced by either Asians or Hispanics. African Americans are exposed to much higher levels of segregation than the other two groups, and unlike with Asians and Hispanics the vast majority of African American segregation cannot be explained by economic factors. Meanwhile, HDS 2000 documented substantially higher levels of discrimination against Asians in sales markets and Hispanics in rental markets than against African Americans.

Further, the declines in segregation over the last few decades are not consistent with the observed declines in housing discrimination in terms of either the timing or the location of those declines. African American homeowners in the 1980s moved away from central city neighborhoods toward higher-income suburban neighborhoods (Bostic and Martin 2005). This shift and the accompanying declines in racial segregation during the 1970s and 1980s occurred in spite of the high levels of discrimination documented by the national paired testing studies conducted in 1977 and 1989. Meanwhile, the pace of improvements in racial segregation did not change appreciably during the 1990s (Iceland 2004), a period in which housing market discrimination against African Americans declined markedly. Further, Galster and Ross (2007) found that that the decline in discrimination against African Americans was largest in metropolitan areas with the smallest increases in Hispanic population, while Card, Mas, and Rothstein (2008b) found that racial tipping points increased, and therefore segregation decreased, the most in metropolitan areas with growing Hispanic populations.

Countervailing Views

Naturally, the arguments above reflect my interpretation of the evidence, and other scholars believe that housing discrimination is still an important factor behind the high levels of racial segregation in the United States. Below, I present the three most common arguments made to support the idea that housing discrimination contributes to racial segregation today.

First, it has been argued that metropolitan areas with high levels of housing discrimination also tend to have high levels of segregation. Using data from HDS 1989, Galster (1991) examined the relationship between housing discrimination against African Americans and both the centralization and residential segregation of the African American population in selected U.S. metropolitan areas. He found that African Americans have much higher levels of centralization and segregation in metropolitan areas where he predicted high levels of discrimination in the sales market. However, he also found a negative relationship between rental market discrimination and African American centralization and segregation, which raises questions about how to interpret these results.[13] Further, Galster and Ross (2007) examined changes in racial segregation between 1990 and 2000 and housing discrimination between HDS 1989 and 2000, only to find little evidence of any correlation between these changes for either the sales or rental markets.

Second, discrimination in rental markets is still a very serious problem. HDS 2000 found high levels of discrimination in rental housing against Hispanics and Native Americans. Further, the decline in discrimination against African Americans in the rental market may not represent a meaningful increase in opportunities. The reader needs to remember that the key service provided by a rental agent is the provision of rental housing, while paired testing can only assess the amount and nature of information provided to the testers during their initial in-person inquiry about the advertised rental unit. It is impossible to know whether discrimination against African Americans has declined or instead has been moved to other stages of the transaction that are not captured by traditional testing efforts. For example, Massey and Lundy (2001) found that testers who speak "Black English" are less likely to be able to make an appointment to see available rental housing over the phone, and Galster and Ross (2007) found that local HUD-funded enforcement activities were associated with a decline in adverse treatment of African Americans in the rental market, possibly because land-lords shift discrimination until later in the rental process in order to avoid detection.[14]

Naturally, the first response to concerns about discrimination in the rental market as a source of segregation is to note that HDS 2000 did capture substantial discrimination against Hispanics, and yet Hispanics experience substantially lower levels of segregation than African Americans. Further, a large fraction of Hispanic segregation can be explained by differences in economic resources and immigration. In addition, racial discrimination in the sales market fell between 1989 and 2000. Almost 70 percent of U.S. households are homeowners, and this share is even higher in suburban areas. As noted by Fischer (2008), most of the decline in racial segregation has occurred in central cities, where rentals are a larger share of the housing market. These facts suggest that major discriminatory barriers to further integration of the African American population must be found either in the market for owner-occupied housing or in other markets that are crucial to the transition to homeownership, such as the home mortgage market.[15]

The declines in sales market discrimination identified by HDS 2000 appear quite compelling. Unlike rental agents who might withhold housing at later stages of the transaction, real estate agents in the sales market provide services that are easily observed during testing, and the remaining discrimination against African Americans and Hispanics in this segment of the market appears quite low. The job of a real estate agent is to provide information on homes that are available for purchase, as well as to provide homeseekers with physical access to those properties. The sales tests directly examine these treatments and allow for both a follow-up visit by the tester and follow-up contact by the real estate agent. Substantial declines in sales market discrimination were observed for both African Americans and Hispanics. Further, Galster and Ross (2007) did not find any evidence that these declines in sales market discrimination were associated with fair housing enforcement activities, suggesting that real estate agents did not need to hide discriminatory activities.

Finally, many advocates point to the substantial evidence of racial steering by real estate agents during HDS 2000 and in the NFHA study. As discussed above, steering rose between 1989 and 2000 for the metropolitan areas studied in HDS 2000. Further, the NFHA study and Galster and Godfrey (2005) found evidence of extensive commentary by real estate agents. Even if minorities are shown units in white neighborhoods, segregation might be reinforced and maintained if African Americans and whites are consistently pushed toward selecting houses in racially homogeneous neighborhoods.

However, while steering against African Americans did increase during the 1990s, racial differences in steering based on the locations of units recommended or shown were approximately five percentage points in HDS 2000, which is comparable to the low levels of disparate treatment observed for African Americans in the sales markets on most treatments in 2000 and statistically indistinguishable from steering against Hispanics. In fact, the increase in racial steering may in part be due to a number of factors that represent improvements in the housing market. First, the opportunity to steer increased because mainstream real estate agencies increased their representation and advertising of units located in minority neighborhoods between 1989 and 2000, indicating greater willingness of real estate agents to market such units.

Further, the real estate industry has consolidated substantially, reducing the incentives for agents to practice discrimination based on the prejudice of their potential customers.[16] In fact, Galster and Godfrey (2005) found that the majority of commentary was aimed at whites rather than African-American homebuyers. Rather than exclusion from neighborhoods, which may create substantial price premiums, real estate agents today appear to practice a less restrictive form of steering where they provide homebuyers with information on racial and ethnic composition of neighborhoods that in some cases disparages integrated neighborhoods to white homebuyers. This behavior might reinforce the type of "white racism" referred to by Cutler, Glaeser, and Vidgor (1999), but such comments may also be a reflection of the perceived preferences of typical white homebuyers as opposed to systematic actions by real estate agents that shape white preferences.[17]

Stereotypes and the Role of Past Discrimination and Segregation

In my opinion, it is not appropriate to simply end the conversation having described a limited role for current real estate agents. Cutler, Glaeser, and Vidgor (1999) and the work of many others clearly demonstrate that discrimination played a very important role in creating the highly segregated metropolitan areas that exist today. The finding that whites pay higher prices for housing is consistent with whites paying a premium to avoid living in integrated neighborhoods but does nothing to identify why those whites are willing to pay this premium. In a similar vein, would the typical white homeowner have any preference for segregation, or would the typical real estate agent have any economic incentive to discourage whites from visiting housing units in predominantly African American neighborhoods if the U.S. metropolitan environment had not been so terribly distorted by a legacy of very high levels of housing discrimination?[18]

For example, Galster (1991) developed a descriptive model where housing discrimination leads to racial segregation, and the resulting racial segregation contributes to negative outcomes for African Americans in terms of education outcomes, family structure, and the labor market. Cutler and Glaeser (1997), Collins and Margo (2000), and Card and Rothstein (2007) all have documented the negative impact of residential segregation on the African American population. In addition, Collins and Margo (2001) detailed the historical influence of segregation on homeownership and housing values, which may have limited the wealth accumulation of African-American families (Charles and Hurst 2000). In Galster's model, racial segregation is reinforced and maintained by the racial differences in poverty, unemployment, and single parenthood that arise in part from segregation, and once established, high levels of racial segregation can persist even if housing discrimination has been completely eliminated.

Finally, the research of Card, Mas, and Rothstein and also of Ferreira in this volume might be considered in the light of stereotypes that are propagated and maintained by residential segregation. Card, Mas, and Rothstein found evidence of what they refer to as one-sided tipping, where neighborhoods that cross a threshold share of minority residents start moving toward becoming predominantly minority neighborhoods, while neighborhoods below that threshold exhibit substantial stability. One explanation for this phenomenon involves racial composition being used as a signal for neighborhood quality. When racial composition is below the threshold, the signal conveys no information about neighborhood quality and therefore does not have any systematic affect on future changes in racial composition.

Ferriera (this volume) describes research by Ferreira and Saiz (2008) that examines the influence of changing neighborhood ethnic composition on housing prices. Specifically, they estimated the impact of a Hispanic household moving into a neighborhood and found that this move decreases property values in predominantly white neighborhoods and increases property values in predominantly Hispanic neighborhoods. They interpreted these findings as evidence of tastes for self-segregation among both whites and Hispanics. An alternative explanation, however, arises if one considers that the entrance of a Hispanic household provides information about both the direct change in neighborhood composition and the ethnicity of the typical person who is demanding housing in this neighborhood—that is, the ethnicity of the typical person who is negotiating for and helping to set the price of housing in the neighborhood.[19]

In both cases, phenomena that are in part ascribed to preferences concerning racial or ethnic composition may be explained by racial or ethnic differences in preferences for neighborhood quality and potentially by information asymmetries between whites and minorities concerning neighborhood quality. Especially in the case of one-sided tipping, the empirical regularities uncovered appear very consistent with the notion of neighborhood stereotyping or using neighborhood racial or ethnic composition as a noisy signal for neighborhood quality. Such stereotypes clearly can be maintained by the existing high levels of racial segregation in U.S. metropolitan areas and the negative impacts of that segregation on the African American population.

Conclusion

The willingness of whites to live in integrated neighborhoods has improved steadily. The incidence of housing discrimination is down substantially with the exception of discrimination against Hispanics in the rental market, and the observed pattern of prices and outcomes in the housing market suggests that discrimination by real estate agents does not significantly constrain the neighborhood choices of minorities. And yet, residential segregation of African Americans persists at a level far above the level experienced by other minority groups in this country. Improvements in residential segregation have been modest since the 1970s, and there is no evidence of an acceleration in desegregation as discrimination fell during the 1990s. This combination of empirical evidence strongly suggests that the elimination of housing discrimination (while a major accomplishment for other reasons) would do little to mitigate the high levels of racial segregation experienced by many African Americans in our country.

On the other hand, the legacy of past housing discrimination is almost certainly the central factor in explaining the high levels of residential segregation that developed during the last century and likely heavily influences the segregation experienced by African Americans today. While middle-income African Americans have suburbanized over the last two decades, this suburbanization has taken place in a cultural environment distorted by high levels of racial segregation, and accordingly the resulting pattern of African American suburbanization also involves high levels of segregation mirroring that earlier environment (Fischer 2008).

Building on earlier work by Galster (1991) and Ellen (2000), I have suggested that the history of African American residential segregation may be a central force in developing and maintaining the attitudes about individuals and neighborhoods that reinforce and maintain the high levels of racial segregation observed in U.S. metropolitan areas. White households may stereotype African Americans as neighbors and predominantly African American neighborhoods in terms of the quality of the neighborhood environment, which is based on the segregated urban environment that arises from such attitudes. The frequency and severity of such stereotyping may be exacerbated because whites may have difficulty evaluating neighborhood quality in predominantly minority neighborhoods due to cultural differences. Information asymmetry concerning neighborhood quality has been understudied in research on racial segregation and may be especially important for explaining why racial segregation in housing has been so persistent as general attitudes have improved and housing discrimination has declined.

Notes

Chapter 3. Educational Interventions

Portions of an earlier version of this chapter were published in Brian A. Jacob, and Jens Ludwig. "Improving Educational Outcomes for Poor Children." In *Changing Poverty, Changing Policies*. © 2009 Russell Sage Foundation, 112 East 64th Street, New York, NY 10065. Reprinted with permission.

1. Standard deviation units are a common way of expressing effect sizes. For comparison, the standard deviation is 15–16 points for a typical IQ test and 100 points for the SAT.

2. This section is based on the excellent summary of Project STAR research by Schanzenbach (2006/7).

Chapter 4. Before or After the Bell?

The authors wish to thank Marie Chevrier, Kurt Beron, Harriet Newburger, Wim Vijverberg, and various seminar participants for helpful comments and suggestions. This research has been supported by grants from the Texas Higher Education Coordinating Board and the Institute of Educational Studies, U.S. Department of Education.

1. For technical details of the transformation, see Vijverberg (2004).

2. The graph for percentage of adults who are college graduates is quite similar.

3. The full regression results underlying Figure 4.5 are available from the authors upon request.

4. The full regression results underlying Figures 4.6 and 4.7 are available from the authors upon request.

Chapter 5. Neighborhoods, Social Interactions, and Crime

The authors thank Liz Furbush for invaluable research assistance.

1. Violent offenses include murder, manslaughter, rape, sexual assault, robbery, assault, extortion, and other violent offenses, while property offenses include burglary, larceny, motor vehicle theft, fraud, possession and selling of stolen property, destruction of property, trespassing, vandalism, and other property offenses. Drug-related offenses include possession, manufacturing, trafficking, and other drug offenses. The data are reported in the *Sourcebook of Criminal Justice Statistics* but are gathered from *The FBI Uniform Crime Reports* for the relevant years.

2. The chart tracks reported rates of property crimes (burglary, larceny, motor vehicle theft, fraud, possession and selling of stolen property, destruction of property, trespassing, vandalism, and other offenses) and violent crimes (murder, manslaughter, rape, sexual assault, robbery, assault, extortion, and other offenses) and drug-related arrests for possession, manufacturing, trafficking, and other offenses. The recent data come from the U.S. Federal Bureau of Investigation (FBI), Uniform Crime Reporting Program, Crime in the United States 2005 (at www.fbi.gov/ucr/05cius/index.html); historical data have been compiled by the U.S. Census Bureau, Statistical Abstract, Table H-23 on crime rates (www.census.gov/statab/hist/) and the U.S. Bureau of Justice Statistics for drug arrests (at www.ojp.usdoj.gov/bjs/dcf/enforce.htm).

3. See Sampson, Morenoff, and Gannon-Rowley (2002) for a thorough discussion of the different sources of influence of social interactions on crime and the problems in identifying their effects.

Chapter 7. Exploring Changes in Low-Income Neighborhoods in the 1990s

1. Much of the analysis in this chapter is drawn from an earlier paper, "Reversal of Fortunes? Low-Income Urban Neighborhoods in the 1990s," which is forthcoming in *Urban Studies*. We are grateful to Rachel Meltzer and Keren Horn for excellent research assistance in helping us extend the analyses in that earlier paper.

2. Note that this theory is similar to the theory of neighborhood change posited by the sociologists that formed the Chicago School of the 1920s (Park, Burgess, and McKenzie 1925).

3. The census defines as institutionalized those individuals living under the care and authority of others, i.e., patients and inmates.

4. Because we relied on metropolitan area data for 1970, 1980, 1990, and 2000, our analysis was restricted to metropolitan areas that were designated as metropolitan areas in all four of our decades. (Note that a few metropolitan areas were also excluded because of missing income data in the NCDB.)

5. A weakness of average income is its sensitivity to changes at the tails of the distribution. An increase in average household income may arise from upward shifts in the distribution of household income, or increased income polarization, which should be kept in mind when interpreting our findings. Unfortunately, median household income was not available for all of the four census years examined.

6. Similar measures were used in Fogarty (1977) and in Brueckner and Rosenthal (2005) and Rosenthal (2006), for example.

7. We arrived at these cutoffs by creating quintiles of the data, pooled over all four decades. Specifically, we arrayed all of our tracts (all decades) in ascending order of their relative income, and then created quintiles from the poorest to the wealthiest tracts. We then use the cutoffs from this pooled population to establish constant definitions of our categories, which we then applied to each decade. This approach can be distinguished from Rosenthal (2006) and Brueckner and Rosenthal (2005), who defined quintiles for each decade, so that lowest-income neighborhoods are always the bottom fifth of neighborhoods in a particular metropolitan area. While their quintile approach is appealing, the shift in neighborhood income distribution between 1970 and 2000 (discussed below) would make such an approach problematic for us.

8. We replicated our results for alternative cutoffs and found that our results are not sensitive to choice of cutoff.

9. Note that the pattern was somewhat different for very low-income tracts in the *suburbs*. While the proportion of very low-income suburban tracts that experienced a gain in income was higher in the 1990s than in the 1980s, their likelihood of improving was highest in the 1970s.

10. When large change is defined as a 15 percentage point change, the same pattern of results emerges.

11. As will be discussed below, this is partly because it was the very poorest, or very lowest income tracts, within the lowest-income category that tended to experience gains in income during the 1990s.

12. Jargowsky (2003) and Kingsley and Pettit (2003) each credit the deconcentration of poverty to the economic expansion.

13. While its impact was of smaller magnitude, the real minimum wage also increased during this time period.

14. The HOPE VI program, for instance, demolished many large public housing developments, relocated original low-income tenants to other neighborhoods, and rebuilt lower-scale developments designed for a mix of market-rate and low-income occupants. More generally, public housing authorities changed their eligibility criteria to admit a greater number of working families.

15. For a discussion of the trends and literature, see Levitt, 2004.

16. For this analysis we included all census tracts for which we had 1990 and 2000 tract and MSA data. This sample was larger than those tracts for which we had full data going back to 1970, the basis for Table 7.1.

17. In addition, higher-status residents and higher rates of homeownership are likely to be correlated with superior public services (such as schools), which will both make a neighborhood more attractive to higher-income households and perhaps make it a place where lower-income residents are more likely to succeed.

18. This is consistent with simple tabulations showing that the tracts in the lowest-income category gained during the 1990s had higher poverty rates and higher black proportions in 1990 than tracts in the lowest-income category that didn't experience gains.

19. The coefficient on Northeast is only significant in some of the models, however. The inclusion of the share of the population that is foreign born captures the bulk of regional variation in the likelihood of low-income neighborhoods gaining economically.

20. When we restricted our analysis to the very lowest-income tracts (those with income less than half of the MSA average), we found an even stronger relationship.

21. When we included both change in poverty rate and the per capita number of LIHTC units, both were significantly related to the probability of gain for the broader set of lower-income neighborhoods.

Chapter 9. Reinventing Older Communities

1. Place-based policies may be initiated by the federal government, e.g., HOPE VI, a housing program designed to replace public housing with mixed-income housing with the goal of improving neighborhood quality. State programs generally try to promote economic development, e.g., the Keystone Opportunity Zones in Pennsylvania, which provide tax abatements and low-interest loans for firms who locate in designated zones; or the city of Philadelphia's ten-year tax abatement for the construction of new or rehabilitated housing units. Such state and local programs are found throughout the United States.

2. Much of the pre-2000 data herein was collected for Pack (2002) and has been updated through the 2000 census.

3. Glaeser and Gottlieb (2008) considered federal policies intended to strengthen particular places. The authors concluded that "targeted policies . . . seem to have an effect, but they are expensive relative to their achievements. The most promising area for a national place-based policy is to impede the tendency of highly productive areas to restrict their own growth through restrictions on land use" (quotation from the abstract).

4. William Frey (2005) has been a major contributor to this literature.

5. Per capita income changes over a ten-year period—while they may somewhat over- or under-state the change—will be relatively accurate welfare indicators, unless there has been a very long or very deep recession.

6. The explanation here may lie in the nature of the change in population, in particular a large immigration during these years (Frey 2005).

7. Obviously individual places can introduce policies, e.g., enterprise zones, mixed income housing, neighborhood policing, "bidding" against other places for businesses of various sorts—an automobile plant or a sports stadium, for example. What we are providing is a context for thinking about policy directed at reinventing older communities more generally. See, for example, Calanog and Oberholzer-Gee (2006).

8. As indicated earlier, poverty and unemployment rates will rise or fall, depending upon general economic conditions. However, to be well above or below the overall average rates is a major indicator of vulnerability and, therefore, poverty and unemployment rates are appropriately included in the definitions of distress and well-being. The education variables are not included in the index, given the earlier analysis that shows that these are the most important determinants of urban growth and well-being.

9. The number of areas characterized as distressed, as defined above, has clearly increased in 1990 and 2000, compared with 1970 and 1980. As we shall see below, the number of well-off metropolitan areas is more erratic— decreasing between 1970 and 1980, then increasing substantially, and then falling back to its 1970 number.

10. The definitions are the same as those for metropolitan areas, using deviations from city averages.

11. It should be kept in mind that these figures are based upon definitions that depend upon the values of three variables and their deviation from average values: per capita income, unemployment rate, and poverty rate. As has been shown earlier, cities generally look worse on all three variables than do their suburbs.

Chapter 10. An Overview of Moving to Opportunity

Support for the research reviewed and summarized in this chapter was provided by the Russell Sage Foundation, the William T. Grant Foundation, the U.S. Department of Housing and Urban Development, the Princeton Industrial Relations Section, the Princeton Center for Health and Wellbeing, the National Institute of Child Health and Development and the National Institute of Mental Health (R01-HD40404 and R01-HD40444), the National Science Foundation (9876337 and 0091854), the MacArthur Foundation, the Robert Wood Johnson

Foundation, the Smith Richardson Foundation, and the Spencer Foundation. We thank the U.S. Department of Housing and Urban Development for continued access to MTO data and to products resulting from these data. The contents of this chapter represent the views of the authors, and do not necessarily reflect the views or policies of the U.S. Department of Housing and Urban Development or the U.S. government.

1. A competitive process selected these five cities for participation: Baltimore, Boston, Chicago, Los Angeles, and New York. Eligibility for the voluntary MTO program was limited to low-income families with children living in public housing or Section 8 project-based housing that was located in census tracts with poverty rates of at least 40 percent. To meet its research goals, HUD took advantage of the excess demand for Section 8 rental assistance by determining receipt of vouchers via a random lottery. This random selection has been central to HUD's ability to support rigorous research efforts to understand the MTO program's causal impact on participating families.

2. See http://www.hud.gov/offices/pih/programs/hcv/ for more information about HUD's Section 8 program.

3. See the U.S. Department of Housing and Urban Development, http://www.hud.org, as well as http://mtoresearch.org.

4. For the nonexperimental literature, see Sampson, Morenoff, and Gannon-Rowley 2002; Kawachi and Berkman 2003; Leventhal and Brooks-Gunn 2000; Ellen and Turner 2003. Most of this research has focused on adolescents, although for young children there has been some evidence that the presence of affluent neighbors in particular affects cognitive and achievement outcomes (Brooks-Gunn et al. 1993; Duncan et al. 1994; Chase-Lansdale and Gordon 1996; Chase-Lansdale et al. 1997). Particularly striking are Crane's (1991b) findings from cross-sectional data from the census claiming that high school dropout rates increase sharply (that is, nonlinearly) in the most disadvantaged neighborhoods. Sampson, Morenoff, and Gannon-Rowley (2002) suggest that the strongest evidence of neighborhood effects is on criminal behavior. The Gautreaux program is discussed in this volume by Briggs et al.

5. See Kling, Liebman, and Katz (2007b), Section E, for a more detailed description of internal validity and threats to experimental estimates in the context of MTO.

6. See Orr et al. 2003. Also see Kling, Liebman, and Katz 2007a; Kling, Ludwig, and Katz 2005; Ludwig and Kling 2007; and Sanbonmatsu et al. 2006.

7. All estimates are regression-adjusted, controlling for a range of individual and local characteristics measured at study entry or baseline.

8. Results presented as "percentage points" in the text are presented as "proportions" in Figures 10.1, 10.2, 10.4, and 10.5.

9. The Psychological Distress index (K6) was normalized and converted into a z-score. The K6 ranges from zero to 24, thus if Adult A scored 3 and the standard deviation for the sample is 2 and the average score among all adults is 12, then the normalized score for Adult A would take the value $(3–12)/2 = -4.5$.

10. For more detail, see justification and related documents submitted to OMB at http://www.reginfo.gov/public/do/PRAViewDocument?ref_nbr= 200708-2528-003.

11. Administrative data will also allow us to compare the dynamics of impacts for youth who moved through MTO at different ages to try to distinguish treatment heterogeneity by time since moving versus by age at moving.

Chapter 11. How Does Leaving High-Poverty Neighborhoods Affect the Employment Prospects of Low-Income Mothers and Youth?

1. Rubin (1978) shows that when the no-interference assumption does not hold, causal models require a different value of assignment realization for each potential value of the outcome variable, not just the T (number in discrete treatment group) assignment values. The number of aggregate outcomes becomes very large. On adjustments for interference, see Sobel (2003).

2. Kling, Liebman, and Katz (2007:109) compared experimental and nonexperimental results from different survey populations, concluding that "Although numerous nonexperimental studies document strong associations between neighborhood characteristics and individual outcomes, these associations appear to be much weaker in the studies with the most credible identification strategies."

3. Per Orr et al. (2003:B8–9), the TOT estimate (or its standard error) for a given site is the ITT measure divided by the site lease-up rate (experimental group: 35 percent Chicago, 64 percent Los Angeles; comparison group: 67 percent Chicago, 76 percent Los Angeles). Thus, the t-statistic is unchanged by this transformation.

Chapter 12. Teens, Mental Health, and Moving to Opportunity

1. I also replicated the results for all five sites using a model similar to that used in the MTO interim report. I used virtually the same set of covariates, the same weights, and robust standard errors. However, I used a narrower age category (14–19), and I added a separate test to look at the difference in treatment effect by gender.

2. Siblings are included in this count, but they were taken out in the model, bringing the sample size down further.

3. Comparing the entire experimental group to the control group was critical to maintaining the experimental nature of the analysis. With random assignment of households to the experimental and control groups, we expected a similar distribution of baseline characteristics across the households in the two groups and could attribute differences in outcomes for the two groups to the treatment rather than to differences in household characteristics. Were we to have compared only the subset of experimental households that took up the voucher offer with control households, we would not have been able to assume that the subset had the same distribution of observed and unobserved characteristics as the control group.

4. A list of covariates is available from the author. The covariates in the model controlled for baseline characteristics and improved the precision of the estimates but should not, given random assignment, have affected estimates of experimental impacts. These include the teens' age at random assignment, school performance measures, and parental characteristics such as employment status and educational attainment. By using robust standard errors, the presence of siblings in the sample was adjusted for. All the estimates were computed using sample weights. These weights have three components, and they are described in detail in Orr et al. (2003), Appendix B.

I included interaction terms for gender and treatment group in the model, since this analysis explores differential treatment effects by gender. Let Y be the outcome of interest, $G=1$ if female, 0 if not, and Z be membership in the experimental group. Equation (1) shows a simple regression model used to esti-mate the control means (β_{10} and β_{12}) and the ITT differences between the experimental and control groups (β_{11} and β_{13}) for girls and boys, respectively.

$$Y_i = G_i\beta_{10} + G_iZ_i\beta_{11} + (1 - G_i)\beta_{12} + (1 - G_i)G_i\beta_{13} + \epsilon_{1i} \tag{1}$$

Estimating the treatment effect for both genders simultaneously allows a simple correction of standard errors for correlation in outcomes between siblings.

In order to increase precision of the estimates and control for any small sam-ple differences in baseline covariates (X), I used regression-adjusted effects, as estimated using equation (2).

$$Y_i = G_i\beta_{20} + G_iZ_i\beta_{21} + (1 - G_i)\beta_{22} + (1 - G_i)Z_i\beta_{23} + X_i\beta_{24} + \epsilon_{21} \tag{2}$$

The difference in treatment effects between males and females is β_{23}—β_{21}. This difference and its standard error were calculated using Stata's lincom function.

5. Similar data were collected in Chicago.

6. Analysis available from author.

7. With regard to observed differences, adult "compliers" were more likely to be younger, enrolled in school, living in smaller households, and dissatisfied with their baseline neighborhood environments than noncompliers (Clampet-Lundquist and Massey 2008). The presence or absence of major family dysfunc-tion is an example of an unobserved factor that might affect outcomes—including the likelihood that a family will be able to use a voucher if one is offered.

8. The experimental complier group of teens had lived at their current resi-dence for an average of 2.8 years, while the control group of teens had lived at their current residence for an average of 6 years.

9. The initial coding was primarily descriptive rather than analytic. Coders met weekly to ensure the reliability of the coding process. We imported inter-view material from the topical fields into NVivo for more detailed analytical coding. At this stage, one coder read through the data and systematically ana-lyzed the coded material for patterns by gender and treatment group. These patterns were not derived from highly structured items but rather from material across the narratives. While the bulk of the data came from the narratives of the teenagers in the sample, there are some cases where data from the parent inter-views and/or field notes from the interviewer were used to supplement the teens' stories.

10. Another related issue that control teens may have struggled with was their relocation from public housing. The MTO families in Baltimore mainly lived in public housing developments at baseline which were slated for HOPE VI redevelopment. Those control teens who moved may have perceived their relo-cation from public housing as less voluntary compared to the experimental com-pliers. On the other hand, this move would have occurred three to five years before the interview and no teens mentioned it.

11. This is not including the times spent incarcerated in a juvenile detention facility for assault or other charges.

12. A number of studies have documented a link between ADHD and anger (Richards, Deffenbacher & Rosen 2002; Braaten & Rosen 2000; Kitchens, Rosen, & Braaten 1999; Biederman, Newcorn, & Sprich 1991), and lead paint poisoning and aggression or delinquent behavior (Needleman et al. 2002; Nee-dleman et al. 1996).

13. On the other hand, there were several examples in the qualitative analysis where the actions of biological fathers or adult male family members had extremely negative effects on the female and male teens in the control group.

Chapter 13. Changing the Geography of Opportunity by Helping Poor Households Move Out of Concentrated Poverty

1. More sophisticated studies employ either instrumental variables, differencing, fixed effects, or comparisons of siblings, several of which are discussed in the Johnson chapter earlier in this volume.

2. In other cases (Yonkers, e.g.), there are limitations in the range of neighborhoods to which participants moved because of where subsidized housing was located. This reduces the ability of statistical tests to discern neighborhood effects.

3. Gennetian et al. (this volume) note that this issue will be addressed in the final MTO evaluations forthcoming.

4. Quigley and Raphael (2008) have developed a statistical model of how much distance between residences and jobs might affect the employment rate of black workers and conclude that the experimental treatment involved in MTO ex post (after subsequent moves by the treatment group) could not be expected to yield detectable differences in employment outcomes.

5. For example, see Clampet-Lundquist and Massey (2008) as well as Galster et al. (2007), who use the neighborhood poverty rate averaged over all years of childhood as a predictor of multiple outcomes for young adults.

Chapter 14. Are Mixed Neighborhoods Always Unstable?:

1. We express the change in white population as a fraction of the total tract population in 1970. Minorities are defined as nonwhites and white Hispanics.

2. The older data are available for only a small fraction of the cities studied by CMR, and it can be difficult to harmonize census tract definitions across decades. These three cities were among the earliest to be tracted and had fairly stable tract boundaries between 1940 and 1960.

3. Because tract boundaries changed in many cities between 1960 and 1970, we have not calculated 1960 tipping points.

4. For a somewhat more mathematical treatment of this model, see Card, Mas, and Rothstein (2008b).

5. In math, this corresponds to negative first partial derivatives of the two inverse demand functions: $\partial b^w(n^w, m)/\partial n^w < 0$ and $\partial b^m(n^m, m)/\partial n^m < 0$.

6. Demand specificity will be less important when a neighborhood is small relative to the set of close substitutes, with few unique locational, cultural, or other amenities. These conditions may be more likely to arise in suburbs than in central city areas.

7. With a fixed number of homes in each neighborhood, the number of white buyers can increase only if the number of minority buyers falls. We can thus rewrite the white bid function to depend on the number of homes left after all n^m minorities have purchased homes: $b^w(N - n^m, m)$, where N is the total number of homes in the neighborhood. Moreover, in any equilibrium it must be the case that $m = n^m/N$. Thus, if we normalize the total supply of houses to unity, an integrated neighborhood in equilibrium must have $b^w(1 - m, m) = $

$b^m(m, m)$; an all-white neighborhood must have $b^w(1, 0) > b^m(0, 0)$; and an all-minority neighborhood must have $b^w(0, 1) < b^m(1, 1)$.

8. This is a consequence of the fact that market-level inverse demand functions are nonincreasing functions of the quantity sold.

9. Schelling (1971) considered a case where there are N current white owners of the homes in a neighborhood, and each white has a threshold m_i beyond which his or her demand falls to 0. In this case, assuming m_i is distributed with distribution function F, the white inverse demand (of current owners) is horizontal for m in the interval from 0 to m^*, where $F(m^*) = 1\text{-}m^*$, and then falls to 0.

10. In principle whites may view a modest minority share as a positive amenity. In that case, the social interaction effect will cause the white bid function to be increasing in the minority share at low levels of m, even in the absence of demand specificity.

11. CMR assume that the inverse demand functions for whites and minorities for homes in neighborhood n in city c can be written as $b^w_{nc} = b^w_c(1 - m_{nc}, m_{nc}) + e^w_{nc}$, $b^m_{nc} = b^m_c(m_{nc}, m_{nc}) + e^m_{nc}$, where e^w_{nc} and e^m_{nc} represent neighborhood-specific demand shocks. Thus, the demand curves in different neighborhoods are all vertical translations of city-specific base functions. This implies that there is a city-specific tipping point.

12. Formally, a candidate tipping point is a fixed point in the differential equation describing the evolution of the neighborhood's relative composition.

13. In technical terms, the 1980 distribution of minority shares relative to the 1970 tipping point in the $\geq m^*$ group stochastically dominates that in the $< m^*$ group.

14. One reason for this attenuation is that our procedure for identifying tipping points typically picks out a candidate point even if the city is not tipping. While there are extreme nonlinearities in the change in white population around candidate tipping points, on average, and most cities have tipping points, there may be cities for which we have identified a candidate tipping point where neighborhoods are not actually tipping. In these cases the change in white population in relation to initial minority share exhibits smoothness, whereby low minority areas tend to experience higher growth of white population relative to higher minority areas, but without any pronounced nonlinearities. In such cases, the candidate tipping point will be relatively large, so that when we restrict the sample to high tipping points, these nontipping cities tend to be disproportionately represented in the sample.

Chapter 15. Preferences for Hispanic Neighborhoods

I would like to thank Blake Willmarth and Igar Fuki for outstanding research assistance. I also would like to thank the Research Sponsor Program of the Zell/Lurie Real Estate Center at the Wharton School of the University of Pennsylvania for financial support.

Chapter 16. Increasing Diversity and the Future of U.S. Housing Segregation

1. Massey and Denton (1988) surveyed twenty different measures of segregation. They classified them into five groups, with the measures in each group capturing a different dimension of segregation. The five dimensions of segregation are termed evenness, exposure, concentration, centralization, and cluster-

ing. The isolation index falls in the exposure category, while the dissimilarity index is in the evenness category. Exposure refers to the degree of potential contact or possibility of interaction between minority and majority group members. Evenness measures compare the spatial distributions of different groups among units in an MSA. The dissimilarity index captures the degree to which the racial composition of census tracts within an MSA differs from the racial composition of the overall MSA. If all census tracts had a racial composition exactly equal to the MSA's, then the dissimilarity index would equal zero. www.census.gov/hhes/www/housing/housing_patterns/housing_patterns.html contains data on isolation indexes used in the study.

2. The formula for the isolation index is, $\sum_{i=1}^{n} [(\frac{x_i}{X})(\frac{x_i}{t_i})]$, where x_i is the minority population of census tract i, X is the total minority population in the MSA, and t_i is the total population of census tract i. As an example of calculating the isolation index, assume that there are two census tracts in an MSA. One census tract has 150 African Americans and a total population of 500, the other an African American population of 300 and a total population of 1000. The isolation index would in this case equal $[(150/450)*(150/500)] + (300/450)*(300/1000) = 0.3$.

3. Detailed discussions of the 2000 segregation data can be found in Glaeser and Vigdor (2002), Logan, Stults, and Farley (2004), and Charles (2003).

4. The entropy score for a given metro area, D_m, is equal to: $\sum_{i=1}^{n} \Pi_i \ln(1/\Pi_i)$, where Π_i is the population share of a mutually exclusive racial or ethnic group i in metro area m and ln refers to the natural log. A higher value of D indicates more diversity. The maximum value for D equals the natural log of the number of groups and occurs when each racial and ethnic group has an equal population share in the MSA.

5. Entropy scores for each MSA for the years 1980, 1990 and 2000 are available at www.census.gov/hhes/www/housing/housing_patterns/housing_patterns.html.

6. Blalock and others (e.g., Tolnay and Beck 1995) have noted that whites are a heterogeneous group that need not view an increased minority presence only as a threat. For example, white elites might welcome more minorities because they represent relatively cheap labor compared to lower-class whites. Yet these elites also might fear solidarity between minorities and lower-class whites in struggles for resources, power and status, and thus support control measures that split the groups. Lower-class whites are thought to back control measures, since they probably view minorities as direct competitors for economic resources as well as for status, given that both groups are near the bottom of the social hierarchy.

7. Conceptual discussions in the literature of possible nonlinearities have been confined to political and economic threats and have normally ignored social status competition. We follow this tradition.

8. The full effect of a change in a minority's share on the change in segregation equals the estimated coefficient on the change in the minority's share plus the estimated coefficient on the interaction between diversity and change in minority share times the level of diversity. Using the values in the Appendix Table for black-white segregation, for example, this equals $.0143 - (.0036 \times$ diversity). Because the data for diversity were standardized for the analysis, with mean equal to 0 and standard deviation equal to 1, setting the value for diversity

at zero (its average value) yields the "mid diversity" value of .0143 shown in Figure 16.4. Setting the value for diversity at plus one standard deviation (+1) and minus one standard deviation (−1) gives the racial threat effect for the "high diversity" and "low diversity" scenarios shown in Figure 16.4. These equal .0143 − .0036 and .0143 + .0036, respectively. The same procedure using the estimated coefficients for Hispanic-white segregation was carried out to obtain the values shown in Figure 16.5.

Chapter 17. Understanding Racial Segregation

1. The dissimilarity index is a measure of segregation that captures what percentage of a group's population would need to move in order to obtain complete integration. The high levels of segregation were accompanied by the concentration of African Americans in central cities. Collins and Margo (2001) documented that this concentration depressed the homeownership rates of African Americans between 1940 and 1960.

2. For example, Sniderman and Piazza (1993) found that half of whites surveyed endorsed some negative stereotypes of African Americans and over one in five held uniformly negative views. Similarly, Bobo and Kluegel (1997) found that over half of whites surveyed rated African Americans relatively lower than whites on intelligence and higher on laziness and violent tendencies, and over three-quarters rated African Americans as relatively more likely to prefer living off welfare.

3. Similarly for Hispanics, Baugh (2007) found that individuals with Chicano or Mexican dialects faced substantial stereotyping, being assessed to have lower intelligence than whites, and Charles (2000) and Bobo and Zubrinsky (1996) suggested that white preferences for segregation limited the housing market opportunities of Hispanic households.

4. Phase I of the 2000 study piloted tests for Asian and Native Americans, and Phase II, which was conducted in 2001, included a national study of discrimination against Asian Americans. Finally, Phases III and IV conducted more limited analyses of the treatment experienced by Native Americans and the disabled. Also see Yinger (1993), Smith (1993), and Boggs, Sellers, and Bendick (1993) for histories of testing in the housing market.

5. A direct comparison cannot be made between the 1977 and 1989 studies because they were conducted in different markets and used different methodologies, but the levels of adverse treatment in the 1989 study appeared comparable to 1977 (Yinger 1995).

6. The composite results presented here are based on a hierarchy of 14 treatment variables where availability of the advertised unit is first, followed by ability to inspect the advertised unit. See Turner, Ross, Galster, and Yinger (2002) for details.

7. These declines in discrimination appeared to be most pronounced in metropolitan areas that had stable or slowly growing Hispanic populations (Galster and Ross 2007). This finding suggests that discrimination should have risen based on current trends and that the decline in discrimination was likely associated with broad changes in racial attitudes and in the structure of the real estate industry (Ross and Turner, 2005).

8. A third significant change arose because real estate agents substantially increased the amount of financial assistance being offered to prospective homebuyers. This increase was substantially smaller for Hispanic testers than for

white or African American testers and so adverse treatment of Hispanic testers increased markedly on the financial assistance measures (Turner et al. 2002; Ross and Turner 2005).

9. The NFHA report explicitly acknowledged that their measures of discrimination did not capture the national incidence of discrimination.

10. For example, NFHA found that African Americans and Hispanics were denied access or given limited information in 20 percent of tests, but this finding is broadly comparable to findings in HDS 2000 that approximately 15 percent of white, black, and Hispanic testers were told that the advertised unit was not available when their partner was told that the unit was available, suggesting net measures of adverse treatment near zero. The NFHA report does present net measures for number of units inspected, with African Americans and Hispanics seeing about three units fewer than whites, but HDS 2000 also identified substantial differentials on number of units inspected for African Americans.

11. Admittedly, the net measure may underestimate discrimination because sometimes minorities are favored for systematic reasons, such as a white not being shown the requested unit because it is located in a minority neighborhood. In Phase II of HDS 2000, tests with three testers, two of the same race, were conducted at two sites. These tests provide a same-race comparison, allowing the elimination of random differences in treatment without the problems associated with the traditional net measure. The revised net measure based on the same race comparison yielded very similar results to the traditional net measure, favoring the use of the net measure for studying discrimination (Turner and Ross 2003).

12. The NFHA study (2006) found that comments about schools were a very important component of racial steering, but Galster and Godfrey (2005) found that only 5 percent of comments were related to schools.

13. Galster faced the very difficult task of testing for the influence of discrimination on segregation or centralization when in fact segregation and centralization can influence discrimination, and that difficult problem is compounded by the fact that all three variables are products of the same metropolitan environment and therefore probably all heavily influenced by unobserved cultural and historical factors.

14. Further, Galster and Ross (2007) did not find any evidence that enforcement lowered rental market discrimination against Hispanics, which is consistent with the fact that Hispanic-targeted enforcement activity was only one-fifth the level of African American-targeted activity.

15. See Ross et al. (2008), Ross (2006), and Ross and Yinger (2002) for discussions of the evidence regarding racial discrimination in mortgage markets.

16. Ross and Turner (2005) argued that the counterintuitive steering of African Americans toward white neighborhoods in 1989 may have arisen from customer-based discrimination, where agents act to protect potentially vulnerable neighborhoods and are more likely to exclude minorities from neighborhoods that already have some minority residents than from all white neighborhoods. Multivariate analyses of the 1989 HDS and earlier testing efforts have generated numerous findings consistent with discrimination based on the prejudice of real estate agents' white customers, such as Yinger (1986, 1995), Roychoudhury and Goodman (1992), and Page's (1995) finding that minority couples face more discrimination when they have children, Yinger's (1986) finding that discrimination was high in integrated neighborhoods that were not experiencing an influx of African Americans, and Ondrich, Ross, and Yinger's (2002) finding that dis-

crimination decreases with the distance between the housing unit and the real estate agent's office.

17. The steering observed in 2000 may have been the result of statistical discrimination, where real estate agents believe the likelihood of a sale is increased by steering homebuyers toward or away from minority neighborhoods (Ondrich, Ross, and Yinger 2003). For HDS 2000, Zhao, Ondrich, and Yinger (2006) on sales and Choi, Ondrich, and Yinger (2005) on rentals found substantial evidence of neighborhood exclusion based on minority composition and income, which would appear to be consistent with statistical discrimination.

18. As an illustration, Bayer, McMillan, and Ruben (2005) estimated a structural model of residential location choice. This analysis shows that the neighborhood choices available in current metropolitan areas dramatically limit the options of upper- and middle-income African Americans, causing them to consume much lower levels of neighborhood amenities than would otherwise have been expected. Specifically, high-income and high-education neighborhoods with substantial African American populations simply do not exist. This concentration of African Americans of all income levels into potentially lower amenity neighborhoods would naturally limit the willingness of whites to live in integrated neighborhoods.

19. Instead of an empirical analysis that examines the effect of adding a Hispanic to a white or Hispanic neighborhood, the empirical exercise may effectively be thought of as involving an anticipated large change in the ethnic composition (from white to Hispanic) and the associated neighborhood unobservables for a white neighborhood that is attracting new Hispanic homebuyers. Alternatively, Hispanics may simply have a lower willingness to pay for unobserved (from the researcher's perspective) neighborhood attributes that correlate with ethnic composition, or possibly are less able to evaluate neighborhood quality in a predominantly white neighborhood. This phenomenon would lead to falling prices relative to levels that might have been established when whites formed a larger share of potential homebuyers.

Bibliography

Aaronson, Daniel. 1997. "Sibling Estimates of Neighborhood Effects." In Jeanne Brooks-Gunn, Greg J. Duncan, and J. Lawrence Aber, eds., *Neighborhood Poverty, Volume 2: Policy Implications in Studying Neighborhoods.* New York: Russell Sage Foundation.

————. 1998. "Using Sibling Data to Estimate the Impact of Neighborhoods on Children's Educational Outcomes." *Journal of Human Resources* 33 (4): 915–946.

————. 2001. "Neighborhood Dynamics." *Journal of Urban Economics* 49 (1): 1–31.

Aaronson, Daniel, Lisa Barrow, and William Sander. 2007. "Teachers and Student Achievement in the Chicago Public High Schools." *Journal of Labor Economics* 25 (1): 95–136.

Abrams, Charles. 1955. *Forbidden Neighbors: A Study of Prejudice in Housing.* New York: Harper.

Abt Associates. 2003. *Exploring the Impacts of the HOPE VI Program on Surrounding Neighborhoods.* Cambridge, Mass.: Abt Associates.

Achilles, C. M., Barbara A. Nye, Jayne B. Zaharias, and B. Dewayne Fulton. 1993. "The Lasting Benefits Study (LBS) in Grades 4 and 5 (1990–91): A Legacy from Tennessee's Four-year (K–3) Class Size Study (1985–1989), Project STAR." HEROS, Inc.

Adda, Jerome, T. Chandola, and M. Marmot. 2003. "Socio-economic Status and Health: Causality and Pathways." *Journal of Econometrics* 112: 57–63.

Adler, Nancy E., et al. 2007. *Reaching for a Healthier Life: Facts on Socioeconomic Status and Health in the U.S.* John D. and Catherine T. MacArthur Foundation Research Network on Socioeconomic Status and Health.

Aizer, Anna and Janet Currie. 2004. "Networks or Neighborhoods? Correlations in the Use of Publicly-Funded Maternity Care in California." *Journal of Public Economics* 88: 2573–2585.

Aizer, Anna, Laura Stroud, and Stephen Buka. 2008. "Biology, Stress, and the Intergenerational Transmission of Economic Status." Unpublished manuscript. Providence: Brown University.

Alaniz, M. L., et al. 1998. "Immigrants and Violence: The Importance of Neighborhood Context." *Hispanic Journal of Behavioral Sciences* 20: 155–174.

Altonji, Joseph, Todd Elder, and Christopher Taber. 2005. "Selection on Observed and Unobserved Variables: Assessing the Effectiveness of Catholic Schools." *Journal of Political Economy* 113 (1): 151–184.

Anderson, E. 1999. *Code of the Street: Decency, Violence, and the Moral Life of the Inner City.* New York: Norton.

Anderson, Michael L. 2008. "Multiple Inference and Gender Differences in the

Effects of Early Intervention: A Reevaluation of the Abecedarian, Perry Pre-school, and Early Training Projects." 2008. *Journal of the American Statistical Association.* 103 (484): 1481–1495.

Ando, Y. 1988. "Effects of Daily Noise on Fetuses and Cerebral Hemisphere Specialization in Children." *Journal of Sound and Vibration* 127: 411–417.

Aneshensel, Carol S., and Clea A. Sucoff. 1996. "The Neighborhood Context of Adolescent Mental Health." *Journal of Health and Social Behavior* 37: 293–310.

Argys, L. M., D. I. Rees, and D. J. Brewer. 1996. "Detracking America's Schools: Equity at Zero Cost?" *Journal of Policy Analysis and Management* 15: 623–645.

Arias, O., K. F. Hallock, and W. Sosa-Escudero. 2001. "Individual Heterogeneity in the Returns to Schooling: Instrumental Variables Quantile Regression Using Twins Data." *Empirical Economics* 26: 7–40.

Ash, Michael, and T. Robert Fetter. 2004. "Who Lives on the Wrong Side of the Environmental Tracks? Evidence from the EPA's Risk-Screening Environmental Indicators Model." *Social Science Quarterly* 85: 441–462.

Attar, Beth K., Nancy G. Guerra, and Patrick H. Tolan. 1994. "Neighborhood Disadvantage, Stressful Life Events, and Adjustment in Urban Elementary-School Children." *Journal of Clinical Child Psychology* 23: 391–400.

Bailey, Martin. 1959. "Note on the Economics of Residential Zoning and Urban Renewal." *Land Economics* 35 (3): 288–292.

Bailey, Martin J. 1966. "Effects of Race and of Other Demographic Factors on the Values of Single-Family Homes." *Land Economics* 42 (2): 215–220.

Bailey, N., A. Haworth, T. Manzi, O. Paranagamage, and M. Roberts, 2006. *Creating and Sustaining Mixed Income Communities.* Coventry, England: Chartered Institute of Housing/Joseph Rowntree Foundation.

Barghaus, K., D. Cutler, R. Fryer, and E. Glaeser. 2007. "Understanding Racial Differences in Life Expectancy." Mimeo. Cambridge, Mass.: Harvard University.

Barker, R. G., and H. F. Wright. 1951. *One Boy's Day: A Specimen Record of Behavior.* New York: Harper and Brothers.

Barnett, Jonathan. 2003. *Redesigning Cities: Principles, Practice, Implementation.* Chicago: Planners Press.

Barnett, W. S., and Leonard Masse. 2007. "Comparative Benefit–Cost Analysis of the Abecedarian Program and Its Policy Implications." *Economics of Education Review* 26 (1): 113–125.

Bauder, Harald. 2001. " 'You're Good with Your Hands, Why Don't You Become an Auto Mechanic?': Neighborhood Context, Institutions, and Careers Development." *International Journal of Urban and Regional Research* 25 (3): 593–608.

Baugh, John. 2007. "Linguistic Profiling: Implications for Future Research." In J. Goering, ed., *Fragile Rights Within Cities: Government, Housing, and Fairness.* Lanham, Md.: Rowman and Littlefield.

Bayer, Patrick, Fernando Ferreira, and Robert McMillan. 2007. "A Unified Framework for Measuring Preferences for Schools and Neighborhoods." *Journal of Political Economy* 115 (4): 588–638.

Bayer, Patrick, Robert McMillan, and Kim S. Ruben. 2004. "What Drives Racial Segregation? New Evidence Using Census Microdata." *Journal of Urban Economics* 56: 514–535.

Becker, Gary S., and Kevin M. Murphy. 2000. *Social Economics: Market Behavior in a Social Environment.* Cambridge, Mass.: Belknap Press.

Berry, Brian J. L. 1976. "Ghetto Expansion and Single-Family Housing Prices: Chicago, 1968–1972." *Journal of Urban Economics* 3 (4): 397–423.

Berry, Steven, James Levinsohn, and Ariel Pakes. 1995. "Automobile Prices in Market Equilibrium." *Econometrica* 63: 841–890.

Bertrand, Marianne, Erzo Luttmer, and Senhil Mullainathan. 2000. "Network Effects and Welfare Cultures." *Quarterly Journal of Economics* 115: 1019–1056.

Berube, Alan. 2005. *Mixed Communities in England: A U.S. Perspective on Evidence and Policy Prospects.* York, England: Joseph Rowntree Foundation.

Berube, Alan, ed. 2007. *MetroNation: How U.S. Metropolitan Areas Fuel American Prosperity.* Washington, D.C.: Brookings Institution.

Bhattacharya, Debopam, and Bhashkar Mazumder. 2007. "Nonparametric Analysis of Intergenerational Income Mobility with Application to the United States." Working Paper, Series WP-07-12. Federal Reserve Bank of Chicago.

Bhattacharya, Jayanta, and Janet Currie. 2001. "Youths at Nutritional Risk: Malnourished or Misnourished?" In Jonathan Gruber, ed., *Risky Behavior Among Youths: An Economic Analysis.* Chicago: University of Chicago Press for National Bureau of Economic Research.

Biederman, Joseph, Jeffrey Newcorn, and Susan Sprich. 1991. "Comorbidity of Attention Deficit Hyperactivity Disorder with Conduct, Depressive, Anxiety, and Other Disorders." *American Journal of Psychiatry* 148 (5): 564–577.

Birch, David, et al. 1979. *The Behavioral Foundations of Neighborhood Change.* Washington, D.C.: U.S. GPO/U.S. Department of Housing and Urban Development.

Blaisdell, Carol, Robert LoCasale, Ana Gu, and Sheila Weiss. 2007. "Risk Areas for Pediatric Acute Care: Asthma Differs from Upper and Lower Respiratory Illness." *Health and Place* 13 (2): 404–416.

Blalock, H.M. 1956. "Economic Discrimination and Negro Increase." *American Sociological Review* 21: 584–588.

———. 1957. "Percent Non-White and Discrimination in the South." *American Sociological Review* 22: 667–682.

———. 1967. *Toward a Theory of Minority Group Relations.* New York: John Wiley and Sons.

Blanchard, T. C. 2007. "Conservative Protestant Congregations and Racial Residential Segregation: Evaluating the Closed Community Thesis in Metropolitan and Nonmetropolitan Counties." *American Sociological Review* 72: 416–433.

Blank, Rebecca. 2002. "Evaluating Welfare Reform in the United States." *Journal of Economic Literature* 40 (4): 1105–1166.

Bleakley, Hoyt. 2007. "Malaria Eradication in the Americas: A Retrospective Analysis of Childhood Exposure." Working Paper. Bogotá, Colombia: CEDE/Universidad de Los Andes.

Bobo, Lawrence. 2001. "Racial Attitudes and Relations at the Close of the Twentieth Century." In N. Smelser, W.J. Wilson, and F. Mitchell, eds., *America Becoming: Racial Trends and Their Consequences.* Washington, D.C.: National Academy Press.

Bobo, Lawrence, and James Kluegel. 1997. "Status, Ideology, and Dimensions of Whites' Racial Beliefs and Attitudes: Progress and Stagnation." In *Racial Attitudes in the 1990s: Continuity and Change*, ed. S. Tuch and J. Martin. Westport, Conn.: Praeger.

Bobo, Lawrence, and Camille L. Zubrinsky. 1996. "Attitudes Toward Residential Integration: Perceived Status Differences, Mere In-Group Preference, or Racial Prejudice?" *Social Forces* 74: 883–909.

Boggs, Roderic V. O., Joseph M. Sellers, and Marc Bendick, Jr. 1993. "Use of Testing in Civil Rights Enforcement." In *Clear and Convincing Evidence: Testing for Discrimination in America*, ed. M. Fix and R. Struyk. Washington, D.C.: Urban Institute Press.

Bolster, A., S. Burgess, Rucker Johnson, K. Jones, C. Propper, and R. Sarker. 2004. *Neighborhoods, Households and Income Dynamics.* CMPO Working Paper Series no. 04/106. Bristol, England: University of Bristol.

Bonnie, R. J., C. E. Fulco, and C. T. Liverman, eds. 1999. *Reducing the Burden of Injury.* Washington D.C.: Institute of Medicine.

Borman, Geoffrey D., Robert E. Slavin, Alan C. K. Cheun, Anne M. Chamberlain, Nancy A. Madden, and Bette Chambers. 2007. "Final Reading Outcomes of the National Randomized Field Trial of Success for All." *American Educational Research Journal* 44 (3): 701–731.

Bostic, Raphael, and Richard Martin. 2003. "Black Homeowners as a Gentrifying Force? Neighborhood Dynamics in the Context of Minority Homeownership." *Urban Studies* 40 (12): 2427–2449.

———. 2005. "Have Anti-Discrimination Housing Laws Worked? Evidence from Trends in Black Homeownership." *Journal of Real Estate Finance and Economics* 31: 5–26.

Bowly, Devereaux. 1978. *The Poorhouse: Subsidized Housing in Chicago, 1895–1976.* Carbondale, Ill.: Southern Illinois University Press.

Boyd, Donald, Pamela Grossman, Hamilton Lankford, Susanna Loeb, and James Wyckoff. 2005a. "How Changes in Entry Requirements Alter the Teacher Workforce and Affect Student Achievement." NBER Working Paper no. 11844. Cambridge, Mass.: National Bureau of Economic Research.

Boyd, Donald, Hamilton Lankford, Susanna Loeb, and James Wyckoff. 2005b. "Explaining the Short Careers of High-Achieving Teachers in Schools with Low-Performing Students." *American Economic Review* 95 (2): 166–172.

Braaten, Ellen B., and Lee Rosen. 2000. "Self-Regulation of Affect in Attention Deficit-Hyperactivity Disorder (ADHD) and Non-ADHD Boys: Differences in Empathic Responding." *Journal of Consulting and Clinical Psychology* 68 (2): 313–321.

Branas, C. C., T. Richmond, C. Schwab, and D. Wiebe. 2005. "Getting Past the 'F' Word in Federally Funded Public Health Research." *Injury Prevention* 11 (3): 191.

Branas, C. C., Dennis Culhane, Therese S. Richmond, and Douglas J. Wiebe. 2008. "Novel Linkage of Individual and Geographic Data to Study Firearm Violence." *Homicide Studies* 12: 298–320.

Branas, C. C., Dennis Culhane, Michael R. Elliott, Therese S. Richmond, and Douglas J. Wiebe. 2009a. "Alcohol Consumption, Alcohol Outlets, and the Risk of Being Assaulted with a Gun." *Alcoholism: Clinical and Experimental Research* 11 (4): 1–10.

Branas C. C., M. R. Elliott, T. S. Richmond, D. Culhane, T. R. Ten Have, D. J. Wiebe. 2009b. "Investigating the Link Between Gun Possession and Gun Assault." *American Journal of Public Health* 99 (11): 2034–2040.

Breslow, N. E. 1996. "Statistics in Epidemiology: The Case-Control Study." *Journal of the American Statistical Association* 91 (433): 14–28.

Briggs, Xavier de Souza. 1997. "Moving Up Versus Moving Out: Neighborhood Effects in Housing Mobility Programs." *Housing Policy Debate* 8 (1): 195–234.

———. 1998. "Brown Kids in White Suburbs: Housing Mobility and the Many Faces of Social Capital." *Housing Policy Debate* 9: 177–221.

———. 2005a. *The Geography of Opportunity: Race and Housing Choice in Metropolitan America.* Washington, D.C.: Brookings Institution.

————. 2005b. "Policy and Politics: Changing the Geography of Opportunity." In Xavier de Souza Briggs, ed., *The Geography of Opportunity: Race and Housing Choice in Metropolitan America.* Washington, D.C.: Brookings Institution.

Briggs, Xavier de Souza, and Benjamin Keys. 2005. "Did Exposure to Poor Neighborhoods Change in the 1990s? Evidence from the Panel Study of Income Dynamics." Paper presented at the annual meeting of the Association for Public Policy Analysis and Management, Washington, D.C.

Brock, William A., and Steven N. Durlauf. 2001. "Discrete Choice with Social Interactions." *Review of Economic Studies* 68: 235–260.

Bronfenbrenner, Urie. 1986. "Ecology of the Family as a Context for Human Development: Research Perspectives." *Developmental Psychology* 22: 723–742.

Bronzaft, Arline L., and Dennis P. McCarthy. 1975. "The Effect of Elevated Train Noise on Reading Ability." *Environmental Behavior* 7 (4): 517–527.

Brooks-Gunn, Jeanne, and Greg Duncan. 1997. "The Effects of Poverty on Children." *The Future of Children* 7: 55–71.

Brooks-Gunn, J., G. Duncan, P. K. Kelbanov, and N. Sealand. 1993. "Do Neighborhoods Influence Child and Adolescent Development?" *American Journal of Sociology* 99(2): 353–395.

Brophy, Paul C., and Rhonda N. Smith. 1997. "Mixed-Income Housing: Factors for Success." *Cityscape: A Journal of Policy and Development Research* 3 (2): 3–31.

Browning, Christopher, Seth Feinberg, and Robert Dietz. 2004. "The Paradox of Social Organization: Networks, Collective Efficacy, and Violent Crime in Urban Neighborhoods." *Social Forces* 83: 503–534.

Brueckner, Jan. 1977. "The Determinants of Residential Succession." *Journal of Urban Economics* 4 (1): 45–59.

Brueckner, Jan and Stuart Rosenthal. 2005. "Gentrification and Neighborhood Cycles: Will America's Future Downtowns Be Rich?" Working Paper. Irvine: University of California, Irvine.

Buchinsky, M. 2001. "Quantile Regression with Sample Selection: Estimating Women's Return to Education in the U.S." *Empirical Economics* 26: 87–113.

Buck, N. 2001. "Identifying Neighborhood Effects on Social Exclusion." *Urban Studies* 38: 2251–2275.

Bui, Linda T. M., and Christopher J. Mayer. 2003. "Regulation and Capitalization of Environmental Amenities: Evidence from the Toxic Release Inventory in Massachusetts." *Review of Economics and Statistics* 85 (3): 693–708.

Bureau of Justice Statistics. 2003. *Key Facts at a Glance: Direct Expenditures by Level of Government.* http://www.ojp.usdoj.gov.bjs/glance/tables/expgovtab.html.

Bureau of Labor Statistics. 2006. Labor Force Statistics from the Current Population Survey. http://data.bls.gov/PDQ/servlet/SurveyOutputServlet.

Buron, Larry, Diane K. Levy, and Megan Gallagher. 2007. *Housing Choice Vouchers: How HOPE VI Families Fared in the Private Market. Brief 3.* Washington, D.C.: Urban Institute.

Buron, Larry, Susan Popkin, Diane Levy, Laura Harris, and Jill Khadduri. 2002. *The HOPE VI Resident Tracking Study: A Snapshot of the Current Living Situation of Original Residents from Eight Sites.* Washington, D.C.: Urban Institute.

Bursik, R. J. and H. G. Grasmick. 1993. *Neighborhoods and Crime: The Dimensions of Effective Community Control.* New York: Lexington.

Burtless, G. 1996. "Introduction and Summary." In G. Burtless, ed., *Does Money Matter? The Effect of School Resources on Student Achievement and Adult Success.* Washington, D.C.: Brookings Institution.

Burton, Linda. 1997. "Ethnography and the Meaning of Adolescence in High-Risk Neighborhoods." *Ethos* 25 (2): 208–217.

Calanog, Victor Franco, and Felix Oberholzer-Gee. 2006. "Bidding for Business: A Field Experiment." Working Paper. Philadelphia and New York: University of Pennsylvania and Columbia University.

Calvó-Armengol, Antoni, and Yves Zenou. 2004. "Social Networks and Crime Decisions: The Role of Social Structure in Facilitating Delinquent Behavior." *International Economic Review* 45: 939–958.

Campbell, Frances A., Shari Miller-Johnson, Elizabeth Puhn Pungello, Craig T. Ramey, and Joseph Sparling. 2002. "Early Childhood Education: Young Adult Outcomes from the Abecedarian Project." *Applied Developmental Science* 6 (1): 42–57.

Card, D. and A. Krueger. 1992. "Does School Quality Matter?" *Journal of Political Economy* 100: 1–40.

Card, David, Alexandre Mas, and Jesse Rothstein. 2008a. "Are Mixed Neighborhoods Always Unstable? Two-Sided and One-Sided Tipping." NBER Working Paper no. 14470. Cambridge, Mass.: National Bureau of Economic Research.

Card, David, Alexandre Mas, and Jesse Rothstein. 2008b. "Tipping and the Dynamics of Segregation." *Quarterly Journal of Economics* 128: 177–218.

Card, David and Jesse Rothstein. 2006. "Racial Segregation and the Black-White Test Score Gap." NBER Working Paper no. 12078. Cambridge, Mass.: National Bureau of Economic Research.

———. 2007. "Racial Segregation and the Black-White Test Score Gap." *Journal of Public Economics* 91: 2158–2189.

Carmichael, J. T. 2005. "The Determinants of Jail Use Across Large U.S. Cities: An Assessment of Racial, Ethnic, and Economic Threat Explanations." *Social Science Research* 34: 538–569.

Carneiro, Pedro, and James J. Heckman. 2003. "Human Capital Policy." In James J. Heckman and Alan B. Krueger, eds., *Inequality in America: What Role for Human Capital Policies?* Cambridge, Mass.: MIT Press.

Carneiro, Pedro, Costas Meghir, and Matthias Parey. 2007. "Maternal Education, Home Environments and the Development of Children and Adolescents." IFS Working Paper W07/15. London: Institute of Fiscal Studies.

Case, Anne, and L. Katz. 1991. "The Company You Keep: The Effects of Family and Neighborhood on Disadvantaged Families." NBER Working Paper no. 3705. Cambridge, Mass.: National Bureau of Economic Research.

Case, Anne, Darren Lubotsky, and Christian Paxson. 2002. "Economic Status and Health in Childhood: The Origins of the Gradient." *American Economic Review* 92 (5): 1308–1334.

Caulkins, Jonathan P., and Sara Chandler. 2006. "Long-Run Trends in Incarceration of Drug Offenders in the United States." *Crime and Delinquency* 52 (4): 619–641.

Ceraso, Karen. 1995. "Is Mixed-Income Housing the Key?" *Shelterforce Online* March–April. http://www.nhi.org/online/issues/80/mixhous.html.

Chambers, Daniel N. 1992. "The Racial Housing Price Differential and Racially Transitional Neighborhoods." *Journal of Urban Economics* 32 (2): 214–232.

Charles, Camille Zubrinsky. 2003. "The Dynamics of Racial Residential Segregation." *Annual Review of Sociology* 29: 167–207.

Charles, Kerwin Kofi, and Erik Hurst. 2000. "The Transition to Home Ownership and the Black-White Wealth Gap." *Review of Economics and Statistics* 8: 281–297.

Chase-Lansdale, P. L., and R. A. Gordon. 1996. "Economic Hardship and the Development of 5- and 6-year-olds: Neighborhood and Regional Perspectives." *Child Development* 67: 3338–3367.

Chase-Lansdale, P. L., R. A. Gordon, J. Brooks-Gunn, and P. K. Klebanov. 1997. "Neighborhood and Family Influences on the Intellectual and Behavioral Competence of Preschool and Early School-Age Children." In J. Brooks-Gunn, G. J. Duncan, and J. L. Aber, eds., *Neighborhood Poverty: Context and Consequences for Children* (Vol. 1, 79–118). New York: Russell Sage Foundation.

Chay, Kenneth Y. and Michael Greenstone. 2003a. "Air Quality, Infant Mortality, and the Clean Air Act of 1970." NBER Working Paper no. 10053. Cambridge, Mass.: National Bureau of Economic Research.

———. 2003b. "The Impact of Air Pollution on Infant Mortality: Evidence from Geographic Variation in Pollution Shocks Induced by a Recession." *Quarterly Journal of Economics* 118 (3): 1121–1167.

Chernichovsky, Dov, and Arleen Liebowitz. 2008. "Integrating Public Health and Personal Care in a Reformed U.S. Health Care System." Unpublished manuscript. Los Angeles: UCLA.

Chicago Housing Authority. 2008. *FY2008 Annual Plan: Plan For Transformation Year 9.* Chicago: Chicago Housing Authority.

Cisneros, Henry G. and Lora Engdahl, eds. 2009. *From Despair to Hope: HOPE VI and the New Promise of Public Housing in America's Cities.* Washington, D.C.:Brookings Institution Press.

Clampet-Lundquist, Susan. 2004. "HOPE VI Relocation: Moving to New Neighborhoods and Building New Ties." *Housing Policy Debate* 15: 415–447.

Clampet-Lundquist, Susan, and Douglas Massey. 2006. "Neighborhood Effects on Economic Self-Sufficiency." Paper presented at the annual meetings of the Eastern Sociological Society, Boston.

———. 2008. "Neighborhood Effects on Economic Self-Sufficiency: A Reconsideration of the Moving to Opportunity Experiment." *American Journal of Sociology* 114 (1): 107–143.

Clampet-Lundquist, Susan, Kathryn Edin, Jeffrey Kling, and Greg Duncan. 2006. "Moving At-Risk Teenagers Out of High-Risk Neighborhoods: Why Girls Fare Better Than Boys." Working Paper no. 509, Industrial Relations Section. Princeton, NJ: Princeton University.

Clapp, John, and Stephen L. Ross. 2004. "Schools and Housing Markets: An Examination of Changes in School Segregation and Performance." *Economic Journal* 114: 425–440.

Clopton, P. 2000. "Texas Mathematics Education in Transition." *Texas Education Review* Fall.

Clotfelter, Charles T., Helen F. Ladd, and Jacob L. Vigdor. 2006. "Teacher-Student Matching and the Assessment of Teacher Effectiveness." *Journal of Human Resources* 41: 778–820.

Cochran, A. B., and Thomas M. Uhlman. 1973. "Black Populations and School Integration—A Research Note." *Phylon* 34: 43–48.

Cohen, D., et al. 2000. "'Broken Windows' and the Risk of Gonorrhea." *American Journal of Public Health* 90 (2): 230–236.

Cohen, Sheldon, Joseph Schwartz, Elissa Epel, Clemens Kirschbaum, Steve Sidney, and Teresa Seeman. 2006. "Socioeconomic Status, Race and Diurnal Cortisol Decline in the Coronary Artery Risk Development in Young Adults (CARDIA) Study." *Psychosomatic Medicine* 68: 41–50.

Collins, Rebecca L. 1996. "For Better or Worse: The Impact of Upward Social Comparison on Self-Evaluations." *Psychological Bulletin* 119 (1): 51–69.

Collins, William J., and Robert A. Margo. 2000. "Residential Segregation and Socioeconomic Outcomes: When Did Ghettos Go Bad?" *Economics Letters* 69: 239–243.

————. 2001. "Race and Home Ownership: A Century-Long View." *Explorations in Economic History* 38: 68–92.

Comey, Jennifer. 2007. *HOPE VI'd and On the Move.* Brief No. 1. Washington, D.C.: Urban Institute.

Cook, T., S. Shagle, S. Degirmencioglu, C. Coulton, J. Korbin, and M. Su. 1997. "Capturing Social Process for Testing Mediational Models of Neighborhood Effects." In J. Brooks-Gunn, G. Duncan, and L. Aber, eds., *Neighborhood Poverty: Vol. II, Policy Implications in Studying Neighborhoods.* New York: Russell Sage Foundation.

Corcoran, M., R. Gordon, D. Laren, and G. Solon. 1990. "Effects of Family and Community Background on Economic Status." *American Economic Review* 80: 362–366.

Corzine, J., J. Creech, and L. Corzine. 1983. "Black Concentration and Lynchings in the South: Testing Blalock's Power-Threat Hypothesis." *Social Forces* 61: 774–796.

Coulton, C., J. Korbin, and M. Su. 1999. "Neighborhoods and Child Maltreatment: A Multi-Level Study." *Child Abuse and Neglect* 23: 1019–1040.

Crane, Jonathan. 1991a. "Effects of Neighborhood on Dropping Out of School and Teenage Childbearing." In C. Jencks and P. E. Peterson, eds., *The Urban Underclass.* Washington, D.C.: Brookings Institution.

————. 1991b. "The Epidemic Theory of Ghettos and Neighborhood Effects on Dropping Out and Teenage Childbearing." *American Journal of Sociology* 96 (5): 1226–1259.

Crowder, K., and S. J. South. 2003. "Neighborhood Distress and School Dropout: The Variable Significance of Community Context." *Social Science Research* 32: 659–698.

Crump, J. 2002. "Deconcentration by Demolition: Public Housing, Poverty, and Urban Policy." *Environment and Planning D: Society and Space* 20: 581–596.

Cullen, Julie, and Steven Levitt. 1999. "Crime, Urban Flight, and the Consequences for Cities." *Review of Economics and Statistics* 81 (2): 159–169.

Cummings, Jean L., and Denise DiPasquale. 1999. "The Low-Income Housing Tax Credit: An Analysis of the First Ten Years." *Housing Policy Debate* 10 (2): 251–307.

Currie, Janet. 2001. "Early Childhood Education Programs." *Journal of Economic Perspectives* 15 (2): 213–238.

————. 2009. "Healthy, Wealthy, and Wise? Socioeconomic Status, Poor Health in Childhood, and Human Capital Development." *Journal of Economic Literature* 47 (1): 87–122.

Currie, Janet, and V. Joseph Hotz. 2004. "Inequality in Life and Death: What Drives Racial Trends in U.S. Child Death Rates?" In Kathryn Neckerman, ed., *Social Inequality.* New York: Russell Sage Foundation.

Currie, Janet, and Wanchuan Lin. 2007. "Chipping Away at Health: More on the Relationship Between Income and Child Health." *Health Affairs* 26 (2): 331–344.

Currie, Janet and Enrico Moretti. 2007. "Biology as Destiny? Short and Long-Run Determinants of Intergenerational Transmission of Birth Weight." *Journal of Labor Economics* 25 (2): 231–263.

————. 2003. "Mother's Education and the Intergenerational Transmission of Human Capital: Evidence from College Openings." *Quarterly Journal of Economics* 118 (4): 1495–1532.

Currie, Janet, and Matthew Neidell. 2005. "Air Pollution and Infant Health:

What Can We Learn From California's Recent Experience?" *Quarterly Journal of Economics* 120 (3): 1003–1030.

Currie, Janet, and Duncan Thomas. 1995. "Does Head Start Make a Difference?" *American Economic Review* 85 (3): 341–364.

Currie, Janet, and Aaron Yelowitz. 2000. "Are Public Housing Projects Good For Kids?" *Journal of Public Economics* 75 (1): 99–124.

Cutler, David M., and Edward L. Glaeser. 1997. "Are Ghettos Good or Bad?" *Quarterly Journal of Economics* 112: 827–872.

Cutler, David M., and Grant Miller. 2005. "The Role of Public Health Improvements in Health Advances: The Twentieth-Century United States." *Demography* 42 (1): 1–22.

Cutler, David, Edward Glaeser, and Jesse Shapiro. 2003. "Why Have Americans Become More Obese?" *Journal of Economic Perspectives* 17 (3): 93–118.

Cutler, David M., Edward L. Glaeser, and Jacob L. Vigdor. 1999. "The Rise and Decline of the American Ghetto." *Journal of Political Economy* 107 (3): 455–506.

D'Alessio, S.J., D. Eitle, and L. Stolzenberg. 2005. "The Impact of Serious Crime, Racial Threat, and Economic Inequality on Private Police Size." *Social Science Research* 34: 267–282.

D'Imperio, Rhonda L., Eric F. Dubow, and Maria F. Ippolito. 2000. "Resilient and Stress-Affected Adolescents in an Urban Setting." *Journal of Clinical Child Psychology* 29 (1): 129–142.

Datcher, L. 1982. "Effects of Community and Family Background on Achievement." *Review of Economics and Statistics* 64: 32–41.

Deaton, Angus, and Darren Lubotsky. 2002. "Mortality, Inequality and Race in American Cities and States." *Social Science and Medicine* 56 (6): 1139–1153.

DeFina, R. and L. Hannon. 2009. "Diversity, Racial Threat and Housing Segregation." *Social Forces* 88(1):373–394.

DeLuca, S., G. Duncan, R. Mendenhall, and M. Keels. 2010. "*Gautreaux* Mothers and Their Children." *Housing Policy Debate* 20 (1): 7–25.

Deming, David. 2007. "Early Childhood Intervention and Life-Cycle Skill Development." Working Paper. Cambridge, Mass.: Harvard University.

DeSantis A.S., E. K. Adam, L. D. Doane, S. Mineka, R. E. Zinbarg, and M. G. Craske. 2007. "Racial/Ethnic Differences in Cortisol Diurnal Rhythms in a Community Sample of Adolescents." *Journal of Adolescent Health* 41 (1): 3–13.

De Sena, J. N. 1990. *Protecting One's Turf: Social Strategies for Maintaining Urban Neighborhoods.* Lanham, Md.: University Press of America.

Downs, Anthony. 1973. *Opening Up the Suburbs: An Urban Strategy for America.* New Haven: Yale University Press.

Dreier, Peter, John Mollenkopf, and Todd Swanstrom. 2004. *Place Matters,* 2nd ed. Lawrence: University of Kansas Press.

Duncan, G. 1994. "Families and Neighbors as Sources of Disadvantage in the Schooling Decisions of Black and White Adolescents." *American Journal of Education* 103 (1): 20–53.

Duncan, G., J. Connell, and P. Klebanov. 1997. "Conceptual and Methodological Issues in Estimating Causal Effects of Neighborhoods and Family Conditions on Individual Development." In J. Brooks-Gunn, G. Duncan, and J. Aber, eds., *Neighborhood Poverty: Volume 1, Context and Consequences for Children.* New York: Russell Sage Foundation.

Dynarski, Mark, Roberto Agodini, Sheila Heaviside, Timothy Novak, Nancy Care, Larissa Campuzano, Barbara Means, Robert Murphy, William Penuel,

Hal Javitz, Deborah Emery, and Willow Sussex. 2007. "Effectiveness of Reading and Mathematics Software Products: Findings from the First Student Cohort." Mathematica Policy Research for the U.S. Department of Education, NCEE 2007–4005. http://www.mathematica-mpr.com/publications/PDFs/effectread.pdf.

Edin, Kathryn, and Laura Lein. 1997. *Making Ends Meet: How Single Mothers Survive Welfare and Low-Wage Work*. New York: Russell Sage Foundation.

Eide, E., and M. H. Showalter. 1998. "The Effect of School Quality on Student Performance: A Quantile Regression Approach." *Economics Letters* 58: 345–350.

Ellen, Ingrid Gould. 2000. *Sharing America's Neighborhoods: The Prospects for Stable Racial Integration*. Cambridge, Mass.: Harvard University Press.

———. 2008. "Continuing Isolation: Segregation in America Today." In J. H. Carr and N. K. Kutty, eds., *Segregation: The Rising Costs for America*. New York: Routledge.

Ellen, Ingrid Gould, and Margery Austin Turner. 2003. "Do Neighborhoods Matter and Why?" In John Goering and Judith D. Feins, eds., *Choosing a Better Life? Evaluating the Moving to Opportunity Social Experiment*. Washington, D.C.: Urban Institute Press.

Ellen, Ingrid Gould, Katherine O'Regan, and Ioan Voicu. 2009. "Siting, Spillovers, and Segregation: A Re-examination of the Low Income Housing Tax Credit Program." In Edward Glaeser and John Quigley, eds., *Housing Markets and the Economy: Risk, Regulation, Policy; Essays in Honor of Karl Case*. Cambridge, Mass.: Lincoln Institute for Land Policy.

Elliott, D., W. Wilson, D. Huizinga, A. Elliott, and B. Rankin. 1996. "The Effects of Neighborhood Disadvantage on Adolescent Development." *Journal of Research in Crime and Delinquency* 33 (4): 389–426.

Ellwood, David. 1986. "The Spatial Mismatch Hypothesis: Are there Jobs Missing in the Ghetto?" In Richard Freeman and Harry Holzer, eds., *The Black Youth Employment Crisis*. Chicago: University of Chicago Press.

———. 2001. "The Impact of the Earned Income Tax Credit and Social Policy Reforms on Work, Marriage, and Living Arrangements." In B. Meyer and D. Holtz-Eakin, eds., *Making Work Pay: The Earned Income Tax Credit and Its Impact on America's Families*. New York: Russell Sage Foundation.

Emerson, Michael O., Karen J. Chai, and George Yancey. 2001. "Does Race Matter in Residential Segregation? Exploring the Preferences of White Americans." *American Sociological Review* 66 (6): 922–935.

Ennett, S. T., R. L. Flewelling, R. C. Lindrooth, and E.C. Norton. 1997. "School and Neighborhood Characteristics Associated with School Rates of Alcohol, Cigarette, and Marijuana Use." *Journal of Health and Social Behavior* 38: 55–71.

Eriksen, Michael D., and Stuart S. Rosenthal. 2007. "Crowd Out, Stigma, and the Effect of Place-Based Subsidized Rental Housing." Working Paper. Athens, Ga: University of Georgia.

Evans W. N., W. Oates, and R. M. Schwab. 1992. "Measuring Peer Group Effects: A Study of Teenage Behavior." *Journal of Political Economy* 100: 966–991.

Evans, G. W., M. Bullinger, and S. Hygge. 1998. "Chronic Noise Exposure and Physiological Response: A Prospective Study of Children Living Under Environmental Stress." *Psychological Science* 9: 75–77.

Farley, Reynolds, and William H. Frey. 1994. "Changes in the Segregation of Whites from Blacks During the 1980s: Small Steps Toward a More Integrated Society." *American Sociological Review* 59: 23–45.

Farley, Reynolds, Charlotte Steeh, Maria Krysan, Tara Jackson, and Keith Reeves. 1994. "Stereotypes and Segregation: Neighborhoods in the Detroit Area." *American Journal of Sociology* 100: 750–780.

Fauth, R., T. Leventhal, and J. Brooks-Gunn. 2003a. "Short-term Effects of Moving from Public Housing in Poor to Affluent Neighborhoods on Low-Income, Minority Adults' Outcomes." Unpublished paper, National Center for Children and Families. New York: Columbia University.

———. 2003b. "They're Moving Out, Are They Moving Up? Early Impacts of Moving to Low-Poverty Neighborhoods on Low-Income Youth." Unpublished paper, National Center for Children and Families. New York: Columbia University.

Felson, M. 1986. "Routine Activities, Social Controls, Rational Decisions and Criminal Outcomes." In D. Cornish and R. V. Clarke, eds., *The Reasoning Criminal*. New York: Springer Verlag.

———. 1987. "Routine Activities and Crime Prevention in the Developing Metropolis." *Criminology* 25: 911–931.

Fernandez, Roberto M., and Celina Su. 2004. "Space in the Study of Labor Markets." *Annual Review of Sociology* 30: 546–569.

Ferreira, Fernando, and Alberto Saiz. 2008. "The Importance of Being 'Ernesto': Do Hispanics Affect the Housing Market?" Working Paper. Wharton School, University of Pennsylvania.

Fischer, Claude S. 2002. "Ever-More Rooted Americans." *City and Community* 1 (2): 175–193.

Fischer, Mary J. 2008. "Shifting Geographies: Examining the Role of Suburbanization in Blacks' Declining Segregation." *Urban Affairs Review* 43: 475–496.

Fischer, Paul. 2002. *Where Are The Public Housing Families Going? An Update.* Lake Forest, Ill.: Lake Forest College.

Florsheim, P., P. Tolan, and D. Gorman-Smith. 1998. "Family Relationships, Parenting Practices, the Availability of Male Family Members, and the Behavior of Inner-City Boys in Single-Mother and Two-Parent Families." *Child Development* 69 (5): 1437–1447.

Fogarty, Michael S. 1977. "Predicting Neighborhood Decline Within a Large City: Application of Discriminant Analysis." *Environment and Planning A* 9 (5): 579–584.

Follain, James R., and Stephen Malpezzi. 1981. "Another Look at Racial Differences in Housing Prices." *Urban Studies* 18: 195–203.

Freeman, Richard B. 1996. "Why Do So Many Young American Men Commit Crimes and What Might We Do About It?" *Journal of Economic Perspectives* 10 (1): 25–42.

———. 2001. "The Rising Tide Lifts . . . ?" NBER Working Paper no. 8155. Cambridge, Mass.: National Bureau of Economic Research.

Freeman, Richard B., and William M. Rodgers III. 2000. "Area Economic Conditions and the Labor Market Outcomes of Young Men in the 1990s Expansion." In Robert Cherry and William M. Rodgers III, eds., *Prosperity for All? The Economic Boom and African Americans*. New York: Russell Sage Foundation.

Frey, William. 2005. "Metropolitan Magnets for International and Domestic Migrants." In Alan Berube, Bruce Katz, and Robert E. Lang, eds., *Redefining Urban and Suburban America: Evidence from Census 2000*. Washington, D.C.: Brooking Institution Press.

———. 2007. *America: A Social Atlas*. New York: Longman.

Frey, W. H., and R. Farley. 1996. "Latino, Asian and Black Segregation in U.S.

Metropolitan Areas: Are Multiethnic Metros Different?" *Demography* 33: 35–50.

Friedrichs, J. 1998. "Do Poor Neighborhoods Make Their Residents Poorer? Context Effects of Poverty Neighborhoods on Their Residents." In H. Andress, eds., *Empirical Poverty Research in a Comparative Perspective*. Aldershot: Ashgate.

Friedrichs, J., G. Galster, and S. Musterd. 2003. "Neighborhood Effects on Social Opportunities: The European and American Research and Policy Context." *Housing Studies* 18 (6): 797–806.

Fryer, Roland G., Paul S. Heaton, Steven D. Levitt, and Kevin M. Murphy. 2005. "Measuring the Impact of Crack Cocaine." NBER Working Paper no. 11318. Cambridge, Mass.: National Bureau of Economic Research.

Fuchs, Victor, R. 1993. "Poverty and Health: Asking the Right Questions." In D. E. Rogers and E. Ginzberg, eds., *Medical Care and the Health of the Poor*. Boulder, Colo.: Westview Press.

Galster, George. 1977. "A Bid-Rent Analysis of Housing Market Discrimination." *American Economic Review* 67 (2): 144–155.

———. 1987. *Homeowners and Neighborhood Reinvestment*. Durham, N.C.: Duke University Press.

———. 1991. "Housing Discrimination and Urban Poverty of African-Americans." *Journal of Housing Research* 2: 87–122.

———. 2001. "On the Nature of Neighborhood." *Urban Studies* 38 (12): 2111–2124.

———. 2002. "An Economic Efficiency Analysis of Deconcentrating Poverty Populations." *Journal of Housing Economics* 11(4): 303–329.

———. 2004. "The Effects of Affordable and Multifamily Housing on Market Values of Nearby Homes." In Anthony Downs, ed., *Growth Management and Affordable Housing*. Washington, D.C.: Brookings Institution Press.

———. 2005. *Neighborhood Mix, Social Opportunities, and the Policy Challenges of an Increasingly Diverse Amsterdam*. Amsterdam: University of Amsterdam, Department of Geography, Planning, and International Development Studies. http://www.fmg.uva.nl/amidst/object.cfm/objectid = 7C149E7C-EC9F-4C2E-91DB7485 C0839425.

Galster, George, and Erin Godfrey. 2005. "By Words and Deeds: Racial Steering by Real Estate Agents in the U.S. in 2000." *Journal of the American Planning Association* 71: 251–268.

Galster, George, and Sean Killen. 1995. "The Geography of Metropolitan Opportunity: A Reconnaissance and Conceptual Framework." *Housing Policy Debate* 6 (1): 7–43.

Galster, George, and Stephen L. Ross. 2007. "Fair Housing Enforcement and Changes in Discrimination between 1989 and 2000." In J. Goering, ed., *Fragile Rights Within Cities: Government, Housing, and Fairness*. Lanham, Md.: Rowman and Littlefield.

Galster, G., J. Cutsinger, and R. Malega. 2008. "The Costs of Concentrated Poverty: Neighborhood Property Markets and the Dynamics of Decline." In N. Retsinas and E. Belsky, eds., *Revisiting Rental Housing: Policies, Programs, and Priorities*. Washington, D.C.: Brookings Institution Press.

Galster, George, Roberto Quercia, Alvaro Cortes, and Ron Malega. 2003. "The Fortunes of Poor Urban Neighborhoods." *Urban Affairs Review* 39 (2): 205–227.

Galster, George, Dave Marcotte, Marv Mandell, Hal Wolman, and Nancy Augustine. 2007. "The Influence of Neighborhood Poverty During Childhood on Fertility, Education and Earnings Outcomes." *Housing Studies* 22 (5): 723–752.

Garces, Eliana, Duncan Thomas, and Janet Currie. 2002. "Longer Term Effects of Head Start." *American Economic Review* 92 (4): 999–1012.

General Accounting Office. 1997. *Tax Credits: Opportunities to Improve Oversight of the Low-Income Housing Program (GGD/RCED-97-55).* Washington, D.C.: GAO.

———. 2001. *Federal Housing Assistance Programs: Costs and Housing Characteristics.* Report GAO-01–901R. Washington, D.C.: GAO.

Gennetian, Lisa A., Pamela A. Morris, Johannes M. Bos, and Howard S. Bloom. 2005. "Constructing Instrumental Variables from Experimental Data to Explore How Treatments Produce Effects." In Howard S. Bloom, ed., *Learning More from Social Experiments.* New York: Russell Sage Foundation.

Geolytics. 2004. *Census CD Neighborhood Change Database, 1970–2000.* East Brunswick, N.J.: Geolytics.

Gephart, M. 1997. "Neighborhoods and Communities as Contexts for Development." In J. Brooks-Gunn, G. Duncan, and J. Aber, eds., *Neighborhood Poverty, Vol. 1, Context and Consequences for Children.* New York: Russell Sage Foundation.

Geronimus, A. T. 2006. "Invited Commentary: Using Area-Based Socioeconomic Measures—Think Conceptually, Act Cautiously." *American Journal of Epidemiology* 164 (9): 835–840.

Geronimus, Arline, Margaret Hicken, Danya Keene, and John Bound. 2006. "'Weathering' and Age Patterns of Allostatic Load Scores Among Blacks and Whites in the United States." *American Journal of Public Health* 96 (5): 826–833.

Glaeser, Edward, and Joshua Gottlieb. 2008. "The Economics of Place-Making Policies." Working Paper, March.

Glaeser, Edward L., and Jose A. Scheinkman. 2003. "Non-Market Interactions." In M. Dewatripont, L. P. Hansen, and S. Turnovsky, eds., *Advances in Economics and Econometrics: Theory and Applications, 8th World Congress, Vol. 1.* Cambridge: Cambridge University Press.

Glaeser, Edward L., Bruce Sacerdone, and José A. Scheinkman. 1996. "Crime and Social Interactions." *The Quarterly Journal of Economics* 111 (2): 507–548.

Glazer, Nathan. 1986. "Education and Training Programs and Poverty." In Sheldon Danziger and Daniel Weinberg, eds., *Fighting Poverty: What Works and What Doesn't.* Cambridge, Mass.: Harvard University Press.

Glazerman, Steven, Tom Silva, Nii Addy, Sarah Avellar, Jeffrey Max, Allison McKie, Brenda Natzke, Michael Puma, Patrick Wolf, and Rachel Ungerer Greszler. 2006. "Options for Studying Teacher Pay Reform Using Natural Experiments." No. ED-04-CO-0112/0002. Washington, D.C.: Mathematica Policy Research.

Glied, Sherry. 2001. "The Value of Reductions in Child Injury Mortality in the U.S." In David M. Cutler and Ernst R. Berndt, eds., *Medical Care Output and Productivity.* Chicago: University of Chicago Press.

Gluckman, P. D. and M. Hanson. 2005. *The Fetal Matrix: Evolution, Development, and Disease.* Cambridge: Cambridge University Press.

Goering, John, and Judith D. Feins, eds. 2003. *Choosing a Better Life? Evaluating the Moving to Opportunity Experiment.* Washington, D.C.: Urban Institute Press.

Goetz, Edward. 2003. "Housing Dispersal Programs." *Journal of Planning Literature* 18 (1): 3–16.

Golub, Andrew, and Bruce D. Johnson, 1994, "A Recent Decline in Cocaine

Use Among Youthful Arrestees in Manhattan, 1987 Through 1993." *American Journal of Public Health* 84 (8): 1250–1254.

Gonzales, N. A., A. M. Cauce, R. J. Friedman, and C. A. Mason. 1996. "Family, Peer, and Neighborhood Influences on Academic Achievement Among African-American Adolescents: One-Year Prospective Effects." *American Journal of Community Psychology* 24: 365–387.

Gordon, Robert, Thomas J. Kane, and Douglas O. Staiger. 2006. "Identifying Effective Teachers Using Performance on the Job." Hamilton Project Discussion Paper 2006–01. Washington, D.C.: Brookings Institution.

Gould, Eric D., Bruce A. Weinberg, and David B. Mustard. 2002. "Crime Rates and Local Labor Market Opportunities in the United States: 1979–1997." *Review of Economics and Statistics* 84 (1): 45–61.

Graham, K., K. et al. 1998. "Current Directions in Research on Understanding and Preventing Intoxicated Aggression." *Addiction* 93 (5): 659–676.

Granovetter, Mark. 1974. *Getting a Job: A Study of Contacts and Careers.* Cambridge, Mass.: Harvard University Press.

Green, D. P., D. Z. Strolovitch and J. S. Wong. 1998. "Defended Neighborhoods, Integration and Racially Motivated Crime." *American Journal of Sociology* 104: 372–403.

Grogger, Jeffrey. 1998. "Market Wages and Youth Crime." *Journal of Labor Economics* 16 (4): 756–791.

———. 2003. "The Effect of Time Limits, the EITC and Other Policy Changes on Welfare Use, Work and Income Among Female Headed Households." *Review of Economics and Statistics* 85 (2): 394–408.

Grogger, Jeff, and Michael Willis. 2000. "The Emergence of Crack Cocaine and the Rise in Urban Crime Rates." *Review of Economics and Statistics* 82 (4): 519–529.

Grossman, Michael. 2000. "The Human Capital Model." In Anthony Culyer and Joseph P. Newhouse, eds., *The Handbook of Health Economics.* Amsterdam: North Holland.

Guarino, Cassandra M., Lucrecia Santibanez, and Glenn A. Daley. 2006. "Teacher Recruitment and Retention: A Review of the Recent Empirical Literature." *Review of Educational Research* 76 (2): 173–208.

Guerra, Nancy G., L. Rowell Huesmann, Patrick H. Tolan, Richard Van Acker, and Leonard D. Eron. 1995. "Stressful Events and Individual Beliefs as Correlates of Economic Disadvantage and Aggression Among Urban Children." *Journal of Consulting and Clinical Psychology* 63 (4): 518–528.

Hägerstrand, T. 1970. "What About People in Regional Science?" *Papers in Regional Science* 24 (1): 6–21.

———. 1974. "The Domain of Human Geography." In R. Chorley, ed., *New Directions in Geography.* Cambridge: Cambridge University Press.

Haile, G., and N. A. Nguyen. 2008. "Determinants of Academic Attainment in the U.S.: A Quantile Regression Analysis of Test Scores." *Education Economics* 160: 29–57.

Halfon, Neal, and Miles Hochstein. 2002. "Life Course Health Development: An Integrated Framework for Developing Health, Policy, and Research." *Milbank Quarterly* 80 (3): 433–479.

Hannerz, Ulf. 1969. *Soulside: Inquiries into Ghetto Culture and Community.* New York: Columbia University Press.

Hanushek, Eric A. 1986. "The Economics of Schooling: Production and Efficiency in Public Schools." *Journal of Economic Literature* 24: 1141–1177.

Hanushek, Eric A. 1996. "Measuring Investment in Education." *Journal of Economic Perspectives* 10: 9–30.

Hanushek, Eric A., John F. Kain, J. M. Markman, and S. G. Rivkin. 2003. "Does Peer Ability Affect Student Achievement?" *Journal of Applied Econometrics* 18: 527–544.

Hanushek, Eric, John F. Kain, Daniel M. O'Brien, and Steven G. Rivkin. 2005. "The Market for Teachers." NBER Working Paper no. 11154. Cambridge, Mass.: National Bureau of Economic Research.

Harris, Douglas N. 2009. "Would Accountability Based on Teacher Value Added Be Smart Policy? An Examination of the Statistical Properties and Policy Alternatives." *Education Finance and Policy* 4 (4) (forthcoming).

Harris, Douglas N., and Tim R. Sass. 2007. "What Makes for a Good Teacher and Who Can Tell?" Unpublished manuscript. Tallahassee, Fl.: Florida State University.

Hart, K. D., S. J. Kunitz, R. R. Sell, and D. B. Mukamel. 1998. "Metropolitan Governance, Residential Segregation, and Mortality Among African Americans." *American Journal of Public Health* 88 (3): 434–438.

Hartung, J. M., and J. R. Henig. 1997. "Housing Vouchers and Certificates as a Vehicle for Deconcentrating the Poor: Evidence from the Washington, D.C., Metropolitan Area." *Urban Affairs Review* 32: 403–419.

Haynie, Dana L. 2001. "Delinquent Peers Revisited: Does Network Structure Matter?" *American Journal of Sociology* 106 (4): 1013–1057.

Hayward, Mark D., and Melonie Heron. 1999. "Racial Inequality in Active Life Among Adult Americans." *Demography* 36: 77–91.

Heckman, James J. 2007. "The Technology and Neuroscience of Capacity Formation." *Proceedings of the National Academy of Sciences* 104 (33): 13250–13255.

Henly, Julia R. 2002. "Informal Support Networks and the Maintenance of Low-wage Jobs." In Frank Munger, ed., *Laboring Below the Line.* New York: Russell Sage Foundation.

Herr, Toby, and Suzanne L. Wagner. 2007. *Beyond Barriers to Work.* Chicago: Project Match.

Hertz, Tom. 2005. "Rags, Riches, and Race: The Intergenerational Economic Mobility of Black and White Families in the United States." In Samuel Bowles, Herbert Gintis and Melissa Osborne Groves, eds., *Unequal Chances: Family Background and Economic Success.* Princeton, NJ: Princeton University Press.

Hill, Heather C. 2007. "Learning in the Teaching Workforce." *The Future of Children* 17 (1): 111–127.

Hines, John R., Jr., Hilary W. Hoynes, and Alan B. Krueger. 2001. "Another Look at Whether a Rising Tide Lifts All Boats." In Alan B. Krueger and Robert M. Solow, eds., *The Roaring Nineties: Can Full Employment Be Sustained?* New York: Russell Sage Foundation.

Hirsch, Arnold R. 1998. *Making the Second Ghetto: Race and Housing in Chicago 1940–1960.* Chicago: The University of Chicago Press.

Hogan, James. 1996. *Scattered-Site Housing: Characteristics and Consequences.* Seattle, Washington: Prepared for the United States Department of Housing and Urban Development, Office of Policy Development and Research.

Holin, Mary Joel, and Jean Amendolia. 2001. *Interim Assessment of the HOPE VI Program: Case Study of Ellen Wilson Dwellings in Washington, D.C.* Cambridge, Mass.: Abt Associates.

Holt, D., et al. 1996. "Area Homogeneity and the Modifiable Areal Unit Problem." *Geographical Systems* 3: 181–200.

Holt, Steve. 2006. *The Earned Income Tax Credit at Age 30: What We Know.* Urban Institute. http://www.urban.org/url.cfm?ID = 1000970.

Holzer, Harry J., Paul Offner, and Elaine Sorensen. 2005. "Declining Employment Among Young Black Less-educated Men: The Role of Incarceration and Child Support." *Journal of Policy Analysis and Management* 24 (2): 329–350.

Horowitz, Carol, Kathryn A. Colson, Paul L. Hebert, and Kristie Lancaster. 2004. "Barriers to Buying Healthy Foods for People with Diabetes: Evidence of Environmental Disparities." *American Journal of Public Health* 94 (9): 1549–1554.

Iceland, J. 2004. "Beyond Black and White: Metropolitan Residential Segregation in Multi-ethnic America." *Social Science Research* 33: 248–271.

Ihlanfeldt, Keith R. 1999. "The Geography of Economic and Social Opportunity Within Metropolitan Areas." In A. Altshuler, W. Morrill, H. Wolman, and F. Mitchell, eds., *Governance and Opportunity in Metropolitan America.* Washington, D.C.: National Academy of Sciences.

———. 2002. "Spatial Mismatch in the Labor Market and Racial Differences in Neighborhood Crime." *Economics Letters* 76: 73–76.

———. 2007. "Neighborhood Drug Crime and Young Males' Job Accessibility." *Review of Economics and Statistics* 89 (1): 151–164.

Ihlanfeldt, Keith R., and Benjamin P. Scafidi. 2004. "White Neighborhood Racial Preferences and Neighborhood Racial Composition in the United States: Evidence from the Multi-City Study of Urban Inequality." *Housing Studies* 19: 325–359.

Ihlanfeldt, Keith R., and David Sjoquist. 1998. "The Spatial Mismatch Hypothesis: A Review of Recent Studies and Their Implications for Welfare Reform." *Housing Policy Debate* 9 (4): 849–892.

Imazeki, Jennifer. 2007. "Attracting and Retaining Teachers in High-Needs Schools: Do Financial Incentives Make Financial Sense?" Working Paper. San Diego, CA: San Diego State University, Department of Economics.

Jacob, Brian. 2004. "Public Housing, Housing Vouchers and Student Achievement: Evidence from Public Housing Demolitions in Chicago." *American Economics Review* 94 (1): 233–258.

———. 2005. "Accountability, Incentives and Behavior: the Impact of High-Stakes Testing in the Chicago Public Schools." *Journal of Public Economics* 89 (5–6): 761–796.

———. 2007. "The Challenges of Staffing Urban Schools with Effective Teachers." *The Future of Children* 17 (1): 129–153.

Jargowsky, Paul A. 1996. "Take the Money and Run: Economic Segregation in U.S. Metropolitan Areas." *American Sociological Review* 61 (6): 984–998.

———. 1997. *Poverty and Place: Ghettos, Barrios and the American City.* New York: Russell Sage Foundation.

———. 2003. "Stunning Progress, Hidden Problems: The Dramatic Decline of Concentrated Poverty in the 1990s." Report for the Living Cities Census Series. Washington, D.C.: Brookings Institution.

Jencks, Christopher. 1986. "Education and Training Programs and Poverty." In Sheldon Danziger and Daniel Weinberg, eds., *Fighting Poverty: What Works and What Doesn't.* Cambridge, Mass.: Harvard University Press.

Jencks, Christopher, and Susan Mayer. 1990. "The Social Consequences of Growing Up in a Poor Neighborhood." In Lawrence Lynn and M. G. H. McGeary, eds., *Poverty in the United States.* Washington, D.C.: National Academy Press.

Jepsen, Christopher, and Steven G. Rivkin. 2002. "What Is the Tradeoff Between

Smaller Classes and Teacher Quality?" NBER Working Paper no. 9205. Cambridge, Mass.: National Bureau of Economic Research.

Johnson, Robert A., Dean R. Gerstein, Rashna Ghadialy, Wai Choy, and Joseph Gfoerer. 1996. "Trends in the Incidence of Drug Use in the United States, 1919–1992." Rockville, Md.: U.S. Department of Health and Human Services, Substance Abuse and Mental Health Services Administration, Office of Applied Studies.

Johnson, Rucker C. 2007. "Health Dynamics and the Evolution of Health Inequality Over the Life Course: The Importance of Neighborhood and Family Background." Unpublished manuscript. Berkeley: University of California, Berkeley.

———. 2008a. "The Place of Race in Hypertension: How Family Background and Neighborhood Conditions During Childhood Impact Later-life Health." Unpublished manuscript. Berkeley: University of California, Berkeley.

———. 2008b. "Race Differences in the Incidence and Duration of Exposure to Concentrated Poverty Over the Life Course: Upward Mobility or Trapped in the Hood?" Unpublished manuscript. Berkeley: University of California, Berkeley.

———. 2008c. "Inequality in Men's Mortality: The Influence of Young Adult Neighborhood and Family Socioeconomic Factors." Unpublished manuscript. Berkeley: University of California, Berkeley.

Johnson, Rucker C., and Robert F. Schoeni. 2007. "The Influence of Early-Life Events on Human Capital, Health Status, and Labor Market Outcomes Over the Life Course." Working Paper. Ann Arbor, MI: National Poverty Center.

Johnson, Rucker C., Robert F. Schoeni, and Jeannette Rogowski. 2008. "Neighborhoods and the Health of Elderly Americans." Unpublished manuscript. Berkeley: University of California, Berkeley.

Joseph, Mark. 2006a. "Is Mixed-Income Development an Antidote to Urban Poverty?" *Housing Policy Debate* 17 (2): 209–234.

———. 2006b. "The Rationale for Mixed-Income Development: Early Findings from Chicago." Unpublished manuscript.

———. 2008. "Early Resident Experiences at a New Mixed-Income Development in Chicago." *Journal of Urban Affairs* 30 (3): 229–257.

———. 2010. "Creating Mixed-Income Developments in Chicago: Developer and Service Provider Perspectives." *Housing Policy Debate* 20(1):88–115.

Joseph, Mark, Robert J. Chaskin, and Henry S. Webber. 2007. "The Theoretical Basis for Addressing Poverty Through Mixed-Income Development." *Urban Affairs Review* 42 (3): 369–409.

Kain, John F. 1968. "Housing Desegregation, Negro Employment, and Metropolitan Decentralization." *Quarterly Journal of Economics* 32: 175–197.

———. 1992. "The Spatial Mismatch Hypothesis: Three Decades Later." *Housing Policy Debate* 3 (2): 371–460.

Kane, Thomas J., Jonah Rockoff, and Douglas Staiger. 2006. "What Does Certification Tell Us About Teacher Effectiveness? Evidence from New York City." NBER Working Paper no. 12155. Cambridge, Mass.: National Bureau of Economic Research.

Kasinitz, Phillip and Jan Rosenberg. 1996. "Missing the Connection: Social Isolation and Employment on the Brooklyn Waterfront." *Social Forces* 43: 180–195.

Katz, Lawrence, Jeff Kling, and J. B. Liebman. 2001. "Moving to Opportunity in Boston: Early Results of a Randomized Mobility Experiment." *Quarterly Journal of Economics* 116 (2): 607–654.

Kawachi, Ichiro, and Lisa F. Berkman, eds. 2003. *Neighborhoods and Health.* New York: Oxford University Press.

Keels, Micere, Greg J. Duncan, Stefanie DeLuca, James Rosenbaum, and Ruby Mendenhall. 2005. "Fifteen Years Later: Can Residential Mobility Programs Provide a Permanent Escape from Neighborhood Crime and Poverty?" *Demography* 42 (1): 51–73.

Kemple, James J., and Judith Scott-Clayton. 2004. *Career Academies: Impacts on Labor Market Outcomes and Educational Attainment.* New York: MDRC.

Khadduri, Jill. 2001. "Deconcentration: What Do We Mean? What Do We Want?" *Cityscape: A Journal of Policy Development and Research* 5 (2): 69–84.

King, Thomas A., and Peter Mieszkowski. 1973. "Racial Discrimination, Segregation, and the Price of Housing." *Journal of Political Economy* 81 (3): 590–606.

Kingsley, G. Thomas. 2009. "Appendix A." In Henry G. Cisneros and Lora Engdahl, eds., *From Despair to Hope: HOPE VI and the New Promise of Public Housing in America's Cities.* Washington, D.C.: Brookings Institution Press.

Kingsley, G. Thomas, and Kathryn Pettit. 2003. "Concentrated Poverty: A Change in Course." *Neighborhood Change in Urban America.* Washington, D.C.: Urban Institute.

———. 2007. "Destination Neighborhoods of Multi-Move Families in the Moving To Opportunity Demonstration." Seattle: Paper presented at the Urban Affairs Association annual meeting.

Kirschenman, Joleen, and Kathryn Neckerman. 1991. "'We'd Love to Hire Them, But . . .': The Meaning of Race for Employers." In Christopher Jencks and Paul E. Peterson, eds., *The Urban Underclass.* Washington, D.C.: Brookings Institution Press.

Kitchens, S. A., Lee Rosen, and Ellen B. Braaten. 1999. "Differences in Anger, Aggression, Depression, and Anxiety Between ADHD and Non-ADHD Children." *Journal of Attention Disorders* 3 (2): 77–83.

Klein, Stephen, et al. 2000. "What Do Test Scores in Texas Tell Us?" Santa Monica: RAND Corporation.

Kleit, Rachel. 2001a. "Neighborhood Relations in Scattered-Site and Clustered Public Housing." *Journal of Urban Affairs* 23: 409–430.

———. 2001b. "The Role of Neighborhood Social Networks in Scattered-Site Public Housing Residents' Search for Jobs." *Housing Policy Debate* 12 (3): 541–573.

———. 2002. "Job Search Networks and Strategies in Scattered-Site Public Housing." *Housing Studies* 17 (1): 83–100.

———. 2005. "HOPE VI New Communities: Neighborhood Relationships in Mixed-Income Housing." *Environment and Planning A* 37: 1413–1441.

Kling, Jeffrey R., Jeffrey B. Liebman, and Lawrence F. Katz. 2007a. "Experimental Analysis of Neighborhood Effects." *Econometrica* 75 (1): 83–119.

———. 2007b. "Supplement to Experimental Analysis of Neighborhood Effects." Web Appendix. *Econometrica* 75 (1): 83–119.

Kling, Jeffrey R., Jens Ludwig, and Lawrence F. Katz. 2005. "Neighborhood Effects on Crime for Female and Male Youth: Evidence from a Randomized Housing Voucher Experiment." *Quarterly Journal of Economics* 120 (1): 87–130.

Kling, Jeffrey, Jeffrey Liebman, Lawrence Katz, and Lisa Sanbonmatsu. 2004. "Moving to Opportunity and Tranquility: Neighborhood Effects on Adult Economic Self-Sufficiency and Health from a Randomized Housing Voucher Experiment." NBER Working Paper. Cambridge, Mass.: National Bureau of Economic Research.

Knies, G. 2007. "Keeping up with the Schmidts: Do Better-off Neighbours Make People Unhappy?" Paper presented at the workshop Neighborhood Effects Studies on the Basis of European Micro-data, Humboldt University, Berlin.

Knudsen, Eric I., James J. Heckman, Judy L. Cameron, and Jack P. Shonkoff. 2006. "Economic, Neurobiological, and Behavioral Perspectives on Building America's Future Workforce." *Proceedings of the National Academy of Sciences* 103: 10155–10162.

Kohen, Dafna, Jeanne Brooks-Gunn, Tama Leventhal, and Clyde Hertzman. 2002. "Neighborhood Income and Physical and Social Disorder in Canada: Associations with Young Children's Competencies." *Child Development* 73 (6): 1844–1860.

Koretz, Daniel, and Sheila Barron. 1998. "The Validity of Gains in Scores on the Kentucky Instructional Results Information System (KIRIS.)" Santa Monica: RAND Corporation.

Koretz, Daniel, et al. 1991. "The Effects of High-Stakes Testing: Preliminary Evidence About Generalization Across Tests." Chicago: American Educational Research Association.

Kozol, Jonathan. 1991. *Savage Inequalities: Children in America's Schools.* New York: Crown.

Krieger, N., et al. 2002. "Geocoding and Monitoring of U.S. Socioeconomic Inequalities in Mortality and Cancer Incidence: Does the Choice of Area-Based Measure and Geographic Level Matter? The Public Health Disparities Geocoding Project." *American Journal of Epidemiology* 156 (5): 471–482.

Krivo, L. J. and R. L. Kaufman. 1999. "How Low Can It Go? Declining Black-White Segregation in a Multiethnic Context." *Demography* 36: 93–109.

Krueger, Alan B., and Diane M. Whitmore. 2001. "The Effect of Attending a Small Class in the Early Grades on College-Test Taking and Middle School Test Results: Evidence from Project STAR." *Economic Journal* 111 (January): 1–28.

———. 2002. "Would Smaller Classes Help Close the Black-White Achievement Gap?" In John Chub and Tom Loveless, eds., *Bridging the Achievement Gap.* Washington, D.C.: Brookings Institution Press.

Krysan, Maria. 2002. "Whites Who Say They'd Flee: Who Are They, and Why Would They Leave?" *Demography* 39 (4): 675–696.

Kuh, D. J. and M. E. Wadsworth. 1993. "Physical Health Status at 36 Years in the British National Birth Cohort." *Social Science and Medicine* 37 (7): 905–916.

LaGrange, R. L., et al. 1992. "Perceived Risk and Fear of Crime: Role of Social and Physical Incivilities." *Journal of Research in Crime and Delinquency* 29 (3): 311–334.

Lantz, P., Lynch, J., House, J., Lepkowski, J., Mero, R., Musick, M., and D. Williams. 2001. "Socioeconomic Disparities in Health Change in a Longitudinal Study of U.S. Adults: The Role of Health-Risk Behaviors." *Social Science and Medicine* 53 (1): 29–40.

Laub, John H., Robert J. Sampson, and Gary A. Sweeten. 2006. "Assessing Sampson and Laub's Life-Course Theory of Crime." In Francis T. Cullen, John Paul Wright, and Kristie R. Blevins, eds., *Advances in Criminological Theory, Vol. 15.* New Brunswick, N.J.: Transaction Publishers.

Laurenti, Luigi. 1960. *Property Values and Race.* Berkeley: University of California Press.

Leventhal, Tama, and Jeanne Brooks-Gunn. 2000. "The Neighborhoods They Live In: The Effects of Neighborhood Residence on Child and Adolescent Outcomes." *Psychological Bulletin* 126 (2): 309–337.

Levin, Henry. 1977. "A Decade of Policy Developments in Improving Education and Training for Low-Income Populations." In Robert Haveman, ed., *A Decade of Federal Anti-Poverty Policy: Achievements, Failures, and Lessons.* New York: Academic Press.

Levin, J. 2001. "For Whom the Reductions Count: A Quantile Regression Analysis of Class Size and Peer Effects on Scholastic Achievement." *Empirical Economics* 26: 221–246.

Levitt, Steven. 2004. "Understanding Why Crime Fell in the 1990s: Four Factors That Explain the Decline and Six That Do Not." *Journal of Economic Perspectives* 18 (1): 163–191.

Levy, J. I., L. K. Welker-Hood, J. Cougherty, R. Dodson, S. Steinbach, and H. P. Hynes. 2004. "Lung Function, Asthma Symptoms and Quality of Life for Children in Public Housing in Boston: A Case-Series Analysis." *Environmental Health* 3 (13): n.p.

Lin, Nan. 2001. *Social Capital: A Theory of Social Structure and Action.* Cambridge: Cambridge University Press.

Linn, Robert, et al. 1990. "Comparing State and District Results to National Norms: The Validity of the Claim that 'Everyone Is Above Average.'" *Educational Measurement: Issues and Practice* 9 (3): 5–14.

Livingston, M. 2008. "A Longitudinal Analysis of Alcohol Outlet Density and Assault." *Alcoholism: Clinical and Experimental Research* 32 (6): 1074–1079.

Lochner, Lance, and Enrico Moretti. 2004. "The Effect of Education on Crime: Evidence from Prison Inmates, Arrests, and Self-Reports." American Economic Review 94 (1): 155–189.

Logan, J. R., B. J. Stults, and R. Farley. 2004. "Segregation of Minorities in the Metropolis: Two Decades of Change." *Demography* 41: 1–22.

Longley, Paul A., Michael F. Goodchild, David J. Maguire, and David W. Rhind. 2005. *Geographical Information Systems and Science,* 2nd ed. New York: Wiley.

Lopez, Russell, and Patricia Hynes. 2006. "Obesity, Physical Activity, and the Urban Environment: Public Health Research Needs." *Environmental Health* 5 (1): 25–35.

Löytönen, M. 1998. "GIS, Time Geography and Health." In A. C. Gatrell and M. Löytönen, eds., *GIS and Health.* Philadelphia: Taylor and Francis.

Ludwig, Jens, Greg J. Duncan, and P. Hirschfield. 2001 "Urban Poverty and Juvenile Crime: Evidence from a Randomized Housing-Mobility Experiment." *Quarterly Journal of Economics* 116 (2): 655–679.

Ludwig, Jens, Greg J. Duncan, and Helen Ladd. 2003. "The Effects of MTO on Children and Parents in Baltimore." In John Goering and Judith D. Feins, eds., *Choosing a Better Life? Evaluating the Moving to Opportunity Experiment.* Washington, D.C.: Urban Institute Press.

Ludwig, J., G. Duncan, and J. Pinkston. 2000. "Neighborhood Effects on Economic Self-Sufficiency: Evidence from a Randomized Housing-Mobility Experiment." JCPR Working Paper no. 159. Chicago: Joint Center for Poverty Research, Northwestern University and University of Chicago.

Ludwig, J., H. Ladd, and G. Duncan. 2001. "The Effects of Urban Poverty on Educational Outcomes: Evidence from a Randomized Experiment." In W. Gale and J. R. Pack, eds., *Brookings-Wharton Papers on Urban Affairs.* Washington, D.C.: Brookings Institution.

Ludwig, Jens, and Jeffrey R. Kling. 2007. "Is Crime Contagious?" *Journal of Law and Economics* 50 (3): 491–518.

Ludwig, J., Jeffrey Leibman, Jeffrey Kling, Greg Duncan, Lawrence Katz, Ronald

Kessler, and Lisa Sanbonmatsu. 2008. "What Can We Learn About Neighborhood Effects from the Moving To Opportunity Experiment?" *American Journal of Sociology* 114 (1): 144–188.

Ludwig, Jens, and Douglas L. Miller. 2007. "Does Head Start Improve Children's Life Chances? Evidence from a Regression-Discontinuity Design." *Quarterly Journal of Economics* 122 (1): 159–208.

Luttmer, Erzo F. P. 2005. "Neighbors as Negatives: Relative Earnings and Well-Being." *Quarterly Journal of Economics* 120 (3): 963–1002.

Maantay, J. 2001. "Zoning, Equity, and Public Health." *American Journal of Public Health* 91 (7): 1033–1041.

Manski, Charles F. 1993. "Identification of Endogenous Social Effects: The Reflection Problem." *The Review of Economic Studies* 60 (3): 531–542.

———. 1995. *Identification Problems in the Social Sciences.* Cambridge, Mass.: Harvard University Press.

———. 2000. "Economic Analysis of Social Interactions." *Journal of Economic Perspectives* 14: 115–136.

Marsh, Herbert W., and John W. Parker. 1984. "Determinants of Student Self-Concept: Is It Better to Be a Relatively Large Fish in a Small Pond Even if You Don't Learn to Swim as Well?" *Journal of Personality and Social Psychology* 47 (1): 213–231.

Martinez, J., and P. Richters. 1993. "The NIMH Community Violence Project: II. Children's Distress Symptoms Associated with Violence Exposure." *Psychiatry* 56: 22–35.

Massey, D. S. and N. A. Denton. 1988. "The Dimensions of Racial Segregation." *Social Forces* 67: 281–315.

———. 1993. *American Apartheid: Segregation and the Making of the Underclass.* Cambridge, Mass.: Harvard University Press.

Massey, Douglas S., and Mary J. Fisher. 2003. "The Geography of Inequality in the United States, 1950–2000." In William G. Gale and Janet Rothenberg Pack, eds., *Brookings–Wharton Papers on Urban Affairs, 2003.* Washington, D.C.: Brookings Institution Press.

Massey, D. S., and A. B. Gross. 1991. "Explaining Trends in Racial Segregation, 1970–1980." *Urban Affairs Quarterly* 27: 13–35.

Massey, Douglas S., and Garvey Lundy. 2001. "Use of Black English and Racial Discrimination in Urban Housing Markets: New Methods and Findings." *Urban Affairs Review* 36: 452–469.

Matsueda, Ross L., and Kathleen Anderson. 1998. "The Dynamics of Delinquent Peers and Delinquent Behavior." *Criminology* 36: 269–308.

Mauer, Marc, and Tracy Huling. 1996. "Young Black Men and the Criminal Justice System: A Growing National Problem." Washington, D.C.: Sentencing Project.

Mauer, Marc, and Sentencing Project (U.S.). 1999. *Race to Incarcerate.* New York: New Press.

Mayer, Susan E. and Christopher Jencks. 1989. "Growing Up in Poor Neighborhoods: How Much Does It Matter?" *Science* 243 (4897): 1441–1445.

Mayer, T. 1960. "The Distribution of Ability and Earnings." *Review of Economics and Statistics* 42: 189–195.

McClure, Kirk. 2006. "The Low-Income Housing Tax Credit Program Goes Mainstream and Moves to the Suburbs." *Housing Policy Debate* 17 (3): 419–446.

McConnochie, Kenneth, Mark Russo, John McBride, Peter Szilagyi, Ann-Marie Brooks, and Klaus Roghmann. 1999. "Socioeconomic Variation in Asthma Hospitalization: Excess Utilization or Greater Need?" *Pediatrics* 10 (6): 75–82.

McCreary, L., P. England, and G. Farkas. 1989. "The Employment of Central City Male Youth: Nonlinear Effects of Racial Composition." *Social Forces* 68: 55–75.

McFadden, Daniel. 1973. "Conditional Logit Analysis of Qualitative Choice Behavior." In *Frontiers in Econometrics*. New York: Academic Press.

———. 1978. "Modeling the Choice of Residential Location." In A. Karlquist et al., eds., *Spatial Interaction Theory and Planning Models*. New York: Elsevier North-Holland.

McGinnis, M.J., P. Williams-Russo, and J. R. Knickman. 2002. "The Case for More Active Policy Attention to Health Promotion." *Health Affairs* 21 (2): 78–93.

Meade, S. M., and R. J. Earickson. 2000. *Medical Geography*. 2nd ed. New York: Guilford.

Mendenhall, Ruby. 2004. "Black Women in Gautreaux's Housing Desegregation Program." Ph.D diss., Northwestern University.

Metropolitan Planning Council. 2003. *CHA Plan for Transformation July 2003 Progress Report*. Chicago: Metropolitan Planning Council.

Michalopoulos, Charles. 2005. "Precedents and Prospects for Randomized Experiments." In Howard S. Bloom, ed., *Learning More from Social Experiments*. New York: Russell Sage Foundation.

Moffitt, R. 1998. "Policy Interventions, Low-Level Equilibria and Social Interactions." Baltimore: Johns Hopkins University, Department of Economics.

Monsivais, Pablo and Adam Drewnowski. 2007. "The Rising Cost of Low-Energy-Density Foods." *Journal of the American Dietetic Association* 107 (12): 2071–2076.

Moore, Latetia, and Ana V. Dize Roux. 2006. "Associations of Neighborhood Characteristics with the Location and Type of Food Stores." *American Journal of Public Health* 96 (2): 325–331.

Morenoff, Jeffrey, and Robert Sampson. 1997. "Violent Crime and the Spatial Dynamics of Neighborhood Transition: Chicago, 1970–1990." *Social Forces* 76 (1): 31–64.

Morenoff, J., R. Sampson, and S. Raudenbush. 2001. "Neighborhood Inequality, Collective Efficacy, and the Spatial Dynamics of Homicide." *Criminology* 39 (3): 517–560.

Morland, Kimberly. 2002. "The Contextual Effect of the Local Food Environment on Resident's Diets: The Atherosclerosis Risk in Communities Study." *American Journal of Preventive Medicine* 92 (2): 1761–1767.

Mouw, Ted. 2000. "Job Relocation and the Racial Gap in Unemployment in Detroit and Chicago, 1980 to 1990." *American Sociological Review* 65: 730–753.

Musterd, S., and R. Andersson. 2005. "Housing Mix, Social Mix and Social Opportunities." *Urban Affairs Review* 40 (6): 761–790.

Muth, Richard. 1972. "A Vintage Model of the Housing Stock." *Regional Science Association Papers and Proceedings* 30 (2): 141–156.

National Center for Education Statistics. 2007. "The Nation's Report Card, Mathematics 2007: National Assessment of Educational Progress at Grades 4 and 8." NCES 2007–494. U.S. Department of Education, Institute of Education Sciences.

National Fair Housing Alliance. 2006. *Unequal Opportunity: Perpetuating Housing Segregation in America*. Washington D.C.: National Fair Housing Alliance.

National Opinion Research Center. 2006. *Resident Relocation Survey: Phase III First Follow-Up: Findings and Methodology*. Chicago: National Opinion Research Center.

Needleman, H., and B. Gatsonis. 1991. "Meta-analysis of 24 Studies of Learning Disabilities Due to Lead Poisoning." *Journal of the American Medical Association* 265: 673–678.

Needleman, Herbert L., Julie A. Reiss, Michael J. Tobin, Gretchen E. Biesecker, and Joel B. Greenhouse. 1996. Bone Lead Levels and Delinquent Behavior. *Journal of the American Medical Association* 275 (5): 363–369.

Needleman, Herbert L., Christine McFarland, Roberta B. Ness, Stephen E. Fienberg, and Michael J. Tobin. 2002. "Bone Lead Levels in Adjudicated Delinquents: A Case Control Study." *Neurotoxicology and Teratology* 24 (6): 711–718.

Neidell, Matthew. 2004. "Air Pollution, Health, and Socio-Economic Status: The Effect of Outdoor Air Quality on Childhood Asthma." *Journal of Health Economics* 23 (6): 1209–1236.

Newacheck, Paul. 1994. "Poverty and Childhood Chronic Illness." *Archives of Pediatric and Adolescent Medicine* 148: 1143–1149.

Newacheck, Paul, and Neil Halfon. 1988. "Prevalence and Impact of Disabling Chronic Conditions in Childhood." *American Journal of Public Health* 88 (4): 610–617.

Newman, Katherine S. 1999. *No Shame in My Game: The Working Poor in the Inner City.* New York: Knopf and Russell Sage Foundation.

Newman, Katherine S., and Rebekah Peeples Massengill. 2006. "The Texture of Hardship: Qualitative Sociology of Poverty, 1995–2005." *Annual Review of Sociology* 32: 423–446.

Newman, Sandra, and Ann Schnare. 1997. ". . . and a Suitable Living Environment: The Failure of Housing Programs to Deliver on Neighborhood Quality." *Housing Policy Debate* 8 (4): 703–741.

Nye, B., B.D. Fulton, J. Boyd-Zaharias, and V. A. Cain. 1995. "The Lasting Benefits Study, Eighth Grade Technical Report." Nashville: Center of Excellence for Research and Policy on Basic Skills, Tennessee State University.

Oakes, J. M. 2004. "The (Mis)Estimation of Neighborhood Effects: Causal Inference for a Practicable Social Epidemiology." *Social Science and Medicine* 58: 1929–1952.

Oates, Wallace. 1969. "The Effects of Property Taxes and Local Public Spending on Property Values: An Empirical Study of Tax Capitalization and the Tiebout Hypothesis." *Journal of Political Economy* 77: 957–971.

Oberholzer-Gee, Felix, and Miki Mitsunari. 2006. "Information Regulation: Do the Victims of Externalities Pay Attention?" *Journal of Regulatory Economics* 30 (2): 141–158.

O'Campo, P. 2003. "Invited Commentary: Advancing Theory and Methods for Multilevel Models of Residential Neighborhoods and Health." *American Journal of Epidemiology* 157 (1): 9–13.

Openshaw, S. 1984. "The Modifiable Areal Unit Problem." *Concepts and Techniques in Modern Geography* 38: 41–54.

O'Regan, K. M., and J. M. Quigley. 1996. "Spatial Effects upon Employment Outcomes." *New England Economic Review* May: 41–64.

Oreopoulos, Philip. 2003. "The Long-Run Consequences of Living in a Poor Neighborhood." *Quarterly Journal of Economics* 118 (4): 1533–1575.

Orr, Larry, Judith D. Feins, Robin Jacob, Erik Beecroft, Lisa Sanbonmatsu, Lawrence F. Katz, Jeffrey B. Liebman, and Jeffrey R. Kling. 2003. *Moving to Opportunity: Interim Impacts Evaluation.* Washington, D.C.: U.S. Department of Housing and Urban Development.

Os, Jim Van. 2004. "Does the Urban Environment Cause Psychosis?" *British Journal of Psychiatry* 184: 287–288.

Owens, Ann. 2008. *Neighborhoods and Schools as Competing and Reinforcing Contexts in Educational Attainment.* Unpublished master's thesis, Sociology and Social Policy. Cambridge, Mass.: Harvard University.

Pack, Janet Rothenberg. 1998. "Poverty and Urban Public Expenditures." *Urban Studies* 35 (11): 1995–2019.

———. 2002. *Growth and Convergence in Metropolitan America.* Washington, D.C.: Brookings Institution Press.

Pader, Ellen, and Myrna Breitbardt. 2003. "Transforming Public Housing: Conflicting Visions for Harbor Point." *Places* 8 (4): 34–41.

Patterson, Orlando. 1997. *The Ordeal of Integration: Progress and Resentment in American's "Racial" Crisis.* New York: Civitas/Counterpoint.

Pattillo, Mary. 2007. *Black on the Block: The Politics of Race and Class in the City.* Chicago: University of Chicago Press.

Pendall, Rolf. 2000. "Why Voucher and Certificate Holders Live in Distressed Neighborhoods." *Housing Policy Debate* 11 (4): 881–910.

Perlin, Susan A., Ken Sexton and David W. S. Wong. 1999. "An Examination of Race and Poverty for Populations Living Near Industrial Sources of Air Pollution." *Journal of Exposure Analysis and Environmental Epidemiology* 9 (1): 29–48.

———. 2001. "Residential Proximity to Industrial Sources of Air Pollution: Interrelationships Among Race, Poverty, and Age." *Journal of the Air and Waste Management Association* 51 (3): 406–421.

Pernanen, K. 1998. "Prevention of Alcohol-Related Violence." *Contemporary Drug Problems* 25: 477–509.

Plotnick, Robert and Saul Hoffman. 1999. "The Effect of Neighborhood Characteristics on Young Adult Outcomes: Alternative Estimates." *Social Science Quarterly* 80 (1): 1–18.

Pocock, S. J., M. Smith, P. Baghurst. 1994. "Environmental Lead and Children's Intelligence: A Systematic Review of the Epidemiological Evidence." *British Medical Journal* 309 (6963): 1189–1197.

Popkin, S. J. 2007. Testimony before the U.S. Senate Subcommittee on Housing, Transportation, and Community Development, and the U.S. House Subcommittee on Housing and Community Opportunity. http://www.urban.org/ UploadedPDF/901088_HOPE_VI.pdf.

Popkin, Susan J., Mary Cunningham, and Martha Burt. 2005. "Public Housing Transformation and the Hard-to-House." *Housing Policy Debate* 16 (1): 1–24.

Popkin, Susan J., Laura E. Harris, and Mary K. Cunningham. 2002. *Families in Transition: A Qualitative Analysis of the MTO Experience.* Washington, D.C.: Urban Institute.

Popkin, Susan J., Tama Leventhal, and Gretchen Weismann. 2006. "Girls in the 'Hood: Evidence on the Impact of Safety." *Poverty and Race Research Action Council* newsletter, September–October.

———. 2008. "Girls in the 'Hood: The Importance of Feeling Safe." Urban Institute Metropolitan Housing and Communities Center. http://www.urban .org/publications/411636.html.

Popkin, Susan J., James E. Rosenbaum, and Patricia M. Meaden. 1993. "Labor Market Experiences of Low-Income Black Women in Middle-Class Suburbs: Evidence from a Survey of Gautreaux Program Participants." *Journal of Policy Analysis and Management* 12 (3): 556–573.

Popkin, Susan J., Larry F. Buron, Diane K. Levy and Mary K. Cunningham. 2000. "The Gautreaux Legacy: What Might Mixed-Income and Dispersal Strategies Mean for the Poorest Public Housing Tenants?" *Housing Policy Debate* 11 (4): 911–942.

Popkin, Susan J., Victoria Gwiasda, Lynn Olson, Dennis Rosenbaum, and Larry Buron. 2000. *The Hidden War: Crime and the Tragedy of Public Housing in Chicago.* New Brunswick, N.J.: Rutgers University Press.

Popkin, S., G. Galster, K. Temkin, C. Herbig, D. Levy, and E. Richter. 2003. "Obstacles to Desegregating Public Housing: Lessons Learned from Implementing Eight Consent Decrees." *Journal of Policy Analysis and Management* 22 (2): 179–200.

Popkin, Susan J., Bruce Katz, Mary Cunningham, Karen D. Brown, Jeremy Gustafson, and Margery Turner. 2004. *A Decade of HOPE VI: Research Findings and Policy Challenges.* Washington, D.C.: Urban Institute and Brookings Institution.

Prelow, Hazel M., Sharon Danoff-Burg, Rebecca R. Swenson, and Dana Pulgiano. 2004. "The Impact of Ecological Risk and Perceived Discrimination on the Psychological Adjustment of African American and European American Youth." *Journal of Community Psychology* 32 (4): 375–389.

Putnam, R. D. 2007. "*E Pluribus Unum*: Diversity and Community in the Twenty-first Century. The 2006 Johan Skytte Prize Lecture." *Scandinavian Political Studies* 30: 137–174.

Quigley, J., and S. Raphael. 2008. "Neighborhoods, Economic Self-Sufficiency, and the MTO." Unpublished paper. Berkeley: University of California, Berkeley, Department of Economics.

Quillian, Lincoln. 2003. "How Long Are Exposures to Poor Neighborhoods? The Long-Term Dynamics of Entry and Exit from Poor Neighborhoods." *Population Research and Policy Review* 22: 221–249.

Rainwater, Lee. 1970. *Behind Ghetto Walls: Black Families in a Federal Slum.* Chicago: Aldine.

Ramey, Craig T. and Frances A. Campbell. 1979. "Compensatory Education for Disadvantaged Children." *The School Review* 87 (2): 171–189.

———. 1984. "Preventive Education for High-Risk Children: Cognitive Consequences of the Carolina Abecedarian Project." *American Journal of Mental Deficiency* 88 (5): 515–523.

Rankin, Bruce, and James Quane. 2000. "Neighborhood Poverty and the Social Isolation of Inner-city African-American Families." *Social Forces* 79 (1): 139–164.

Raphael, Steven. 1998. "The Spatial Mismatch Hypothesis and Black Youth Joblessness: Evidence from the San Francisco Bay Area." *Journal of Urban Economics* 43: 79–111.

Raphael, Steven, and John Quigley. 2008. "Neighborhoods, Economic Self Sufficiency, and the MTO." *Brookings-Wharton Papers on Urban Affairs* 9: 1–46.

Raphael, Steven and Melissa Sills. 2006. "Urban Crime, Race, and the Criminal Justice System in the United States." In Richard Arnott and Dan McMillen, eds., *Companion to the Handbook of Urban Economics.* Oxford: Blackwell.

Raphael, Steven, and Michael Stoll. 2002. "Modest Progress: The Narrowing Spatial Mismatch Between Blacks and Jobs in the 1990s." Washington, D.C.: Brookings Institution.

———. 2009. "Why Are So Many Americans in Prison?" in Steven Raphael and Michael A. Stoll, eds., *Do Prisons Make Us Safer? The Benefits and Costs of the Prison Boom.* New York: Russell Sage Foundation: 27–72.

Raphael, Steven, and R. Winter-Ebmer. 2001. "Identifying the Effect of Unemployment on Crime." *Journal of Law and Economics* 44 (1): 259–283.

Rasmussen, D. W. 1994. "Spatial Economic Development, Education and the New Poverty." *International Regional Science Review* 14: 107–117.

Reed, J. S. 1972. "Percent Black and Lynching: A Test of Blalock's Theory." *Social Forces* 50: 356–360.

Reider, J. 1985. *Canarsie: The Jews and Italians of Brooklyn Against Liberalism.* Cambridge, Mass.: Harvard University Press.

Reyes, Jessica. 2005. "The Impact of Prenatal Lead Exposure on Health." Working Paper. Amherst, Mass.: Amherst College, Department of Economics.

Richards, T. L., J. L. Deffenbacher, and Lee Rosen. 2002. "Driving Anger and Other Driving-Related Behaviors in High and Low ADHD Symptom College Students." *Journal of Attention Disorders* 6 (1): 25–38.

Richters, P., and J. E. Martinez. 1993. "The NIMH Community Violence Project: I. Children As Victims of and Witnesses to Violence." *Psychiatry* 56: 7–21.

Rohe, William, and Lance Freeman. 2001. "Assisted Housing and Residential Segregation: The Role of Race and Ethnicity in the Siting of Assisted Housing Developments." *Journal of the American Planning Association* 67 (3): 279–292.

Rosen, Kenneth T., Grace J. Kim, and Avani A. Patel. 2003. "Shopping the City: Real Estate Finance and Urban Retail Development." Washington, D.C.: Brookings Institution.

Rosen, Sherwin. 1974. "Hedonic Prices and Implicit Markets: Product Differentiation in Pure Competition." *Journal of Political Economy* 82 (1): 34–55.

Rosenbaum, E. 1996. "Racial/Ethnic Differences in Home Ownership and Housing Quality, 1991." *Social Problems* 43: 403–426.

Rosenbaum, E., L. Harris, and N. Denton. 2003. "New Places, New Faces: An Analysis of Neighborhoods and Social Ties Among MTO Movers in Chicago." In J. Goering and J. Feins, eds., *Choosing a Better Life? Evaluating the Moving To Opportunity Experiment.* Washington, D.C.: Urban Institute Press.

Rosenbaum, J. 1991. "Black Pioneers: Do Moves to the Suburbs Increase Economic Opportunity for Mothers and Children?" *Housing Policy Debate* 2: 1179–1213.

———. 1995. "Changing the Geography of Opportunity by Expanding Residential Choice: Lessons from the Gautreaux Program." *Housing Policy Debate* 6 (1): 231–269.

Rosenbaum, James, Stefanie DeLuca, and Tammy Tuck. 2005. "New Capabilities in New Places: Low-Income Black Families in Suburbia." In Xavier de Souza Briggs, ed., *The Geography of Opportunity: Race and Housing Choice in Metropolitan America.* Washington, D.C.: Brookings Institution Press.

Rosenbaum, J., L. Reynolds, and S. DeLuca. 2002. "How Do Places Matter? The Geography of Opportunity, Self-Efficacy, and a Look Inside the Black Box of Residential Mobility." *Housing Studies* 17 (1): 71–82.

Rosenbaum, James E., Linda K. Stroh, and Cathy Flynn. 1998. "Lake Parc Place: A Study of Mixed-Income Housing." *Housing Policy Debate* 9 (4): 703–740.

Rosenbaum, J., S. Popkin, J. Kaufman, and J. Rusin. 1991. "Social Integration of Low-Income Black Adults in Middle Class Suburbs." *Social Problems* 38: 448–461.

Rosenthal, Stuart. 2006. "Old Homes, Externalities, and Poor Neighborhoods: A Model of Urban Decline and Renewal." Working Paper. Syracuse, N.Y.: Syracuse University.

Ross, Stephen L., and Margery A. Turner. 2005. "Housing Discrimination in

Metropolitan America: Explaining Changes Between 1989 and 2000." *Social Problems* 52: 152–180.

Ross, Stephen L., Margery A. Turner, Erin Godfrey, and Robin Smith. 2008. "Mortgage Lending in Chicago and Los Angeles: A Paired Testing Study of the Pre-Application Process." *Journal of Urban Economics* 63: 902–919.

Rossman, Gretchen B., and Bruce L. Wilson. 1994. "Numbers and Words: Being 'Shamelessly Eclectic.'" *Quality and Quantity* 28: 315–327.

Rubin, Donald. 1978. "Bayesian Inference for Causal Effects: The Role of Randomization." *Annals of Statistics* 6 (1): 34–58.

Rubinowitz, Leonard, and James Rosenbaum. 2000. *Crossing the Class and Color Lines: From Public Housing to White Suburbia.* Chicago: University of Chicago Press.

Rutter, M. 2006. *Genes and Behavior: Nature-Nurture Interplay Explained.* Oxford: Blackwell.

Ryan, William, Allan Sloan, Mania Seferi, and Elaine Werby. 1974. *All In Together: An Evaluation of Mixed-Income Multi-Family Housing.* Boston: Housing Finance Authority.

Saiz, Albert, and Susan Wachter. 2006. "Immigration and the Neighborhood." Mimeo. Philadelphia: University of Pennsylvania, The Wharton School.

Sampson, R. J. 1997a. "Collective Regulation of Adolescent Misbehavior: Validation Results for Eighty Chicago Neighborhoods." *Journal of Adolescent Research* 12 (2): 227–244.

———. 1997b. "The Embeddedness of Child and Adolescent Development: A Community-level Perspective on Urban Violence." In Joan McCord, ed., *Childhood and Violence in the Inner City.* Cambridge: Cambridge University Press.

———. 2003. "The Neighborhood Context of Well-being." *Perspectives in Biology and Medicine* 46 (3 Suppl): S53–64.

———. 2008. "Moving to Inequality: Neighborhood Effects and Experiments Meet Social Structure." *American Journal of Sociology* 114 (1): 189–231.

Sampson, R., and W. B. Groves. 1989. "Community Structure and Crime: Testing Social Disorganization Theory." *American Journal of Sociology* 94 (4): 774–802.

Sampson, Robert J. and John H. Laub. 1993. "Structural Variations in Juvenile Court Processing: Inequality, the Underclass, and Social Control." *Law and Society Review* 27 (2): 285–312.

———. 2003. "Life Course Desisters? Trajectories of Crime Among Delinquent Boys Followed to Age 70." *Criminology* 41 (3): 301–340.

———. 2005. "A Life Course View of the Development of Crime." *Annals of the American Academy of Political and Social Science* 602: 12–45.

———. 2005. "When Prediction Fails: From Crime-Prone Boys to Heterogeneity in Adulthood." *Annals of the American Academy of Political and Social Science* 602: 73–79.

Sampson, Robert J., and Jeffrey Morenoff. 2006. "Durable Inequality: Spatial Dynamics, Social Processes and the Persistence of Poverty in Chicago Neighborhoods." In Samuel Bowles, Steven N. Durlauf, and Karl Hoff, eds., *Poverty Traps.* Princeton, N.J.: Princeton University Press.

Sampson, Robert J., Jeffrey D. Morenoff, and Thomas Gannon-Rowley. 2002. "Assessing Neighborhood Effects: Social Processes and New Directions in Research." *Annual Review of Sociology* 28: 443–478.

Sampson, Robert J., and Steve Raudenbush. 1999. "Systematic Social Observation of Public Spaces: A New Look at Disorder in Urban Neighborhoods." *American Journal of Sociology* 105: 603–651.

Sampson, R. J., et al. 1997. "Neighborhoods and Violent Crime: A Multilevel Study of Collective Efficacy." *Science* 277 (5328): 918–924.

Sanbonmatsu, Lisa, Jeffrey R. Kling, Greg J. Duncan, and Jeanne Brooks-Gunn. 2006. "Neighborhoods and Academic Achievement: Results from the Moving To Opportunity Experiment." *Journal of Human Resources* 41 (4): 649–691.

Sard, Barbara, and Leah Staub. 2008. *House Bill Makes Significant Improvements in "HOPE VI" Public Housing Revitalization Program: Provisions to Overcome Employment Barriers Need Strengthening.* Washington, D.C.: Center on Budget and Policy Priorities.

Schanzenbach, Diane Whitmore. 2006/7. "What Have Researchers Learned from Project STAR?" In Thomas Loveless and Frederick Hess, eds., *Brookings Papers on Education Policy*, 205–228. Washington, D.C.: Brookings Institution Press.

Schell, Lawrence, and Melinda Denham. 2003. "Environmental Pollution in Urban Environments and Human Biology." *Annual Review of Anthropology* 32: 111–134.

Schelling, Thomas. 1971. "Dynamic Models of Segregation." *Journal of Mathematical Sociology* 1: 143–186.

Schill, M. 1997. "Chicago's New Mixed-Income Communities Strategy: The Future Face of Public Housing?" In W. Van Vliet, ed., *Affordable Housing and Urban Redevelopment in the United States.* Thousand Oaks, Calif.: Sage.

Schnare, Ann B. 1976. "Racial and Ethnic Price Differentials in an Urban Housing Market." *Urban Studies* 13: 107–120.

Schoeni, R., J. House, G. Kaplan, and H. Pollack, eds. 2008. *Making Americans Healthier: Social and Economic Policy as Health Policy.* New York: Russell Sage Foundation.

Schuman, Howard, Charlotte Steeh, Lawrence Bobo, and Maria Krysan. 1997. *Racial Attitudes in America: Trends and Interpretations*, rev. ed. Cambridge, Mass.: Harvard University Press.

Schubert, Michael F., and Alison Thresher. 1996. "Lessons from the Field: Three Case Studies of Mixed-Income Housing Development." Working Paper, Great Cities Institute. Chicago: University of Illinois at Chicago.

Schweinhart, Lawrence J., Jeanne Montie, Zongping Xiang, W. Steven Barnett, Clive R. Belfield, and Milagros Nores. 2005. *Lifetime Effects: The High/Scope Perry Preschool Study Through Age 40.* Ypsilanti, Mich.: High/Scope Press.

Scribner, R. 2000. "Small Area Analysis and GIS Technology: Incorporating Group Level Effects into Explanatory Models." In *NIAAA Research Monograph 36: The Epidemiology of Alcohol Problems in Small Geographic Areas.* Bethesda, Md: National Institute on Alcohol Abuse and Alcoholism.

Scribner, R. A., et al. 1995. "The Risk of Assaultive Violence and Alcohol Availability in Los Angeles County." *American Journal of Public Health* 85 (3): 335–340.

Seidman, Edward, Hirokazu Yoshikawa, Ann Roberts, Daniel Chesir-Teran, Larue Allen, Jennifer Friedman, and J. Lawrence Aber. 1998. "Structural and Experiential Neighborhood Contexts, Developmental Stage, and Antisocial Behavior among Urban Adolescents in Poverty." *Development and Psychopathology* 10 (2): 259–281.

Shaw, Clifford R., and Henry D. McKay. 1942. *Juvenile Delinquency in Urban Areas.* Chicago: University of Chicago Press.

Shepard, Lorrie. 1990. "Inflated Test Score Gains: Is the Problem Old Norms or Teaching the Test?" *Educational Measurement: Issues and Practice* 9 (3): 15–22.

Shonkoff, Jack, and Deborah Phillips, eds. 2000. *From Neurons to Neighborhoods: The Science of Early Childhood Development.* Washington, D.C.: National Academy Press.

Silverman, E.,R. Lupton, and A. Fenton. 2005. *A Good Place for Children? Attracting and Retaining Families in Inner Urban Mixed Income Communities.* London: Chartered Institute of Housing/Joseph Rowntree Foundation.

Silverman, I. W. 2003. "Gender Differences in Delay of Gratification: A Meta-Analysis." *Sex Roles* 49: 451–463.

Skogan, W. G., and M. G. Maxfield. 1981. *Coping with Crime: Individual and Neighborhood Reactions.* Beverly Hills: Sage.

Small, Mario Luis, and Katherine Newman. 2001. "Urban Poverty After *The Truly Disadvantaged*: The Rediscovery of the Family, the Neighborhood, and Culture." *Annual Review of Sociology* 27: 23–45.

Smith, Alistair. 2002. *Mixed-Income Housing Developments: Promise and Reality.* Cambridge, Mass.: Joint Center for Housing Studies of Harvard University.

Smith, James P. 1999. "Healthy Bodies and Thick Wallets: The Dual Relation between Health and Economic Status." *The Journal of Economic Perspectives* 13 (2): 145–166.

———. 2004. "Unraveling the SES: Health Connection." *Population and Development Review Supplement: Aging, Health, and Public Policy* 30 (1): 108–132.

Smith, Sandra Susan. 2005. "'Don't Put My Name on It': Social Capital Activation and Job-Finding Assistance Among the Black Urban Poor." *American Journal of Sociology* 111 (1): 1–57.

———. 2007. *Lone Pursuit: Distrust and Defensive Individualism Among the Black Poor.* New York: Russell Sage Foundation.

Smith, Shanna L. 1993. "The Fair-Housing Movement's Alternative Standard for Measuring Housing Discrimination: Comment." In *Clear and Convincing Evidence: Testing for Discrimination in America*, ed. M. Fix and R. Struyk. Washington, D.C.: Urban Institute Press.

Smolensky, E. 2007. "Children in the Vanguard of the U.S. Welfare State." *Journal of Economic Literature* 45: 1011–1023.

Sniderman, Paul M., and Thomas Piazza. 1993. *The Scar of Race.* Cambridge, Mass.: Harvard University Press.

Sobel, Michael S. 2003. "What Do Randomized Studies of Housing Mobility Demonstrate? Causal Inference in the Face of Interference." Unpublished paper. New York: Columbia University.

South, Scott J., and Kyle Crowder. 1997. "Escaping Distressed Neighborhoods: Individual, Community, and Metropolitan Influences." *American Journal of Sociology* 102 (4): 1040–1084.

Speer, P. W., et al. 1998. "Violent Crime and Alcohol Availability: Relationships in an Urban Community." *Journal of Public Health Policy* 19 (3): 303–318.

Stack, Carol B. 1974. *All Our Kin: Strategies for Survival in the Black Community.* New York: Harper & Row.

Stecher, Brian M., and Sheila I. Barron. 1999. "Quadrennial Milepost Accountability Testing in Kentucky." Los Angeles: Center for the Study of Evaluation, University of California, Los Angeles.

Steele, Jennifer, Richard Murnane, and John Willet. 2009. "Do Financial Incentives Help Low-Performing Schools Attract and Retain Academically Talented Teachers? Evidence from California." NBER Working Paper no. 14780. Cambridge, Mass.: National Bureau of Economic Research.

Stegman, Michael. 1991. "Excessive Cost of Creative Finance: Growing Inefficiencies in the Production of Low–Income Housing." *Housing Policy Debate* 2 (2): 357–373.

Stevenson, Howard. 1997. "'Missed, Dissed, and Pissed': Making Meaning of Neighborhood Risk, Fear, and Anger Management in Urban Black Youth." *Cultural Diversity and Mental Health* 3 (1): 37–52.

Stucky, T. D. 2005. "Local Politics and Police Strength." *Justice Quarterly* 22: 139–169.

Summers, A. A., and B. L. Wolfe. 1977. "Do Schools Make a Difference?" *American Economic Review* 67: 639–652.

Suttles, G. D. 1972. *The Social Construction of Communities.* Chicago: University of Chicago Press.

Sweeney, James. 1974. "A Commodity Hierarchy Model of the Rental Housing Market." *Journal of Urban Economics* 1: 288–323.

Swidler, Ann. 1986. "Culture in Action: Symbols and Strategies." *American Sociological Review* 51: 273–286.

Takahashi, L. M., et al. 2001. "Navigating the Time-Space Context of HIV and AIDS: Daily Routines and Access to Care." *Social Science and Medicine* 53 (7): 845–863.

Taylor, A. F., A. Wiley, F. E. Kuo, and S. C. Sullivan. 1998. "Growing Up in the Inner City: Green Spaces as Places to Grow." *Environment and Behavior* 30: 3–27.

Teitler, J. O., and C.C. Weiss. 1996. "Contextual Sex: The Effect of School and Neighborhood Environments on the Timing of First Intercourse." Paper presented at the annual meetings of the Population Association of America, New Orleans.

Thernstrom, Stephen and Abigail Thernstrom. 1997. *America in Black and White: One Nation Indivisible.* New York: Simon and Schuster.

Tiebout, Charles M. 1956. "A Pure Theory of Local Expenditures." *Journal of Political Economy* 64: 416–424.

Tienda, Marta. 1991. "Poor People and Poor Places: Deciphering Neighborhood Effects on Poverty Outcomes." In J. Huber, ed., *Macro-Micro Linkages in Sociology.* Newbury Park, Calif.: Sage.

Tilly, Chris, Phillip Moss, Joleen Kirschenman, and Ivy Kennelly. 2001. "Space as a Signal: How Employers Perceive Neighborhoods in Four Metropolitan Labor Markets." In Alice O'Connor, Chris Tilly, and Lawrence Bobo, eds., *Urban Inequality: Evidence from Four Cities.* New York: Russell Sage Foundation.

Tolnay, Stewart E. 2001. "African Americans and Immigrants in Northern Cities: The Effects of Relative Group Size on Occupational Standing in 1920." *Social Forces* 80: 573–604.

Tolnay, Stewart E., and E. M. Beck. 1995. *A Festival of Violence: An Analysis of Southern Lynchings, 1882–1930.* Urbana: University of Illinois Press.

Tolnay, Stewart E., E. M. Beck, and James L. Massey. 1989. "Black Lynchings: The Power Threat Hypothesis Revisited." *Social Forces* 67: 605–623.

Tonry, Michael H. 1995. *Sentencing Matters.* New York: Oxford University Press.

Turbov, Mindy, and Valerie Piper. 2005. *HOPE VI and Mixed-Finance Redevelopments: A Catalyst for Neighborhood Renewal.* Washington, D.C.: Brookings Institution.

Turner, Margery Austin. 1998. "Moving Out of Poverty: Expanding Mobility and Choice through Tenant-Based Housing Assistance." *Housing Policy Debate* 9 (2): 373–394.

———. 2008. Presentation to the Funders' Exchange for Community Change,

Poverty Reduction and Prosperity Promotion. San Diego: Funders' Exchange for Community Change.

Turner, Margery A., and Stephen L. Ross. 2003. *Discrimination in Metropolitan Housing Markets: Phase II—Asians and Pacific Islanders*. Washington D.C.: Department of Housing and Urban Development.

———. 2004. *Discrimination in Metropolitan Housing Markets: Phase III—Native Americans*. Washington D.C.: Department of Housing and Urban Development.

Turner, Margery A., Carla Herbig, Deborah Kaye, Julie Fenderson, and Diane Levy. 2005. *Discrimination against Persons with Disabilities: Barriers at Every Step*. Washington D.C.: Department of Housing and Urban Development.

Turner, Margery A., Stephen L. Ross, George Galster, and John Yinger. 2002. *Discrimination in Metropolitan Housing Markets: National Results from Phase I of the HDS 2000*. Washington D.C.: Department of Housing and Urban Development.

U.S. Centers for Disease Control. 2003. "Children's Blood Lead Levels in the United States." National Center for Environmental Health. http://www.cdc.gov/nceh/lead/research/kidsBLL.htm.

U.S. House of Representatives Committee on Ways and Means. 2004. *2004 Green Book: Background Material and Data on the Programs Within the Jurisdiction of the Committee on Ways and Means*. Washington, D.C.: Government Printing Office.

Uniform Crime Reports, Federal Bureau of Investigation. http://www.fbi.gov/ucr/00cius.htm.

Vale, Lawrence. 2006. "Comment on Mark Joseph's 'Is Mixed–Income Development an Antidote to Urban Poverty?'" *Housing Policy Debate* 17 (2): 259–269.

Van Kempen, E. 1997. "Poverty Pockets and Life Chances." *American Behavioral Scientist* 41 (3): 430–449.

Varady, David, and Carole Walker. 2003. "Housing Vouchers and Residential Mobility." *Journal of Planning Literature* 18 (1): 17–30.

Varady, D. P., J. A. Raffel, S. Sweeney, and L. Denson. 2005. "Attracting Middle-Income Families in the HOPE VI Public Housing Revitalization Program." *Journal of Urban Affairs* 27 (2): 149–164.

Vartanian, Thomas, and Philip Gleason. 1999. "Do Neighborhood Conditions Affect High School Dropout and College Graduation Rates?" *Journal of Socio-Economics* 28: 21–41.

Venkatesh, Sudhir A. 2000. *American Project: The Rise and Fall of a Modern Ghetto*. Cambridge, Mass.: Harvard University Press.

Venkatesh, Sudhir A., Isil Celimli, Douglas Miller, Alexandra Murphy, and Beauty Turner. 2004. "Chicago Public Housing Transformation: A Research Report." Working Paper. New York: Columbia University Center for Urban Research and Policy.

Vijverberg, Wim P. M. 2004. "Early Human Capital Skills and Labor Market Entry." Unpublished manuscript. Dallas: University of Texas, Dallas.

Vrijheid, Martine. 2000. "Health Effects of Residence Near Hazardous Waste Landfill Sites: A Review of Epidemiologic Literature." *Environmental Health Perspectives Supplements* 108 (S1): 101–112.

Weinberg, B., P. Reagan, and J. Yankow. 2004. "Do Neighborhoods Affect Work Behavior? Evidence from the NLSY79." *Journal of Labor Economics* 22 (4): 891–924.

What Works Clearinghouse. 2007a. "Intervention Report: Everyday Mathematics." Washington, D.C.: Institute of Education Sciences, U.S. Department of Education.

————. 2007b. "Topic Report: Middle School Math." U.S. Department of Education.

Wheaton, B., and P. Clarke. 2003. "Space Meets Time: Integrating Temporal and Contextual Influences on Mental Health in Early Adulthood." *American Sociological Review* 68 (5): 680–706.

White, Michael J. 1987. *American Neighborhoods and Residential Differentiation.* New York: Russell Sage Foundation.

Wikström, Per-Olof, and Robert J. Sampson. 2003. "Social Mechanisms of Community Influences on Crime and Pathways in Criminality." In Ben Lahey, Terrie Moffitt, and Avshalom Caspi, eds., *Causes of Conduct Disorder and Serious Juvenile Delinquency.* New York: Guilford Press.

Williams, Jenny, and Robin C. Sickles. 2002. "An Analysis of the Crime as Work Model: Evidence from the 1958 Philadelphia Birth Cohort Study." *Journal of Human Resources* 37 (3): 479–509.

Williams, Kale, Paul Fischer, and Mary Ann Russ. 2003. *Temporary Relocation, Permanent Choice: Serving Families With Rent Vouchers During the Chicago Housing Authority Plan for Transformation.* Chicago: Commissioned by the Metropolitan Planning Council for the Chicago Housing Authority.

Wilson, James Q., and George L. Kelling. 1982. "Broken Windows." *Atlantic Monthly* 249 (3): 29–38.

————. 1989. "Broken Windows." In R. Dunham and G. Alpert, eds., *Critical Issues in Policing: Contemporary Readings.* Prospect Heights, Ill: Waveland Press.

Wilson, William Julius. 1987. *The Truly Disadvantaged: The Inner City, the Underclass, and Public Policy.* Chicago: University of Chicago Press.

————. 1996. *When Work Disappears: The World of the New Urban Poor.* New York: Alfred A. Knopf.

Wong, D. 1991. "The Modifiable Areal Unit Problem in Multivariate Statistical Analysis." *Environment and Planning A* 23 (7): 1025–1034.

Wood, Joanne V. 1989. "Theory and Research Concerning Social Comparisons and Personal Attributes." *Psychological Bulletin* 106 (2): 231–248.

Woodruff, Tracey J. 1998. "Public Health Implications of 1990 Air Toxics Concentrations Across the United States." *Environmental Health Perspectives* 106 (5): 245–251.

Word, David, and Colby Perkins. 1996. "Building a Spanish Surname List for the 1990's—A New Approach to an Old Problem." Technical Working Paper no. 13. Washington, D.C.: U.S. Bureau of the Census, Population Division.

Wrigley, N. 1995. "Revisiting the Modifiable Areal Unit Problem and Ecological Fallacy." In A. Cliff, P. Gould, A. Hoare, and N. Thrift, eds., *Diffusing Geography.* Oxford: Blackwell Scientific.

Yinger, John. 1978. "The Black-White Price Differential in Housing: Some Further Evidence." *Land Economics* 54 (2): 187–206.

————. 1986. "Measuring Discrimination with Fair Housing Audits: Caught in the Act." *American Economic Review* 76: 881–893.

————. 1993. "Access Denied, Access Constrained: Results and Implications of the 1989 Housing Discrimination Study." In M. Fix and R. Struyk, eds., *Clear and Convincing Evidence: Testing for Discrimination in America.* Washington, D.C.: Urban Institute Press.

————. 1995. *Closed Doors, Opportunities Lost: The Continuing Costs of Housing Discrimination.* New York: Russell Sage Foundation.

Zenk, Shannon, Shuming Bao, Barbara A. Israel, Sherman A. James, Amy J. Schulz, and Mark L. Wilson. 2005. "Neighborhood Racial Composition,

Neighborhood Poverty, and the Spatial Accessibility of Supermarkets in Metropolitan Detroit." *American Journal of Public Health* 95 (4): 600–607.

Zhao, Bo, Jan Ondrich, and John Yinger. 2006. "Why Do Real Estate Brokers Continue to Discriminate?" *Journal of Urban Economics* 59: 394–419.

Zielenbach, Sean. 2003. "Catalyzing Community Development: HOPE VI and Neighborhood Revitalization." *Journal of Affordable Housing* 23 (2): 40–80.

Zimmer, R. W., and E. F. Toma. 2000. "Peer Effects in Private and Public Schools Across Countries." *Journal of Policy Analysis and Management* 19: 75–92.

Zubrinsky, Camille L., and Lawrence Bobo. 1996. "Prismatic Metropolis: Race and Residential Segregation in the City of Angels." *Social Science Research* 25: 335–374.

Contributors

Eugenie L. Birch is Lawrence C. Nussdorf Professor of Urban Research and Education, chairs the Graduate Group in City and Regional Planning at PennDesign, and is Co-Director of the Penn Institute for Urban Research. Her research focuses on urban revitalization.

Charles C. Branas is associate professor of epidemiology at the University of Pennsylvania and a senior scholar at Penn's Center for Clinical Epidemiology and Biostatistics. Among other topics, his research explores healthcare systems as well as the impacts of violence and aggression.

Xavier de Souza Briggs is associate director of the Office of Management and Budget in the White House and an associate professor of sociology and urban planning (on leave) at the Massachusetts Institute of Technology. His books include *Democracy as Problem-Solving* and *Moving to Opportunity.*

David Card is the Class of 1950 Professor of Economics at the University of California, Berkeley. His current research interests include the causes and consequences of racial segregation, the economic impacts of immigration and the effects of health insurance on health care utilization and health.

Susan Clampet-Lundquist is an assistant professor of sociology at Saint Joseph's University. Her research focuses on urban neighborhoods, families, adolescent risk behavior, and social policy. Much of her research has focused on the effects of housing mobility initiatives.

Elizabeth Cove is an analyst at the Government Accountability Office. While working as a research associate at the Urban Institute, her research examined relationships among poor neighborhoods, employment, and earnings, as well as the effect of public housing revitalization initiatives such as HOPE VI on the lives of children and families.

Janet Currie is the Sami Mnaymneh Professor of Economics and chair of the Department of Economics at Columbia University. She is the Director of the Program on Children and Families at the National Bureau of Economic Research and on the Advisory Board of the National Children's Study. Her work evaluates the extent to which federal programs for poor children and families can be viewed as successful social investments.

Robert DeFina is a professor in the sociology department at Villanova University. His main teaching and research interests include poverty, inequality, the social safety net, and housing segregation. His research appears in the *Review of Economics and Statistics, Social Forces, Social Science Research,* and the *Review of Income and Wealth.*

Cynthia Duarte is a Faculty Fellow at the Institute for Latino Studies and Visiting Assistant Professor of Sociology at the University of Notre Dame. She is an urban sociologist interested in the relationship between poor neighborhoods, employment and earnings as well as the integration and residential mobility patterns of later generation Latinos.

Mohamed El Komi is a doctoral candidate in public policy at the University of Texas at Dallas (UTD). He worked as a researcher at the Texas Schools Project at UTD during 2006 and 2007. His research interests are poverty eradication, microfinance and Islamic finance, as well as using experimental economics in evaluating developmental programs.

Ingrid Gould Ellen is an associate professor of public policy and urban planning at New York University's Robert F. Wagner Graduate School of Public Service and Co-Director of NYU's Furman Center for Real Estate and Urban Policy. She teaches microeconomics, urban economics, and urban policy. She has written on racial integration, housing policy, and the neighborhood spillover effects of various place-based government investments, among other subjects.

Fernando Ferreira is an assistant professor in the Real Estate Department of the University of Pennsylvania's Wharton School. His current research interests include the participation of Spanish-speaking residents in the housing market, the effect of local politics on housing markets, efficiency and inequality in the provision of local public goods, and racial discrimination in the housing market.

George Galster is the Hilberry Professor of Urban Affairs in the Department of Geography and Urban Planning at Wayne State University. He has written extensively on the topics of metropolitan housing markets, racial discrimination and segregation, the causes and effects of neighborhood dynamics, residential reinvestment, community lending and insurance patterns, and urban poverty.

Lisa Gennetian is senior research director in the Economic Studies program at the Brookings Institution. She currently is co-directing the long-term evaluation of the Moving to Opportunity project.

Lance Hannon is an associate professor and director of the Criminology, Law, and Society graduate program at Villanova University. His research focuses on theoretically predicted nonlinearities in criminology and sociology. His recent work appears in *Social Forces, Criminology, Social Science Quarterly,* and *Social Science Research.*

Brian A. Jacob is the Walter H. Annenberg Professor of Education Policy, a professor of economics, and the director of the Center on Local, State and Urban Policy at the Gerald R. Ford School of Public Policy at the University of Michigan. His primary fields of interest are labor economics, program evaluation, and the economics of education.

Paul A. Jargowsky is a professor of public policy at the University of Texas at Dallas and a senior research affiliate at the National Poverty Center at the University of Michigan. In the spring of 2009, he was a Visiting Scholar at the Urban Institute in Washington, D.C. His principal research interests are inequality, the geographic concentration of poverty, and residential segregation by race and class.

Rucker C. Johnson is an economist and assistant professor at the Goldman School of Public Policy at the University of California, Berkeley. His research considers the role of poverty and inequality in affecting life chances. His work investigates the long-run consequences of growing up poor; the extent of intergenerational mobility; socioeconomic determinants of health; and the societal consequences of incarceration.

Mark L. Joseph is an assistant professor at the Mandel School of Applied Social Sciences and a faculty associate of the Center on Urban Poverty and Community Development at Case Western Reserve University. His research focuses on comprehensive community revitalization initiatives and mixed-income development as a means of addressing urban poverty.

Jens Ludwig is the McCormick Foundation Professor of Social Service Administration, Law, and Public Policy at the University of Chicago, a nonresident senior fellow at the Brookings Institution, and research associate of the National Bureau of Economic Research. His research in the area of social policy focuses on urban poverty, education, crime, and housing.

Alexandre Mas is an associate professor at the Haas School of Business and the Department of Economics at the University of California, Berkeley, and a Faculty Research Fellow with the National Bureau of Economic Research. His research interests are in labor and personnel economics.

Harriet B. Newburger is a Community Development Research Advisor in the Community Affairs Department of the Federal Reserve Bank of Philadelphia. She was a member of the economics department at Bryn Mawr College for twenty years and, earlier, worked as a research economist in HUD's Office of Policy Development and Research. She has also served as a Senate fellow on the Joint Economic Committee, where she focused on housing issues. Her recent research has focused on low-income homeownership and its sustainability.

Katherine O'Regan is associate professor of public policy and director of the Public and Nonprofit Management and Analysis Program at the New York University Wagner Graduate School of Public Service. Her research focuses on issues and programs affecting the urban poor and the neighborhoods in which they live, including issues of isolation, affordable housing, and neighborhood change.

Janet Rothenberg Pack is a professor of business, public policy and real estate at the University of Pennsylvania's Wharton School, a nonresident fellow at the Brookings Institution, co-coordinator of the Brookings-Wharton Conference on Urban Affairs, and co-editor of the Brookings Wharton Papers on Urban Affairs. Her current research focuses on disentangling spatial mismatch from skills mismatch in explaining unemployment, the increasing role of the private sector in providing services traditionally provided by local governments, and changes in urban development.

Steven Raphael is a professor of public policy at the University of California, Berkeley. His research interests include labor and urban economics, specifically homelessness, the economics of discrimination, and the relationships between racial segregation in housing markets and employment prospects. Additional research interests are access to transportation and employment outcomes, unemployment and crime, peer influences and youth behavior, and trade unions and wage structures.

Stephen L. Ross is a professor of economics at the University of Connecticut. Ross's primary research interests include mortgage lending and housing discrimination. Other interests include urban economics, specifically racial differences in homeownership, racial segregation, minority education gaps, and urban labor markets.

Jesse Rothstein is an assistant professor of economics and public affairs at Princeton University and a faculty research fellow of the National Bureau of Economic Research. A public and labor economist, his research focuses on education and tax policy. Much of his research examines racial and socioeconomic gaps in educational outcomes. In 2009–10, he will be serving as a senior economist at the Council of Economic Advisers.

Lisa Sanbonmatsu is a postdoctoral fellow at the National Bureau of Economic Research. Her research focuses on social policies that affect low-income families and their children.

Michael A. Stoll is professor and chair of public policy in the School of Public Affairs and associate director of the Center for the Study of Urban Poverty at the University of California, Los Angeles. His main research interests include the study of urban poverty and inequality, specifically the interplay of labor markets, race and ethnicity, geography, and policy.

Margery Austin Turner is Vice President for Research at the Urban Institute. Turner served as Deputy Assistant Secretary for Research at the Department of Housing and Urban Development from 1993 through 1996. Her publications include *Public Housing and the Legacy of Segregation*.

Susan M. Wachter is the Richard B. Worley Professor of Financial Management and Professor of Real Estate Finance at The Wharton School; and Professor of City and Regional Planning at PennDesign; as well as Co-Director, Penn Institute for Urban Research. She served as Assistant Secretary for Policy Development and Research at the U.S. Department of Housing and Urban Development. Her research focuses on housing and real estate finance.

Douglas J. Wiebe is an assistant professor of epidemiology at the University of Pennsylvania and a senior scholar in Penn's Center for Clinical Epidemiology and Biostatistics. Wiebe's research interests include environmental risk factors for injury and the impact of daily routines on health-related behavior.

Index

Page numbers in italics represent tables and figures in the text.

Acknowledgments

Neighborhood and Life Chances: How Place Matters in Modern America is the ninth volume in the University of Pennsylvania Press's The City in the Twenty-First Century book series, organized through the Penn Institute for Urban Research (Penn IUR). Many of the ideas here were first aired at the symposium on the economic challenges facing older communities hosted biennially by the Federal Reserve Bank of Philadelphia. On March 26–28, 2008, "Reinventing Older Communities: How Does Place Matter" brought together leaders from the private sector, mayors from the United States and several other countries, policy experts and academics.

Penn IUR was pleased to bring together academics, policymakers and practitioners and to foster their interaction in the symposium's research track. The research that this volume represents would not have been possible without the support of the Federal Reserve, its President and CEO, Charles Plosser, its Executive Vice President, Rick Lang, its Vice President and Community Affairs Officer, Dede Myers, and the efforts of all those who participated in the symposium.

Penn IUR is indebted to the continued support of its Advisory Board, the President's Office, and the Provost's Office at the University of Pennsylvania. Their commitment to developing and disseminating the forms of knowledge necessary for sound urban policy and revitalized cities makes publications like this one possible. The editors of the volume are grateful to the authors, whose rigor and intelligence this book showcases; to Penn IUR staff Amy Montgomery, Greg Scruggs, and Daniel Stout for helping bring this project to completion; and to the leadership and staff at Penn Press, particularly Peter Agree, and the development editors, Audra Wolfe and Edward J. Blum, whose thoroughness and care helped guide and shape the volume.

The views expressed in this volume are those of the individual authors and not those of our sponsor organizations.